Marcus M. Spiegel

# A Jewish Colonel in the Civil War

MARCUS M. SPIEGEL OF THE OHIO VOLUNTEERS

Marcus M. Spiegel

*Edited by*

JEAN POWERS SOMAN

*and*

FRANK L. BYRNE

University of Nebraska Press
Lincoln and London

© 1985 by The Kent State University Press. © 1994 by Jean P. Soman.
Manufactured in the United States of America

♾ The paper in this book meets the minimum requirements of American National Standard for Information Sciences—Permanence of Paper for Printed Library Materials, ANSI Z39.48-1984.

First Bison Book printing: 1995
Most recent printing indicated by the last digit below:
10    9    8    7    6    5    4    3    2    1

Library of Congress Cataloging-in-Publication Data
Spiegel, Marcus M., b. 1829.
[Your true Marcus]
A Jewish colonel in the Civil War: Marcus M. Spiegel of the Ohio Volunteers /
Marcus M. Spiegel; edited by Jean Powers Soman and Frank L. Byrne.
p.   cm.
Originally published: Your true Marcus. Kent, Ohio: Kent State University Press, c1985.
Includes bibliographical references and index.
ISBN 0-8032-9232-5 (pa: alk paper)
1. United States—History—Civil War, 1861–1865—Personal narratives, Jewish.   2. Jewish soldiers—United States—Correspondence.   3. Jews—United States—Correspondence.   4. Spiegel, Marcus M., b. 1829.   I. Soman, Jean Powers.   II. Byrne, Frank L. (Frank Loyola), 1928–   .   III. Title.
E540.J5S65   1995
973.7'81—dc20
[B]
95-5381   CIP

Reprinted from the original 1985 edition by The Kent State University Press, titled *Your True Marcus: The Civil War Letters of a Jewish Colonel*.

# Contents

Foreword by Dr. Jacob R. Marcus                    vii

Preface                                            ix

Abbreviations Used in Footnotes                    xii

CHAPTER 1:    From Germany to Ohio                 1

CHAPTER 2:    From Warehouseman to Warrior         10

CHAPTER 3:    "Who wouldent be a Soldier?"         20

CHAPTER 4:    "After Stonewall Jackson"            59

CHAPTER 5:    "Attached to McClellan's grand army" 110

CHAPTER 6:    "The 120th will do to bet on"        173

CHAPTER 7:    "No Peace Democrat"                  224

CHAPTER 8:    "My boys will follow me anywheres"   265

CHAPTER 9:    "I will be 'Starred'"                306

Selective Bibliographic Essay                      342

Index                                              346

# Foreword

Jean Powers Soman has asked me to write a foreword to this book containing the Civil War letters of Marcus M. Spiegel, her great-great-grandfather. I do so gladly for a number of reasons. The more source material we have on this conflict the more we will be able to evaluate what really happened during those four eventful years. Personally I am very much interested in the fine collection of over one hundred letters of this Civil War officer because for years I have followed with interest the career of this notable Ohioan.

Spiegel was born in a German village in 1829, the son of a rabbi who staunchly maintained the traditions of his ancestors. The rabbinate in those days was no bed of roses; young Marcus was reared in a disciplined home but was given sufficient education to value secular learning and libertarian ideals. When the revolution of 1848 erupted in reactionary Germany he joined wholeheartedly in the effort to bring the spirit of enlightenment and egalitarianism to the larger Germany. After the republican revolution failed he set sail for America in 1849. Here, like many of his compatriots who lacked skills, he turned to peddling and finally became a modest shopkeeper in Ohio. It was almost inevitable that this émigré, with his love for freedom, would become an ardent American patriot and would volunteer as a soldier in 1861 when the call to arms was sounded. In steady progression he rose in a relatively short time from the humble rank of second lieutenant in the Sixty-seventh Ohio Volunteer Infantry to colonel of the 120th Ohio Infantry.

It is a tribute to the United States that a German immigrant was able to rise to the command of a regiment in a little more than a decade after his arrival on these shores. His career is comparable to that of the German Jew, Louis A. Gratz, who came to this country in 1861, peddled for a few months, and then joined up as a soldier. Gratz was then about twenty-one years of age. In just over a year he became commanding officer of a regiment of cavalry with the title of major. Spiegel and Gratz are not important solely because they rose to the top so rapidly; George Armstrong Custer was a general at the age of twenty-four. The careers which distinguished foreign-born Gratz and Spiegel were possible only in the United States.

What then is the importance of this collection of the letters of Marcus M. Spiegel? Spiegel's career takes on significance when it is realized that he moved forward in this country in a generation when many looked askance at Jews. A treaty with the Swiss in 1855 ignored the rights of American Jewish citizens; during the Civil War rabbis could not serve as chaplains in the armed forces until 1862, and in that very year Gen. Ulysses S. Grant expelled Jews from the Department of the Tennessee because some were buying cotton from Southern planters. Yet, despite these difficult events, Spiegel's merits were recognized. The promises inherent in Jefferson's Declaration of Independence still dominated American thoughts and hopes. Despite old prejudices America could well prove to be a land of opportunity for almost anyone with intelligence and moral courage. Spiegel was almost brevetted a brigadier general; at least four other American Jewish officers were inducted into this honorary one-star rank.

The war as revealed in these letters of a Jew shows that the Children of Israel could succeed in the profession of arms, a field of endeavor that had been alien to them since the days of the Maccabees when a handful of patriots defeated the Syrian armies. The war taught Jews to have faith in themselves, to forget the disabilities under which they had labored in Germany. The new Jew who emerged from the fratricidal conflict in the U.S. was a complete American. He believed in himself; he insisted on equality; he had emancipated himself from the ghetto mentality. For immigrants, for Jews, the war was an Americanizing forcing house. That is why these letters merit reading; they reflect more than the hazards and adventures of a Civil War officer. Thank you, Jean P. Soman, for giving us this opportunity to read the letters of your distinguished ancestor.

JACOB R. MARCUS

*American Jewish Archives*
*September 1981*

# Preface

A historical event as related through the voice of a participant is vibrant and alive; it becomes human. The historian writing a century later can seldom capture the aura of excitement as did the person writing about the events as they occurred. Such an eyewitness to history was Marcus M. Spiegel, one of the few Jewish colonels during the American Civil War. During the two and a half years he served in the Union army, he wrote more than one hundred and fifty letters to his wife Caroline and to others. Caroline Spiegel wisely had his letters mounted and bound in a black leather album. For five generations, this album has been preserved and passed down from mother to daughter. Jean Soman vividly remembers how, as a child growing up in Miami, Florida, she saw this great old book of letters, covered with dust, perched high on a shelf in her mother's closet. Despite the heat and humidity, the letters remained in miraculously good condition and, for the most part, legible. Along with the letters was a box containing relics belonging to the Spiegel family, the family Bible, and a Hebrew prayer book.

It is hard to believe that only twelve years prior to the writing of these letters, Spiegel arrived in America from Germany with little, if any, knowledge of English. He very rapidly developed an extensive vocabulary and an impressive command of his new country's language. At times his writing is almost poetic and his vivid narrative descriptions are often works of art. He is able to paint a detailed picture of the day-to-day life of a Union soldier in camp and on the battlefield. The trials and tribulations of war are brilliantly described in his eloquent and lucid letters. Living conditions good and bad; sweet victory and agonizing defeat; many aspects of the war in both its eastern and western theaters can be seen in Spiegel's letters. This perceptive observer comments in great depth on politics, including the issue of the abolition of slavery. Especially revealing is his gradual change in attitude toward emancipation. Interwoven throughout Spiegel's writings are his extreme feelings of patriotism, his love for his family and fellow man, and his general philosophy of life. Never did he abandon his belief in God or in the Jewish religion. A Renaissance man in his interests, he was adventurous and brave, hardworking and dutiful, compassionate, romantic, and to his beloved wife ever true. Despite all the hardships encountered, he remained an eternal optimist.

The historical importance of the letters became apparent to Colonel Spiegel's great-great-granddaughter, Jean Soman, after her freshman year at the University of Wisconsin. Her brother-in-law, James Soman, a Civil War buff, read the letters in their entirety and encouraged her to do something of significance with them. As a junior majoring in history, she wrote a paper based on them for a course on the Civil War. Intrigued by the writings of Marcus Spiegel, she continued to research his life. The idea of compiling this book of letters became an obsession for Jean. For more than a decade, the project has dominated her free time. Her most difficult task was deciphering these difficult to read, handwritten letters and putting them into typed form. Caroline Frances Powers, Jean's mother, who was named after Marcus's wife, instilled in her an early appreciation for history and a great interest in her great-great-grandfather. Unfortunately, Caroline passed away before the publication of this book, but her encouragement and assistance will be forever appreciated. Marcus Spiegel has given Jean a feeling of deep respect for her American Jewish heritage and extreme love for her country. For this she will be eternally grateful.

It has been especially rewarding for Jean to travel with her husband and daughters to many of the locations mentioned in the letters. While touring the battlefield in Vicksburg, Mississippi, she walked through the area where the Ohio regiments were stationed. She approached a large, handsome granite monument and was completely astonished when she read the engraving across the front: "One Hundred and Twentieth Infantry, Col. Marcus M. Spiegel." It was absolutely thrilling to discover this historic remembrance located on the exact piece of land that Colonel Spiegel had described in his letters during the siege of Vicksburg.

Frank L. Byrne, a Civil War historian, has spent the past four years coediting the letters with Jean Soman. While studying the life and times of Marcus Spiegel, he too has become a sincere admirer of the colonel.

In carrying out their work, the editors have incurred many scholarly debts. Both editors note with sincere thanks the kind assistance of the following people and institutions: Paul H. Rohmann, Director of the Kent State University Press, for his belief in the historical importance of this book and for his extreme patience and invaluable advice; Dr. Jacob R. Marcus, Director of the American Jewish Archives and Professor of American Jewish History at Hebrew Union

College, for his beautiful Foreword and for all of the additional information he has provided, but most of all for his encouragement; Rabbi Michael B. Eisenstat, Temple Judea, Coral Gables, Florida, for all his helpful advice and translations and for introducing Jean Soman to Dr. Marcus; Allan Peskin of Cleveland State University; Harold Schwartz of Kent State University; Michelle Finkelstein, Director of the Chicago Jewish Archives; Gary Williams, Clerk of Sussex, Virginia Courthouse; Charles Lanford, Vicksburg, for his photograph of the Vicksburg monument; the late Mrs. Jeanette Freiler, Chicago; Ms. Elizabeth Stein, Chicago; Mr. Modie Spiegel, Chicago; Mr. and Mrs. Leon Alschuler, Beverly Hills, Ca.; Martha Givner, New York City; John J. Patrick of Youngstown, Ohio; Werner Baum and family, Rochester, N.Y.; and James Soman, Fennimore, Wisconsin. Special thanks to Laura Nagy and Jeanne West, Editors at the Kent State University Press, for all of their devotion and hard work, to Carol Horner of the Kent State University Press for her assistance, and to all the staff of the Press. We further appreciate the help of the staffs of the American Jewish Archives, Akron Public Library, Holmes County *Farmer-Hub,* Library of Kent State University, Mansfield Public Library, National Archives, Washington, D.C., New York Public Library, Ohio Historical Society, Wayne County Library, and the Library of the Western Reserve Historical Society. Thanks also to Nancy Eisenstat and Patricia Bonavia, Miami, Florida, for their help.

Jean Soman wishes to express her deepest gratitude to her husband, Bill, for all his love, encouragement, and advice. She is forever grateful to her daughters, Jennifer and Jill; her father, Gabriel Powers; late mother, Caroline Powers; sister, Susan Scott; and niece, Nancy Everhart, for their interest and help. Frank Byrne wishes to thank his wife, Marilyn, for her support.

Many friends and relatives have been a great source of strength and wisdom regarding this new publication. Special thanks to: Barry Halpern and his wife, Sheila, for all the patience, advice, and interest; Miriam and Rodney Teichner for their translations and encouragement; Pat and Paul Bonavia for their concern and support; Sara Soman Flack and her family; and to Ira and Brenda Abrams. Additional thanks to: Betty Soman; the late Walter Soman; Jim, Fred, Dan, and John Soman and their families; Larry and Fran Blum; Arthur and John Bovarnick; John and Jane Barbe; Bob and Susan Alschuler; Lischa Stein; Richard and Penny Thurer; Gerard and Joyce Kaiser; Gary Eisenberg; Roy Krochmal; Rodger Aidman; Arthur Teitelbaum; Randy Nimnicht; Dr. Henry Green; Gary and Barbara Cohen; Martin and Linda Cohen; Dan and Nancy Greenberg; Harvey and Rona Simovitch; Adrian and Natalie Weiss; Rhoda Malsin; Fred and Ruth Friendly; Elie Wiesel; Rabbi Herbert Baumgard; Rabbi Mark Kram; Rabbi Jon Kendall; Mitchell Kaplan; Dr. Abraham Peck; Mark and Nedra Oren; Mark and Rusty Slavin; Mel Young; Len Scher; Robert Coorsh; and again thanks to Dr. Jacob Rader, Marcus and Rabbi Michael and Nancy Eisenstat. We greatly appreciate the support of all our friends at the University of Miami, the *Miami Herald,* and the *Miami News.*

# Abbreviations Used in Footnotes

AJA — American Jewish Archives, Hebrew Union College, Cincinnati, Ohio

DAB — Allen Johnson and Dumas Malone, eds. *Dictionary of American Biography.* 20 vols. New York: Scribner's, 1928–36

GB — Ezra J. Warner, *Generals in Blue: Lives of the Union Commanders.* Baton Rouge: Louisiana State University Press, 1964

MF — *Millersburg Holmes County Farmer*

MR — *Millersburg Republican*

OAGC — Ohio, Adjutant General, Correspondence, Ohio Historical Society, Columbus, Ohio

OR — United States, War Department. *The War of the Rebellion: A Compilation of the Official Records of the Union and Confederate Armies.* 70 vols. in 128, Washington, D.C.: Government Printing Office, 1880–1901

OR Atlas — United States, War Department. *Atlas to Accompany the Official Records of the Union and Confederate Armies.* Washington, D.C.: 1891–95. Reprint, New York: T. Yoseloff, 1958

Roster — Ohio, Roster Commission. *Official Roster of the Soldiers of the State of Ohio in the War of the Rebellion, 1861–1866.* 12 vols. Akron: Werner Co., 1886–95

Soman Coll. — The Soman Collection, in the possession of Jean Soman, Miami, Florida

WRHS — Western Reserve Historical Society, Cleveland, Ohio

# CHAPTER ONE

# From Germany to Ohio

In the tiny hamlet of Abenheim, Germany, located near the Rhine River northwest of the ancient and historic city of Worms, Marcus M. Spiegel was born on December 8, 1829 to a family that could trace its roots to sixteenth-century Frankfurt. According to family legend, Meyer, an ancestor, had a large "spiegel," German for mirror, in front of his home, so that during the time of Napoleon, when Jews were given surnames, it became meaningful for the family to adopt the name Spiegel.[1]

Moses Spiegel, the father of Marcus, was a well-educated and wise man who served as village rabbi for Abenheim's several Jewish families.[2] Rabbi Spiegel and his devoted wife, Regina Herz Spiegel, lived in this peaceful Rhineland village until the mid 1840s with their five children, Marcus, Sarah, Minna, Theresa, and Joseph; three other children died in infancy. Marcus, the eldest son, was given the Hebrew name Gershon after his grandfather, who was also a rabbi.

During this period in history Germany was a disunited group of independent principalities. After the defeat of Napoleon at Waterloo in 1815, the ideals of the French Revolution—liberty, equality, and fraternity—were no longer practiced by the majority of autocratic German rulers, who once again instituted and enforced medieval restrictions on Jews. The philosophy of the Enlightenment and the Rights of Man were short-lived in the German states at this time. Jews were forced to pay extremely heavy taxes, were deprived of citizenship, and were permitted to reside only in specific areas. In many instances, they were restricted in the type of occupation they could pursue and limited in their ability to travel. A set number of Jewish matrimonies were permitted at any one period of time and many couples were unable to get married when they so desired. Expulsions

---

1. Orange A. Smalley and Frederick D. Sturdivant, *The Credit Merchants: A History of Spiegel, Inc.* (Carbondale: Southern Illinois Univ. Press, 1973), 2.

2. *Selbstverlag der Landesarchivverwaltung Rhineland Pfalz* (Koblenz, 1975), 156. Copy in the American Jewish Archives, Hebrew Union College, Cincinnati, Ohio. Hereafter cited as AJA. The Jewish population of Abenheim in 1824 was 60 out of a total population of 1,133.

and confiscations of property were extremely common occurrences and many Jews were conscripted into the army, but forbidden to become officers.

In 1845 a widespread depression swept across Europe, creating discontent everywhere. Historically, the Jewish people have frequently been viewed as scapegoats for various social ills and calamities, and once again they were placed in this role. Moses Spiegel perceptively recognized that the outlook was not promising for his family in Germany, and he made the momentous decision to journey with his wife and four of their children—young Marcus stayed behind—across the Atlantic to America. In this promised land, he hoped they would live free from the prejudices and lack of personal freedom that they had already experienced in Germany and which seemed to be increasing. In 1846, the Spiegels left Abenheim, travelled to Hamburg, and from there embarked upon a long and treacherous ocean voyage to New York City.[3] The German Jews were part of a great wave of migration to the United States which significantly increased the foreign-born population generally and the Jewish population in particular. Between 1850 and 1860, American Jews would triple in number to 150,000 in a national population of 31.5 million.[4] Spiegel and his family joined the clusters of other Jewish immigrants who settled on the later famous lower east side of Manhattan. While living in this urban environment, dotted with tenement houses, neighborhood groceries, and clothing stores, Moses began peddling needles and cloth to make a living. Admired and respected by the many co-religionists who inhabited this area, he was soon asked to serve as the neighborhood rabbi.

The German Jews brought with them to America the idea of Reform Judaism, and Spiegel's rabbinate reflected these changes. Leopold Mayer, a fellow immigrant, observed, "How happy I was when I reached the promised land of freedom where the laws at least are the same for Jews and non-Jews. . . . In New York, my best friend and former teacher, . . . Moses Spiegel, took me to the first Jewish Reform Temple I had ever visited. . . ."[5] The German Jews attempted

---

3. Lizzie T. Barbe, "Memoirs," 1. Typescript in AJA. Barbe cites 1846 for the arrival of Moses Spiegel and family but other sources mention 1847 or 1848. Much of the family information on the following pages comes from the Barbe "Memoirs."

4. Bertram Wallace Korn, *American Jewry and the Civil War* (Philadelphia: Jewish Publication Society of America, 1951), 1, 11.

5. Leopold Mayer, 1827–1903, like the Spiegels was from Abenheim and later settled in Chicago where he was an incorporator of the Reform Temple

to modernize Judaism by adapting it to nineteenth-century thought. In their synagogues, they innovated the ritual, used the vernacular (German and later English), instituted organ music, and held religious school on Sunday. Men and women were seated together in the synagogue, yet many still observed dietary laws in their homes.

While Moses Spiegel was establishing the family's roots in New York, eighteen-year-old Marcus, an idealistic young man who desired to join the movement for Liberal reform, participated in the Liberal Revolution of 1848 and fought to overthrow the Prussian dynasty. Marcus and many of his fellow revolutionaries believed that if more power were given to the middle class, a freer and more tolerant society would exist and conditions for the Jews might ameliorate. Much to his disappointment, the revolution failed dismally; Germany was not unified and the disunited states with their individual despots offered little hope for the Jews. As a result of this abortive revolution, many Jews and non-Jews involved in the Liberal movement sought refuge in America, and Marcus Spiegel was among them. By the spring of 1849, he had arrived in New York City to join his family on the lower east side.[6]

Apparently, life in this crowded urban ghetto of immigrants soon became too confining for adventurous young Marcus. While he had received a fine education in Germany, he did not have a profession. In 1850, he travelled westward to the growing city of Chicago, where his sister Sarah had settled with her husband, Michael Greenebaum, a plumber by trade, who was well-established, successfully operating a hardware and tinsmith shop.[7] Michael's brothers, Elias and Henry, worked as clerks in the banking firm of Richard I. Swift and eventual-

---

Sinai Congregation. The New York temple mentioned was Emanu-El. Morris U. Schappes, *A Documentary History of the Jews in the United States, 1654–1875*, 3 vols. (New York: Citadel Press, 1950), 647. The quotation is from Jacob R. Marcus, *Memoirs of American Jews, 1775–1865* (Philadelphia: Jewish Publication Society of America, 1955), 2:282.

6. Smalley and Sturdivant, *Credit Merchants*, 4.

7. Michael Greenebaum (1824–94), Sarah's first cousin, had in 1846 moved from Germany to Chicago where he was one of the first Jews to settle. In 1851, he founded the Hebrew Benevolent Society and also was a founding member of Temple Sinai. An opponent of slavery, he led a crowd of citizens which in 1853 freed a fugitive slave held by a United States marshal. He later became an active Republican, whereas his brother, Henry, was like Marcus Spiegel a supporter of Stephen A. Douglas. Schappes, *Documentary History*, 313, 648.

ly became two of Chicago's leading bankers.[8] These relatives were among the first Jewish settlers in Chicago, and were instrumental in the establishment of the first Reform Temple there, with Rabbi Bernard Felsenthal, a relative of Marcus's, as their spiritual leader.[9] When Marcus's parents also moved to Chicago, Moses Spiegel became teacher of the congregation's religious school.[10]

Hard-working and industrious immigrants, the Greenebaums struggled to earn a living. As was customary in America at this time, the more established immigrants helped new arrivals get an economic start in their adopted country, and the Greenebaums aided young Spiegel. Peddling was a popular occupation for newcomers because it was relatively easy to learn, required no formal training or command of the English language, and demanded little initial capital. The Greenebaums outfitted Marcus with a peddler's necessities: a pack and a stock of such goods as calico, muslin, needles, thread, and linen. He was assigned to the territory of Ohio.[11]

As could be imagined, the life of an immigrant peddler in 1850 was difficult and at times extremely lonely. Young Spiegel tramped over the unfamiliar Ohio terrain from farmhouse to farmhouse and village to village, carrying his pack of wares, alone in a new country, with little knowledge of English. The most important stop he made while peddling his goods was at the farmhouse of Stephen Hamlin, a refined Quaker gentleman, near Uniontown, Stark County, Ohio. Hamlin, true to his heritage, had built the farmhouse in the architectural style of the Old South, and Southern hospitality and cooking were always observed. The Hamlin family had come to

---

8. They eventually formed the Greenebaum Brothers banking firm. Smalley and Sturdivant, *Credit Merchants,* 6.

9. Rabbi Bernhard Felsenthal (1822–1908), born in Munchweiler, Germany, became a leader of Reform Judaism. His first job when he came to Chicago was with the Greenebaum Brothers Banking House. In 1858, he founded the Jüdische Reformverein which developed into the Sinai Congregation of Chicago. He was a strong advocate of the abolition of slavery. Isidore Singer, ed., The *Jewish Encyclopedia* . . . , 12 vols. (New York and London: Funk and Wagnalls, 1901–6), 5:361; Korn, *American Jewry,* 22–23.

10. Memorial resolutions on Moses Spiegel, *The Occident,* 15(April 1858). This memorial by Congregation Kehilah Anshe Maariv of Chicago recalled "his efficient and successful labors as a teacher in Israel—one who has promulgated a thorough devotion to the Jewish faith. . . ."

11. Smalley and Sturdivant, *Credit Merchants,* 6.

America from England in 1637 and settled in Sussex County, Virginia. They had emancipated their slaves as early as the 1780s, some of the first Americans to do so.[12] In 1807 Stephen Hamlin had married Elizabeth (Lizzie) Felts and moved from Virginia to Ohio. Many Quakers were then making a similar move, possibly because they were farmers and Virginia's soil was depleted but also perhaps because they felt uncomfortable in a slaveholding society. In Ohio, the Hamlins' home became a mecca where travelers would often stop for a warm welcome and a good meal. Marcus Spiegel became a frequent visitor. Here he found warmth and comfort, but more important, he found Caroline Frances, Hamlin's lovely young auburn-haired daughter. Marcus was captivated.

The story of the courtship of Marcus Spiegel and Caroline Hamlin is retold by their daughter, Lizzie Barbe, in her "Memoirs." As the story goes, Spiegel remarked after first meeting Caroline, "I'll be back to marry you some day." When he first proposed marriage to her, she laughed and said she would never marry a "Dutchman,"[13] a nickname given to German immigrants because they spoke "Deutsch," but after the romance had continued for some time, a mature Caroline, now twenty, finally accepted the marriage proposal. Elated with her acceptance, Spiegel returned to Chicago to inform his relatives of the engagement. Quite shocked to hear that Spiegel was to marry a Quaker girl, Henry Greenebaum, his cousin, was sent by the family to Ohio to try to dissuade the young couple from marrying. Evidently Caroline made a positive impression because Greenebaum returned to Chicago and informed the concerned relatives that, if Spiegel did not marry her, he would try to win Caroline for himself. This glowing report appeased and satisfied the family's concern.

On August 7, 1853, Marcus M. Spiegel and Caroline Frances Hamlin were married by a Justice of the Peace in Stark County, Ohio. Shortly thereafter the newlyweds travelled to Chicago, where Caroline began studying Judaism and was subsequently converted[14] in one

---

12. Hamlin emancipation document, original in Sussex County Courthouse, Sussex, Virginia; copy in possession of Jean Soman, Miami, Florida. Hereafter cited as Soman Coll. Additional information on the Hamlins is from the Barbe memoirs cited above and from family tradition. Caroline Hamlin was born near Limaville in Stark County on July 27, 1833.

13. Barbe, "Memoirs," 2.

14. The original conversion document has been preserved; original in Spiegel Papers, AJA, copy in Soman Coll.

of the first ceremonies of its kind in the history of the city. While living in Chicago, Caroline was instructed by her new relatives in the art of German-Jewish cooking, and taught the German language, a necessity because her new friends and relatives spoke German exclusively. Spiegel, on the other hand, easily settled into a position as a clerk in Francis Clark's Dry Goods Emporium, the Marshall Fields of that day.

As the conversion of his wife might suggest, Spiegel intended that he and his family should remain true to Judaism, and he did so throughout his life. While living in Chicago, Spiegel helped to organize the Hebrew Benevolent Society, was for a time its president, and was a member of one of the first Reform congregations in the city. It is not known whether he and Caroline kept a kosher home, but later, while in the army, either by choice or out of necessity, he did not observe the Jewish dietary laws; in his letters he mentions that he could eat almost everything, including pork. A religious man, Marcus did adhere to the traditions of Judaism whenever possible, and his letters show that he was able occasionally to attend services even in the field. In 1862 he planned to journey twelve miles from camp to Norfolk, Virginia in order to attend High Holiday services. He sent Caroline explicit instructions to keep their children home from school on Rosh Hashanah and Yom Kippur and reminded her to observe Passover. While at war in the South, Spiegel prayed to the "God of Israel" for safe deliverance from the enemy, and also enjoyed socializing with Jews among the Southerners. It remained important for him to set a good example for his children and to leave them a legacy of strong religious faith and tradition.

In the late spring of 1854 when Caroline Spiegel—pregnant with their first child—returned to Ohio to visit her family, Marcus Spiegel again demonstrated his commitment to Judaism. "Ah, my sweet little darling," he reminded her, "do not forget that you are a Jehudah [Jew]." Recalling that "you carry our offspring beneath your heart," he hoped that God would "give us the blessing of being enabled to raise him or her, as a good Citizen and Jehudah." Despite his reference to both sexes, he frequently referred to their eagerly awaited child as "our little son." He also often expressed deep affection—indeed passion—for his wife (". . . if I could only now see you and give you a good lon——g kis——s"). As later during the Civil War, he urged her to write more frequently, while she occasionally gave voice to doubts that he really missed her. "I do not think your letter was

Marcus Spiegel and Caroline Hamlin Spiegel, at
about the time of their marriage in 1853

quite so affectionate as usual," she wrote, "are you not almost used to
live without me." Marcus Spiegel hastened to assure her that life was
tasteless without her; for him even the fraternal lodges and theaters
had temporarily lost their attraction.

More important for the Spiegels' future than their pangs of separa-
tion was their discussion of where they should live and work. On the
one hand, Marcus Spiegel at first asked his wife to inquire among his
relatives and friends in Ohio as to business prospects there for him.
But on the other hand, he believed he had good prospects at the
Clark store in Chicago and eventually on his own, and he made evident his enjoyment at living in the rapidly growing metropolis of
Illinois. One reason for his ultimate decision might have been his
wife's homesickness for her native state. Another most certainly was
her report that some people in Limaville, Ohio, had expressed scorn
of the couple. Her offended husband angrily exclaimed that the talk
of such "dam, dam fools" made him "allmost raging mad." He concluded, "The best thing for to stop their talk and make them burst for
jealousy is to start a Store some place in Ohio and show them how to
live and how to dispice them." In mid-summer, he joined Caroline in

Ohio and, with the probable aid of Ohio friends, attempted to become a successful entrepreneur.[15]

The young Spiegels settled in the village of East Liberty in Green Township, located about ten miles south of Akron, and opened up a general country store. Besides retailing goods and buying produce, Spiegel also became postmaster of the Summit Post Office, which he probably maintained in his store.[16] How happy they were a short time later when Hamlin, their first child, was born in 1854. Spiegel, a husband and now a father, assumed the same role the Greenebaums had several years earlier: the older established immigrants who wholeheartedly volunteered to help outfit the many young German newcomers with their basic peddling articles. Identifying strongly with these enterprising young men, he gladly offered them food and lodging, never forgetting his responsibility to his compatriots. Unfortunately, the men whom Spiegel backed did not always understand how to make money to repay him. According to his daughter, "They charged goods for the farmer with the red barn, or with the white fence, and that was poor identification in a land of red barns and white fences."[17]

Spiegel's appointment as a postmaster, a patronage position, accurately indicates that he had become politically active. While in Chicago, he had talked with Republicans and ardent opponents of slavery, among them Michael Greenebaum, but such was not Marcus's political disposition. Instead, like the majority of German-Americans, he rejected the party whose ranks included many recruits from the antiforeign Know-Nothing movement. After becoming a citizen on March 27, 1857,[18] he supported the Democracy. As his letters indicate, his political idol was the chieftain of the Democrats of the Old Northwest, Stephen A. Douglas. Like many Democrats, he was apathetic to the plight of the Negro slave, of which in any event

15. Ten of the letters that Spiegel wrote to his wife in 1854 are in an album of Jeanette Freiler of Chicago, at publication in the possession of Elizabeth Stein who courteously made it available. The first quotes from Marcus Spiegel are from his letter of [May? 1854]. The words quoted from Caroline Spiegel are repeated by her husband in his letter of Monday Evening, 9 o'clock P.M. [June 1854]. The quotes regarding Limaville gossip and a store are from his letter of Tuesday, 11 o'clock A.M. [June 1854].

16. Copy of postmaster's commission dated Nov. 10, 1855, in Soman Coll.; original in Spiegel Papers, AJA.

17. Barbe, "Memoirs," 4.

18. Copy of naturalization certificate in Soman Coll.

Spiegel and his associates had no firsthand knowledge. Moreover, many Ohio Democrats believed that the Negro, if freed, would move north and take jobs away from white workers. Marcus Spiegel, influenced by his party and fellow citizens, was no abolitionist in the 1850s—though by 1864 he would evolve into an ardent supporter of emancipation.

Preoccupied with their own affairs, the Spiegels lived the life of a typical village couple. It was commonplace in their society to hire a servant, and a copy of the indentured-servant contract between Sarah Foust, in behalf of her twelve-year-old daughter, Elizabeth, and Marcus Spiegel, which was signed in 1855, has been preserved.[19] The terms of this agreement state that this young girl was to live in the Spiegel household and help with the housework and children in return for meals, clothing, schooling, and lodging until she reached the age of eighteen. Elizabeth was treated as a member of the family, and Spiegel's frequent inquiries about her in his letters indicate his concern for her welfare. Elizabeth Foust's duties grew greater in 1856 when the Spiegels' first daughter, Lizzie, was born. A year later, Spiegel mourned the death of his father, who died at Cleveland on November 1, 1857 while travelling to visit Marcus, Caroline, and the grandchildren.[20] By 1860, when the Spiegels' third child, Moses, was born, they had moved to Akron. With his good personality and winning smile, Spiegel soon became popular in his new hometown. He was an officer in the Summit Lodge of Independent Order of Odd Fellows, and was also a Mason.[21] He continued to buy and sell produce and claimed to own real estate worth $3,000.[22] Still, he hoped to do better and was willing to move again to seek his fortune.

---

19. Copy in Soman Coll.

20. *The Occident,* 15(April 1858). Caroline's father, Stephen Hamlin, had died a year earlier in Stark County on Nov. 21, 1856.

21. Smalley and Sturdivant, *Credit Merchants,* 7.

22. U.S. Census, 1860, manuscript return for Summit County, 293, microfilm copy at the Western Reserve Historical Society, Cleveland, Ohio, hereafter cited as WRHS. A check mark obscures the first number of the real estate evaluation but it appears to be a "3." Spiegel may not necessarily have been free of debt for this property.

CHAPTER TWO

# From Warehouseman to Warrior

"We have been personally acquainted with Mr. S. for a number of years," remarked an editor in May 1860, "and it affords us great pleasure to assure the people of Holmes County that he is a gentleman in every sense of the word, and a thorough business man; one," concluded Democrat and newspaper editor James A. Estill, "in whom the utmost confidence may be placed." Spiegel came to Holmes County as a participant in a firm formed by moneyed men from nearby Akron and Ravenna, intending to do business as E. Steinbacher and Co., Produce and Commission Merchants. By locating in Millersburg at the end of what was then a branch-line railroad, the new company would be able to tap the abundant resources of the surrounding agricultural region. As agent for the firm, Spiegel would sell certain staples and buy wool produced by Holmes County's many sheep and grain to supply the expanding mills of Akron. He would do business in a leased warehouse, a two-story, red-painted frame building next to the railroad tracks. As he began, he received another editor's encouraging testimonial that "his experience and agreeable manners are certain guarantees of success anywhere."[1]

Much about Spiegel's new home held out hope of success and satisfaction. This picturesque part of Ohio was reminiscent of Germany, with its lofty rolling hills, dotted with carefully tended farms. Millersburg, a village of 1,160 on the east bank of Killbuck Creek, was similar in size to Abenheim and, little more than a generation beyond its establishment, was still a raw, growing community. Though its streets

---

1. Spiegel's business associates were Weimer & Steinbacher and Buel & Taylor. The quotations are from the *Millersburg Holmes County Farmer* (hereafter abbreviated MF), May 17 and 31, 1860, the latter issue quoting the *Akron Summit Democracy*. See also MF for June 7, 1860. Estill (1837–83) was a Pennsylvania-born lawyer and politician. Marguerite Dickinson, "Obituaries Abstracted from Holmes County Ohio Papers in Farmer Hub Office, Millersburg Library, Holmes County Historical Society, Western Reserve Historical Society," 26, typescript in WRHS. For the appearance of the warehouse, see J. A. Caldwell, *Caldwell's Atlas of Holmes Co. Ohio from Actual Surveys . . .* (Condit, Ohio: J. A. Caldwell, 1875), 31.

were dusty or muddy depending upon the season, it boasted of being the county seat and was the trading center of a predominantly agricultural district. Holmes County had been little affected by the economic and political changes which were bringing manufacturing and Republicanism, often in tandem, to other parts of the state. Spiegel, an ardent Democrat, could easily relate to a strongly Democratic town which still without fail commemorated the anniversary of Andrew Jackson's victory at New Orleans.[2] Indeed, the businesses themselves suggested by their names the electorate's loyalty to Stephen A. Douglas; one clothing store marked itself with "the Sign of the Little Giant" and another, using a Douglas slogan, called itself the Young America Clothing House. Many in Millersburg shared Spiegel's political views, including his support for Douglas and hostility to antislavery politicians. As to the slaves and to blacks generally, Millersburg residents took at best a dim view of their capabilities, and at worst, like editor James A. Estill, were near rabid with Negrophobia. While few blacks lived in Millersburg, the town held a remarkable diversity of whites. From the beginning of settlement, Virginians had mingled with Pennsylvanians, including Amish and Mennonites, and Swiss and Germans had arrived directly from Europe to farm in the vicinity. The frequent use of German dialects created opportunities for merchants able to communicate with these potential customers. Several German and Jewish storekeepers had already opened shops. In joining them, Spiegel would find both business associates and friends.[3]

By late summer of 1860, Spiegel had bought a house for about $900 and moved in with his wife and three children. Among his near neighbors and soon-to-be friends were Benjamin Cohn, tailor and clothing dealer, and Henry Herzer, partner in a grocery and restau-

2. For population, MF, Apr. 4, 1861; for the appearance of Millersburg, L. R. Critchfield to Marcus Spiegel, Feb. 21, 1862, in the Spiegel Papers, AJA; for economy and politics, Andrew Jackson Stiffler, *The Standard Atlas of Holmes County* . . . (Cincinnati: Standard Atlas Publishing, 1907), 12.

3. See advertisements in *Millersburg Republican* (hereafter cited as MR), May 8, June 20, 1861; for Estill's racial views, see MF, Oct. 25, 1860; for political and ethnic background, see Fred W. Almendinger, *An Historical Study of Holmes County, Ohio*, M.A. thesis, University of Southern California, 1938 ([Millersburg]: Library Archives of Holmes County, Ohio, 1962), 23, 49–51, 79–80; Catherine Joss, *Autobiography of Catherine Joss* . . . (Cleveland, 1891), 13–14, 40.

rant.[4] These men were also Spiegel's brothers in the local Masonic lodge. Quickly winning a reputation as a "jolly fellow" and "powerful eater," Spiegel was an obvious choice to help arrange the Masonic "Pic-Nic." He earned the advanced degree of Royal Arch Mason and also continued to join other fraternal groups. When the Sons of Malta spread to Millersburg, the jovial businessman almost inevitably became a leader in one of the first funmaking secret societies. Its main activity was putting new recruits through a rowdy and strenuous initiation.[5] With many of his fraternal and business associates, including Herzer, Cohn, and Estill, Spiegel joined in the campaign to elect Stephen A. Douglas to the American presidency. He attended conventions and rallies and on September 21, 1860 was one of the German speakers before a crowd of over five thousand which gathered in the German and Swiss village of Weinsberg (later Winesburg), Ohio.[6]

A minority in Holmes County opposed Douglas. In fact, a delegate from this Democratic county to the Republican national convention played a key role in nominating Douglas's most dangerous opponent. Dr. Robert K. Enos, Millersburg physician and banker, helped arrange the sudden shift of Ohio votes which made Abraham Lincoln the party's nominee. Despite this local interest, however, most of the county's votes went to the Democrats and the majority doubtless shared editor Estill's disgust at Lincoln's victory, which put them "for four years under Black Republican rule, provided the Union lasts so long." As Estill had feared, Southern states reacted to Lincoln's election by leaving the Union. In April 1861, when the rebel attack on

4. For house, see MF, Aug. 23, 1860; advertisements for Herzer and Cohn are in ibid., Sept. 5, 1861, and MR, May 8, 1862. Cohn, who was thirty-five, and Herzer, who was twenty-four, were both of German birth, married men with children. U.S. Census, 1860, manuscript return for Holmes County, 317, 326.

5. For Spiegel's Masonry, see Benjamin Cohn to Major General Canby, May 26, 1864, copy in the Spiegel Papers, AJA; MF, Jan. 3, Dec. 19, 1861. The quoted words describing Spiegel are from a satirical letter signed "Jonathan Q. Smith," probably written by Estill, in MF, Jan. 24, 1861. It said of Spiegel: "He is a rale [real], clever, holesoled, jolly fellow but he is a powerful eater." Cohn was said to be "terrible on logger [lager] and switzer cheese." For Sons of Malta, see MF, Aug. 29, 1861, and Albert C. Stevens, *The Cyclopedia of Fraternities* . . ., 2d ed. (New York: E. B. Treat, 1907, rpt. Detroit: Gale Research Co., 1966), 284.

6. MF, June 28, July 12, Aug. 16, Sept. 27, 1860.

Fort Sumter brought war, Estill quickly dropped his initial idea that Republicans should do all of the fighting and joined the great bulk of his fellow citizens in a cry to uphold "THE CONSTITUTION, THE UNION AND THE ENFORCEMENT OF THE LAWS."[7]

Spiegel did not join the first company of troops to leave Millersburg. A man of his age, with a wife and three small children, might well have thought it both unwise and unnecessary to join the rush of youths to fight in the expected brief campaign. Moreover, his business affairs were at a turning point. He and Henry Herzer were in the process of buying out Spiegel's original associates and by summer were operating as partners. Spiegel not only helped run the "Red Warehouse," as they called it, but also rode into neighboring counties to buy wool. On one occasion he broke two ribs in a fall. Another day, hot and dust-covered, he was turned away at a hotel. "Being a good liver, and possessing ponderous capacity of stomach," according to Estill, he wished to eat and sleep at the Kenyon House in Mount Vernon. "'Lantlort,' he called out, 'coust you feet me and my horses and dis uner feller all night.'" The proprietor, seeing them dusty and with a large package in the buggy, mistook them for peddlers and refused to keep them, whereupon they parted in ill temper. Perhaps this affair represented one of Spiegel's few recorded contacts with what may have been antiforeign or anti-Jewish prejudice. Yet more representative of the atmosphere of tolerance (at least toward whites) in which Spiegel moved was the editor's headlining the story "Bad Luck to the Kenyon House" and urging Holmes County people to boycott the place.[8]

---

7. D. P. Garber, *The Holmes County Rebellion* (n.p., 1967), 2. While at the Republican convention, delegate Enos was the victim of a pickpocket, according to the Democratic editor, who chortled that he "got 'Chicagoed' at that interesting city." As indicated below, Spiegel had financial relationships with Pennsylvania-born Robert K. Enos, 1806–84. A physician, lawyer, and businessman, Enos became one of Millersburg's wealthier men. His friendship with the influential Simon Perkins of Akron had helped to secure the railroad for Millersburg. *Commemorative Biographical Record of the Counties of Wayne and Holmes, Ohio.* . . . (Chicago: J. H. Beers, 1889), 610–15; MF, May 24, 1860. For reactions to election and secession, see issues of Nov. 8, 1860 (first quote), Apr. 18 and 25 (second quote), 1861.

8. For the new partnership, MF, May 23, 30, and Nov. 21, 1861; Spiegel's fall, Oct. 3, 1861; hotel, Sept. 26, 1861. Estill did not specifically say that the rejected buyer was Spiegel but concluded, "For further particulars we refer the reader to M. M. Speigel [*sic*]." (Even those who knew Spiegel well mis-

While social problems were rare, economic difficulties were frequent. As Spiegel's later letters indicate, there was concern over debts to the bankers Enos, Brown Company and to his friend Cohn, a worry to him and evidently even more to Caroline Spiegel. The depression following the Panic of 1857 and the economic confusion at the war's beginning made it a difficult time for a new business. Thus, when the North failed to achieve a quick triumph and called for more troops, Spiegel had economic as well as patriotic reasons for responding. For him as well as others, steady pay, especially as an officer, might mean financial salvation. Above all, as a German-Jewish immigrant, he felt it was his duty to preserve the American Union for his children.[9]

Spiegel might well hope to be an officer. It is unclear whether he had had military experience in the German Revolution of 1848, but in the United States eleven years later, when Gov. Salmon P. Chase had reorganized the Ohio militia, Spiegel had obtained a commission as brigade major, and in the ensuing years his political connections with both Democrats and Republicans from his area had if anything improved.[10] His first thought was to become quartermaster of the Forty-fifth Ohio Volunteer Infantry, a position well suited to his mercantile background. He was able to get the endorsement of the prominent men on the local Military Committee, part of the statewide system to

---

spelled his name in several ways.) There is no evidence that Spiegel or other Millersburg Jews faced the bias described as existing in Buffalo, New York, in David A. Gerber, "Cutting Out Shylock: Elite Anti-Semitism and the Quest for Moral Order in the Mid-Nineteenth Century American Market Place," in *Journal of American History* 69(December 1982):615–37. For more on prejudice, see also John Higham, *Send These to Me: Jews and Other Immigrants in Urban America* (New York: Atheneum, 1975), 138–43.

9. James M. McPherson, *Ordeal By Fire: The Civil War and Reconstruction* (New York: Knopf, 1982), 200–201, 251, 372–73.

10. A Democratic editor in an article encouraging recruiting by Spiegel claimed that the latter had been "an officer under Gen. Seigel [Franz Sigel] in the German Revolution of 1848." *Cleveland Plain Dealer*, quoted in MF, Nov. 21, 1861. For the reorganization of the militia, see Eugene H. Roseboom, *The Civil War Era, 1850–1873*, vol. 6 of Carl Wittke, ed., *The History of the State of Ohio* (Columbus: Ohio Historical Society, 1944), 383. A photocopy of Spiegel's commission dated Aug. 12, 1859 is in the Soman Coll., the original being in the Chicago Jewish Archives. The commission is incorrectly made out to "Martin Speigle" but Spiegel properly signed the oath on the reverse. He dated the oath Sept. 1, 1859, early enough so that he may have participated in the encampment of the Second Brigade, Eighteenth Division at Akron later that month. *Akron Summit Beacon*, Sept. 21, 1859.

coordinate recruiting, and even to secure the intervention of the governor's military aide, Martin Welker, a Republican lawyer and politician formerly from Millersburg. But Welker reported that Gov. William Dennison, a Republican, had promised the much-sought-after post to someone else and Spiegel settled for becoming a recruiting lieutenant.[11] In eye-catching advertisements, Spiegel called for men to "Rally under the Good Old Flag your Forefathers Defended" and also reminded them of the $100 bounty for enlisting. The great bulk of his recruits were Democrats from Holmes County. Among them were many of Spiegel's German compatriots, including several army veterans. After Spiegel and his company left on December 11, 1861, Amish customers still occasionally came inquiring, "Where ish der Spiegel?" A friend replied, "Fighting the battles of his country against the damned rebels."[12]

---

11. For the military committee system, see a message of Adj. Gen. C. P. Buckingham, Sept. 27, 1861, reprinted in MF, Oct. 17, 1861; for recommendation of the Military Committee of Holmes County, see Robert Long to Gov. William Dennison, Oct. 28, 1861, in Ohio, Adjutant General, Correspondence, Ohio Historical Society, Columbus (hereafter cited as OAGC). This collection contains evidence of vigorous competition to become quartermaster of various regiments. M. Welker to Major Spiegel, Oct. 28 and 30, 1861, in Soman Coll. Welker, born in Knox County, Ohio, in 1819, read law and practiced in Millersburg. He was a Whig and later a Republican. In 1857, he moved to Wooster and also was elected lieutenant-governor under Chase. (As such he would have been in a position to obtain Spiegel's commission as major.) Enjoying close relations with Dennison, he subsequently won three terms in Congress and became a federal district judge. George I. Reed, *Bench and Bar of Ohio: A Compendium of History and Biography,* 2 vols. (Chicago: Century Pub., 1897), 1:225–28. For Spiegel's commissioning as lieutenant, see Robert Long to [Governor of Ohio?], [Nov. 12, 1861], in OAGC, which certified that Spiegel was "of good moral character and possesses sufficient qualifications to command a company" and also had the approval of the regimental commander.

12. Announcing Spiegel's recruiting, James A. Estill hailed him as "one of our best citizens, and he is not only the right man in the right place, but he is the right man in any place that may be assigned him." Anxious to prove that Democrats were as patriotic as Republicans, the editor ironically added, "He is, however, a rank secessionist, having voted the Democratic ticket at the recent election." MF, Nov. 21, 1861. For Spiegel's advertising and the political and ethnic composition of his company, ibid., Dec. 12 and 26, 1861, Jan. 16, 1862. The final quotation is from L. R. Critchfield to Marcus Spiegel, Feb. 21, 1862, in Spiegel Papers, AJA.

Going by rail to Cleveland, Spiegel and his recruits became part of the force being gathered by Alvin C. Voris, a thirty-three-year-old lawyer. Born in Stark County, Voris had attended Oberlin College for two years. He settled in Akron, read law, and became a partner of the politically significant Gen. Lucius V. Bierce. In 1859 he had been elected as a Republican member of the Ohio House of Representatives. From legislator to lieutenant colonel of the Forty-fifth Ohio was an easy transition—easier, as it turned out, than recruiting the thousand men necessary to fill the regiment. When the state adjutant general decided to consolidate several incomplete units, the men of the Forty-fifth found themselves greatly outnumbered by the more than seven hundred recruits gathered in the Toledo area for the Sixty-seventh Ohio. Perforce they lost their identity to the larger regiment, and Voris became second in command. A Columbus editor noted that there was "considerable fluttering" among the officers of the merged units but supported the consolidation "no matter whose feathers fly." In the feuding common in Civil War regiments, Spiegel and others of the minority from the old Forty-fifth might well have ended as plucked birds.[13]

Fortunately for Spiegel, the attitudes of the original members of the Sixty-seventh Ohio presented opportunity rather than menace. Shortly after the regiment began recruiting at Toledo, Governor Dennison had sent as its commander a dubious figure. Otto Buerstenbinder, a native of Hamburg, Germany and about thirty years old, claimed to have had formal military training and experience in the wars of Europe. In ordinary times, his claims to have held high positions in Mexico and El Salvador during the 1850s might have been investigated, but in the crisis of the Union a colonel's commission was quickly forthcoming. Initially well received at Toledo, Buerstenbinder soon antagonized part of the community and some of his officers, forcing the reassignment of the regiment's original lieutenant colonel. By Christmas Eve, 1861, when the Sixty-seventh left Toledo, at least part of its men had lost confidence in their colonel. While they were at Columbus, some came to question the authenticity of his military

---

13. "General A. C. Voris," in *Magazine of Western History* 4(August 1886):507–15; A. C. Voris to [Governor], Nov. 29, 1861, in Ohio, Governors' Papers, Ohio Historical Society, Columbus (microfilm copy at Kent State University, Kent, Ohio); Rodney J. Hathaway, "History of the 67th Reg. O.V.I.," 2, typescript in WRHS; *Columbus Journal* quoted in *Daily Toledo Blade*, Dec. 19, 1861.

record, noting that he gave commands to the regiment seldom and then made mistakes. There were complaints of "petty tyranny" and "love of drink." Those aggrieved within the Sixty-seventh, added to those drawn from the old Forty-fifth, might well have been a majority of the consolidated regiment. For Spiegel and even more for his friend Lieutenant Colonel Voris, a chance existed to gain the confidence of the disaffected Toledoans. All this was still in the future, however, as the men of the former Forty-fifth joined the Sixty-seventh at Camp Chase on the edge of Columbus.[14]

There on January 2, 1862 Spiegel, who had been made a captain two weeks earlier, was mustered with his men into the United States service as Company C, Sixty-seventh Ohio Volunteer Infantry. Captain Spiegel was a handsome officer. His black curly hair was cut stylishly short. While in the army, he sometimes shaved his chin but always wore side whiskers and a long mustache curving over his rather full lips. His eyes were dark; his nose fairly long. Spiegel was of middling height with a relatively slight frame. At the time he entered the military, good living had thickened his midriff. Before he and his men left Camp Chase, they were armed and uniformed.[15]

While still at Columbus, Spiegel began to write the series of letters with which, like many a soldier of the Civil War, he would form a record of his military adventure. Through their content, he clearly indicated why he would succeed as an officer. Helpful, of course, were his political connections and even his ethnic background in dealing with many of his men. He faced little overt anti-Semitism. Even more important in explaining his success were his geniality, his paternal concern for his "boys" and the physical courage without which no company officer could keep his men's respect. Additional factors facilitated his rise to higher commands. Especially significant were his intelligence and ability to acquire technical skills, his stability and free-

---

14. For Buerstenbinder's background, *Daily Toledo Blade*, Oct. 19, 1861; for Sixty-seventh Ohio's departure and controversy involving Buerstenbinder, ibid., Dec. 21, 23, 26, 28, and 31, 1861, Jan. 21, Feb. 5, 1862. An early critique of Buerstenbinder is S. A. Raymond to Governor Dennison, Nov. 13, 1861, in Ohio, Governors' Papers.

15. Ohio, Roster Commission, *Official Roster of the Soldiers of the State of Ohio in the War of the Rebellion, 1861–1866,* 12 vols. (Akron: Werner Co., 1886–95), 5:578. Hereafter cited as Roster. The description of Spiegel is based on contemporary photographs in Soman Coll., and on references to his girth cited above. For equipping the regiment, *Daily Toledo Blade*, Jan. 3, 1862.

dom from such weaknesses as drunkenness, and his usefulness to Republican leaders as a cooperative Democrat. Not surprisingly, Spiegel showed through his letters a growing fondness for the role in which he was achieving so much.

He also demonstrated more or less constant tensions with his wife over this very point. Possibly Caroline Spiegel's Quaker origins may have caused some of her evident wish that her husband should leave the war. Surely her worries over their debts and general financial situation also were involved. Moreover, caring for their children, while expecting new ones, and the effects of simple loneliness were enough to explain her unhappiness, which Spiegel would so often try to assuage while undiplomatically making it obvious that he would not resign as she so much wished. Spiegel's younger brother, Joseph, moved to Millersburg shortly after Marcus went to fight in Virginia. Joseph helped Caroline with the children and also assisted at the warehouse. Marcus Spiegel constantly expresses his love and concern for his younger brother, and throughout his writing this bond is strengthened. Thus on a personal level, the Spiegel letters trace the difficulties of a family in wartime. In the political sphere, they demonstrate the shifting attitudes of a Democrat toward the Lincoln administration, slavery, and even Holmes County neighbors. On the military plane, they give glimpses of combat in both east and west and of camp life, including some rare information on the sutlers or travelling storekeepers who sold to the troops. Weeks, months, and years of correspondence develop these themes, a time span unanticipated by Spiegel when he began writing the letters.

In preparing Spiegel's letters for publication, the editors have pursued a course between the extremes of a complete, literal reproduction of the whole collection, perhaps best achieved by printing photocopies, and the correcting, improving kinds of revision which an editor might give to the work of a living author. It would have been needlessly expensive and historically useless to print repetitious descriptions of the same event, similar comments on politics and personalities, and the oft-repeated endearments, injunctions, and inquiries that recur in most families' letters. Accordingly we have omitted entirely a few letters and parts of many others, indicating deletions except for the omission of military headings. As to the material included, we have thought it important to demonstrate the extent to which Spiegel had mastered written English, the continuing influence on his writing of his ethnic background, and the improvement in style so characteristic of prolonged Civil War correspondence. Accordingly we have reproduced verbatim the first two letters and the last letters for each year, five in all. On the other hand, we have considered it unhelpful to the reader to copy Spiegel's routine misspellings and frequent run-on sentences. Therefore in all letters except the five mentioned, we have regularized to some extent spelling and punctuation and spelled out abbreviations, much as newspaper editors had already done for those Spiegel letters which we have taken from the nineteenth-century press. We have retained, however, phonetic spellings likely to be characteristic of Spiegel's pronunciation, mainly avoiding the use of "*sic*" so as not to break the flow of the letters. Occasional translations from German, Hebrew, and Yiddish have been indicated. We hope that we have served the needs both of scholars, who may in any event wish to consult the originals,[16] and of the varied readers who we hope will enjoy getting to know Marcus Spiegel.

---

16. Most of the original Spiegel letters are in the Spiegel Papers, AJA, while original photographs and additional letters are in Soman Coll.

# CHAPTER THREE

# "Who wouldent be a Soldier?"

Camp Chase near Columbus[1]
Sunday December 29/61

My dear & much beloved Wife and Children!

Last night we arrived here at about 10 o'clock after a ride of 8 hours from Cleveland, and we came here found that Lieut Chapman[2] had a good Supper prepared for the Boys. (I send Chapman 1 day sooner). here we have Barracks large & Comodius   I consider them as decidedly superior to the Tents, the Barracks for the Boys are prepared so as to accommodate 18 the[y] have Bunks to sleep on three in a Bunk and 2 Bunks in one length & 3 length over each other leaving a Room in front as large as our Kitchen   My quarters are prepared with Bunk also & as warm as can be. I have nothing to wish for but my family & friends I left at home   if I could only see you and the children onced a day, I would feel as happy as I could wish   But as I have taken it upon me to be a bold Soldier Boy I must feel resigned and I feel it my dear Cary that I will come ere soon and neither you or any of my friends will feel sorry or ashamed that I have enlisted in my Countrys cause.

Lt. Col. Voris is a true & tried friend to me, all the time he has to spare he spends in my company all consultations he makes with me & in short I know his heart is right   by the way the most heart rendering Scene I have seen yet since the opening of this Campayne was the parting Scene of Voris and his wife at Akron, it was awfull, he is not going home untill after the war is over.

It looks now as though we would stay here about 2 Mos. at least.

---

1. The first two letters are reproduced verbatim.
2. 1st Lt. John B. Chapman. Roster 5:578.

By the way, when I went to dinner to day at the Boarding house on Camp I was talking to Chapman and when my name was mentioned a very fine looking Gentleman got up aproached me very cordially and introduced himself as our Colonel Burstenbinder and said a great many nice & flattering things to me, he is a perfect Gentleman & I know him and I will be friends. I saw all the Liberty Boys Harringtons, Remely, Cline, Foust, & other as soon as they heard I had come they came & want me to try & have them transferred in my Company also Frank Manderbach (tell Jacob).[3]

Gensdarm Jacob Graesley[4] is still my servant & he makes a first rate one   he takes the best kind of care of me and my things. I intend to come the latter part of the week and tell you a great many pretty things.

While I write to you I can hear 2 Bands playing and the drummers beating. This is most a magnificent day and the Guard mounting & dress parade to day was splendit, I wish to God you and the Children and Onkel Joseph[5] were here what a nice time we would have. I hope that the children are all hearty and behave well so that I will hear no complaint I hope they will make their dear mother no trouble, because she has trouble enough while their Papa is away, o but I will love them so well if they are right good children.

My dear wife I bid you for the sake of the love I bear towards you be easy, dont trouble yourself any, but take the times as easy as you possible can & let us hope and trust that the day will not be far distant when we will live together again never to be separated again and without any of

---

3. Men from East Liberty, Spiegel's former home village, who were not in the Sixty-seventh Ohio. Spiegel probably refers to Eli, William F., or Theodore N. Harrington, Frederick C. or Christian Remley, William Cline, George Foust, and Benjamin F. Manderback, all of the Twenty-ninth Ohio. Roster 3:367, 378, 379, 380, 388.

4. Pvt. Jacob Grassly, to whom Spiegel gives an ironic title. Roster 5:581.

5. Joseph Spiegel, Marcus's younger brother, born in 1839. As the following letters indicate, he had recently come to Millersburg from New York. Marcus was fond of him and also felt responsible for his economic welfare. Marcus refers to him by varying names, including Josey and Jo.

those pecuniary troubles that I have had for the last 3 years. Farewell my loves & remember your ever loving husband & father.

Marcus

Give my best wishes to Onkle Jo & Elizabeth.[6]

HeadQuarters Color Comp.
67th Regt. Camp Chase Jan. 3/62

My dear & much beloved Wife and Children

I just have a few minutes to tell you that as I was ready to start for home to day I recd. orders from Head Quarters that I was not permited to leave untill after the inauguration of the new Governor[7] in which occasion we are to have grand review.

I am well & feel as hearty as I ever dit in my life & if could only see you and the children onced every hour would not wish it any better pecuniary as well as respectable.

My Company is Comp. C the Color Company of the Regt. & we feel proud of it.[8] The new Col. is very favorably disposed towards me and I think would do anything to please me. I shall have no difficulty in getting the Quarter-Master ship either for me or Henry & Joseph.[9]

I can not say wether I can come Home after the Inauguration, but I send you $10 and if you would only make up your mind to come here Friday night the 11th [10th] I would call for you at the depot & you could stay and see the inauguration of the Governor elect & I know you would have a good time with me, you might bring Hamlin & Lizzie

6. Elizabeth Foust, originally of East Liberty, the Spiegels' former "bound girl," maid, and member of their household.

7. David Tod, elected on the Union party ticket and, like Spiegel, a prewar Democrat and supporter of Stephen A. Douglas. Roseboom, *Civil War Era*, 392.

8. When the regiment was formed in line of battle, its flag would be located in Company C.

9. Henry Herzer, Spiegel's business partner, and Joseph, Marcus's brother, both of Millersburg.

along or leave them at home if you bring them I can find
somebody to take care of them & I take care of you. Let me
know right off wether you will come or not, I wish to God
you would I know you would enjoy it better than anything
you ever done.

I am doing very well only I would like to see you awfull
well, I am really homesick for you. I drilled the Boys all day
& am getting to be quite a Soldier. my men love me & are
willing to swear by me.

My love to all the Children, kiss them for me & say to
them to be good children, & I will be all right.

Ever loving & true
Your
Marcus

Head Quarters Company C
67th Reg. or in other
words "at my lonely
barracks"
January 9th 1862

My dear and much beloved Wife! and good children!

It is the Evening of [a] musty and foggy day, after Company Drill in the forenoon, Battalion Drill and Dress Parade
in the afternoon and then only after I am permitted (in
consequence of an order issued to my company to day of
which you find a copy enclosed) [not found] to set in my
own Quarters with nobody but Jacob with me to address
you a few lines. I intend to give you a history of every thing
that happened since we are here, that is a Synopsis and I
know my dear wife that you will not be displeased with it,
more especially if you enjoy my letters half as much as I do
yours. Nothing has given me so much real happiness since I
am a Soldier, as your letter. I read it about 5 times a day at
least. It is full of essence of life for me, just like you, love,
advice and full of practical Good sense. I think I have in my
last letter given you a description of our arrival and I now
propose to follow up and if I reiterate any already given to
you in my last, I hope you will forgive me.

Allow me here to say that the officers of the 67th Regiment are as good, clever, and gentlemanly set of men as I ever met. They are men of the right stamp, men of means and of hearts and I do not know which one to mention to you as the best except it be Captain H. G. Ford who is about as fine a looking man as I ever saw, and as good as he is handsome, a Knight Templar and an intimate friend of mine already. He may probably come home with me.[10]

I think [I] have already given you a history of our New Year's evening consolidation Feast and dedication of our Regiments Messroom. If I have not, allow me here to say that it was as pleasant a night as I ever spent in a company of men; everything passed off most happy and the consolidation was complete, not only of men of the 45th and 67th Regiments but of hearts and Souls of brother Officers, until 12 o'clock, when every body retired, satisfied that no happier choice could possibly have been made. By the way the Officers' Mess Room is an institution started upon the suggestion of the worthy Colonel Buerstenbinder and is conducted on the following manner: all the Field, Line and Staff Officers are united in one Mess; they appoint a Committee of one Captain, and 1st Lieutenant and one 2nd Lieutenant who buy the provisions, superintend the cooking and preside at the table and render account to the Mess. We have breakfast at 7, Lunch at 12 o'clock and Dinner at 6 o'clock P.M. We get Ham and Eggs, Buck Wheat cakes and so forth for Breakfast; Soup and cold meats for Lunch and splendit table for our Dinner which I however call Supper. There being 40 Officers in the Regiment, the average expenses are about from $2.50 to 2.75 per week and the boarding could not be any better and I might as well here say that I never had better appetite in my life, as we have our regular time for Drill 3 hours in the forenoon and 3 hours in the afternoon, which I regularly attend. My Quar-

---

10. Hyatt G. Ford of Company B. The Knights Templars were a Masonic group composed only of Christians. Roster 5:572; Stevens, *Cyclopedia of Fraternities*, 41.

ters I had to fix up this week so that they are now just as good as our house in Millersburg with the exception of my dear family.

My Company is making very efficient progress in drill; there is no Company in the Regiment that can beat them. The Boys are all right and I am not saying too much when I say that they love me, like they would a father. I have no difficulty at all in keeping them under strict military discipline and had only onced placed one in the Guard house, whom I discharged from the Company for he was a thief. His name is Rose, he was from Fredericksburg and was enlisted by Chapman and John Irvine on Christmas day.[11] Next Tuesday we have to march to Columbus for Inauguration. My Company is the Color Company of the Regiment and I tell you the boys feel proud of it. I have only been to Columbus twiced since I am here and that was on business onced and in Lodge once with 16 of our Officers. By the way we are starting a Lodge for our Regiment; we have 20 Masons in our Regiment that we know of. Our Colonel will not allow scarcely any of the officers nor men to leave Camp. One of my friends, Captain Platt,[12] went to town yesterday without leave and dit not come back till to day. When he returned the Colonel ordered him to report himself under arrest, deliver up his sword and stand a Court martial. I am very sorry for him, for he is a good fellow and meant no harm but such is military discipline.

I intend to come home after this week if I dare and stay a week at least. You have no idea how bad I long to see you all and tell you everything, but I will have to wait till my Superiors say so.

My prospects are O.K., everything will be all right. I get the best of treatment from Colonel down to Camp Carpenter. Jacob is a first rate Servant, he does anything in the

11. Probably William B. Rose, discharged on surgeon's certificate of disability on Jan. 2, 1862. Roster 5:583. Irvine was not in the Sixty-seventh. Possibly he was a private in the First Ohio Light Artillery. Ibid., 10:425.

12. Edwin S. Platt of Company E. Roster 5:591.

world for me and treats me as a friend. The Boys are all well and feel well except 1 or 2 that have bad cold. We had good snow but it is all gone. Colonel Voris just now came in my room and is raising the devil, going through Sword Exercises. As I said to you he is all right, a better and truer friend I never had and I know you will be satisfied with the way he sees me through. . . .

On the day of the gubernatorial inauguration, Spiegel obtained leave to visit his family. Through the *Millersburg Farmer* he announced that his men were well, thus showing the feel for community relations characteristic of effective commanders of locally raised Civil War units. While he was at home, a minor crisis erupted in Virginia. That state, whose capital of Richmond was also the Confederate capital, had been the site of the first great rebel victory at Bull Run and a major Southern army was still encamped outside Washington. But Union forces had already occupied much of the area west of the Alleghenies from which would be carved the new state of West Virginia. Pushing east through the Alleghenies along the Baltimore and Ohio Railroad and south from the Potomac River, the Federals menaced the Shenandoah Valley. Rich in itself, the Valley was also close to the heart of eastern Virginia. The commander of the Confederate's Valley District, Gen. Thomas Jonathan "Stonewall" Jackson, took the offensive against the Federals, driving them from Romney on the South Branch of the Potomac on January 14, 1862. When Spiegel returned from leave, he found that the 67th Ohio was among the Union reinforcements hurriedly ordered to the rescue.[13]

Camp Lander, New Creek, Va.[14]

January 27/1862

My dear and much beloved Wife and Children!

Onced more after a longer lapse of time than I can justify, am I permitted to say to you my beloved ones that I am hale and hearty and God only knows that I love you more than ever!

---

13. MF, Jan. 16, 1862; McPherson, *Ordeal by Fire*, 159–61; Frank E. Vandiver, *Mighty Stonewall* (New York: McGraw-Hill, 1957), 189.

14. This and several other Virginia towns mentioned in the following letter became part of the state of West Virginia.

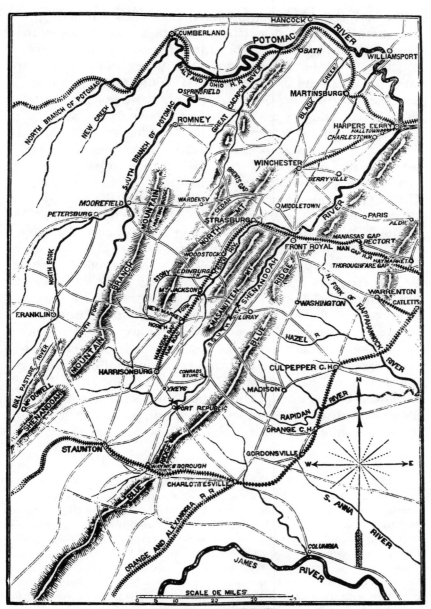

Operations in the Valley (from *Harper's
Pictorial History of the Civil War*)

When I arrived at Camp Chase, Columbus, we had marching Orders and as I have very little confidence in the Orders that we get through some officers, I doubted very much that we should move for some time, yet therefore delayed writing until as I supposed [I] could give you some positive information. But Saturday night we got Orders to draw 2 days' rations and be ready to move to the State House, Columbus, to draw our pay and leave for Romney, Virginia. We left Camp Chase Sunday 11 o'clock A.M. and we came to Columbus. They only had time to pay off 4 Companies and unfortunately mine was not one of them. Our 6 Companies were hurried off, to meet the Enemy which, it was said was bearing heavy on the few Union troops.[15] When however we came to Bellaire and crossed over to Benwood, Virginia, the Water was so high (the Ohio River) that we could not go on. Had to take Quarters in cattle and freight Cars. At 1 o'clock Monday night the Water got so high that they had to remove our train 1-1/2 miles from Benwood. When day light came on and we were informed that we could get no further on account of Breakage in the Railroad, I ordered my boys to pitch their tents right on the side of the Railroad track, instead of staying in the dirty Cars. No sooner had my boys pitched their Tents when the Colonel saw it; he ordered the Regiment to pitch Tents on [a] very pretty piece of ground along the Banks of the noble Ohio. We were permitted to stay until we were

---

15. Some of the men in the six unpaid companies of the Sixty-seventh Ohio threatened to wait for their money. Through a patriotic speech, Lieutenant Colonel Voris persuaded them of their duty to go to the rescue of endangered comrades. He thereby also demonstrated his growing influence over what was still nominally Buerstenbinder's regiment. *Daily Toledo Blade,* Feb. 1, 1862. A soldier in Spiegel's company praised Voris, saying, "I do not think there is a man in the regiment who does not love and respect him." Besides Voris's speech at Benwood, the soldier liked his lieutenant colonel's friendliness to the men. "If the lowest private salutes him, he returns the compliment. Not so with our Colonel, Bustenbinder [*sic*]; why I have seen a commissioned officer salute him and he not regard it with the least notice." He described Spiegel as "a gentlemen and a soldier." *Akron Summit Beacon,* Feb. 6, 1862.

fixed when an Order came from General Lander[16] to move on to Patterson Creek, Virginia, forth with. We got ready at twelve o'clock at midnight, crawled into a lot of freight cars and rode without stopping until we got to Grafton at noon next day where we stopped 2 hours and from which place I sent a telegram which I hope you received. From Grafton we went along and when night came it was reported we were to stop at Oakland, Maryland, but that was not done and when we dit stop it was 2 o'clock in the morning. Lieutenant Chapman and myself being tired laying in the Car and anxious to learn where we were, got out and walked along the track until we came to the first picket Guard. They of course halted us and through them we were informed that [we] were near New Creek, Virginia, and that our Millersburg Band was near.[17] We could scarcely wait until morning [as] the Guard would not let us pass, but as soon as day we went. [We] found them all in Bed but not long and such a welcome it would have done your Soul good to see. We got a nice breakfast and eat some of Mother Tysher's apple butter. We pitched our Tents that day, Saturday, right on the Banks of the north western wing of the Potomac; before us Hills, on our side Mountains and all around us very large Elevations of dirt and Rocks. Mrs. Southworth[18] ought to be here [to] see the beautiful caves

---

16. Frederick West Lander of Massachusetts, an engineer, had helped survey transcontinental railroad routes in the 1850s. After serving as an aide during the fighting in western Virginia, he had been commissioned brigadier general of volunteers. Ezra J. Warner, *Generals in Blue, Lives of the Union Commanders* (Baton Rouge: Louisiana State Univ. Press, 1964), 274–75. Hereafter cited as GB.

17. The Millersburg Band had attached itself to the First Virginia Cavalry (Union). MF, Sept. 26, 1861.

18. Emma D. E. N. Southworth, a popular novelist who often wrote sympathetically about Virginia and the South. Beatrice K. Hofstadter, "Southworth," in Edward T. James et al., eds., *Notable American Women, 1607–1950, A Biographical Dictionary*, 3 vols. (Cambridge, Mass.: Harvard Univ. Press, 1971), 3:327–28. Mrs. Southworth often included descriptions of mountains, gorges, and caverns. Regis Louise Boyle, *Mrs. E. D. E. N. Southworth, Novelist* (Washington, D.C.: Catholic Univ. of America Press, 1939), 80–81.

and everything for a splendit romance except Woman. Of that class of humanity I have not seen but one old nigger wench since I left Columbus.

I will not say to you much more. I shall write to you again day after tomorrow and give you details of myself and everything.

I never in my life have been kept as busy and constantly engaged. No place to write and no rest if I had place, for [listening to a] thousand questions of the Boys. Only let me say to you: be easy, everything is working well and you and all my friends will be pleased. Just keep in mind that my only hope of success is the conviction of your happiness and welfare and that of our beloved children. O, just for one half hour with you and the little ones.

Your ever true and loving,<br>Marcus

My good little wife it is just 2 o'clock. I have written a letter for the <u>Farmer</u>[19] since and 4 more. Everybody sleeps I suppose you do. Pleasant dreams and 1000 kisses to you and the children from your ever true Marcus. . . .

Camp Lander, New Creek, Va.<br>January 30th 1862

My dear beloved Wife!

It is been quite a time indeed, since I heard from you except through Brother Joseph of whom I had a letter to day.

Our mails are very irregular and I almost had the blues, as some of my friends call it "Homesickness", but otherwise

---

19. Millersburg's Democratic newspaper. This may well have been Spiegel's first published letter, as he said "it would do me good to see a letter of mine in print once in my life." While generally paralleling the above letter to his wife, he was more diffident. He did not wish to be held responsible "in a grammatical or orthographical viewpoint." As to the scenery, "were I anything of a sentimental writer I would give you a glowing description of the Baltimore & Ohio Railroad line; but since it is admitted that my eloquence is best displayed when judging good Lager, you would not ask me to spread on rocks, creeks, laurels, & c." MF, Feb. 6, 1862.

I feel well. There is nothing ailing me, except a Boil on a certain unpleasant place where I had so many all ready and I miss you my love, my only comfort, to say a good word to me and doctor me.

My dear Wife keep up your Spirits and take care of yourselves, my good Wife and Children, a bright day is dawning. Charges and Specifications have been filed against our Colonel Buerstenbinder which will send him h——l wards.[20] Lieutenant Colonel Voris will be Colonel and then I am all right. I have concluded to accept the Quarter Mastership, send for Brother Joseph and make all that I can lawfully and justly out of it and keep out of danger and that all for your sake, my love, as I have promised to you. If it were not for that my love or if I had left you and my good children in a way so that you were independent, I would like nothing better than try my hand in the military. I am a tolerable good Soldier and of my courage and bravery I think lots, if only I would dare to try it.

You must not feel bad when I say to you that I would like to be at home just now, for I think I have been a little homesick, yet I keep up Spirits.

We are pretty comfortably situated now in our Camp as I have written to you, between the Potomac and the Mountains. We are within 14 miles of the enemy but no fear of

---

20. Nearly all of the regiment's captains had signed charges that Buerstenbinder seldom drilled or otherwise exercised command over the regiment and that when he did, he was inefficient. They also charged him with petty tyranny and falsification, including compelling a lieutenant to file a fraudulent muster roll. The governor of Ohio accepted the validity of the accusations and forwarded them to the War Department for action. An editor previously favorable to Buerstenbinder remarked, "such a man is not the proper person to entrust with the lives of one thousand men." *Daily Toledo Blade*, Feb. 5, 1862. In the same issue of the MF that published Spiegel's first letter, Estill reported "with good authority" the dissatisfaction of the Sixty-seventh Ohio with its colonel. Instead of the "tyrannical and ignorant" Buerstenbinder, he like Spiegel recommended Voris, "an excellent man and an excellent officer." MF, Feb. 6, 1862.

an attack from the Rebels, neither from us on them, as the Roads are impassible for the transport of things. . . .

Tuesday last I was Brigade Officer of the day for the first time in my life in an Enemy's country. The duties of the Brigade Officer of the day is to see to everything about all the troops present; all the Guards, Pickets and Outposts are under his control. I rode all day on my Friends Sam Yates horse,[21] saw all the Pickets in day time, give them Instructions and Countersign and Parole [password]. At midnight I had to go out again and see whether the Outposts, Pickets and Guards understand their Business. My Orderly, "Wiggins",[22] rode with me. We were well armed with Revolvers and so forth but saw no Enemy. The Outposts and so forth are from 2 [to] 5 miles and it takes about 20 miles riding to get around. I stood it like a man, only I think the big ride is the father of my "Boil." Dr. Ebright[23] is coming to see me Sunday and stay over night.

Allow me here to say that Lieutenant Colonel Voris is as true a friend as I ever had. He knows you and me and our circumstances and helps to make it all right. I think shortly to have the boys, Joseph and Henry, here. We are looking daily for the Pay master to pay me off and then I want to pay that note with the Bank where my Friend Cohn is Bail on and then I am all right and you too, just keep your spirits. My dear and sweet wife, this is the only time that I can see a clear way of getting money enough to make us comfortable. If only God spares my health and Keeps my dear

---

21. Samuel Yates, one of the "principal musicians" of the Millersburg Band. MF, Sept. 26, 1861.

22. William J. Wiggins, orderly or first sergeant of Company C. Roster 5:578.

23. Thomas McBride Ebright of Millersburg, a surgeon with the Eighth Ohio. Roster 2:237. Born in 1824 in Pennsylvania, he was a graduate of the Starling Medical College at Columbus, Ohio. After 1864 he moved to Akron where he became a prominent physician under the name "McEbright." William Henry Perrin, ed., *History of Summit County, with an Outline Sketch of Ohio* (Chicago: Baskin and Battey, 1881), 748.

family all right, by the time this is over we can live comfortable and happy together. . . .

South Branch of the Potomac<br>
French's Store, Feby 5/62

My dear and beloved Cary
My sweet children!

. . . You are undoubtedly anxious to know how we came here to this beautiful spot of creation. Well Monday we got Orders to draw 3 days rations, strike tents, cook the rations and be packed up and ready to move within 2 hours. You had better believe they huzzled them selves. We were ordered to report ourselves at Patterson Creek, Virginia, 8 miles below Cumberland, Maryland. We got there at 5 o'clock in the eve, when we were ordered to report ourselves at this place to Brigadier General Tyler,[24] my old friend from Ravanah [Ravenna, Ohio] who is now our Brigadier General. (I saw him and you had better believe he was pleased to see me) and he told me he would try and have our Regiment in his Brigade. That's lucky for me. When we got here, however, at 12 o'clock night before last, Tyler had gone with 6000 men to attack the Rebels but when he got to the place they had left. Had we arrived here an hour sooner, we might have had the pleasure of a night march to the enemy but unfortunately we were too late and had to wait all night. The Cars being open stock cars and awfully crowded, I preferred sleeping on 3 Rails in front of an awful big fire yesterday. I felt tolerably good yesterday, all except the crevices on my body from the soft side of a rail. It rained all day yesterday, and sometimes we had Orders to unload and pitch tents and sometimes not, still waiting Orders to march across the mountains after the Enemy or rather to reinforce Tyler. But at 10 last night we heard

---

24. Erastus Barnard Tyler, a businessman who had helped to raise and become colonel of the Seventh Ohio, at this time commanded a brigade but did not formally become a brigadier general until May 14, 1862. GB, 515.

our forces were coming back and found no enemy and I had made preparations in a freight car for Chapman and myself. I slept "bully" and never felt better in my life than I do this morning, as bright as a dollar. My "bile [boil] is busted" and I am all right. We have sent a new [communication?] for the removal of our Colonel and are looking for his arrest, as charges and specifications are made sufficient to arrest and court martial any man.

I can say nothing about the folks about and through the country wherever we have been, from the fact that neither my Lieutenants nor myself make a practice of going through the country as a great many officers do, to get familiar with families and so forth. We stay with the Boys all the time.

Write to 67th Regiment Western Virginia.

Just now we received orders to move further down the road towards Hancock. . . .

Camp New Burg
Morgan Co. Va. Feby. 8/62

My dear and much beloved Wife,

The enclosed letter we wrote on board of the Cars and was sent off with the Regimental letters and we supposed them to their respective destinations when to our dismay he returned this morning saying that he could not get through our lines to take or bring us any mail. We have heard nothing, that is we have had no mail since the 2nd of this month. We pitched our tents yesterday and are to a measure comfortable again. The Millersburg Band came up to us last night at 12 o'clock. They slept with us scattered among my Boys and this morning I invited the whole Band and their Colonel who is a splendit man and a very good friend of mine,[25] to breakfast with me, in my tent. My boys

25. Colonel Henry Anisansel, First Virginia Cavalry. United States, War Department, *The War of the Rebellion, A Compilation of the Official Records of the Union and Confederate Armies*, 70 vols. in 128 (Washington, D.C.: Government Printing Office, 1880–1901), ser. 1, vol. 12, pt. 3, 492. Hereafter cited as OR with all citations from series 1, unless otherwise indicated.

killing 3 young hogs during the night, gave me a couple of
nice hams which with other things made us a splendit re-
past.

I begin to feel very uneasy and quite unhappy for not
hearing anything from you since I saw you last. If you can,
do write 4–5 letters every week. Tell me every little thing;
you do not know how it interests me to hear from you
everything that happens, about our little children and everybody else.

Bodily I never felt better in my life, I am not as fat as I
was by a good deal but stout, rugged and hardy.

As I am writing, the Report comes our Colonel is under
arrest. Hope to God it may be so; if not to day it will be to
morrow. . . .

The mail sergeant just now comes in my tent and says he
is now going to try again to get our mail off; hope he will
succeed and this may reach you. I will kiss this right
here   Kiss it off. My love to all my children and say to
them their father is well and hopes to see them soon. Keep
up spirit my love, all will be right. I will come out of this
with honor and Money. All I am sorry for is that our Colonel was so worthless; that keeps our Boys back and I am
feared we will never have the pleasure of being in front of
a Battle but always away off.

If we stay here two days we will be paid.

Good buy my sweet, my good, my dear little Cary, may
God bless you and keep you in good health so that you may
enjoy a many, many pleasant time in the Arms and on the
Breast of your ever true and loving,

Marcus. . . .

Camp Paw Paw, Va.<br>Feb. 13, 1862

My dear beloved Wife
My faithful Caroline!

You will see by the above that our watchword is onward,
onward. We are now in front of the celebrated Paw Paw
Tunnel. Our Camp is situated this time [with] the Potomac

Caroline Spiegel

and Baltimore and Ohio Railroad now back or to our West, an awful Hill or mountain in front or on the East side, the Paw Paw Tunnel and its mountain on the north and any amount of camps on our South.

There must be 20,000 troops in this camp, artillery say 40 Cannons of all sizes, plenty of Cavelery, and Infantry. The drums and fifes, Bugles and trumpets and the numerous Brass Bands are continually heard over the voices of the Commanders of Divisions, Brigades, Regiments, Battalions, Companies and Squads. Guard mounting here, and drill in the manual of Arms there and every thing is practiced here to make one think and ask "who wouldent be a Soldier?"

After giving you a rough outline of our Camp situation I will commence and describe to you how I came here or rather give you a history of what had happened since I last wrote to you my dear.

I had just mailed two letters to you, one of which I had sent off 4 or 5 days and came back when I received notice that I had to sit as President of a Regimental Court Martial

over 3 privates and while we were examining the witnesses
of the first case Lieutenant Colonel Voris came in and said
we just received orders to march immediately without our
tents and probably would have a fight that night and also
gave me a letter from you, my love and kind wife. And
when I say to you there never was a streak of fortune nor
any thing in this world that had a more electrifying influence than that letter had upon me, I was a new man,
could have licked a thousand Rebels myself. I read it and
such a letter, so kind and so encouragingly [worded] and
just at a time when I expected to meet the enemy. When I
came to the words: "be careful of your health, be brave, be
kind, be noble and be generous but above all be cautious," I
called out Company C in a hurry, had them drawn in a line
and they could not think what made me feel so good. I told
them, that I just received a letter from my good wife and
read to them the above Passage. They gave 3 cheers for the
Captain's wife and we marched out and were the first Company in the line of battle, all of us feeling good. I never felt
better in my life.

We marched 9 miles on the Railroad track when we were
taken to our "file left" up to a considerable of an elevation
where I think I saw a very pretty sight: about 8000 men all
in Regimental line having big fires in front and their arms
back of them; the men laying down on the snow in front of
the fire and the Snow about a foot deep; the men all evidently well satisfied with their situation. We were marched
in front where we took up our position by Companies the
same as the rest, build big fires. I got 3 Rails, spread my
Blanket and laid in front of the fire but my boys insisted on
me taking 3 more blankets and I slept tolerably well, except
that the pointy side of one of the rails would not soften
down. The first time I ever slept in the winter on the snow
out doors, but I had a letter from you and when I tell you I
felt as good and as well satisfied as though I slept in a
downy feather bed. My conscience is clear and I had just
heard my family was well.

The next morning when our Scouts returned they

brought the news that the Enemy had fallen back. We were therefore ordered about a half a mile along the Railroad where we were told to try and make ourselves as comfortable as possible under the circumstances. Our Boys fixed themselves shanties out of Rail, one end on the ground the other up about 4 feet high and covering the same with pine and spruce brush, also spreading pine and spruce on the floor and they slept in [them] two nights. They fixed me a shanty, a big fire in front. The 3d day I was ordered with my Company about 3 miles on Picket guard, to report myself first to head quarters. I there saw the celebrated General Lander, the Commander of all these forces, a very nice looking General and a Gentleman. I received my instructions from him, went out and spread my Company in Picket Posts of from 4 to 8 on every little road and so forth for 4 miles, with instructions if they see anything or get attacked [to] fire and fall back to my quarter which was on the side of a hill where I kept my body guard of about 10 men and my 1st Lieutenant. We had not much happen to us of any note. At 8 o'clock at night I sent one of my men in to see whether the mail had come in. I thought what a pretty thing it would be to get a letter from home and lo behold I got your and Oncle Joseph's 2nd letter. You might as well make up your mind I felt bully. When we returned next day to Camp all safe and sound when after I received a compliment from General Lander's Aide-de-Camp that I was the best Officer on Picket that he had met for a great while. We found our tents and baggage had come.

We commenced pitching them and last night I slept in my own bunk on a lot of fine Spruce and pine Sprouts, 3 Quilts over them and 4 woolen Blankets over me. I slept like a baby and feel good.

I am none the worse for wear, feel exceedingly good, take good care of myself, quarrel with nobody except Colonel Buerstenbinder whom I despise worse than any other man I ever knew, but we had additional assurance from the Governor last night, that as soon as the war department in Washington can reach them he will go to h——l and that will be in a few days.

I had a good deal of trouble with my Cooks. I tried several and none was worth a d——n. We have a good one now,
one of my boys. We had a nice chicken soup and some
pork. Sometimes our eating is hard but I can eat most anything now. I have eat boiled cabbage (boiled with pork) and
beef) like a major. In short you may rest perfectly easy as
far as I am concerned. I am sure I will get out of this in
good health and with plenty of tin. Tell Oncle Joseph that
my letters to you are intended for him and tell him also
that I expect in a few days to be able to send money
enough home to make everything all right and tell him not
to be out of humor, that whatever I do good for me I do
for him, and that I soon expect to be able to call him to my
side.

Tell Hamlin that I was very much pleased to hear that he
is such a good boy and that as soon as [I] come home and if
I am in the war yet when summer comes, if he is a good
boy he may stay with me <u>four weeks</u>. Tell Lizzie that I felt
so good when I heard that she is such a good child and that
the teacher speaks so well of her, that I almost cried. Tell
Mosey I am anxious to see him and that Pa Pa is at Paw
Paw.

I am writing on a chair on my lap and must close for to
day, the Parade roll beats.

Ever your love,<br>Marcus

Paw Paw, Va. Feby. 17/62

My dear and much beloved Wife
My good and sweet Children!

This is Monday morning amid raining, a regular blue
Monday. I am sitting on my bunk, have a book on my lap,
paper on the book and am communicating with my dear
once at home.

You may probably ask how it came I dit not write yesterday (Sunday); the answer I was on duty as officer of the
day, (and a regular Summer day it was), had no time until
after 10 o'clock last night when, feeling very tired, I laid
down on my virtuous couch and slept fine, dreaming of my

good wife and children and friends I left at home and a sweet dream it was.

I had just mailed my last letter to you when the Long Roll was beaten, which is a signal of alarm and calls every Soldier out armed and equipped, when we were informed to provide ourselves with 3 days' rations and march down to the Capon [Cacapon] River and attack the enemy.[26] I never yet was sick since I am in the service except on the day I wrote to you the last letter. I had one of my old fashion headaches on the left side of my forehead over my eye, feeling as though it would "bust", but when we got the order to march I said nothing, cheered my boys and got ready, taking a piece of chicken which our cook had ready and a hard cracker in my Havresack, my Revolver and Sword and started on the Head of my company, which position I held during the whole of the march, without once complaining. We were marched right behind the 13th Indianah Regiment, Colonel Sullivan.[27] We started here at 4 o'clock in the afternoon on Thursday, mud knee deep for the first 2 miles until we got on the Winchester Pike. There it was not muddy, but a soft slippery snow. We were led on the Pike for 3 miles when the Order was given to turn off to the left through a rough and newly made road through the woods. We marched on this road about 4-1/2 miles when we were ordered to counter march to where we turned off and take the Pike in order to cut off the Retreat of the Enemy, who would be attacked on the other side from the first Virginia Cavelery, the 7th Virginia, 4th and 8th Ohio Infantry (the latter Dr. Ebright's Regiment). We marched on the Pike until 2 o'clock in the morning when we were ordered to halt, squad right down, and go to sleep if we could on our arms.

---

26. The movement which Spiegel next describes was part of an attack led by General Lander on a Confederate position at Bloomery Gap in the mountains south of the Potomac. GB, 274.

27. Jeremiah Cutler Sullivan, brigade commander and later general. GB, 487–88.

Hold on, I forgot to tell you that on our march we had to climb a Hill of at least 3-1/2 miles long and awful high, a grand Scenery to behold by moonlight; an awful hill, all the time on one side of high Rocks and Scattered Pine and Spruce trees and on the other Side the grandest precipice down, down, as far as men could see, with an awful rolling of Water which at first sight, would naturally stop a person and make him look, admire and chill at the awful, romantic and fearful sight. If I had not had an advantage I should never have got up the Hill; the advantage was that by stepping 3 paces forward I only slit two backward, gaining one pace every time. Had it been Visa Versa I never should have got up. But I got up the foeremost of my Company too, with an awful Headache, the Sweat pouring down off my forehead almost equal to the East Liberty Spring and when we got on top we stopped, rested, I wiped the sweat, blowed off and at once my Headache was gone and I felt extremely good, free, light, and healthy and not a bit tired, as though I just got out of bed after a good night's rest.

Now let us go back to where we stopped and think of the happiness I enjoyed when George Wygand[28] stepped up and told me that he and 2 other boys of my Company, had taken a Blanket apiece from my Bed and brought them with them for me. I then laid down, one Blanket that I had under me and 3 Blankets that the Boys brought over me and slept as good as ever I dit in my life, nice and warm and soft until the Sergeant major came to me a little before the Break of day and told me, let my Company fall in quietly and march on.

After marching about a mile we came to the north River close by the fork of the Capon [Cacapon] River. It had no Bridge and we had to wade it. I jumped in, called for the Boys to follow the Captain, water up to my hips, a rapid stream, and sang Dixie and crossed it over first; Christ Keller,[29] the boy that stayed at our house one night, 2nd. I

---

28. Cpl. George Weigam. Roster 5:580.
29. Pvt. Christian Keller. Roster 5:582.

think I never done any thing since I am a Soldier that endeared me as much to my Boys as that crossing the River.

We were marched on from there and halted in front of the big Capon [Cacapon] River, awaiting to hear the booming of the cannon on the other side and then cross it and give the Rebels fits.

We were allowed however to build big fires and try [dry] our clothing and for the first time I left the Company and went with Dr. Westfall[30] in a House close by and got a room with a big old fashion fire place, where I stripped and tried [dried] off. My drawers, stockings, pants and so forth felt bully after we got all try. Mrs. Loy, the lady of the House, was [a] very fine old lady, very kind and a Union lover, (as she said).

When I say to you that my boys, my officers and your humble servant felt keen for a fight I say to you only that which is true. If we had been permitted to cross the River and have a little fight on our own hook, we agreed as soon as the fight commenced to throw off our Blankets and over coats and go it. I felt just as certain of success and that I could give you a description of a Battle as I am now giving you a sketch of our march. But we dit not get into the fight any nearer that 1/2 mile and as the Rebels had been informed by some spy or other of our position they changed their road and dit not come to us. The Cavelery done all the fighting; they killed about 40, took 58 prisoners and wounded some 40 or 50. Our folks lost 2 killed and have two wounded. When we waited until about 3 o'clock in the afternoon, our other forces met us and we were ordered to march back to camp. We waded the River and camped in the woods for an hour and made a big fire and tried ourselves.

Since I wrote on the opposite page, I was called to dinner; Lieutenant Chapman cooked dinner to day. We had fresh beef soup with desicated vegetables and desicated

---

30. James Westfall, assistant surgeon. Roster 5:565.

potatoes in, fried hominy, fried desicated potatoes, beef, blackberry pie (which the Boys traded for cream), opened the can of peaches which Werner of Berlin[31] gave me for the Surgeon General, coffee, crackers and molasses. A bully bully dinner of which I eat harty and after dinner we were called to Head Quarters to hear a dispatch read from Washington stating our troops took 15,000 prisoners and gave them H——l generally.[32]

This desicated vegetables are pressed and tried [dried] vegetables consisting of Cabbage, Carrots, turnips, onions, salat, and so forth pressed in the shape of a "Butterkooche" [butter cookie] which if you soak will swell up and make a french soup. Desicated potatoes are tried and pressed and by boiling swell and are like other potatoes. We draw them of the Quarter Master as well as Molasses, Coffee, Sugar, Candles, Soap, Beans, Rice, Peas, Pork, Bacon and occasionally fresh Beef. We buy of the Quarter Master for Lieutenant Chapman, Lieutenant Childs[33] and myself. It is hard sometimes on account of getting nothing but pork for weeks and still if we had Bread instead of the Sole leather crackers ["hard tack"], I think we would do bully.

I have trespassed on your patience with eatings and now go back to our march. We left the woods this side of north River at 3 o'clock and reached here at 10 o'clock. Nothing happened on the march back of any note except that the Boys of the 60th Ohio hearing of our returning send a lot of whiskey and give every Boy of the 67th, their older sister,[34] a horn of whiskey.

---

31. A village in Holmes County. Werner is unidentified.

32. On the previous day, the federal forces had captured Fort Donelson, Tennessee, with its garrison. E. B. Long, *The Civil War Day by Day, An Almanac, 1861–1865* (Garden City, N.Y.: Doubleday, 1971), 171–72.

33. 2d Lt. George L. Childs.

34. Despite its lower number, the Sixtieth had been mustered in later than the Sixty-seventh. Robert S. Harper, *Ohio Handbook of the Civil War* (Columbus: Ohio Historical Society for the Ohio Civil War Centennial Commission, 1961), 62.

We arrived in our Camp at 10 o'clock Friday eve, an absence of 30 hours, having marched 41 miles over the mountains, slept on the ground and waded the river twiced and had a fair prospect of a fight and I am happy to say I felt strong and good and now 3 days after the march I feel better every day. I was somewhat disappointed after I came home in the Eve; and making big calculations on a nice roost in my bunk and finding it occupied by Colonel Anisansel, a friend of mine (the Colonel of the 1st Virginia Cavelery where our Bandboys belong) who got ruptured in the fight that day and my friend Kolbe[35] was very carefully attending him and I had consequently to sleep on the floor but slept bully.

Their tents not being here yet, he and Kolbe stayed with me till last night when they got their tents, the Band boys stopping with my boys, except Tip Irvine[36] who was quite unwell stopped with my 2nd Lieutenant.

Our Regimental affairs are still undecided. We had a letter from our Messenger who went to Columbus that the Governor sent him to Washington and he intends to be back by tomorrow with the Order of the Suspension of Colonel Buerstenbinder's Command. Would to God he may succeed. I hate and despise that man as I ever hated or despised man and you know I don't very often hate. Him and I are at the nicest quarrelling relations.

Lieutenant Colonel Voris and I still continue to be as good friends as ever was born; he is a friend, a man and my style. Our Major Bond and myself are very intimate; he is a jolly good fellow.[37] I like all the officers of the Regiment except 4; the 4 I only dislike but one I hate above all.

You may tell Hamlin that I am well and very anxious to

---

35. Carl F. Kolbe, one of the "principal musicians" of the Millersburg Band. MF, Sept. 26, 1861.

36. Probably William H. Irvine, a band member. MF, Sept. 26, 1861.

37. John R. Bond, formerly adjutant of the Twentieth Ohio Infantry and an officer of the Sixty-seventh Ohio before its consolidation with the Forty-fifth Ohio. Roster 5:565.

see him. Tell him that I marched off for a battle, with Cannons and Cavelery; the Cannons loaded and the Guns all loaded and tell him I felt like fighting for him. Tell him that I have a nice Revolver that shoots five times at once. Tell him it would kill a cow across the Killbuck.[38] Tell him when the War is over and I do not lose it, he shall have it to keep providing he is a very good boy and behaves himself first rate to you while I am gone.

Tell Lizzie that she must be a very good Girl, that before I come home I will get a Sesesh [Secessionist] Relic for her, which must be very nice. She must be a very good child and mind you and then she will get the nicest thing she ever saw. Tell Hamlin to write a letter to me in his A B C book style, and I will be very much pleased. Tell Mosey about me so that he won't forget me and kiss them all [a] thousand times for me.

Of course Oncle Joseph will read my letters that I write to you; they are no secret. Tell him that I often wish he was with me and tell him to keep in good Spirit and not leave Millersburg till I send for him. We do not want to leave Millersburg. If the war ends by Summer, I can raise quite a nice little pile of money and we stay in the Warehouse; we do not want to sell the Warehouse. I will send home about $700 shortly. I do not feel like selling the warehouse; if we owe anything to Henry and I should not succeed in getting the Quarter mastership for Henry, I will send the money.[39] We are making out our January and February Payrolls. Things will soon be all right.

We may probably stay here for some time, tell Oncle Josey that my fortune is his and what I make he shall have his share, just live well and feel easy.

Tell Elizabeth to keep herself in good trim, be a good girl; and say to her, if she is first Rate, for her she may

---

38. A creek at Millersburg.

39. While Spiegel evidently still had an interest in the business, Henry Herzer after Oct. 30, 1861, listed himself alone as owner of the "Red Warehouse." MF, Mar. 13, 1862.

have my 3d Sergeant for her husband, the best boy in the Regiment.

When I tell you my sweet good wife that my thoughts, my all, my very life concentrates in your wellbeing and that of my little children and my brother, mother, and sisters, I mean more particularly that you should take good care of yourselves and keep up your Spirits. Just feel that I am all right and that if you just take my advice you will write often, sing, laugh, and dream of me as I do of you. I had a letter from Cohn; he says that you were all well as far as he knew. How does that come? Does he not know whether my family is well for sure?

Have you done anything about my boots? If you have not sent them yet send a pair for Geo Wygam along, his wife knows all about.

You may send me something nice to eat in the Box; it will not cost any more. A bottle of something to drink won't hurt anybody. You may direct the Box to Cumberland, Maryland, and write me about it. Direct all your letters for the time being [to] Paw Paw, Virginia.

My good wife and children, good Brother and all, having written 3 sheets of nonsense I hope you will excuse and write soon to

Your true and loving,
Marcus

Paw Paw Feby. 19/62

My dear Brother Moses[40]

I suppose you think I have forgotten you, but not so. There is not an hour passing but I think of you and frequently have I dreamed of you and very often in the day I see your form standing right before me; a friend as you have always been to me is not to be forgotten. I suppose you think "Why dit you not write then" but dear Moses in

---

40. Moses Joseph of Uniontown, Ohio; a cousin and good friend of Spiegel's.

my new calling as a Soldier I really have so far had but very little time for me so as to recreate or even write to my friends. Thousand things to do and to attend drill and Parade, marching and countermarching, requisitions and descriptive lists, clothing accounts and Regimental orders and everything has to be attended to. You know I am a Captain of Company C, the Color Company of the 67th Regiment and I will now give you a little history of the past, present and future of my military life, if I do not break down.

When I went into the service I calculated on being Quarter-Master of the 45th Regiment which by order of the Adjutant General was consolidated with the 67th and the 67th formed, by which arrangement my Quartermastership of course nocked into a cocked hat, to the great displeasure of many of my friends, and [it] then rather chagrined me.

But since that I am not sorry as I think besides the Sutler[41] there is no position outside of military in a Regiment that pays. Sutler must pay from $50 to $100 per day as they sell from $100 to 300 per day at enormous prices and their money as sure as the State Railroad of Ohio whether the law protects them or not. I was home on a visit from 16th to 18th of last month and the day that I started for Uniontown I got a dispatch to join my Company forthwith as we had moving orders. When I returned to Columbus we left next day for Virginia in order to reinforce several Regiments who were in danger from an attack of the Rebel General Jackson. . . .

We got along pretty comfortable but for Mars stern commands. [On February 10,] I was ordered on outpost picket Guard with my whole Company which I cheerfully done, as it was something I had not done in the service yet. Nothing occurred that night safe a trunken [drunken] (I suppose) Aide-de-Camp party who endeavored to pass my Head

---

41. A civilian permitted to sell food, drink, and a variety of merchandise to the troops. Francis A. Lord, *They Fought for the Union* (New York: Bonanza Books, 1960), 130–31.

Quarters by all means, when I got my 3 nearest Posts, 27 in number, and gave the Command: prime, ready, aim, when Mr. Aide-de-Camp and party [of] 8 on horses thought best to retreat, by first however saying, don't shoot we meant no harm. Next day I got Complimented by General Lander who commands this Division of the Potomac, by saying I, that is your humble servant, "Was the best Officer he had met since he took this command. . . ."

Paw Paw, Va. Feby. 19/62

My dear and good Wife!

. . . This has been an unpleasant day, raining all day, so much so that the mud is almost a foot deep in our camp and our tent floor is covered with mud from the many coming in with muddy Boots and shoes.

Chapman and I get along about as well as any two "mail" folks could get along. We never yet quarreled for "keeps" but are always abusing each other for fun and as soon as one is out of sight of the other for 10 minutes, the other is on the hunt of the one. My Lieutenant Childs is a very quiet unassuming Christian Gentlemen, very pleasant and a good fellow. Of course my orderly Wiggins you know is a brick, no discount on him.[42] We board together and right here I must "countermand" of what I said in my last about our good "Grubb". Since Monday last we dit not live very fat. Getting tired of pickled Pork, we have nothing but Rice, Coffee and Crackers, Crackers, Coffee and Rice. Our Quartermaster has not been very flush and we feel as though we

---

42. In a letter to the editor dated March 9, Spiegel more fully described these comrades: "Chapman is, as you all know, a gay and gallant fellow, a gentleman of extraordinary 'poetical power,' as well as a bold soldier boy. Lieut. Childs is a young man of the strictest orthodox church discipline; yet, a very active and brave soldier. I have regular morning and evening devotions, conducted by Lieut. Childs, assisted by Orderly Wiggins, Corporal [Leroy] Osborn, and others. Childs is a K.T. [Knight Templar]; Wiggins is a brick, and the best Orderly [Sergeant] in the world, and since he has left off profanity, I think he has a better appetite." MF, Mar. 20, 1862.

came here to save our money and not to spend it and I at any case, feeling like dieting somewhat, just as leave do without meat a week.

What are you doing? How do you spend your time? Are you in good Spirits? Is Oncle Joseph in good humor? If he is tell him for my sake to be wide awake and pleasant. I feel bodily as well as ever I dit and think this War will improve me in two respects. In the first, I can eat most anything; cornbread and cabbage is first rate. In the 2nd, I think I will not be half as much of a "Complainer" but always [in] good humor if you agree to be. In spirit I feel well and if only I hear once or twice a week from you all is right and if this War would only give me employment even in the position I hold now a year longer, I would have about $2000 of my own earnings subject to nobody and loans paid for and the Warehouse partly and all would be right.[43] All is right anyhow. I would like to have you safe all my letters I write so as to show me something of the War after it is over.

To night our messenger is coming back from Washington and brings us intelligence in regard to our Colonel. We all hope it may be cheering. While I write and sit comfortably by my little stove and a little camp stove presented to me by Lieutenant Colonel Voris, it blows and rains furiously out doors and I pity the poor boys on Guard.

I have at present 12 of my Boys sick in the hospital with measles and mumps and about 8 unfit for duty in the tents. Soldiering is hard sometimes and more especially at first; when they get hardened to Camp life, it is pleasanter.

While you would go through our Camp at this time 8 o'clock P.M., raining and blowing, you would hear passing the tents coughing like everything, the fiddle, singing, 3 cheers, probably all in one tent; snoring, some fellow telling

---

43. A captain's basic pay and allowances totaled $118.50 per month, plus $10 when commanding a company. J. H. Eaton, *The Army Paymaster's Manual . . . With Tables of the Monthly Pay, Subsistence & c . . . Revised to Include June 30, 1864* (Washington, D.C., 1864), 127.

a funny story; half of the boys laughing like every thing and the rest snoring in sweet repose. Really it is sad, strange, awful and amusing. . . .

Paw Paw, Va. Feby. 25/62

My dear Wife
and sweet children:

. . . I say as you, dear Wife, I think the War will soon be over. Yet I do not think we will be mustered out of Service very soon, neither do I care much, as long as I am safing $125 per month, think that is about as well as a man can do, considering hard times, and would it not be for being away from my family I would not care if I would have to stay 3 years, but I am really getting to feel as though I ought to go home and see you. It would be such a delight; nobody can appreciate it, as I could. I have not seen but 2 families since I came to Virginia and both of them were not very sociable. I am in hopes that I can go home in April and stay during Wool season as I have a very nice "Family Arrangement" to report on which I am sure our Commanding General Lander will excuse me and grant me a furlough.[44]

There has nothing of any military importance transpired here since I have written to you last, only that there is an Order here from the War Department at Washington for the investigation of the charges against our Colonel. We were examined once before a Military Commission and they have reported to court martial him, so far so good. By the way we have a new Flag presented to us by the Ladies of Cleveland, which the Commanding General Lander presented to our Regiment on the 22nd with a very nice Speech.[45]

---

44. Spiegel refers to the anticipated birth of their next child.

45. A veteran later recalled that the flag had been sent by friends in Toledo. *The Sixty-Seventh Ohio Veteran Volunteer Infantry, A Brief Record of Its Four Years of Service in the Civil War, 1861–1865* ([Massillon, Ohio: Ohio Printing, 1922]), 6.

Dr. Ebright and myself are together almost daily and I believe we enjoy our visits pretty well.

I think I might as well tell you, that I had the biggest bile [boil] I ever had right in the back of my neck, as big as a hen Egg. It has been running now for 5 days and the core is not yet out. My Lieutenants Chapman and Childs have poltest [poulticed] it regular with Linseed or Flaxseed poltess, washed it twice a day with Cast Steel [castile] Soap and squeezed it and been just as good to me as you ever saw, but before it was open I was almost homesick. They say it was so much fun to squeeze it as it ran out by spoonfulls. It does not hurt me anymore, I am still poltessing to get the core out.[46]

This is my day for "Officer of the Day" and it is now 11 o'clock in the Eve and I will soon have to make the "Grand Rounds" and then go to bed. We get paid the 2nd of March so the Paymaster said this week and then I will send you some money, or all that is over after I pay the note in [the] Bank. I want Brother Joseph to hold on and not get the "blues" as I will soon see him. Can he not get something to do in Millersburg for awhile? I have no idea that we leave here until the Roads get better, as they are too muddy to move men, horses, or artillery. I think you can not complain of me now, as I write twice every week. . . .

I do not care if you do not write me anything about the Millersburg News as I generally hear all that is going on; only write me about you, you my dear, the children what they say and do, oncle Joseph and Elizabeth. Let me know every little thing going on in the family, every thing; write often and long loving letters; you have no Idea how refreshing they are, to a Soldier and more especially to such a one as me, whose whole soul is home, home, Sweet home. . . .

---

46. A common nineteenth-century treatment for boils. One recipe for such a warm poultice included bread and linseed meal to which a little fat or oil might be added. Richard V. Tuson, ed., *Cooley's Cyclopaedia of Practical Receipts and Collateral Information in the Arts, Manufactures, Professions and Trades. . .* , 2 vols., 6th ed. (New York: D. Appleton, 1879), 1:327.

Paw Paw Tunnel, Va.
March 2, 1862

My dear dear Wife and beloved children!

I never in my life felt better or half as well as I do now. Day before yesterday I received a letter, as well as yesterday and to day.

From you, Oncle Joseph and above all from my own "Son" and that house he painted. Your letter my own dear wife was so cheering and full of life's own and full of the good woman and lovely mother that if you were just now here I could kiss you all and hug you "more than you ever saw."

A messenger just now went by my Quarters with the painful news, that our own gallant, brave, noble and generous General Lander breathed his last, about 30 minutes ago. Such is life; 8 days ago, he presented a flag to our Regiment and reviewed 20,000 troops, spoke to all of them and as he came charging along our lines upon his noble steed, erect, powerful and manly, respected and loved by all, one would have thought, O but for a glorious career of glory as the General may expect and all would be well, and to day he is no more, being afflicted with pelurisy and a congestion of the brains.[47]

This accounts for the following circumstances. When I wrote to Oncle Joseph I said to him that if we dit not get Orders to move that night and so forth, I expected we would get paid. We dit get orders that night to cook 3 days rations and get ready to start at one hours notice.

The boys cooked and packed, the wagons were loaded and everything was full of life (though I must say I went to bed and slept soundly till morning). Morning came and we found out the Cavelery, Artillery and 7 Regiments of Infantry had left; our Brigade and several others were ready to move and awaiting orders. The day passed without any

---

47. Lander, who had complained of illness since the movement against Bloomery Gap, died of a "congestive chill"—perhaps pneumonia. GB, 274–75.

orders and last night we went to bed with all our clothes on, expecting to move; that is expecting to hear the "long Roll" beating which calls every Soldier to his feet ready and equipped to march, fight or anything in his line.

Yet, we have not been called to march as yet, but instead of this we received Orders to unpack and those started are ordered back.

Who the successor of General Lander will be I know not, but it maybe General Rosencranz.[48]

As I was telling you, I felt good and do so yet, for my motto is there is plenty of good men to take the places of those going out, only I am really very very sorry.

The reason why I have not written to you ere this is simply this order to move. I expected after a march of 20 or 30 miles new sceneries and everything else as well as the description of an expected but not occurring Battle would be acceptable to you and of a great deal of Interest in your monotony of Millersburg life, for since I last wrote to about our march, our Flag presentation and so forth, there has been nothing but Rumors and Reports and the daily duty of Parade, drill, Inspection, loading and firing, drawing rations and fuel.

I have been out twiced with my men on pretty days climbing the sides of these awful hills through the pine bushes and over the Rocks, practicing as skirmishers and I am satisfied if you would stand on the top of the mountain 5 times as high as the Berlin Hill[49] and see me and my boys come up, not along the road but on the rough side and hear me give the commands, Rally by fours, Rally by platoons, Rally on the Reserve, or deploy into line as skirmishers, fire and load at will and so forth and so forth, as I said before see me come up there without puffing or blowing as I used to, it would make you feel good, or if you would see my boys

---

48. William Starke Rosecrans, who commanded the Department of West Virginia. Mark Mayo Boatner III, *The Civil War Dictionary* (New York: David McKay, 1959), 708.

49. Perhaps the rise behind Millersburg on the road to Berlin.

gather around me when we get marching orders and hear them give me pledges of their faith and fidelity, then and then only you would feel all right. . . .

I have now lost 13 of my men in the General Hospital at Cumberland, Maryland, 60 miles from here; there is none however dangerously ill and all of them are getting along pretty well.

The men I have in the Cleveland and Wheeling Hospitals have come home (that is) to the Regiment. Jacob Grassley is as clever and officious as ever.

I have really nothing of any note of news to say to you. Our lovely Colonel has not yet been arrested but the matters are in the hands of a military board and hope they may send him to h——l, for he is a Scoundrel.

The box I have not yet received but you may safely bet on it that my "mouth is watering" for the contents already. I have sent a man for it to day and have no doubt but it will be here by to morrow and then O God, wont I pitch in? I should think I will.

As far as my debts are concerned, in Millersburg I owe the Bank $500 which I will send as soon as we are paid off and we are mustered for pay and the paymaster is expected daily. You must not give youself any uneasiness about any of my affairs. I am doing well and will be home "wool season" and stay at home 4 or 5 weeks and then we will have a grand old time I'll bet you. Oh but I would like to see you all, yet when I get such loving and sweet letters from all of you, then I feel proud, happy and gay. I am all perfectly well, no boil nor anything else, but as contented as any man in my circumstances could be and as I think of coming home in about 6 or 7 weeks, then I feel gay and well. My appetite is good and I do not seek any Company but those of my boys and Dr. Ebright and Colonel Voris.

The other day Voris, Ebright and myself had a fine horseback ride over these Hills. Voris acting as Division Officer of the Field, Ebright and myself rode with him as Aids and if you would have seen your "gallant Soldier" galloping over the Hills I know you would have felt gay and proud even if I dit stay out at meals a little too long and even if you dit scold me a little when I was at Herzers Grocery too late.[50]

It is now 10 o'clock in the Eve, I am to day Regimental officer of the day and have to make the grand rounds after 12 o'clock and I would like to write to you all night or read your letters all night (by the by I do read them most all day when I am not on duty) but I have several letters to write yet and I do really think I am acting foolish in writing so much nonsense, and so often. Yes I think you can not complain of me not writing enough, because they are often laughing at me for [writing] home all the time.

I am now clearing $120 per month over all Expenses and I think that is doing pretty well, considering the way times are, every where, and as for danger I fear it not. I am just as well satisfied that I am engaged in a glorious cause and will come home with honor and glory, all safe and sound, as I am of my existence. Just give yourself no uneasiness on my account; I will be home better than I left it in health and spirit as well as pecuniary relations and a better man.

While I write on one side of the table Chapman writes on the other a letter to the "Republican".[51] I have a chance of sending this letter by a young man from Akron who will give it to Batton or Palmer. I enclose ten Dollars for you; as soon as I get my money I will send you more. I sold my watch and chain to Chapman for one hundred Dollars. I am glad she is sold; I will get the money the 2nd pay day.

Tell Hamlin that, his House and his letter pleased me so much that I felt as though I could have kissed him one thousand times, it looked so much like a big Son; everybody asked me whether he was as big as a man. He must do as he said in his letter, learn well and be a good, very good

---

50. Mid-nineteenth-century "groceries" often sold drinks as well as food. Charles and Henry Herzer's sold wines, liquor, and ale and had a restaurant. MF, Sept. 5, 1861.

51. Spiegel thus had a friend to represent his interest to the editor of Millersburg's Republican newspaper.

boy; maybe he will get something else than a Pistol. Tell
Lizzie that I am so very much pleased that she is such a
good Girl; that I tell everybody that I have a regular "young
lady daughter"; she will get something nicer than a little
nigger. Tell Mosey to keep Papas chair ready for him; he
will be home to set in it, "pretty soon". If Mr. McCormicks
intentions towards Lizzie are honorable and you and she
thinks she can get him, by all means "smoke him". He will
make a good Husband and is worth having.[52] Elizabeth,
look out; be a good and virtuous Girl and if he is honorable
and you can marry him, do so.

Good night my love, may your dreams be happy and
agreeable and may you rise from your bed strengthened
and hearty and always be happy and may never more a
dreary day or unpleasant occurrence come across your path
of life, but may it be happy indeed and the privilege of
enjoying it with you, be granted to your loving and true

husband Marcus.

Paw Paw, Va. March 4/62
My dear and much beloved wife, my sweet children!

Oh but I had gay living; the box came yesterday and such
greeve [griebe? = cracklings] and gansfleisch [goose meat],
peppernuts [pfeffernüsse cookies] and zukerkuche [sugar
cookies] I never eat before. The Bitters is just the thing as
will make a man feel at home. Everything was in the best of
Order and felt just right. We have had awful rains here
within the last few days but to day it was nice and cold
again. I believe I wrote to you, that I sold my watch and
chain for $100. The chain you may keep until farther orders.

We may move on down the Railroad to Martinsburg. I
wish we would, as it feels too gloomy here since the death
of Lander. By the way General Lander was married to a
celebrated Tragedienne, I think Miss Davenport. She lives in

---

52. Perhaps N. P. McCormick, Millersburg's watch and clock maker.
Advertisement in MF, Nov. 21, 1861.

Washington; wont she play off nice?[53] Yesterday we went
through the funeral ceremonies over the corpse of General
Lander. Just imagine 20,000 troops of all kinds drawn in
line:

<u>Cavelery</u>

<u>Infantry</u>

the procession

<u>Infantry</u>

<u>Artillery</u>

The above is the order. He was in a common box as they
could not get a Coffin.

The procession consisted of 2 Bands of Music (the Millersburg Band as one), then came the master of ceremonies,
the coffin carried by eight Colonels (Voris one of them),
then his staff, his body Guard and 2 Regiments of Infantry
with "arms reversed". It looked truly grand and had it not
been that we had to stand for 4 hours in the cold and
waited for it I think I could have given you a very graphic
description of the performance. I forgot the coffin was
wrapped in the American flag. I hope they will not have
any General die soon and if they do I would like for them
to die and be buried on a warm day.

I am well. It is said to night that the Paymaster will pay
us to morrow. I hope so as it would be quite a relief to a
great many of my boys and to me; we are all mustered and
ready for pay.

A move down the Railroad towards Baltimore would be
quite a treat as the boys have burned all the Rails and wood

---

53. After her husband's death, Jean Davenport Lander (1829–1903) became "lady superintendent" of the Union hospitals in Port Royal, South Carolina. After the war, she resumed her stage career. Boatner, *Civil War Dictionary,* 470; MR, Dec. 18, 1862.

for miles and it is getting hard to get; besides we would see something new and then I could give you a detailed history of it again.

I am well and hearty as a buck bear, eating all day of the good things from home, and if I could only now see you and the children and Joseph for one hour I would feel O.K. . . .

I have been interrupted; had a visit of 3 Captains and 4 Lieutenants. I had a mess with our Colonel to day and they came to ask me whether they can do me any good. I told them let us go in the morning and see whether the Colonel can not be hoisted at once. Oh but he is a Scoundrel, Liar and Imposture. . . .

# CHAPTER FOUR

# "After Stonewall Jackson"

Martinsburg, Va.
March 7, 1862.[1]

My Dear and Much Beloved Wife and Children:

"Onward to Richmond" was the celebrated war cry of certain political generals previous to the memorable Bull Run disaster  Onward seems to be, and now is, the word of the gallant defenders of our glorious Union. Onward to victory! Onward to crush rebellion. Onward to bring this unfortunate and unhappy war, forced upon us by the ambitious leaders of a misguided people, to a successful termination.

In my last I intimated that we might have to march. Even then we were under marching orders, and fearing you might feel uneasy I determined not to say we were going; but determined rather to wait and say we have arrived safely at Martinsburg. Wednesday, the 5th, we were ordered to strike tents within one hour; it being then 8 o'clock A.M. I believe I have never said anything to you about the work of striking tents. In most cases it is a work which is pleasantly performed by the boys, as they are always as eager to strike

---

1. Spiegel addressed this letter, like some others, to his wife but wrote with an eye to publication. Hence he included extra detail and pointed political references, such as his initial thrust at Republican journalist Horace Greeley's "Forward to Richmond" slogan. The originals of this and of subsequent letters published in newspapers no longer exist. An undated note which accompanied this letter does survive. In it Spiegel explained, "The enclosed letter I wrote to you and would like if Brother Joseph would let Estill read it and if he would publish it in the Farmer I would like it very much." Perhaps because of Spiegel's harsh allusions to Buerstenbinder, who was still his superior officer, Estill omitted Spiegel's signature, simply initialing it "M." The same issue contained a letter to the editor dated Mar. 2, 1862, and signed "M. M. Spiegel." In it, in what he called "my good, plain, half dutch way," Spiegel repeated the news given earlier to his wife. MF, Mar. 20, 1862.

tents and move as they are to pitch tents and stay. Great confusion, boxing up, teaming up, singing, and some times a little swearing are the principal features of tent striking. It forcibly reminds one of a first of April in the city of New York. When, after 9 o'clock, we had finished our labor, a severe snow storm, snowing heavy and blowing, violently, came upon us and lasted for three hours; during which time all we could do was to stand out and take it like cows in a thunderstorm.

To disabuse the minds of many who may think military orders are very promptly and minutely executed, I would simply say that when the men get orders to be ready to march at 12 o'clock the men are invariably ready; but the marching may be expected at 4 or 5 o'clock; a military necessity perhaps, of which however, I trust, regiments under a competent leader are not practiced in very much. Finally at 4 o'clock P.M. the train came with single deck cars, such as any Holmes County stock dealer would refuse to accept for his hogs and cattle and we were ordered to pile in; 35 men in a car with tents, cooking utensils and all crowded in. I would, however, here say that many Colonels who have Ohio boys under their command would refuse such accommodations and treatment for their men; but you will occasionally find a Colonel who came from Germany, where he never ranked as high as 7th corporal, but happens to have the brass, impudence and German tailor polish, and just sense enough to buy himself one or two forged recommendations, and with them dupe certain Republican Governors and secure a Colonelcy; which office such scoundrels think is a pass to have men abused, dogged and slaughtered. Such, I am sorry to say, is the case with a certain Regiment. And yet, 8 Captains, 16 Lieutenants and 700 men have placed the facts and their grievances before the Chief Magistrate of the sovereign State of Ohio without obtaining redress. It seems that certain red tape will prevent the investigation of the conduct of the reprobate until most of the men have found their death in dreary hospitals. But enough of this. All I have to ask is, how long will the men of Ohio allow such impositions to be practiced upon their sons by a mere adventurer.

You know that when I write to you, my good wife, I generally express my mind on all matters without coloring, and I hope will pardon me for having spoken so plainly on an unpleasant subject. I will endeavor to avoid the like in future.

We were moved about 48 miles on the railroad, from Paw Paw to Blackcreek, which took us from 4 P.M. to 5 A.M. On our arrival the order was given, "get out and unload immediately," which was done in double quick. After starting fires by the side of the Railroad track and waiting until 8 o'clock we deposited our baggage on the top of a hill, left it in charge of 5 of the weakest men of each company, and crossed Blackcreek; and here I performed the hardest task yet done by me in the service of Uncle Sam; though it would have been fun for many men. Across Blackcreek the Baltimore & Ohio Railroad Co. had built a most solid as well as magnificent bridge, in the most perfect manner of workmanship; but Secesh not being any too anxious to continue.the swift and frequent visits from Yankeedom undermined the arched masonwork of the bridge, and by means of powder blew the work asunder to a considerable extent; which prevented our men from crossing until the damage was repaired. In order, therefore, to push the men forward to Martinsburg it was necessary to construct a temporary pass. This was accomplished by stretching across 4 wire cables, laying planks crosswise and lengthwise over the cables; making a walk 4 feet wide, elevated from 60 to 70 feet above a stream rushing wildly through the rocks. The structure swayed slightly to and fro, and the passage of it made my head swim. Notwithstanding I placed my hand on the knapsack of one of the boys, I was extremely light headed.

After crossing the river we beheld the work of Secesh in its glory. For miles the track of the railroad is torn up, the iron carried away to build a railroad from Harper's Ferry to Winchester, the railroad buildings generally destroyed or badly mutilated, locomotives and cars smashed up and property destroyed. The country looked to us as Canaan must have appeared to the children of Israel, for it is getting out of the wilderness.

After laying for months among the hills and the mountains of Virginia and Maryland it does one good to see a nice, level country with pretty farm houses and big barns. By getting into a nice country we find more violent secession feelings, and more niggers.

On my march yesterday I deviated from my usual practice, and questioned quite a number of fat, sleek and hearty looking slaves. I asked them how they were satisfied, and so forth, and whether they would go North with me. To the first their answer was, pretty well; and to the latter, "guess not massa." I am the more strongly confirmed in my old faith that for the Constitution, the Union and the Flag of my country I will fight to the last; I am ever ready to punish and to shoot traitors; but it is not necessary to fight for the darkies, nor are they worth fighting for.

In Blackcreek town, on the railroad, the only large and pretty Union flag we have encountered since we left Grafton, was displayed from the top of a large building. From Blackcreek we took a southern direction, and after marching a few miles we came to Hedgesville, a town about the size of Canton, Stark County, which contains a great many handsome buildings. The women and children, white and black, congregated in front of every house. I must confess we were not received with very flattering enthusiasm; owing perhaps, to the fact that most of their husbands and sons were in the rebel army. From Hedgesville we marched 15 miles over by-roads and crooks to the Winchester pike, which is in splendid condition. At 12 o'clock at night we reached Martinsburg. . . .

Martinsburg Va
March 9/62

My dear and good wife
My sweet children and beloved brother!

This is Sunday Morning just after Roll Call, and the sun has made its appearance over the eastern Hills in all its magnificance and glory of a Spring morn and as I was just walking for 15 minutes in a Garden attached to the big Store House I occupy, it seemed to me as though I must at once go in and write to you my loved ones, even though only yesterday I sent a long and probably uninteresting letter to all of you.

We have not been two days in this ancient and hallowed town of Martinsburg in the Old Dominion, the home of Faulkner, the late Minister to France under Buchanan,[2] and the Home of the once Member of Congress, Martin of Martinsburgh.[3]

When we came here, night reigned over the sleepy Inhabitants who the day subsequent from all appearances felt quite alarmed as you could scarcely see any one out the whole day, except in the afternoon when the numerous Bands were playing for Dress Parade of the different Regiments, a window was occasionally opened and in less than an hour the Window Shudders of a great many deserted looking Houses were opened and female Heads deliberately exhibited over the window sills. Yesterday the 2nd day the streets were crowded with Civilians and Soldiers. The Ladies

---

2. Charles James Faulkner (1806–84) had also served as a congressman in the 1850s. During the Civil War, he served on the staff of "Stonewall" Jackson. James Elliott Walmsley, "Faulkner," in Allen Johnson and Dumas Malone, eds., *Dictionary of American Biography*, 20 vols. (New York: Scribner's, 1928–36), 3:298–99. Hereafter cited as DAB.

3. As no such man served from Martinsburg, Spiegel may be thinking of Rep. Elbert S. Martin, who lived in Lee County and sat from 1859 to 1861. *Biographical Directory of the American Congress, 1774–1961*, 85 Cong., 2 Sess., House Doc. no. 442 (Washington, D.C.: Government Printing Office, 1961), 174.

such as Dresses in Style are stylish indeed but such as apparently are poor whites dress ten times meaner than the poor women of Millersburg.

The negro women are variagated in their mode of dress; some of them look as gay as a french dancing woman while others look a genuine personification of the Devils Grandmother. I have not made the acquaintance of anybody yet, neither do I intend to. Company C is probably the only Company of the 65 stationed here where all 3 commissioned officers stay with their men all the time.

Chapman, Childs and myself sleep on the countre, stay with the boys all the time, eat with them, sing with them and have a decent joke with them, and yet I claim there is no Captain in the Service that has more the respect and moral as well as military power over his boys than I have. This may seem like bragging but to you I may be open and can therefore say it is true. Over 900 of the Refugees have returned to their homes and fireside since the advance of the Union troops and still they come. Although when the Sesesh troops were here it was not safe for Union families to be here, but during the stay of the Union troops Sesesh families are as much protected as Union, if they only behave themselves, and this is truly just as it should be.

I believe never have I written to you that one of our Regimental Doctors is Westfall, a Brother to the Westfalls of Mount Union School notoriety,[4] whom I have known in former years. He is very kind to me and my boys from old acquaintance sake. He was here yesterday and urged me very strong to come and share quarters with him, as he is with one of the finest families in town. I refused however and told him that I have not had my Uniform on for 4 weeks except on Parade and would not until I could show it

---

4. Spiegel may refer to the seminary which had recently become Mount Union College or to the village in which it was located (later part of Alliance). No Westfalls are mentioned in the early history of the former. *A History of Mount Union College during Its First Thirty Years, 1846–1876* (Cleveland, 1876), passim.

to my wife and family. Except on Parade and Special duty, I wear Blouse and Pants like the boys.

Our Colonel I am fighting and if it were not for our confounded moving and the certain death of General Landers I should have succeeded ere this, but the day "of retribution am a coming" and he will have to walk the pole.

I think these 2 days under Roof has done the boys a great deal of good; they feel bully and I wish all my boys from the Hospital at Cumberland, Maryland, were here; they would get along better here than in Cumberland. If you and the children and Brother Joseph were here we would take such a big ride over the City and country and you could see then, how far men will go when their passions are roused. To see 64 Locomotives of the very best and biggest kind (1 as big as 3 of ours at home) destroyed, willfully, maliciously and feloniously, the nicest Bridges of iron and wood destroyed, a magnificent Depot House as nice as I ever saw in the United States smashed and destroyed, I am satisfied you would feel Secession is awful and must be subdued. We are here 8 miles from Bunker Hill, 15 miles from Charlestown and 24 from Harpers Ferry, the Theater of John Browns fanaticism,[5] 22 miles from Winchester where the Rebels boast of being strongly fortified and ready to receive us. How long we stay here I know not but am thinking not long. Our Baggage, tents and so forth is not here yet; expected to day.

Just now the news is spread through town that Winchester was taken this morning at 5 o'clock by General Banks and his forces.[6] Thus falls one after the other of the boasted

---

5. Spiegel refers to John Brown's raid on the arsenal at Harper's Ferry in 1859, for which Brown was hanged at Charlestown. Boatner, *Civil War Dictionary*, 91.

6. The report of the fall of Winchester was slightly premature. Nathaniel Prentiss Banks (1816–94) commanded the Department of the Shenandoah in which Spiegel was serving. A prewar congressman and Republican governor of Massachussetts, Banks had been appointed major general of volunteers. Spiegel ultimately fought in two theaters commanded by this militarily unsuccessful "political general." GB, 17–18.

stronghold of Seseshdom; they can not withstand the fire, earnestness and enthusiasm of those who gather around the good old flag. I begin to think it will soon be played out. As far as I am concerned I feel stout and hearty and I believe if nothing farther will happen to me, this "my service" will add 10 years to my life. . . .

Since I have finished the other side I went to work and cooked supper for me and Lieutenant Chapman, now mark, I had 6 Eggs. In the first place I boiled water in frying Pan, then put in the Eggs (open), let them boil, put in Salt and Pepper and plenty of butter; Chapman bought a warm lofe of bread and you may laugh but by George we had "poached Eggs" aint that [the] way you cook them? But they were not cooked left handed. I forgot to say that on the march I lived on Gansfleish, tongue, Peppernuts and Zucker Kuche, of which I had my havresack full when we started but empty when I got here.

Your,
Marcus

Near Winchester Va.
March 13/62

My lovely and good Wife,
good Children and dear Brother

You will see by the above that we were not granted to enjoy the so very congenial Air to so many fancy officers of the very pretty town of Martinsburg, but had to advance on the very stronghold of this Section, their Manassas, and as we chased them off in a hurry, I will give you a history of our departure of Martinsburg, our advance and so forth, and if sitting in my tent on the floor, covered with 2 Blankets, a Bayonet stuck in the floor, my Paper on a Company book, my spectacles on, my head bent over, will make it so that it may not be so very interesting, you must not blame me and by the way I do not yet know how to get this to any post office. While in Winchester and 3 days before I was under arrest for which I was at times mad enough to fight, but you must not think I done anything very bad, or done any wrong but in order to fix easy your mind I will give you the facts. In Paw Paw the officer of the Guard arrested one of my men for leaving his Post to satisfy the calls of nature, which he should not have done. While in the Guardhouse, a nasty stinking place, I complained and wanted my man out. Although the Guard Tent is most always full, never before was any of my men in Guard and the Colonel not being a friend of mine wanted to show some of his venomous spirit and told me to prefer charges against my man and he would send him to the Brigade Guard House to have him tried. I told him I had no charges to make; the man that arrested him should make or have made the charges on the Regimental Guardbook and as he had not done it he, the Colonel, had no right to hold my man and I demanded his immediate release. He said there was a Regimental Order compelling me to prefer charges. I told him it dit not make any difference to me about his Regimental Orders when they conflicted with the United States Army Regulations and good sense. He then had me arrested and demanded my sword which I refused and I told him, he was in the habit of arresting officers (5 Captains were under arrest in one week) but since he arrested me, I demanded a Court Martial and so I had to confine myself to my Quarters, not having command of my Company in public. I dit not leave my Quarters at all. All went on well; I dit not care, still hoping to get a chance for a Court Martial as we have 26 Commissioned Officers who would have sworn they dit not believe the Colonel under oath, but the Cuss[?] never reported me to even the Colonel Commanding the Brigade, Colonel Kimbal of Indiana.[7] One day after I wrote to you from our big store and the same Evening that we were ordered to leave the Store and take possession of a big Brick house, 2 story, with a nice Bedroom in it for me and

---

7. Nathan Kimball (1822–98), a physician, had been a captain of volunteers in the Mexican War. At this time colonel of the Fourteenth Indiana, he would soon be a brigadier general. GB, 267–68.

a Bed, Bureau and so forth, I received your very very sweet letter, my dear wife, with a little note from Oncle Joseph in it, after I had gone to bed, which was written on the 26th February and mailed the 4th of March in Millersburg and such a sweet letter. It made me feel as well as I dit the morning I bid you good bye at home after the Atwater Ball when I started with Henry Greenebaum to Chicago, you know yet? When you showed tears the first time? How happy I felt, but this I think rather beats it as I love you more the older I get every day of my life, and every time I get a letter the boys say, look at Captain, see how pleast Captain is; if you want to go anywheres better ask Captain now, he just got a letter from home and so forth, and he will let you go now and it always makes me give the Command better.

Now to business; the Eve when we were fixed in our new house, the Adjutant came and said (then 10 o'clock P.M.) you must draw 3 days rations, cook them and fill your havresacks and be ready to march at 7 o'clock to morrow Morning. We fixed and at 7 A.M. we left the town on the Winchester Pike. The day was delightful and as the Bands of the different Regiments played their patriotic tones, the Colors flying, one felt as though it was a comfort to be a soldier fighting for our glorious union to be possessed yet by our posterity, and as we marched along through the prettiest country a man can see anywheres and see the magnificent palasts [palaces] surrounded by beautiful plantations and negro shanties, all of which at once satisfied and shows to the thinking man, oh what fools were you to bring on a destructive War while everything was surrounding you, that could be wished for; in times of peace you certainly had plenty.

We marched to Bunker Hill 9 miles from Martinsburg, stopped at Bunker Hill for further Orders. We fixed Beds and cooked but no rest for the Soldier when a victory is to be achieved. At 9 o'clock the Couriers came dashing with the news that Stone Wall Jackson as the Rebels calls their General was drawing in Line-o-Battle before Winchester. We

had orders to fall in immediately and the boys felt gay but I
dit not feel as well satisfied as I was still under arrest. We
marched on for 12 miles when [we] were halted within one
mile of the enemies entrenchments and it was a sight never
to be forgotten as Regiment after Regiment came and [was]
assigned its position; Battery after battery swept passed us
and being aligned, the Cavelery posted right and left of the
division; the Country perfectly level, the only elevation is an
easy sloping Hill all around Winchester on which the Enemy
had their Batteries, which was reported to be 64 Cannons
supported by about 20,000 men[8] and as we received the
orders to lay down on our arms and at the least alarm be
ready, we felt good and really I think every man was anxiously awaiting the time to hear the sound of the Cannons'
monotonous music and as I laid down aside of Chapman in
less than 5 minutes I was asleep and dreamed all night
about you my love and the children. I dreamed I was sitting
in our big black rocking chair and you on that little willow
chair, Oncle Josey laying down leaning his elbow on that
square carpet covered stool and the children all around us
and I was telling you all how I was the 2nd on the Ram-
parts planting the Colors and how old General Shields[9]
complimented me and you said when Jo brought the paper
home where you read it how I was praised by everybody
you danced for joy and then I said, come on woman, let us
dance now and we danced and the children all laughed and
just as I was going to jump and cut up, we were called fall
in. It was not yet day light. I woke, dit jump up and told
Chapman all will be right this day. Our Gallant General
Shields, the noble Hero of Mexico, was riding along our

---

8. With less than five thousand men, the Confederates were in fact greatly outnumbered. Vandiver, *Mighty Stonewall*, 197.

9. James Shields (1806–79) was born in Ireland. Settling in Illinois, he
became active in Democratic politics but also eventually a friend of Abraham
Lincoln's. A brigadier general of volunteers in the Mexican War, he entered
the Civil War at the same rank and replaced Lander as division commander.
GB, 444–45.

lines, and encouraged us; he is a noble looking General and I like him better than Lander. Colonel Kimball, our acting Brigadier general, then rode by and I stopped him and told him I was under arrest and he said, I heard of you yesterday. Are you not yet released? I said, no Sir. Says he, Where is that d——n Colonel of yours? On the head of the Column, I said. He galloped off and in less than 2 minutes and I had the comfort of seeing that Cuss [?] of ours come up to me and saying, Captain Spiegel please take command of your Company, and such 3 cheers as my boys gave when they heard me at the head of the Company Call, "Attention Company C", would have done your soul as much good as it was mortifying to Colonel Buerstenbinder to Knucle to me and ask me. He sent me word 3 times the day before, if I would ask him he would release me but I would not do it and at the end I beat him. (Lieutenant Colonel Voris has this afternoon laid the case before General Shields).

March 14, 1862

Since I wrote the above last Eve at 10 o'clock as I felt tired, several matters of Interest have occurred which I will before I close enumerate and now I will commence my narrative.

At the head of my Company, on the nicest day [March 12] I ever saw, the Sun as warm and refreshing as a Warm May noon in Ohio, I marched by the beat of the drums and to the sweet music of the fifes, the noble old flag (which is however brand new and was presented to us by the ladies of Toledo) fluttering gallantly in the Centre of my Company, and after such a sweet dream, going as we supposed to battle, I felt gay and like a Soldier. I knew success would be mine and I would come out of it with credit to myself and all those interested in my welfare. We marched and as we came fairly in view of the Entrenchments, the news came, the Enemy had fled that night in fear of the overwhelming force coming. Disappointment, real, and sorrow were pictured on the eyes of all the Boys as they got the news and they felt loath to believe the report but it was not long until the news was confirmed by our Outposts of Cavelery who rode on without molestation inside the fortifycations and to town, hoisting the Union flag on the Court house and sent a Courier back to inform the General.

Such being the fact we expected to get to town and follow up the Rebels to Strasburg, but disappointment was our doom for that day, as we were ordered by the right flank in a big Hill and led to a very pretty spot high and dry to stack Arms and make fires. We slept there the first night on some old wheat stopples [stubbles] that Wygam, Jac Grassley pulled for me and slept good to the next morning. Some of our Tents came but instead of having a Tent for myself, only one officers Tent came and I have to have both of my Lieutenants in with me and I now sit as I dit last night writing and if my letter is not very intelligible you must excuse my aqued [awkward] position. Winchester, everybody says is a very pretty City; I have not seen it yet and do not know as I shall soon, having no desire to ask our Colonel for a pass and not caring much anyhow as I really enjoy myself among the boys [in] this nice weather, drilling and [doing] exercises in the manual and practice of arms very well and, being very busy through the days, I will write Evenings to my love ones at home. This is a splendit country; from the elevation of our Camp we can see 28 different Camps of Union troops and they say there are plenty of them in and all around Winchester. General Banks, General Rosencranz and our own gallant General Shields are in Winchester and I expect soon to hear that we have met with McClellan.[10] Onward to Richmond I think is our destination, and I would like it indeed, though I have given up all hope of us getting in a fight as we have always missed it.

This morning Colonel Kimball, the Commander of our Brigade, sent me his Compliments, saying he took quite a

---

10. George Brinton McClellan (1826–85), a graduate of West Point whose small successes in western Virginia in 1861 had lifted him to command of the Army of the Potomac. His charisma kept him popular with most of his men and his political orientation was especially acceptable to Democrats like Spiegel. GB, 290–92.

liking to me; he would be pleased to see me. Having been on duty as officer of the day of which I will not be reliefed until 9 o'clock to morrow A.M. I have not called but shall do so to morrow in full Uniform and put on my winning smile.

At 10 o'clock this A.M. rumor came that our outposts were fighting 3 miles from here on the Strasburg Road and it was not long until after we heard the firing and all was alive, expecting to be called out, but about one hour the fight lasted and the Rebels retreated, leaving 17 prisoners and 2 dead in the hands of our boys, none on our side hurt. At our afternoon Parade our Colonel and Lieutenant Colonel Voris had a regular Row, which terminated in our Colonel showing that he was neither a Gentleman and Soldier which facts are reported to-night; charges being preferred every night against our Colonel until finally the War department will have to send him to h——l which they would have done ere this if they had not been so very busy. . . .

Give my love to Cohn and family; my thanks to Mrs. Cohn for the good tongues which were just the thing on a hard march. The Bitters is excellent. I take a horn [drink] every morn and it makes one feel good I tell you. If we only stay here long enough to get our pay, I will be as well pleased as anyone. I think the position of Captain is honorable in the Army; a Captain gets as much respect paid as a Colonel and the pay is $145.50 per month and since Joseph is not coming here I would not take the Quarter Mastership. I think if I come home I can persuade Oncle Josey to go to New York, marry Miss Emden and get some mesumen [money] and him and I will buy out the Warehouse and run it and make money like everything and live happy. I never want to let Oncle Joseph go away from me again; him and I want to stay together for good as long as we are alive and in business until both get as rich so that we need not do business any more.

He must not get out of humor, try and do something for

a little while, maybe clerk for Cherry Holmes[11] or wait until
I get my pay and I will send him some money to "handle"
mit [to do business with]. . . .

Good bye my dear Wife, good night my sweet children,
good nacht bruder Joseph; to Elizabeth good night and I
hope she has the McCormick convinced she would make a
good Mrs. McCormichen.

My love to you all, God bless you.

Ever yours
Marcus

Near Winchester Va.
March 22/62

My dear dear Wife & family!

. . . Colonel Buerstenbinder is under Arrest for the last 4
days and I am satisfied he never will Command this Regiment again, charges preferred against him (which will be
proofen) are sufficient to close out any man from commanding Ohio Boys for ever after and to bring about this
State of affairs, that is, getting him under arrest I tried my
best and done all I could honorably and am happy to say
success crowned our efforts and the Regiment I have no
doubt will be reliefed from the weight of carrying along an
incompetent officer.

We returned last night from a 3 day march to Strousburg
[Strasburg] which was believed and reported to be a strongly
fortified "Rebel Hole", but we were successful in driving
them out and chased them 5 miles South towards Woodstock and as I took some notes in the field, you will permit
me to give you them just as they are and if they seem a little enthusiastic, you must pass on them and make allowances
that they were taken by a Captain proud and elevated by
the noble Spirit of the Boys under his command and at the

---

11. Jacob Cherryholmes ran a general store in Millersburg. MF, Sept. 5,
1861.

moment of the Excitement of the Battlecry. This is Friday morn.[12] Monday Eve we received Marching Orders, that is, to cook 3 days rations and be ready to march without Blankets in 3 hours. Consequently, the Boys commenced cooking. I layed down in the Tents of the Boys and thought as my boy was preparing my rations and my Blankets were Rolled and buckled, my Sword sharpened and my Revolver loaded I would enjoy the 3 hours in sweet repose. Had not been fairly down, but I was sound asleep and the first time I turned round and opened my Eyes it was just daybreak.

I jumped up some what bewildered, thinking I had overslept myself and the Boys probably moved, but it was only for a moment; looking around I saw all my Boys soundly asleep, being however so near day I stayed up and shortly after that Reveillee beat, the Boys arose, Roll was called and it was then ordered to be ready to march by 10 o'clock. Hurrah for Strasburg was the happy response of everybody, after Stone Wall Jackson, the Bold Rebel General, and a true Soldier Spirit was shown all along the lines of the different Camps as far as the Eye could reach. The Cavelery was trotting briskly, the Artillery was moving, Infantry was passing along the pike in front of our Camp and everybody seemed to be alive for the task before them. We all felt, that if we can catch Jackson, we can whip him and his forces. At last the time came when our gallant Boys were led out commanded by our noble and highspirited Lieutenant Colonel Voris.

Never before dit the 67th make so good an appearance as on that day; the Boys all felt that they had somebody who had a Soul and sufficient quantity of Brains to lead them. We were drawn up in line and as our Brigade Commander Colonel Kimball of Indiana, a Gentleman and a Soldier (and by the way a warm friend of mine) passed us, he complimented us highly and we felt proud.

At 10 precisely we started; passed on through Winchester,

---

12. Therefore, this letter should have been dated March 21.

a City which has a regular Old Country City appearance like
Worms, which lay full of Soldiers of Banks division, which
look as though they came just out of a Ben [Band] Box,
not having to share any of the hardships, that we had to
go through with, but were comfortably quartered all
winter. . . .

As we passed through the City of Winchester we received
the hearty cheerings of the Soldiers stationed there, but the
female Citizens (and that is about all there is left as the
male Citizens in this Country have all been pressed or
volunteered in the Rebel Service) dit not seem to relish our
advance much, as undoubtedly they feared we might not
use their father, Husbands, Brothers, or Lovers very kind,
should we meet them on the way.

We halted the first time about 4 miles South of Winchester near 2 of the finest looking Mills I have seen yet in this
Country. It looked for all the World like Millheim near
Abenheim, everything around the Mills and the splendit
houses close by, bespoke wealth of Ages but not of 6 month
growth, like Chicago.[13] And the strangest of all, the pro-
prieters were the strongest Union folks, who had fled and
just returned and then for the first time around Winchester
dit the Ladies wave white Handkerchiefs.

After resting and refreshing ourselves we started on a
merry march; the day was all that could be wished for,
warm and pleasant, and those Virginia Pikes are like our
European Chausee [roads] as even and regular as a floor.
We then passed through the town of Kernstown of the same
shape like most of these towns on the Pike: as long as the
moral Law, only one Street along the Pike; the regular old
fashion Post towns, 2 Or 3 Stage offices or Hotels. About 1
mile South of the town after passing the nicest Country in

---

13. Spiegel perhaps refers to Milltown, actually closer to Winchester than
indicated. United States, War Department, *Atlas to Accompany the Official Records of the Union and Confederate Armies* (Washington, D.C., 1891–95; rpt. New
York: T. Yoseloff, 1958), pl. 43, no. 3 and 49, no. 1. Hereafter cited as OR
Atlas.

America, we came to a plantation which so took me by surprise for its beauty and the Palace it had in its Center struck me so with Admiration that I had to stop and make a minute [memorandum] and from that time commenced my field Notes.

Mrs. Southworth's beautiful Tales located in the Valley of the Shenandoah and the Rapehanick [Rappahannock] in which we thought she stretched a good deal, are daily coming to my mind as we pass through here. Just now we came passed a most grand looking building which would I think fill the description of the mansion of Capitola's[14] Oncle whose name I forgot. The House is large, of Ionic Architecture, [a] finished Mansion of Solid Stones to which Miss Sumner's House near Middlebury or Sam Thomlin's would only be outbuildings in comparison.[15]. The front is supported by heavy Corinthian Pillars and the Windows and Bay Windows of a Gothic Structure. The broad Alley, through an Arched Gate leading, with the Gigantic old Weeping Willows on each Side, the Zink Roof which in the Sun looks like Crystal, and the handsomely finished Hot Greenhouses in front give the beholder an Idea that some Count must live there, or rather hold his sway over the 4 or 500 Blacks who reside in their quarters some distance from the Palace which looks a great deal like the Herrnsheimer Schloss[16] I told you so frequent about. Marching along now as we do in a fine Spring afternoon, on the left of us we behold the beautiful "Blue Ridge" Mountains, which have a Picturesque appearance as they show themselves in a Mountain chain as fair and blue as the Sky in Italy; you behold to our right the Alleghenies as far as the Eye can reach. Quitely we pass along, the Bands playing, our Banner which

---

14. The heroine of *The Hidden Hand* (1859), Mrs. Southworth's most popular novel. Hofstadter, "Southworth," 328.

15. Probably Louise Sumner, a wealthy farmer and stock-raiser of Middlebury, a village later incorporated into Akron. Perrin, *History of Summit County*, 269–70. Sam Thomlin is unidentified.

16. A castle or palace in Germany.

is in my Company proudly and defiantly waving to our front. Just ahead of us we behold now before us on a Hill side the old town of Middletown which like Kernstown is long and ancient. A beautyful Church of Brick has [the] date 1817 on it. We are now South of Middletown and on the battle ground of yesterday between our and the Rebel Cavelery in which my Friend Dr. Ebright was present and captured a Rebel Flag and just now, as we go up quite a little Hill, we hear the Booming of the Cannons some 5 or 6 miles ahead of us and just like an electric Strain it goes through the lines with a Shout of the 12 or 14 Regiments which made the Earth shake and the Heaven tremble. That was enough for the Boys, there was none among them that felt tired. All wanted to go double quick and soon we reached the town of Newtown,[17] a rather Handsome town, something like Middlebury only all in one Street close together. Marching on lively we heard the Sounds which seemed to renew and strengthened the Boys every time. We now came to Cedar Creek with smoking ruins of a handsome Bridge which the Rebels had but shortly burned in Order to detain us, but the ingenuity of our Leaders soon threw the ruins down the Creek, put boards on it and so we crossed single file and as we were briskly advancing on Strousburg we received Orders to halt about an hour after night, lay on our arms and be ready to march at a moments notice. Being right tired I slept soundly as usual with my friend Chapman and at the break of day we were called up, made some Coffee in our Tin Cups and started. As we came within 2 miles of Strousburg we were again halted and ordered to open Ranks. As we led the advance in the move towards Winchester, we have to take the Rear this time and shall not unless a big battle or a flanking movement [is] contemplated get in very soon.[18] As we open our Ranks a

---

17. Spiegel reverses the sequence of the advance through Newton and Middletown. OR Atlas, pl. 49, no. 1.

18. A second "not" which Spiegel erroneously inserted after "contemplated" is omitted.

Courier gallops past with all the appearance of something
up. Now the Bugles of the Artillery sound the Advance,
now the double quick; now they gallop along as fast as the
Horses can go, 6 Horses to a cannon. Just imagine 40 Cannons with 80 Ammunition Wagons, 6 Horses to each,
galloping past while you hear the Enemies batteries playing
at a distant Hill opposite yours, the men hurraing, the
Bugles Sounding, the officers commands and then I ask,
Who wouldn't be a Soldier? Oh it was truly grant; Oh sublime indeed and if ever I live to see the day that I am 80
years old, I think, I can describe that Scene with animation.
Now the Cavelery rushes past; now the Ranks are closed
and, Battalion forward March, is heard from our Lieutenant
Colonel Commanding; forward Company C repeated by me,
and my noble Boys start off with as much alacrity and animation as they would to a 4th of July dance with a pretty
Caroline F. Hamlin with them. Halt is now commanded.
The Rebels still throw their Shells which fall as harmless as
the leaves of a beautiful Rose after it has been lucritive and
sweet. Now Colonel Voris rides up and asks me whether I
want to see the Rebels. I started with him on a big Hill
where on the top of which, to where I went, stands our Noble General Shields and Staff, our and other Brigade Commanders, Colonels and so forth, through Glasses watching
the movements of the Rebels and watching General Shields
directing the advance of our men. The Rebels are at a Hill
right opposite protecting Strousburg; now a shell bursted in
a hallow a great distance below us. Now we see our Artillery
advancing and Cavelery following, between us and the Rebels; now the Rebels see them and pull up stakes. Now the
Command is given, follow up; now we rush to our respective commands. Forward march, on to Strousburg. We are
now in the town, a crooked Streeted old fashion kind of a
town; now the Rebel Cannons are still playing. Now through
the town, up the Hill, where the Rebels was a little while
ago; now off the pike through a long Lane up a Hill, past a
large brick House, through a Barnyard, up another Hill, on
the level; now our Artillery is being planted on an elevation;

now our Brigade is drawn up in line-o-Battle by division [of] 2 Companies; I command the Centre or Color division, my Company and Company H. Oh how big I feel. Now our Artillery commences, boom, boom, boom, more rapid; the Rebels only answer occasionally. Just now General Shields comes galloping apassed our line, commanding our Brigade to double quick down the Side of a Steep Hill of Pinetrees to cut off the retreating Rebels. Now "by the right flank file left, double quick march" down, down as fast as we can get and just as we get on the Pike the 7th Indiana rushes past to get ahead of us. Now Colonel Voris is jumping a high fence with his horse and we follow, double quick through a wheat field, the hardest running I ever done; and now the Balls of the Rebels Cannons are Buzzing over our Heads from Hill top to Hill top, 200 feet over us. Now on the Pike again, over a large Stone Bridge which crosses the north Branch of the Shenandoah River, up a Hill. Here lies 4 dead Horses; 2 Cavelery men are carrying their Saddles passed us, one of them his hand bleeding. Now on top of the Hill; now Halt and rest a little. Now forward march, follow up the fleeing foe, but he is too fast for us, having the Start and knowing the Country. We could not catch them though we chased them for 5 miles; the Infantry never getting a chance to fire at them once. Night coming on, we were ordered back to the big Stone Bridge where we camped in a meddow aside of the River and in less than 1/4 of an hour the Rails of a whole farm [vanished]; as far as the Eye could see folks were camped and the Rails had disappeared. I felt pretty tired; my feet hurt me some and though it was rather rough and chilly, I pulled my boots and soked my feet for 20 minutes in the River, washed my face, neck and Breast, after which I felt Bully. When I came to Camp again, it having commenced to rain, Colonel Voris had built a Rail Pen and covered [it] with our Rubber Blankets, and a good Coffee cooked. One of my boys having been off and pressed 2 Chickens, some Eggs and some flour into the Service, I made a Chicken Zweishel [?] Soup which was bully after which I crept in the Rail pen and though it rained all night I dit not get very wet, but slept as sound as a bug in a Rug all night. In the morning we dit not know which way to march. Finally at 1/2 past 10 the Order came to march back to Winchester to our Camp; it being I suppose not advisable to follow up farther as the Rebels might attack us in the Rear and cut off our Supply. The March back to Camp was made without one stop; just think, marching 25 miles without stopping once. Dr. Ebright whom I met several times the day before, passed and offered me his horse which I refused, but some very nice buisquits with preserves through the middle I excepted. Colonel Voris afterwards insisted that I should ride his horse awhile which I dit for 2 miles.

We reached our Camp at 7 1/2 o'clock sound and hearty, though 11 of my Boys fell back tired out but all came in this morning. I can beat them all on a march. To day I feel as though I could march 50 miles. I take the best kind of care of myself, overdo nothing, but quietly follow the even tenor of my duty, where ever it calls me. . . .

At Camp near Winchester Va.<br>March 22/62

Master Hamlin M. Spiegel
Miss Lizzie T. Spiegel
Master Moses M. Spiegel

My good sweet children:

Yesterday I received the second letter from my dear Son Hamlin and since I know that you can not all of you write yet, I thought best to send you all one letter in Partnership which belongs to you all.

I am very happy indeed that your dear mother always writes me such good news of everyone of you. If she would have to complain of you I would feel very bad, but I always knew that I had just as good Children as there was in the world. I was in a Battle 3 days ago and the Cannon Balls were flying over my head but none hurt me; the good Lord preserved me from any harm and if you will only be right good Children, mind well and pray to the good Lord, I

Hamlin, left, and Lizzie Spiegel

trust soon to see you all well and hearty. Mother writes to me that you all grew nice and learn fast which I hope you will continue to do.

Good buy, my dear Children; may the Lord keep you in good health is the sincerest wish of your Father who loves you dearly.

M. M. Spiegel

When I come home I will try and bring you just such presents as you want.

Winchester Va.<br>March 22/62

My lovely Wife and dear Children
My good Brother!
   . . . I feel good and as happy as a man can be under the Circumstances of being away from those whom he loves dearly. My position is respectable and honorable. I have the Respect of all who know me, am loved by my Boys and feel as though I had the good wishes of many a friend besides my relatives at home and abroad. The position pays and my chance for promotion with influential Friends here to back me is fair, though I will not press it. I could to day take the Quarter Mastership of our Regiment; though it is not a po-

sition very dangerous, yet I will not except it. If I would take any business position in the Army, it should be Adjutant General or Brigade Quarter Master or Sutler, but on the whole if I stay in the Army longer than Spring, I think I shall run my chances as a Soldier. I only wish for you, my dear wife, and for you, my good Brother, to keep up Spirits for a little while and not get disheartened; it grieves my soul to hear you down hearted. You have no occasion for it; I am doing the best for all of you and if Joseph only keeps up for 30 days longer I set him all right. I know I can and he need not leave Millersburg either; just cheer up my boy, dont get disheartened and for a short time dispell the darn blues and you will be all right. The letter my big Son wrote me made me feel happy. I wish he would write often and as I have only this week written a letter to him, I am in hopes that he will not think hard of me for not writing to him as soon as I would if I had more time. . . .

The retirement of Shields's Division from Strasburg to Winchester had attracted the attention of Stonewall Jackson. The Confederate commander correctly interpreted the movement as being part of an attempted shift of much of Banks's force out of the Shenandoah Valley and toward the coast where it could reinforce McClellan's drive on Richmond. Jackson, whose orders were to prevent such a Union transfer, immediately hurried his army north toward Strasburg. His scouts misinformed him as to the strength of the Union forces remaining in the Winchester area. Believing he faced only a rear guard, he threw his 4,200 men against the some 9,000 soldiers of Shields's Division. The resultant battle, which Spiegel and others involved often referred to as "Winchester," would be known to history as "Kernstown" or "First Kernstown."[19]

---

19. Boatner, *Civil War Dictionary*, 456–57; Bruce Catton, *Terrible Swift Sword*, vol. 2 of *The Centennial History of the Civil War* (Garden City, N.Y.: Doubleday, 1963), 265–66.

Strasburg, Va., March 28, 1862[20]

My Dear Beloved Wife and Children,

Brother and Friends:—

I have a painful yet proud duty to perform in giving you
a list of my dead and wounded as well as a history of the
battle so fearfully contested, so gallantly fought and so vic-
toriously won. . . .

All of my boys who were in the battle (except probably
two) fought nobly, standing by my Lieutenants and myself,
maintaining every position we took, never yielding an inch,
gallantly driving the enemy from their position, though
mostly exposed to cross fires, and fearlessly and nobly bearing aloft the colors of the Regiment entrusted to our keeping, and their reward is, that their courage and bravery re-
ceives encomiums from every one in General Shields's Division. Never was an officer prouder of his command than I
am this day of my gallant little band. God bless them. The
coolness, courage and skill of my Lieutenants prevented our
loss from being much greater than it was. I will now give
you a brief account of the battle.

On Saturday afternoon [March 22], when preparing for
dress parade, we heard the firing of the cannon; but paid
no attention to it—supposing it to be artillery practice. In
less than twenty minutes the long roll beat, and the news
spread that Jackson had driven in our pickets. In seven
minutes we were moving at double quick toward Strasburg.
The 67th was the first Infantry Regiment to report itself on
the field, to General Shields. We were therefore deployed as
skirmishers on the left to keep the enemy's right at bay until
other regiments were brought to our support. While we

---

20. Published in MF, Apr. 10, 1862. For another account of Kernstown
which generally parallels Spiegel's, see Franklin Sawyer, *A Military History of
the 8th Regiment Ohio Vol. Inf'y: Its Battles, Marches and Army Movements* (Cleveland: Fairbanks, 1881), 41–43. For a sketch map of the battle, see Vandiver,
*Mighty Stonewell,* 206.

were deploying the enemy showered shell, grape, canister, and round ball among us.—Three shells passed through my company, one of them very close to L. G. Osborn and the color-bearer. None of them did any damage, since they did not burst very near us, and the boys could dodge them. We advanced rapidly but carefully under command of our gallant Lieutenant Colonel Voris, and the enemy gave way slowly, until night, when we halted, and at 12 o'clock we were withdrawn, and fell back a mile and a half. We slept until 4 o'clock when Colonel Voris quietly waked us and ordered us to cook some coffee and be ready to fall in. The boys were quickly up and anxious for further orders. We were delayed until 7 o'clock, when we were marched to the support of Daum's celebrated battery,[21] a position of honor assigned us for being first on the field Saturday evening. We remained at this post until 12 o'clock, and all the time shell was showered at us; but fortunately no one was hurt. At noon we were relieved by the 5th Ohio, and ordered further on to our left wing to guard the movements of the rebel Infantry, where we remained for an hour, and then the enemy attempted to outflank our right by their left and we were ordered with a battery of the 1st Ohio to attack their left. At the same time a part of the 2d Brigade under Colonel [Erastus B.] Tyler, were ordered to prevent the enemy from going any further to the left. We retained this position about half an hour when the enemy made an attempt to go further to the left and a volley of musketry was open on them. The second volley had hardly died away when our Regiment was ordered to advance, which we obeyed, at a double quick, in line-of-battle, under a furious fire of shells, grape and canister shot; but the boys having only victory in contemplation, rushed madly, furiously through the open field into a narrow strip of woods, which lay very high with comparatively few trees. As we came into

---

21. Philip Daum's First Regiment West Virginia Light Artillery (Battery A) (Independent). William Frayne Amann, ed., *Personnel of the Civil War*, 2 vols. (New York: T. Yoseloff, 1961), 2:237.

line with the enemy we discovered that we were too much
to the right. Yet, to our right, in the woods, was the 29th
Ohio and the 110th Pennsylvania, of Tyler's Brigade. They
had no orders to advance. When we were drawn into line
and with others all along to our left open fire it was perfectly awful. We received an unyielding fire from the
enemy's left and left flank.

While we were exposed to a galling fire the Colonel of
the 29th Ohio, who is strictly military, had no orders to advance, and therefore did not advance; though with orders
he might have played on their left flank. Lieutenant Colonel
Voris took the responsibility of moving his Regiment to the
left, under somewhat of a cover. He took the flag, called for
the boys to rally round it, and soon we were in position to
play upon the enemy with fearful effect. Such a fire as we
let them have. The 8th Ohio, who, from their exposed position had to lay flat on the ground, renderered some assistance; and it was not 25 minutes until we made the enemy
give, and then the 8th had full play.

Shortly after this we routed them; they leaving the field
strewn with their dead and wounded, and our boys pursu-
ing them with all haste. They took another stand in a strip
of woods; our boys drove them from this, and pursued
them with the most furious yells and shouts of revenge—
they occasionally making a stand, but to no effect—until
finally they made a stand in a splendid position, high and
commanding, in a strip of woods to their left centre, It was
necessary for us to charge through an open field of probably a hundred acres to reach them, and most of us, in our
eagerness to pursue them, had half crossed the field before
we were aware of our position. It was then that Lieutenant
Colonel Voris said, "Boys if we don't drive them from these
woods, we shall have to go to Richmond or to the d——l.
Let them have it." They were then ordered to fall flat upon
the ground, laying upon their backs to load and whirling
around to take aim at the enemy as they appeared from behind the trees. It then looked most fearful, exposed as we
were to a cross fire, very little chance to do them injury,
and to advance in a body was madness; but

> "When danger looks most severe,
> Then the help of God is near."

So it proved to us. The gallant 13th Indiana had just come up to our left on a cat-like tread, and were not seen until they were opening a murderous fire on the enemy, to the right, which made them falter, wheel and run. Then our boys spread to their feet and run up the field, over the stone fence into another field, through that into the woods, and through that still on, following the panic stricken rebels who threw away guns, bayonets, haversacks, and everything else in order to facilitate their flight. We followed up until dark came on. Our boys were gathered on the field, of which they were complete victors; but how horrible was that field, strewn with dead, and from which came the groans of the wounded and the sighs of the dying. Exhausted and sick at heart we lay down on the field of battle, where we were ordered to remain, and slept without fire or blankets, to awake in the morning stiff and shivering with cold. At day-break we followed the retreating rebels, without anything to eat. They had left their dead and wounded by the way, and at almost every house our Surgeons were called to minister to the wounded men. That night we had some coffee and slept by fires, though without blankets. We started early the next morning and followed until night. On Monday and Tuesday we fought their rear, taking many prisoners.

Thus ended the careful [fearful?] battle of Winchester. It was fearful. Just think of 10,000 muskets fired continually for hours, the chase and the excitement. All our troops engaged did their best. The rebels fought stubornly and with courage, but the Union boys are bound to win, as one of my Sergeants, J. E. Bruce, told a rebel Major after he had shot him on the third charge.

General Shields had his arm shattered the first evening. He is the right man in the right place. On Sunday the command devolved upon Brigadier General Kimball, of Indiana, who acquited himself honorably. Our Regiment was led by Colonel Voris, under whom it is victory or death with our boys.

I am writing this four miles from camp and within three miles of the enemy, where I have been on picket since yesterday; but I expect to be released in an hour.

After we were quartered on Tuesday evening, I went to see General Banks to get permission to look after my dead and wounded. He granted the permission, and shaking my hand said, "I am happy to say, you assisted nobly in gaining a noble victory. . . ."[22] And, in fact, all my boys, except two, should be Colonels, and Sergeant Bruce should be a General.[23]

Good Day,
M. M. SPIEGEL

P.S. Since writing the above it has been ascertained that the gentlemen soldiers from Massachussetts and Connecticut, who have been comfortably quartered about Harper's Ferry, and look as though they had just came out of a band box, laugh at us rough looking Western men and endeavor to steal part of our glory; therefore, we, the officers and men of Shields's Division, feel it is our duty to say to our friends at home that this desperate battle was fought and won by Western men, commanded by Western officers, and planned by Colonel Kimball, of Indiana, after Gen. Shields was wounded. Not until 24 hours after the battle did General Banks arrive with the Eastern troops.[24]

M.M.S.

---

22. In a letter not published here, Spiegel quoted Banks as saying, "Ah your Boys fought nobly. I am well, well pleased." Spiegel to wife, Mar. 26, 1862.

23. James E. Bruce returned the compliment. According to a letter initialed "J.E.B." and almost surely written by him, "Capt. Speigle [sic] continues to be the right man in the right place. He is fast gaining notice by the higher officers in this division. His company are proud of their Captain. . . . 'He is rough but brave, generous and kind.'" *Akron Summit Beacon*, Apr. 10, 1862.

24. Spiegel here expresses the sense of distinctiveness and pride in their military prowess common among Northerners from west of the Appalachians. In reporting the charge of the Sixty-seventh Ohio at Kernstown, an Ohio editor said, "with a terrific Western shout, they pitched in and routed the scamps." *Akron Summit Beacon*, Apr. 10, 1862.

As Spiegel indicates, the battle of Kernstown was both disorganized and furious. "This was emphatically a battle of the boys," Lieutenant Colonel Voris later recalled. "They went in on their own hook and came out on their own motion, in a state of great but glorious confusion." In an explanation which might have been applied to both of the inexperienced, enthusiastic opposing armies, he remarked, "Officers and men were all boys then." Thus, though Shields's men repelled the Confederates' attack and drove them from the field, they were unable to crush their outnumbered foes. Indeed, the Confederates with 700 casualties succeeded in inflicting a heavy loss of 590 on the victors. Ultimately, the Union tactical success at Kernstown led to strategic failure, as the Federals shifted troops back into western Virginia to catch Jackson. The subsequent "Valley Campaign" continued to divert Union strength from McClellan's advance on Richmond, destroyed the reputations of several frustrated United States commanders, and made a Confederate hero of Stonewall Jackson. In the aftermath, the veterans of Shields's Division took lifelong pride in having been the only Union army to vanquish Mighty Stonewall.[25]

Strasburg, Va. March 30/62

My dear dear good Wife
My sweet children
My noble Brother!
. . . I now for the first time since the great fight feel myself as of old bully, and all the horrors are forgotten. That this fight made some impression on me is not to be winced at, though it now seems to me like a dream. I know however that I have acquitted myself to the full satisfaction of all. I was not in the least scared, but energetic and cool. Taking care of myself as much as I possibly could, without heatlessly exposing myself, I was here and there and every where, encouraging all my Boys, seeing them all, leading

---

25. A. C. Voris, "The Battle of the Boys," in Military Order of the Loyal Legion of the United States, Ohio Commandery, *Sketches of War History, 1861–1865, Papers Prepared for the Ohio Commandery of the Military Order of the Loyal Legion of the United States, 1890–1896.* Vol. 4 (Cincinnati: R. Clarke, 1896), 88, quoted words on 98–99; Boatner, *Civil War Dictionary,* 456–57; Catton, *Terrible Swift Sword,* 266–67.

them in front at every change of position, never hiding myself, frequently being in the hottest places and a many,
many well aimed bullet whizzed passed my head and close
by my body everywhere but thanks to God our heavenly
father I came out of it without receiving a scratch. Our
Banner which was always in my Company received 8 Bullets; one just passed through it not 2 inches over my head
while the Colors were proudly waving right over me. I am
well and hearty and the fact that my Company has 4 killed
out of 9 in the Regiment and 5 wounded out of 47 is sufficient that to satisfy anyone that we are fighting boys and
in front.

I just think that I have a lot of the noblest boys that ever
shouldered a musket. My Lieutenants are the right men in
the right places, courageous, brave and cool. Three of my
Sergeants, Wallick, Bruce and Bowman are Boys with whom
I challenge the world; they were as gay and pleasant as a
young woman at a tea party. Wallick I appointed Orderly
on the field of Battle though by the regular Rank of promotion it belonged to Lemon who shortly after the fight commenced hurt his leg (he claims) by getting over a fence
from the Battlefield and dit not join the Regiment until 6
days after the fight, and I believe in rewarding merit, not
Rank.[26] Captain Ford, that very hansome and Interesting
Captain that I wrote you about, was one of the just once
killed. It would be a task for me to describe to you my experience of the Battlefield as it would most likely not
improve your good opinion of military, and I believe I will
wait until I can tell you.

My getting home in May is now a fixed fact; all have such
a good opinion of me that they dare not refuse it. I could
go home to morrow if I desired, but as I can likely only stay
40 days, I have no desire to go and leave again just the time

---

26. Spiegel refers to Sgts. Henry M. Wallick, James E. Bruce, Andrew J.
Bowman, and Marge J. Lemmons. Wallick replaced William J. Wiggins as
orderly or first sergeant. Wiggins had been killed, as indicated later in the
letter. Roster 5:578–79.

when I would not miss being at home for a Colonelship.
The Arrest of the Colonel will undoubtedly lead to his dismissal from the Service which will make Voris Colonel and
the Captain of Company A Major; the Captain of Company
B being dead will make me Captain of Company A or
senior Captain in the Regiment or next to promotion to
Field Officer and the changes, transfers and so forth which
are so frequent gives me a good chance; however I will not
say until I get home as I do not feel like deciding until after
I have seen you all.

Tuesday night I left here and rode Horseback 24 miles to
see my wounded Boys and look after my dead ones, all of
which I found buried but Orderly Wiggins who the Millersburg Band Boys had kept for orders from me, whom I sent
to Millersburg where he has undoubtedly arrived and has
been buried, which I would like to hear in your next.

It is said that he whom the ground covers is gradually
forgotten and so it seems. Since the Boys have made up
their minds, that Friday night Orderly Wiggins Corps arrived at Millersburg and is buried, the last of the fallen
heroes, they are assuming their old gaiyty again, sing and
cut up as much as ever and only when a name of one of
the fallen Nobles is mentioned you can see a spread of
gloom over their faces and I must confess I have not yet
forgotten 5 of my very best boys, who 9 days ago were as
gay as any, are no more, but yet since I got your letter I
feel as though I could enjoy a good joke right hearty. Just
think how much I will have to tell you when I come home!
Been in an awful Battle; just think of the crack of a continuous Musketry of from 15 to 16,000 guns, the Cannonading, the Cavelery dashing, the men yelling and every
thing else; cant I tell you Something? I'll bet I can tell you
as much as you could even if you would go as far as Wooster and you know you always see lots. I have just made up
my mind that I will have as much to tell you as Marshall
and Sally would if they would ride from Lima to Millersburg in a Buggy and you know that is a good deal. Tell
Hamlin that he must be a good Son and I will tell him all

about the big fight; how I seen a Shoe with a foot in, Shot off by a Cannon Ball and lots more. Also Lizzie, I have a great deal to tell her and lots of pretty things to bring her, as well as for Hamlin and Mosey. Oh but I rejoice to see the time when I can take them on my lap and kiss them, but time flies so fast here, moving and removing, tearing down and building up, that I hope it will not be long. Now Brother Joseph, as you stuck out so well, do for my sake and stay and feel happy. I will try and win glory enough to do the whole Spiegel Family and you shall have your share of it and I know it will be for the best for both of us as I will make it all right. I want you to examine my letter and if necessary copy it and place the punctuation before publishing it.[27] Everything except that in lines I would like to have published, look over it and read it. I thought of giving you the history so that you could read it to Caroline and then have it published. Do you ever look in the Akron Beacon? It often has letters from our Akron Boys in the 67th and I am very anxious to see what they say about me, as the little Credit that a Soldier gets is all he has to expect from public opinion and if you see anything worthy of notice about me, which I doubt, have Estill copy it.[28]

It does me good to have the love and confidence of my Boys and the Respect and good will of my Superior Officers and can say without boasting I am gaining daily in the Army.

My dear beloved wife, I dont think ever since we are married dit I do anything for which I had to blush (except Uniontown schocking in former days) [meaning unclear] before you or you to blush for me and I know that my military career as long as it may last will be a career to which we will look back to in after years with pride and satisfac-

---

27. Spiegel refers to the preceding letter, which was evidently sent as an enclosure to this one.

28. Spiegel wishes that any favorable reference to him in the *Akron Summit Beacon*, a Republican weekly, be reprinted in his hometown's Democratic newspaper.

tion. I know you are not sorry you let me go and I know you are not sorry I am neither Quarter Master nor Sutler, but a bold "Soldier Boy". With your fervent prayers, the good wishes of my friends, the encouraging and long letters from home with the pleasing tidings of my sweet and prosperous children, I will get through this in better health, more fully developed, happy and all "O.K." . . .

Strasburg March 31/62

My dear dear good little wife

Though I have only to day sent 2 Letters of 7 or 8 foolscap sheet to you, yet I just now learned that my friend Lieutenant Fahrian[29] is going to Ohio to morrow and I just thought I would give you a few lines to say to you I am bully, bully and that since the great battle I love you more, more much; you are the Idol of my soul, my thoughts by day, my dreams by night, my all, all in all.

God bless you and all our good sweet children, I love them all and God knows want to see them badly.

I live just as I have for a good while. Henry Adams,[30] a young boy from Millersburg or near, cooks for me and attends me. My Lieutenants Chapman and Childs and my self board together. Since we left the Rail Road our board is not so good; we get no Molasses nor Vegetables, only Crackers, fresh and Salt Beef and Pork, Coffee and Sugar. You wanted to know how I wear my whiskers. I have not shaved nor trimmed for 2 Months; my hair is a little longer than usual. I look Sunburned and my hands black. Since the battle I was on Picket and happen to be near a neighborhood where the greatest Pennsylvania Shlemils [simpletons] live that I ever saw; all the Families are the Virginia Dutch so called. We were near a splendit brick house. The Proprietor, as regular John A. Keplar as ever lived in the

---

29. 2d Lt. Gustav W. Fahrion of Company D, Sixty-seventh Ohio. Roster 5:584.

30. A private in Spiegel's company. Roster 5:580.

world,[31] came out and invited me in and asked me to protect him and his property from violence by my boys. I
promised it and made my boys respect my promise. I was
used like a Prince, though I would not accept a bed as I
feared catching cold; I slept on the floor. They have 6
grown girls, as regular John A. Keplars Girls as lived; a
Sarah, Mary Malissa and so forth, their laughing and all;
they talk the same singing dutch. When I left the old Lady
cried; I told them about you and the children and they all
cried.

My coming home, if no preventing providence, is sure
now and God how I long to see the time. You have no
Idea, but patience. George Wygand just came in out of his
bed. He heard his Box had come from home. I hope it has;
he has been lamenting long enough for it.

I have told you yesterday that I dit not fire once during
the Battle. I had once my Revolver cocked but thought of
my promise to you and uncocked it again; from that you
can see that I was perfectly cool and as usual thinking of
you, my love. . . .[32]

Camp in the woods by the Shenandoah River between
Woodstock & Mt. Jackson Va/April 3/62
My lovely and good Wife,
my sweet children and Brother!

As I am setting here in a large woods under cover of
Railpens with Pine brushes and look around me where I can
see the whole of Shield's Division, with the Exception of the
Cavelery, the Boys at home in all manners of houses such as

---

31. Spiegel refers to a mutual acquaintance from Green Township, Ohio,
member of a large "Pennsylvania Dutch" (German) family. Their neighbors
regarded many of the Pennsylvania Dutch as ignorant and superstitious.
Perrin, *History of Summit County*, 598–99, 603.

32. Spiegel may refer to the promise to keep out of danger as much as
possible which he alluded to in his letter of Jan. 30, 1862, or conceivably to a
promise to avoid firing unless unavoidable, which may have had some connection with his wife's Quaker background.

can be shaped out of Rubber Blankets, Rails, Brush and Straw, I felt as though I could not pass my time any more profitable than by writing to you, my loved ones.

We have followed up the Enemy from our old place near Strasburg, starting April 1st A.M., and as we came near Woodstock, the County Seat of Shenandoah County our advance and the Enemy's Rear have been continually fighting almost; the latter slowly retreating and our forces advancing at the same Speed. They burned almost every Bridge as they crossed, doing like a certain Animal drawing its hole in after him, but we prohibited them or rather our Shells [stopped them] from finishing one job of burning a Bridge, on the Railroad which runs from Mount Jackson (I believe) to Manassas Junction. They burned a trussel work almost as large if not larger than the trussel work at near Bristol,[33] a shameful work of destruction, which belongs to the Barbarians of the middle Age.

I can not see how men as intelligent as our Southern Brethen can get so wrathy and self forgetting as to cut off their own noses to spoil the looks of their own faces. Yesterday we had an exciting time firing all day from here to across the River and answered by the Enemy. However considerable of our forces crossed and skirmishing and so forth were kept up all day; 3 of our forces killed and a number wounded; the enemy lost severely.

This morning all was quiet until about an hour ago when the music commenced and every little while the Batteries let loose. When action commences I know not; all I know is that I expect to do my duty. I am in hopes this unwarrantable and unnatural War will soon close. I am satisfied if the people of the South would understand and appreciate our true position, all would be over. We do not want to interfere with their institutions; all we ask is, the Sovereignty of the good old Government. . . .

---

33. Spiegel could be referring to any of several Bristols.

Camp in the Woods near Edenburg Va. April 6/62
My kind beloved and sweet wife!

...We have been here now 4 days right in sight of the
Enemy, skirmish fighting and cannonading daily. Yet I
think there will be no fighting here, as the Enemy is separated from us by the South Branch of the Shenandoah
River [34] and as soon as we advance they will retreat and I
think if General Kimball is correct and he undoubtedly is,
the War will soon be over, as the Enemy is surrounded and
he thinks they will see how they are trapped and must
surrender.

My love I am thinking that I will soon be permitted to see
you. I just feel so, though General Kimball told me to day
when I asked him for a furlough, "indeed Captain we can
not let our best officers go", although he told me a day after the Battle, "I dont think Captain we dare refuse you
anything." Yet in spite of all I think I can engineer a furlough through.

Oh won't we have a gay old time? Eh! Old sweet girl?
Certainly we will or any other man.

What does Oncle Josey say to his gallant Soldier Brother?
I tell you he can not fool me again about my soldiering
when I come home and command him, "about face" "right
face" "left face" "march", he must mind me, or the Guard
house is his doom. My Son Hamlin I hope is doing as well
as he always was and learning and growing fast. My sweet
daughter Lizzie I am sure behaves herself, because she is
the only little Lady I have. Mosey you think would not
know me anymore which indeed would make me feel a kind
[of] awkward[ness]. You must tell him "now pa is coming"
and learn him to run out as though he wanted to meet me
and then he will get used to me.

If I should happen to come home unexpected dont be
scared because I have made up my mind to come as soon as

---

34. Edenburg, later Edinburg, was on the North Fork of the Shenandoah.

can get off and for fear of not getting to go when I want to
I will go when I can. Yet there might be a slight possibility
of not succeeding; if so I will have to yield to powers that
be, but I will try my best and you know I am pretty good at
trying and it would I think go hard with me if I dit not
dare to go as I set my head for going. Besides all this, there
is one thing that is of great help to me; Lieutenant Colonel
Voris is almost as anxious for me to go as I am; he wants
me to go to Columbus and see the Governor for him and
make all things right about his promotion; all he can do will
be done. So you can see we can hope. Keep up your Spirit
and I will mine; in fact I feel as good some how as ever I
dit since I am a Soldier, and well and hearty; can eat like a
trooper. This dinner we had a chicken pot pie but it was
rather heavy; we are baking buisquits without Butter or
cream, use tallow. . . .

     In the field near Woodstock Va. April 27/1862
My dear and good Wife, my good Brother!
My sweet children!
 This is the longest interval of writing to you since I have
been in the Army, and as it is, now I feel sorry and
aggrieved for not keeping up my regular way of corresponding but believe me my dear ones, it was not for any
lack of love or care for you, neither was it negligence, but
simply for the reason of having anticipation of the great
pleasure of surprising you with my great, noble and August
presence, but alas, the ways of humanity as well as that of
providence are frequently hidden from our views and often
our fondest hopes are blasted[?] when we think them almost
accomplished.
 Two weeks ago, I made application for a leave of absence
at the solicitations of Colonel Voris and at the acquiesence
of the pressure of my almost homesick feelings. My request
was approved by Colonel Voris (of course), by Colonel
Mason,[35] Commanding 1st Brigade, by General Kimball

---

35. John Sanford Mason (1824–97), born in Steubenville, Ohio, a West
Point graduate, and colonel of the Fourth Ohio. GB, 313–14.

commanding Division, but General Shields nor Banks either feel disposed to let any Officers go home at present, and this I found out just now and therefore immediately commenced writing.

Since last I wrote to you or rather since Dobbs left,[36] we were in another fight, though not as severe by a good deal as the Winchester, yet in military point of view fully as important, the history of which I enclose to you in a letter to the Holmes County Farmer.[37]

I have been dreaming, thinking and almost living about and on the fond hope of soon seeing you my sweet good and lovely Wife, my beloved Brother whom I respect more every day, and my darling Children, but for the present I must forgo the pleasure and console myself with the hope of soon to have the pleasure but if the neccesity of being compelled to give up this Grim [?] and rainy weather for over 3 days, and being called back from the active field to Police duty, gives me the "blues" somewhat, you will not I hope, feel as though you would want to blame me much. I have come to the conclusion that the fighting part of the 67th Regiment is about played out for this War and we may have to stay here 2 or 3 months, as Colonel Voris is commanding this Post.

I want Oncle Joseph to write me when the wool season commences and what the prospects are. I have written to M. T. Hunter Esq. Schenectedy, N.Y., and to my old friends Hood Troy but received no answer. You had better at once write to Taylor of Cleveland and Suttlef.[38] I presume Henry will have no objection to write in the name of the old Firm as we want to do our Wool Business together again. As soon as Voris has once taken formal possession of the Command of Post, I think he is entitled to issue leave of absence without the long "Rickmeroos" of approvals and rejections.

---

36. A civilian from Millersburg.

37. This did not appear in the *Farmer* and Spiegel's next letter indicates that in fact he never wrote it.

38. Spiegel refers to men to whom he had sold wool.

I have on the other Hand thought best not to urge the matter at present, from the fact that if I would only get leave for 15 days it would not give me time to attend to a certain transaction at home which I would not like to miss and neither would I have time to do any business in wool and the $50 or $60 would be spent in a hurry and very little satisfaction derived from it in return.

We have been 18 miles further and were ordered back, to Guard the Governments Stores and clear the mountainous regions from the Guerillas and Bush whackers.

Since I wrote the above I was taken to New Market as witness on a Court Martial commenced to try Colonel Buerstenbinder but the noble Hamburg Colonel could not be found and therefore the Court was adjourned until next Monday.

I can therefore not go before next week some time. Although I have no leave of absence yet I think I get one.

In New Market I received your kind note and Brother Joseph's letter, with the news of my friend Lieutenant Fahrian iloustrious presence at Millersburg for which I am pleased. He is a fair kind of fellow and when here he always lets on as though he thought "I," that is "Captain Spiegel" was about all the man there is in the Regiment.

My chance for getting to be Major is good providing we can get Colonel Buerstenbinder convicted of which we have no doubt; if we fail and he should return to Regiment, I will unconditionally resign and go home.

I send this morning:
$320 to Enos, Brown Company to credit on my account.
$100 to Mrs. M. M. Spiegel of which I would like to have you pay B. Cohn $30 and give Oncle Joseph as much as he wants. We only were paid till February. We will be paid again the 10th of May when I will be able to close out the most of my pressing old affairs and should I get the Majorship at $200 per month I could in very few months fix it so I would have quite a nice little Capital to go on and do business and, with the Money Oncle Joseph could get in marrying, we could run the nicest institution in Millersburg.

I am very anxious my dear Wife to run a nice even business without any trouble and difficulty, without any
pressure, without the necessity of blushing, without being
compelled to go to a Beerhouse or anywhere else to keep
up appearance, and without bowing my head to any one,
but simply to devote my all, my ambition, my time and my
strength to my dear, dear and beloved family first and to
my business next. I think this military has improved me; I
do really think it made me a better man, both mentally and
fisically, more self dependent, more independent and less
"fractious". I hope you will all agree with me when I come
as to the improvement in everything except my looks. I
think I got homelier.

If Cohn seems to think he ought to have $40 let him have
it as I shall bring money with me when I come home. . . .

Near Woodstock Va May 2/62

My dear good lovely and sweet Wife
My dear Children, dearer than ever
My beloved Brother!

The chief Bugler is just now sounding the Assembly (it
being 3 o'clock P.M.) which means take your Company out
for afternoon drill. The afternoon is warm but pleasant and
somehow I do not feel as though I could do another thing
ere I had written a long letter to you. Therefore Lieutenant
Childs take out the Company and Report me unfit for duty.

I am not sick, yet am not well. There is nothing in the
world wrong with me physically, yet I have seen many,
many days since I have been in the Army, that I felt much
better. My appetite is good, my Victuals of better quality
than I have been wont to have for the last 3 months. Yet
they taste not as relishing to me, as herethefore. I am not
homesick yet I never never in my life felt as much like seeing you all as I do now. I do not think I am at all troubled
about you. Yet for the last week, day and night, your lovely
pictures have been constantly before me and frequently
have my light slumbers been disturbed by dreams about the
children, you and Oncle Joseph, not as pleasant and agree-

able as I like. I really can not say that anything ails me, therefore I can not find a Remedy; yet if you will say nothing about it, I will tell you my private opinion and that is:

A quart of Home would just now do me more good than 5 gallons abroad.

Now it is out, and in Order to relieve my troubled mind I will attempt to write you a long, long, good letter, such as I have been used to write and such as I have only ceased writing from the fact that I thought a great many things I would tell you and for the last 3 weeks I expected to start home every day, but my leave of absence is so slow coming.

Since I have written the above I have been on Dress Parade, took my supper "of smashed up Eggs", my own cooking, listened to the Buglers Retreat and as he or rather they, for there were 5 of them, Sounded "Tattoo" through the quiet, bright, pleasant May Eve, I felt a monotony creep over me as I sat in solitude before my little canvas house, which took one home. I could see you, the sweet children, Oncle Joseph, Elizabeth sitting together and feeling as though you would like to see me and the Picture was a pleasant one and I was aroused from my sweet solitude which I enjoyed for full 1/2 hour, by the lively sound of the Bugle sounding "Taps" which means "blow out the lights" but I have made up my mind not to obey, but got up, from my rough home made bench, told Henry, light up, came in my little lonely House to tell you of it.

I do think if I had never attempted to get leave of absence or if our Regiment was marching on to a Successful assault upon the Enemy, I should not feel quite as uneasy, or if I would get Letters from you as often as I used to, it would relieve my mind, but our mail is very irregular, and we had two mails come in without a word from my sweet ones at home, nor anything at all since the 13th last month and that is hard.

I once told you I would send a letter to Estill giving you a minute description of our last March and Skirmish at Mount Jackson and New Market but I have never done it. Therefore I will now give you a little History, but it is sometime and I may not be so accurate as I should have been some time hence. However as that was in all human probability the last one our Regiment will be engaged in, in this War, and as I have given you pretty impartial catalouges of every movement, where our Regiment has been engaged and as I am anxious to preserve the Record of my Campayne in my family, I will now under take it.[39]

The Morning Mr. Dobbs from Millersburg, who had been with us for quite a time left us, we expected the Paymaster in the afternoon, but at 3 P.M. no Paymaster but a messenger came, instructing our Colonel to have 3 Companies ready with 3 days Rations to move at 6 P.M. and Report at Head Quarters of Colonel Carrols of the 8th Ohio.[40] Colonel Carrol being Ebrights Colonel, I immediately started for Ebrights quarters to find out what was in the wind. Doctor told me, there was fun ahead, that it meant "baging" some Rebels and that he was agoing along. I swiftly returned to Camp, asking Colonel Voris to permit me and my Company to be one of the three Companies but Colonel Voris told me it was not my turn and he had already detailed Companies A, F, and D and, besides all that, we would probably have some fun of our own before another day and he wanted me and my Company with him.

At 6 o'clock that same afternoon another Messenger came and ordered Colonel Voris to have the remainder of his Command ready with 3 days Rations, to fall in at 11 o'clock that night as quietly as possible. Some of the boys were glad while others almost swore and would probably have sworn right out, if it were not that they dare not do so, for fear of hurting the moral feelings of their religious Captain, because they had been disappointed in getting their pay. Yet after all, most of them got ready with pleasure, all but three, and it was the first time since I am in the service that

39. The operation to which Spiegel refers was the occupation by Union forces of Mount Jackson and New Market on April 17. For reports on this operation, see OR, vol. 12, pt. 1, 426–27.

40. Samuel Sprigg Carroll. Roster 2:237.

I came near putting any of my Men in Irons, if they had not changed their notion just in time and told me they would go any wheres I went, though they dit not think the Government used them fairly.

At eleven O'clock just as the moon shed forth its brightest ray over as beautiful Valley as the World ever saw, we fell in, no one speaking above a whisper; the Commands by the Officers was given in "Hamlet's Ghost style", hollow as from the graves. We moved in as easy a tread as we could through the woods, over the Railroad, through Meddow, over a Cloverfield, passed a Wheat field on the Pike. On we went until we got to the Bridge at Edenburg lately burned by the Rebels but rebuilt by the daring Union boys under the constant fire of the Rebels, and as we neared the Bridge, we came to the Buggy and body Guard of the noble old Hero Shields who although severely suffering from his shattered Arm was on hand to give instructions. We halted there until Colonel [John Sanford] Mason of the 4th Ohio, who received his instructions from the old General and then we crossed the Bridge and after marching for about 800 paces, we halted again.

. . . When halted across Stony Creek and we knew within the very limits from where we had seen the Enemy numerous in the afternoon and within 200 paces from where we saw the Enemy throw Shells and Cannon Balls ere night, we felt fun was close at hand and really I never Experienced a more Sublime Spectacle of human bravery and military grandeur. The glistening of the hundreds of Bayonets by the light of the moon, the anxious hearts and the Expectation of a Bloody midnight Battle, something so romantic, really inspired me I believe with true heroism.

The 4th Ohio (rather part of it; part of it having gone at dusk with the so called bagging Expedition) was the only Regiment in our advance and they were divided to the right and left of the pike across the broad field as skirmishers, for a short distance in advance of us, who were marching by the flank in the pike. Slowly but steadily we advanced until

we reached the top of the first Eminence from whence the
Rebel Cannon had been belching forth its harmless Fire
upon our Pickets but 6 hours previous, but nothing was
heard. We descended down and were almost on the foot of
the Hill when, all of a certain and when least expected, the
Report of many rifles right in front of us and whizzing of
as many Bullets apast our ears, and of all Emotions I ever
felt the one felt then was the strangest. It was so unexpected and sounded as clear through the still night air
that it involuntarily produced a strange effect. The first I
dit was to address my company, told them to stand up and
so forth, and also told them that the first man to leave his
Post I would shoot down; at the same time telling Lieutenant Childs to do the same if he saw any of the Boys leaving Ranks, to pop them over. Lieutenant Chapman was not
with us on that trip. Our skirmishers having advanced on
the Rebel outposts just by us, poured a raking fire into the
Enemy whereupon they fled and we pressed after them, but
after we had followed them for about 2 miles, we were
halted and then Ordered to move cautiously and only one
half mile after that time we were again fired into with some
considerable vehemence, when we were ordered to wheel to
the right and give them a "Broad Side" which we dit admirably and as usual they "scatatled". They however had the
advantage of being at home and knowing the Country so as
to take cross lots and it being dark [we] could not see
to follow. It was just shortly before day break and as we
cautiously moved along we all at once saw a Volume of
Smoke rise from a Valley about 1 mile a head of us and
presently the sky was getting red. As far as one could see,
day was dawning and we were permitted to see the Sunrise
on as pretty, rich and furtile a Valley as the Sun Ever shone
on and just as the first Rays of day were visible on the Eastern Horizon we, that is part of our Regiment, just saw the
Blazes light up on a covered Bridge and the Rebels move.
Colonel Mason, Acting Brigadier General of our Brigade,
told Colonel Voris to dispatch his 2 best Companies on dou-

ble quick after them. When of course Captain Spiegel and Captain Buttler[41] were dispatched, I pulled off my Overcoat (that is Chapmans), threw it away, told the Boys, let us give one of our Buckeye yells and after them; it would have done you good. The Bridge was all in flames. We turned to the right, forded the Creek and just crossed in time to give them a Volley of our Muskets. We must have killed and wounded some of them as we saw them put some in Ambulances and run and we after them, when an aid de Camp came and halted us until we could see the Cavelery supporting us to our left on the Pike. By that time the other skirmishers had crossed the Creek to our left and the remainder of our Regiment and 2 Companies were winding their way to our right through the woods. We saw the Cavelery and advanced and as we advanced 400 paces their Artillery threw shells and crape [grapeshot] among us, wounding one of our Boys by a Canister Shot threw the "Rist" from which he subsequently lost his hand. We advanced; I commanded the Division[42] and no one gave me any Orders, so I thought of slowly advancing within fair Musket range and then go double quick with fixed Bayonets and take their old Gun or get whipped. At a fence before us about 100 paces, I ordered the Division to form in 4 platoons and as we were about starting an Aid de Camp to General Kimball came galloping up like——, having lost his hat, shouted, Captain, where in hell are you going to? I answered him, to close out the d——d institution. Yes, says he, "You look like it with a hand full of men; cover yourselves quick," and just then the Rebels discovered us and the way they poured it into us, it was a caution.

Then here we were laying on our Oars, not able to do any thing; not permitted to advance and thinking that probably our other Companies to our right in the Woods might have some fun and need our Assistance, we moved our Di-

---

41. Lewis Butler of Company I. Roster 5:616.
42. That is, the two companies.

vision on our own Responsibilities to the Woods, the Rebels shelling us all this time and we dodging their shells. My Boys got so by this time, they can dodge most any of the Rebel shells.

We reached our Companies and soon were ordered to unite and advance, when shortly we came through the Camp the Rebels had occupied only probably 20 minutes before; their breakfast yet cooking in their messkittles which they left. We advanced, had several other skirmishes that day, awfull hot weather, and had to march until 2 hours after night until we got a chance to stop. Just think of a march from 11 o'clock at night until 10 o'clock next night; it was hard I tell you. When we stopped, my boys soon had plenty of straw where I laid down. The night was warm and I soon slept. About 12 o'clock some of my Boys called me, telling they had a big Supper. On getting up, they told me that they had "bought" a Goose, a Duck and a Chicken; they had cleaned them all and put all of them together in one big kettle which they "borrowed", and then they got some potatoes and some Red Beets, peeled them and put them in the same mess, and then pepper and salt and boiled it, and I tell you it made a splendid mess. I ate hearty, laid down again and slept bully until the Sun shone too hot in my face, which waked me up.

We stayed there that day, when our Boys discovered a Salt Peter mine which I intended to describe to you. From the peculiar situation and romantic aspects, I have no doubt it might prove interesting had I done so right off, but now I have forgotten a good deal. The scenes and movement of the Battle and so forth, I generally take a minute of, as soon as we stop. Next day we were ordered back to Woodstock to get our pay and take charge of the Post until relieved.

Some of the Boys liked it, while others swore about marching back 25 miles from any chance of fighting except Guerillas. As for myself I believe I was not a bit displeased. I felt as though a few weeks rest would not hurt me. Here we are now; our Situation to Woodstock is that of McKees to Millersburg only a little nearer. Woodstock is the County Seat of Shenandoah County, composed mostly of "Secessionists", yet there is but few of the first families here. The town is 150 years old; they have a Church here of 110 years old. I have been acting Provost Marshal of the town for several days and must most likely take charge of the Provost Marshalship altogether to morrow. I was to New Market yesterday and made arrangements for a daily mail here which will be the most pleasing feature in the whole thing. I have not give up the Idea of coming home. I am straining every nerve to get a leave of absence and think I shall accomplish it. I have had lots of fun since I am in the Service and more Especially in Virginia with Yehudim [Jews]. I generally know them by the name as well as ponim [face] and then I go in and take Chapman or Childs along, talk about buying and then say a "loshon hakodesh [Hebrew] word" and you ought to see them jump and ask Yehudah? Yes Sir and then I can assure you they are "[illegible word] Mehanah" [Mekane = envy] and do me all the "covet" [Koved—respect?] in the World. This is Sunday afternoon and [I] was invited down town by two of them for Dinner with all my Lieutenants. I accepted the invitation of Mr. Rosenbaum who has a splendid American Women for a "frau" [wife] and a daughter 14 years and Son 10 years. And such a Dinner would do honor to a King. Mr. Rosenbaum as well as Mr. Heller have invited me to come to town and board with them free of charge but I prefer my own boarding.[43]

While I talk about boarding, I must say to you, the farmers through here, who are mostly like the "Amish" of Holmes County or like William Wise and John Keplar of

---

43. Lewis Rosenbaum was Bohemian-born. Two years earlier he had been forty-six years old and an unaffluent "Peddler of Dry Goods." His wife, Sarah, then thirty-two, was born in Michigan. Much more prosperous was the merchant Adolph Heller, then also forty-six and Austrian-born. His thirty-four-year-old wife, Meahala, was also native American, born in Virginia. U.S. Census, 1860, manuscript return for Shenandoah County, Virginia, 17.

Greentownship,[44] bring daily everything to camp in the line
of Butter, Eggs, Bread and Pie and so forth you could wish.
We can often get 3 dozen of Eggs for a pint of Salt. They
used to pay Seven Dollars for a bushel of Salt and then considered themselves lucky in getting it. Coffee they paid
$1 50/100 per lb, Sugar 50¢, calico 50¢ per Yard and Every-
thing else in proportion.

Most of the Country folks would like to see the War over;
dont care much which side wins. They have not seen any
silver or gold for a year. Everything Shinplaster[45] and I tell
you they love us a little the best, because we have occasionally a quarter in Silver. Enclosed find [fractional curren-
cy] of their money, such they have in 5¢ and 3¢ and 10¢
and so forth.

We have smashed up eggs, poached Eggs, fried Bred,
Cartoffel [potato] Salat, and every thing such as I like and if
I only could go home for 3 weeks I think I could make it
all right.

My love to the children. I will write a letter for the
Special Edification of family use to morrow and will here
after write often. Even if I Expect to go home to morrow,
I will write to day. God bless you. Remember your true,
loving and affectionate

Marcus.

Strictly private
Woodstock Va May 8/1861 [1862]

My good, lovely and abused Wife!

I have no doubt you think that I speak truly when I say
"abused Wife"; [that] a Woman as good and lovely, as
saving and industrious, as kind a wife and good mother as
you are should be left alone hundreds of miles from her
husband who loves her more and with more fervor, zeal

---

44. Wise was about fifty-six years old, a farmer born in Pennsylvania. Ibid.
Summit County, Ohio, 142.

45. That is, depreciated paper money, often of small denomination.

and devotion than any other man can love, just at this time in your situation, with 3 small children and one coming, or that he should leave her at all. That I went to this War I never yet regretted. I think it helped me in my health, reputation and pecuniary [matters], and if just now I were permitted to go home and stay 30 days, I would gladly stay until Fall in the Service. But it does not make me very kind to military authorities if I do not get a leave of absence for some 20 or 30 days pretty soon. If I should not succeed in getting permission to go, I ask of you if you love me, to be as easy as you possibly can be and spend the fifty Dollars which it would cost me to come home for your own benefit and comfort. Get that Woman from Akron to stay with you during that time and if you should bring us a Son give the "Gefattershopt" [godparentage] to Brother Joseph and mother. Call the Boy "George McClellan Spiegel". Buy everything you want to be happy and just console yourself. Yet it seems to me as though such a thing could not be possible without me being there. I would gladly walk 600 miles to see you if they would only say go.

God bless you my love, my sweet, my all; may the blessings of heaven rest upon you. Ever your true and loving

Marcus

My love to the children, Joseph and Elizabeth

A day later, Spiegel succeeded in getting his furlough and by May 12 reached home. His friend James Estill found him to be "the same whole-souled jolly fellow he used to was." While awaiting the birth of his child, Spiegel distributed letters which men in his company had asked him to take to relatives. He and several others travelled to Weinsberg, from which he had recruited several men, where their families and friends entertained him at a lavish dinner.[46] Because he continued to mingle with Democrats and express his traditional political views, he attracted some adverse comment. According to Democrat Estill, one Republican later suggested that "the gallant Capt.

---

46. Compiled service and pension records for Spiegel in Adjutant General's Office, National Archives, Washington, D.C.; MF, May 15 and 22, 1862.

SPEIGEL [*sic*] was a sympathizer with secession." In the increasingly bitter political atmosphere, Estill's insulting response to this barb was to quote an unnamed young man as saying that when he heard anyone talking thus "he felt very much like calling him a liar."[47] Because of what another editor called "family affliction," Spiegel was able to get his leave extended so that he was still at home on June 8 when his fourth child, Hattie, was born.[48]

Preparing then to return to his command, Spiegel first publicly announced his willingness to carry letters and small packages from his soldiers' relatives. Again he demonstrated the almost paternal consideration which endeared him to his men. On June 23, he left Millersburg to rejoin the Sixty-seventh Ohio which in his absence had covered hundreds of miles of northern Virginia. From the Shenandoah Valley to Fredericksburg, back to the Valley again to pursue Jackson, and then to the vicinity of Washington, they had marched and skirmished. Their clothing became so worn that Lieutenant Colonel Voris pointed it out to President Abraham Lincoln during an inspection—thereby strengthening his own popularity with the troops. Spiegel would find his unit ready to join the Peninsula Campaign against Richmond being led by George B. McClellan, the "Young Napoleon."[49]

---

47. MF, June 26, 1862.

48. MR, June 26, 1862; Spiegel Pension File, National Archives. Unlike the Spiegels' earlier children, who were born with the aid of midwives, Hattie's birth was with the assistance of a Millersburg physician.

49. MF, June 12 and 26, July 10, 1862; *Sixty-Seventh Ohio,* 7–8; Spiegel to sister, brother, and friends, July 27, 1862, Spiegel Papers, AJA.

# CHAPTER FIVE

# "Attached to McClellan's grand army"

While Spiegel and the Sixty-seventh Ohio had been campaigning in western Virginia and the Shenandoah Valley, Gen. George B. McClellan had completed the reorganization and rebuilding of the Army of the Potomac. McClellan's force, based in and around Washington, was the main Union army in the Eastern Theater. Its commander, viewing the Confederate capital as his objective, had wished to avoid an overland offensive across the many valleys that lay between Washington and Richmond. Hence he had persuaded the Lincoln administration to permit him to leave only enough troops to protect the United States capital and to move the bulk of his army by water down the Virginia coast to the peninsula between the York and James rivers. Landing there in March 1862, he was close to Richmond and had seaborne supply lines. With caution which minimized casualties and helped endear him to his troops, McClellan had slowly advanced—so slowly that the Confederates had been able to shift the bulk of their forces from northern Virginia to oppose him. Meanwhile Jackson's operations in the Valley had diverted troops which might otherwise have reinforced McClellan. On May 31, the Confederates had unsuccessfully attempted to destroy part of the Army of the Potomac at the battle of Seven Pines outside Richmond. Gen. Robert E. Lee had then replaced the wounded Confederate commander Joseph E. Johnston. Even as Spiegel journeyed toward his regiment's camp outside Washington, Lee was about to begin the climactic battles of the Peninsula Campaign.[1]

Washington D.C. June 25/62

My dear Good Wife
My sweet Children!
I arrived here last Eve and have been very busy all day in the different Departments and writing [riding] about 15

---

1. Boatner, *Civil War Dictionary*, 632–34.

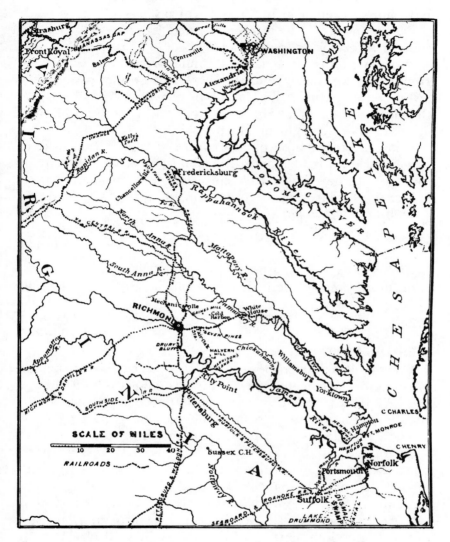

Peninsula Campaign (from *Battles and Leaders of the Civil War*)

miles in 7 Hospitals containing about 3000 sick Soldiers and have not succeeded in finding one of my boys.

Everything so far as I am concerned I think is all right, though I am not quite sure yet.

Our Division is at Manassas 25 miles from here and rumor says we will have to stay here and do guard duty awhile on account of the Hardships our Boys had to go through with. General Shields is here and is going back on an extra train to night in which I think I will get to go.

I have a great many things to write of what I seen to day, which I will do from Camp. But one thing I will tell you: I saw more to day than I have since I have been in America.

Kiss the Children and Mother for me, give my love to Joseph and remember

Your Ever true
Marcus

My next letter will be a <u>buster</u>.
I am more tired to night than I would be after a big march.

Washington D.C.[2]
June 26, 1862

MESSRS. ESTILL—Gentlemen:

Every well-regulated newspaper now a days has its regular Washington Correspondent, and as everybody admits that the FARMER is second to none in importance, I can see no reason why it should be behind the age in this particular.

Allow me, dear sirs; before saying anything else, to thank the people of Holmes county generally, and Weinsberg particularly, for the cheerful and cordial reception given me at my arrival and the unabated kindness shown me during my stay among you. The treatment I received at the hands of my friends at home will ever be to me a talisman, awakening such emotions as to call forth the right kind of action under every circumstance. On my journey hither nothing particular transpired. After I arrived in Pittsburg I began to

---

2. Published in the MF, July 10, 1862.

feel better and my spirits to revive. Somehow I never feel right on the Pittsburg, Fort Wayne and Chicago Railroad. I don't like the road; its conduct never did please me. Take away John McGill, who is as perfect a gentleman as lives, and you have but little worth saving.[3] I will relate a few incidents of my journey, one of considerable importance to the traveling public. In Harrisburg Lager Beer sells at 3 cents a glass. I indulged to the amount of one glass, and found it excellent. I think it would be well for Professor Irvine[4] to stop there awhile on his journey to Washington. I made the agreeable acquaintance of Mrs. Colonel Ellis, of the 1st Missouri Cavalry, so distinguished in the Missouri campaign. She has been through the several battles of Missouri and Arkansas, and gave some very interesting details. She is particularly down on General Fremont, but thinks General Curtis a very good man.[5]

Baltimore does not show any signs of being anywhere near the seat of war; business seems to be thriving and every branch of trade in full bloom—a fair contrast between the parental protection of the outspread wings of the American Eagle and the sneaking reptile monster of Secession.

---

3. A trunk line, already controlled by the Pennsylvania Railroad, with which the branch line from Millersburg connected at Orrville. John F. Stover, *Iron Road to the West: American Railroads in the 1850s* (New York: Columbia Univ. Press, 1978), 122–25, 138. John McGill, presumably a conductor or other employee of the line, does not appear in the 1860 United States census of Ohio.

4. Perhaps William H. Irvine of the Millersburg Band, which had left the army and come home. MR, June 26, 1862.

5. Col. Calvin A. Ellis and half of this regiment had been involved in the campaign against Sterling Price's Confederates. *The Union Army, A History of Military Affairs in the Loyal States 1861–65*, 8 vols. (Madison, Wis.: Federal Publishing Co., 1908), 4:272. John C. Frémont, Republican presidential candidate in 1856, had pursued in Missouri a controversial course which had made him the darling of the Radical Republicans. Samuel Ryan Curtis, a West Pointer originally from Ohio, commanded at the Union victory at Pea Ridge, Arkansas, earlier in 1862. GB, 160–61, 107–8, respectively.

The country situated along the railroad between Baltimore and Washington city at once impresses upon the mind of every one that a large and important, as well as an old city, must be near, and I must confess that when I unexpectedly saw the dome of the Capitol I was completely "taken down". I can now understand why the Rebels venture so much to gain possession of Washington, and why President Lincoln guards it with such jealous care. I had no idea of the grandeur and magnificence of this noble old city, the pride of America. I have seen, and carefully, too, eighteen cities of Europe, including Berlin and Vienna, and in my estimation Washington surpasses them all in magnificence. I do not believe there is a nation in the world that can boast of such a Capitol and such public buildings. God grant that peace may soon be restored, that these monuments of a mighty nation may be enjoyed by a united people.[6]

As I entered the Senate Chamber yesterday about an hour before the Senate convened, I was involuntarily impressed with a feeling of reverential awe, and as I thought of the many glorious and noble statesmen and patriots who have in times past stood there manfully battling for the Constitution and the Union, when I thought of our late beloved leader, Stephen A. Douglas, a pang shot through my heart and, I am not ashamed to say it, tears came to my eyes. Douglas, the noblest of them all, who manfully defended all attacks against the Union by Davis, Benjamin, Slidell and others, oh, that he were here now to battle against Sumner, Wade, Hale, and other Abolitionists, in their unholy efforts to keep us from a re-union for the sake

---

6. Spiegel's patriotism and perhaps his desire to please his American readers impelled him to describe Washington more favorably than did most of those familiar with the great cities of Europe. Foreign travellers seldom were as impressed by the Capitol with its unfinished dome or by the relatively few public buildings scattered across the city's unfilled expanse. Margaret Leech, *Reveille in Washington, 1860–1865* (New York: Harpers, 1941), 5–11.

of the negro.[7] Yesterday I heard his successor, Mr. Browning,[8] make a very able speech against Mr. Sumner's efforts to pass unconstitutional laws against the seceded States. In the House I heard Mr. Sedgwick, of New York,[9] say that he "hoped and trusted that the war would not end until the sun would no longer shine on a single slave in America,". If it is the object of Congress to prolong the war until this is accomplished, I wish they would be honest enough to say so at once, and give us who have engaged in this war for a different purpose a chance to go home.

I am under many obligations to Mr. Nugen and Mr. Edgerton, of Ohio,[10] for their kind treatment. I made the acquaintance of Mr. Richardson, of Illinois, and Voorhes, of Indiana,[11] who are sound on the Union question, and for such sentiments as they advocate I am willing to fight as long as I have life. They are for the Union as it was, and the Constitution as it is.[12] Mr. Lincoln returned here last

---

7. Stephen A. Douglas of Illinois, the idol of many Democrats of the Old Northwest (including Spiegel), had opposed the Republicans and their anti-slavery principles but also had denounced secession. Hence Spiegel's praise for Douglas's defense of the Union against such Southern Democrats as Jefferson Davis, Judah P. Benjamin, and John C. Slidell and his wish that Douglas were still alive to fight Republican Senators Charles Sumner, Benjamin F. Wade, and John P. Hale, who advocated expanding the war from one to save the Union to a crusade against slavery. Spiegel's views were similar to those of many Buckeye Democrats. Roseboom, *Civil War Era*, 364–403 passim.

8. Orville Hickman Browning of Illinois, appointed to the Senate after Douglas's death in 1861. A Republican and friend of Lincoln's, he nevertheless opposed the president's shift toward emancipation as a war aim. Theodore Calvin Pease, "Orville Hickman Browning," in DAB 2:175–76.

9. Charles Baldwin Sedgwick, a Republican. *Biographical Directory of Congress*, 1674.

10. Robert Hunter Nugen, a Democrat from Tuscarawas County, and Sidney Edgerton, a Republican from Summit County, both congressmen from near Spiegel's home. *Biographical Directory of Congress*, 1480, 898, respectively.

11. Representatives William A. Richardson and Daniel W. Voorhees, both Democrats. *Biographical Directory of Congress*, 1607, 1861.

12. A version of a slogan popular among Ohio Democrats, opposing Radical Republican war aims. Eric J. Cardinal, "The Democratic Party of Ohio and the Civil War: An Analysis of a Wartime Political Minority" (Ph.D. diss., Kent State University, 1981), 27.

evening from West Point.[13] Every person except the abolitionists and secessionists, respect and place confidence in
him, believing him to be honest and capable. Yesterday I
visited nine hospitals, containing about 6,000 wounded soldiers. They are conducted in the best style and under splendid management. The Soldiers' Home is an institution
second to none anywhere, but just now it looks rather
gloomy, from the fact that just opposite there are about
1,000 new graves, and as I passed by there were three or
four men digging others.

This morning I started, and got as far as Alexandria,
when I had to return and get a permit from General
Wadsworth[14] to pass a couple of boxes I brought along for
the boys and myself. The boys are thirty miles from here,
near Manassas and ere this reaches you we will in all probability be on our way to Richmond.

I am sorry to find a great deal of feeling here against our
General Shields, as well as Generals Fremont and
McDowell.[15] I hope, however, it will all be settled in due
time, as I understand the whole matter about the late fights
in the Shennandoah Valley is undergoing an examination
before the War Department. General McClellan stands at
the head in this city; everybody praises him and everybody
calls him a Napoleon, and so forth. How long it will last I
do not know; but let us hope for the best.

Yours, truly
M. M. Spiegel

While Spiegel was completing the previous letter, the Seven Days
battles before Richmond had begun. On the outskirts of the rebel

---

13. President Abraham Lincoln had gone to West Point to confer with
retired General Winfield Scott. T. Harry Williams, *Lincoln and His Generals*
(New York: Knopf, 1952), 113.

14. James S. Wadsworth, the military governor of the District of Columbia.
GB, 532.

15. Shields, Frémont, and Irvin McDowell had recently failed to trap
Stonewall Jackson in the Valley Campaign. Boatner, *Civil War Dictionary*,
741–43.

capital, the Confederate Army of Northern Virginia under Robert E. Lee had attacked McClellan's Army of the Potomac. Retreating across the peninsula between the York and James Rivers, McClellan saved his army and finally inflicted upon Lee a bloody repulse at Malvern Hill. He then secured a new supply base at Harrison's Landing on the James and called for reinforcements. Spiegel and the Sixty-seventh Ohio would be part of the North's answer.[16]

On board U.S. Steamer Herald
enroute for City Point, July 2, 1862.[17]
My Dear Wife and Family:

Nothing can be more varied, as well as uncertain than life, except it be the life of a soldier of Shields's division. So varied has been our campaign that you could not astonish a soldier of that much abused and worn out division, if you would tell him that tomorrow he would have to fight a battle on a tightrope; he would at once commence to balance himself. The readiness of the boys is characteristic of their willingness at all times, and under all circumstances to do their duty, their whole duty, though frequently unfit. Within the last 5 days we have been through or past by nearly all the celebrated places, points and objects of the Rebellion around this section of country. Through the once impregnable Manassas by Yankee guns, (of which we saw three), through Centerville, with its chain of abandoned rebellion fortifications stretching for miles. We passed the famous "Bulls Run", where upon its adjoining fields so many of our gallant, brave and noble boys had their bones bleached; noble sacrifices of incompetent leaders.[18] We passed many places of note between Bulls Run and Alexandria, where, as a matter of course, we visited the famous "Marshall House", where the noble but rash, the young and gallant Ellsworth shed his blood upon the stairsteps while

16. Herman Hattaway and Archer Jones, *How the North Won, A Military History of the Civil War* (Urbana: Univ. of Illinois Press, 1983), 193–201.

17. Published in the MF, July 17, 1862.

18. Spiegel refers to the site of the first major battle of the Civil War and to the subsequent fortified Confederate camp outside Washington.

attempting to haul down the Secesh rag and plant instead the defiant Stars and Stripes.[19]

At Alexandria Shields's Division stopped one day, which the boys commemorated by a glorious but fearful drunk.

The embarcation of our Division commenced here, and such a rush and noise, disorder and general display of total carelessness or incompetency on the part of the officers stationed and officially charged with that duty, you can form no idea. It seemed to be their only object to get rid of the d——n soldiers, not looking to their comfort or safety.

The gentlemen in charge of that duty, sent our Regiment and baggage for embarcation to pier number 1, where an old rotten barge called Delaware, of Baltimore, was lying. Our baggage, as well as commissary and ordnance stores were put on board the old thing. Company B, H and my company did not go on board of her. These three companies were put in my charge, and about 10 o'clock, through a darkness Egypt-like, sent to pier 17, and groping our way through the dark found it after marching two miles, when we reported to the Captain of the U.S. Steamer Matamoras. He refused to take us in, as he said he had already more troops than he felt safe in carrying. I started on and called on the steamers Tucker and Sechon, with little success. By this time it commenced to rain furiously, and as dark as it possibly could be. The men having been out since 6 o'clock A.M. were perfectly worn out. I saw U.S. steamer Herald, and found it vacant—took my battalion in for shelter, and started back to report to the commanding General, who ordered me to take my men out again, as that steamer was intended for the 1st Brigade. I told him it was then 1 o'clock A.M., and my men worn out and were then resting their fatigued limbs, that I would not undertake to remove

---

19. E. Elmer Ellsworth (1837–61), organizer of colorful Zouave military units, was shot by the proprietor of the Marshall House, as indicated by Spiegel. His death early in the war had made him a Northern hero. Boatner, *Civil War Dictionary*, 263–64.

them. I must, however, here state that the General commanding our brigade, General Ferry, acted the perfect
gentleman with me, but I cannot say that for his Transportation or Quarter Master, Mr. or Captain Derbin, who being
raised from a poor boy and acting Commissary Sergeant, to
a Quarter Master forgets he ever was poor and looks with
perfect contempt on a soldier who does not belong to his
staff.[20] We left Alexandria on the morning of the 30th, and
taking in tow the barge Delaware, we had a splendid ride
on the beautiful waters of the Potomac and Chesapeake; so
delightful was it to the boys that they were perfectly jubilant
and forgot they ever had hard times before. Singing and
speaking—yea, even dancing were the ruling features of the
day. They did not feel as though there was any danger
ahead, but relying on the old scriptural adage, "sufficient
unto the day is the evil thereof."

The evil came, and in its most terrific form. About 12
o'clock that night the sea became very rough, and the Captain of our steamer found it necessary to change the Barge
from larboard to stern; the shifting of which was a very
hard undertaking, owing to the roughness of the sea and
the utter helplessness of the barge, but finally it was accomplished, and still it continued very severe, and with a crack
the cables attaching the barge to the steamer broke and set
her adrift. Furiously she drifted from us, managed by the
raving waves only, and with a crack only equaled by the
shrieks of the men, her upper deck gave way, and coming
down heavily on the lower deck and beaming, or rather
hanging about half way over the starboard side, in the act
of falling crushed four men severely, and drowning probably as many more, killing five horses and crushing her last

---

20. The general was Orris S. Ferry. Boatner, *Civil War Dictionary*, 278. His
quartermaster may have been Capt. Greene Durbin. Francis B. Heitman,
*Historical Register and Dictionary of the United States Army, From Its Organization,
September 29, 1789, to March 2, 1903*, 2 vols. (Washington, D.C.: Government
Printing Office, 1903), 1:390.

hope, the rudder. For an hour and a half did we attempt to come near or aside the the old rotten tub, but to no purpose; and whenever we got near enough we could hear the lamenting, shrieking and praying voices of the poor boys, exclaiming "save us, we are sinking," and so forth, and we all feared they would have to go before we could save them. The old barge occasionally going from stem to stern as if turning a back summersault, and again looking as though she was going from larboard to starboard, but on the whole sure to go to destruction.

The feelings as depicted upon the face of every one on the Herald, cannot be described, much less the horrors of those on the old barge.

Finally, our Captain succeeded in running our steamer along side of the ill fated vessel, when as the waves rushed her against our vessel the boys jumped on board of the steamer, in this way succeeded in getting all of them safely on board. Colonel Voris, who was with the boys, in his usually cool, brave and courageous manner counseling and consoling them, was the last man to leave the ill-fated barge. After a tour of six hours we reached Fortress Monroe, [Virginia].

Never before did Uncle Sam appear to me to be so gigantic as he did when I beheld Fortress Monroe. The hundreds of steamers and vessels for war and commerce, foreign men-of-war representing all nations, the ordnance stores, quartermaster's supplies, the throng of the many people, and the powerful, magnificent and [im]pregnegable Forts far exceeding anything I ever expected to see. We stopped at this place four hours to give the boys a chance to cook three days rations.

We left the Fort about 3 o'clock P.M. The weather being beautiful we had a pleasant evening. We passed the Rip Raps, Sewell's Point, in the wreck of the Congress, and also that of the Cumberland, which was so gallantly defended by her brave Captain, who would not surrender even to the late monster Merrimac, chosing rather to go down with the gallant ship while the glorious old flag was flying at the mast head.[21]

We anchored last night near Newport News, and we are now traveling on the James River, under protection of the gunboats, for City Point, where we will be attached to McClellan's grand army—I think the left wing.

The most of our boys lost their knapsacks, haversacks, guns and ammunition; many escaping with nothing but their pants.

I am writing this while sitting on a water barrel and crowded by a good many, but I hope and trust it will soon reach you, as a Mr. Barkley, from Philadelphia volunteered to take it along. If, after reading it you will show it to my friend Estill and he sees fit to publish it, he may do so. Neither myself nor any of my boys lost one cents worth. They are all well and in good spirits. We left old Henry Enk and Samuel Townsend in the hospital in Alexandria, not being very well.[22]

Give my love to all my friends, and tell them I feel all right. Kiss the children for me, and give my love to mother and brother, and rest assured I am all right. God bless you and the family, and let us trust that with the kindness of Providence, I may be permitted after doing my duty for my country to live in peace with all of you.

MARCUS . . .

Camp in the Field near
City Point Va.
July 6/62

My dear good Wife, my beloved Children and Brother!

This Sunday A.M., a beautiful but very hot morning, and as I am compelled to lay on my front in consequence of two

---

21. Spiegel refers to the two United States warships destroyed by the Confederate ironclad *Merrimack* (or *Virginia*) which also dueled with the *Monitor* and finally was scuttled. Catton, *Terrible Swift Sword*, 204–15, 280.

22. Privates in Spiegel's Company. The former was at least forty-four years old. Roster 5:581, 584.

monster big "Boils" in the rear and having been forced last night to leave the field 5 miles from here and come down here near the landing among the sick, the cowards and the nuisance Soldiers generally, and as I have about seven among them out of my company, whom I would rather not talk to, I thought there is nothing in the world that could give me more gratification than to "talk" to you for awhile and only stop at times when Henry Beegle puts on the "flax seed".[23] I have written to you on board U.S.S. Herald and there given to you a short sketch of our Sea Voyage, accidents and so forth, and I need only say to you now that we sailed that day from New Port News to a Landing called Harrisons Bar, where after much confusion and waiting and so forth, we were hurried ashore at about 4 O'clock P.M. the 2nd instant. We marched up from the Landing on the James River some distance up a Hill when a beautiful mansion of old fashion structure presents itself to your view, which is the birth Place of old President Harrisons and subsequent residence,[24] a splendit place and surrounded by what was formerly undoubtedly a magnificent plantation, but now a desert covert with thousands of little "Huts".

Since I have written the above I received an order to report to the Field at once, as a Battle was impending. Sick and weary as I was, with 2 Boils about my Stern, the weather to a perfect fever heat, I started and came just in time to see our Pickets driven in by the Rebel Cavelery, whereupon we immediately started out, in line o Battle and they skedatled.

I will now as I lay upon my "belley" on the side of a hill in a rather unpleasant condition give you a short history of our adventures since we arrived here as members of the Grand Army of the Potomack.

As I said to you once before, we were landed at Harrisons

---

23. One of Spiegel's privates. Roster 5:579.
24. William Henry Harrison, while born in Virginia, spent most of his life as a resident of Ohio and Indiana. Dorothy Burne Goebel, "Harrison," DAB 4:348–52.

Bar 4 miles from City Point and were put in a field of
wheat of probably 100 acres which was just harvested and
put on shocks and I am sorry to [say] in less than 5 minutes
all the heavy nice good sheaves of wheat were gone; that is,
taken up by the Boys who rested their weary limbs upon
them. It seems hard, but 5000 men, weary, overheated,
tired out men, must have rest also and nothing seems too
good for the poor boys.

But there is no rest for the wicked. Scarcely had the boys
got into nice snoose after cooking their tin of coffee and
eating a hard cracker, when an order to march came and a
march it was of 6 miles through the meanest, hardest, most
outrageous mud I ever saw. You can have no Idea, neither
can I explain or give you an Idea; the ground is of soft stiff
clay and every step we made we went in various distances
from knee to waist. To draw out a foot was labor of the
hardest kind. It took us 6 hours to walk 5 miles and we
never got to our place of destination, a place in the woods
or rather swamp, until after 12 o'clock at night, when all
that reached that place (though more than half laid down
wore out in the mud before we got there), wrapped themselves in their blanket and gave way to sweet repose. When
scarcely their first dream had ceased, every one was disagre-
ably aware that rain was falling down in torrents upon him
and the blankets were getting heavy and before day light we
got up to fix our blankets as a kind of shelter. When I got
up I found out I was laying in 6 inches of water at least. At
8 A.M. we started through the mud and marched about 3
miles when we halted in a place, not a dry spot within a
mile and there we stayed until about an hour before night
when we marched in the Woods and stacked Arms for the
night as we supposed, but only for awhile as it proved, for
scarcely had we sat down when an orderly came with a message, calling us 5 miles out, in front of the whole line of
General Keys army Corps [25] and about 1 1/2 miles from the

---

25. Maj. Gen. Erasmus D. Keyes's Fourth Corps. GB, 264.

Enemy. Through an almost impassable swamp over fellt [felled] Trees and every imaginable obstacle, we arrived there at 12 o'clock that night, where we found the 62 Ohio Volunteer Regiment already stretched out. The Colonel of the Regiment informed our Colonel [that] our front was well picketed. We laid down in the swamp and at about 1/2 past 2 o'clock the pickets to our right fired and were fired upon, when instantly we were called into line, primed and cocked our Guns and awaited the enemy. We stood thus for about a half hour, when one after an other of the Boys laid down and fell asleep until nearly all slept. At about 1/2 past 3 o'clock, a Company of Rebel Cavalry of probably 1 or 200 who quietly got in front of us fired 2 Guns, thereby arousing us, when in the act of springing to our feet they all fired into our Regiment, killing 2, wounding 2 Lieutenants and 8 men. Their fire was however mainly directed against the right wing of the Regiment. My Company ranking as Company B,[26] we are at the extreme left of the Regiment. [We] dit, thank God not get a wound nor any one killed.

July 7/62

But never in gods world dit men stand up to the fearful work any better than dit my noble Band that night. When most all the Regiment gave way and more especially the right wing, owing to the pressure of the Enemy, I advanced my Company in solid Column, Bayonets fixed, through the dark, only guided by the flash of the Enemies Guns and my Boys dit not fire until we thought we were pretty close and I think it was our firing, that drove the Enemy and sent them kiting. The two nights subsequent we were on the advance Outposts, where we had to fire and were fired on about every ten minutes and in all fighting, skirmishing, Shipwreck and so forth, where our Regiment lost from 25 to 30 men, I have none killed or wounded, thank God. But

---

26. Spiegel refers to Company C's position within the regimental line of battle.

we are most all wore out; the awful heat and suffering for 3 days, we have had no rations, and the water hot and stinky, and no sleep except last night. Yesterday we were relieved from the front and taken back on the Banks of the James River, an awful big River, but the water dirty and stinky.

I really pity my boys in the Bottom of my heart, but yet they are cheerful and lively. While I sit here writing, they sit around me in the best possible humor; they mostly worship me.

The Doctor just now opened my two boils and I feel easier.

If we have much marching to do during this hot weather I shall resign and come home. I would like to get the appointment of Colonel in one of the new Regiments. I have written to Cohn about it; go and see him and talk to him. Urge him to go to Columbus at once and take 4 or five good men along. . . .

> Camp in the Field near
> Harrison Landing
> July 10/62

My dear dear Wife and Children
and Brother if he is there yet.

God bless you! I am well, hearty, cheerful and in better spirit than I have been since I left home. We are still near the Landing but not in front of all the troops. Neither are we in a low miserable swamp, but on a high Bank of the James River in what has been a thriving Cornfield 11 days ago, but is now a vast desert filled with little Canvas houses adorned with pine and oak Brushes which is of a more useful than ornamental nature, helping to make the little houses more comfortable as against the heat. I have been greatly discouraged since we are here owing to the fact that my boys had, even since we have been withdrawn from the lines in front, an unusual amount of labor to perform. Day and night they were at it, chopping or rather slashing trees, digging rifle Pits, throwing up entrenchments and doing various kinds of laborious and toilsome work. The first 4 days of our stay here it looked as though we would have severe fighting to do daily, but somehow or other they would not attack us. If they had attacked us, I think we would have whipped them. You can possibly have no Idea of the slashing of trees there has been done since we came here; 8 or 10 miles of a wild and picturesque forest has been leveled to the ground and the trees felled every way mixed, so as to keep the enemy from using any Artillery and Cavelery against us. I think we have a position now which is impregnable and we are strengthening it daily, so that I came to the conclusion there will be no fight here, neither will we advance until after we get plenty of reinforcement. I never thought it possible that one man could be so beloved by so many thousands of men, as is General McClellan, [whom] the Army of the Potomac fairly Idolizes. He can not show himself any wheres, but the air rings with cheers and huzzas for the Young American Chieftain.

I have again pitched my tent and spread the fly; spread in front and tall limbs of oak and sprigs of pine on the side, which makes it very pleasant and rather agreeable though the heat is awful, yet if I have no particular duty to perform I can keep myself cool. Yet I think I have sweated Barrels of sweat since I have been here and lost much sleep, but since my boils are open, and I am permitted to sleep at nights I feel all right again. Colonel Voris is quite under the weather and I do think if he does not get leave of absence in Order that he may go home and recruit his health, he may be considered "gone". I do sincerely hope leave will be granted him. I have written to Cohn, Critchfield[27] and others to attempt, to getting me a position of Colonel in one of the new Regiments and I do hope he will be successful. Since the War is going on and since I am in, I might as well

---

27. Lyman R. Critchfield, born in 1831 in Knox County, Ohio. Raised in Millersburg, he became an attorney and in 1862 was prosecuting attorney for Holmes County. That fall, he would be elected state attorney general. Like Spiegel, who was his friend, he was an ardent Democrat and a Mason. Stiffler, *Atlas of Holmes County,* 120.

be a little higher inasmuch as I think myself perfectly
adequate for the position.

The Balloons are up every clear day and from them
McClellan gets information as to the position of the Enemy.
I think McClellan is a splendid General, all the Croakers
may say to the contrary notwithstanding. . . .

Harrison Landing Va.
July 11/62

My dear, dear good Wife!

The mail has again been distributed, but no letter for me,
no consoling words from my dear dear Wife, no assurance
of the well being of my sweet angels at home, no repetition
of their innocent baddlings about their Papa; in short no
word which would wear away the gloom of an awful rainy
day.

It is 5 days now since our daily mail commenced and at
every arrival have I, with the greatest anxiety, awaited the
time of distribution of the mail, but alas I had to leave it
disappointed daily.

If I only knew you were all well and hearty, I could feel
perfectly easy but think of it, my good sweet wife, I left you
my love, my joy, my all, the mother of my four beloved
children, one only two weeks old, our sweet Babe, you
scarcely able to stand up, careworn and sad at the departure
of your true husband, troubled as I know you was and subject to those dangerous reverses likely to fall on a woman in
child bed, and then think of me away from home in War
for three long weeks and over, and not a word from you.
May God grant that all is right.

If I hear from you that all is right, I shall feel perfectly
easy. We have rather decent Summer quarters and not likely
to have any trouble shortly as we have a strong position.

I will say no more.

May God our heavenly father ever ever bless you and our
beloved once is the wish of

Your ever true
Marcus

Harrison's Landing Va.
Sunday July 13/62

My dear dear Wife and Children

. . . Since we arrived at this place I have written to you almost daily and waited daily with as much anxiety as any loving husband and father could watch for the uncertainties of the health of those left behind, whom he all loves with the fervour unequalled by few and surpassed by none. Oh my God, are they all well? Is anything wrong? These are the thoughts that occupy my mind through the day and haunt me when asleep at night. God only knows what joy or anguish the answer to those questions could produce. If you do not get letters from me regular you can attribute the same to many reasons, such as marching, picket, guard, officer of the day, member of court martial and so forth and so forth, but when the mail comes regular and many officers and men get their mail regular from home, letters only 2 or 3 days old and none for me, it makes me sad; it makes me feel uneasy and unhappy. You might say there is no use to anticipate trouble or in other words, "sufficient unto the day is the evil thereof", yet a man that loves you as I do, a father whose heart beats with such undescribable love for his beloved Children as does mine, cannot feel satisfied with bare philosophy but wants facts, assurances, something to rely on.

If you are sick or weakly, write often, words only. If anything [is] the matter let me know.

I am well except a boil which is very sore and scarcely have I been relieved from them since I am here. I have really no reason to feel dissatisfied with my situation. My boys are getting better.

Am anxiously awaiting the result of my friends attempt at home, to get me a better situation. Hope they may succeed, in fact I know they will if they do their best.

Ever your true and loving
Marcus

Camp in the Field near
Harrisons Landing Va.
July 18/62

My dear dear good wife and children, good mother,
my good Brother,

You never in all my life was as dear to me as you are this
morning for I just received your loving, good, dear letter of
the 13th which assures me that you all are O.K. My God
what a weight that takes from my mind. I feel young, well,
cheerful and in excellent spirits.

I dit not really think there was anything wrong, yet I
wanted to have it in black and white from you, my love, and
from Brother Joseph. I have not for the last 5 days written
to you, although I felt very much disappointed when the
mail was distributed and I did not get any news, but now I
feel satisfied and find no faults.

I will first of all commence to answer every question in
your letter to the best of my ability. 1st I found my boys
very much disheartened and had I stayed away one week
longer, many of them would have deserted, but my arrival
made it all right and many a sick one was well 2 hours after
my arrival and it is generally admitted that no life man
could receive a more flattering welcome, than I received.

You asked me how Mr. Cohn and I stood when I left
him. I owed him not quite $100; I send him $200 from
Fortress Monroe, which leaves him in our debt about $100.
If you want any money, just get of him what you want. Do
not (for my sake) suffer for anything but live as a good wife
and mother should live, happy and contented, and have
everything you wish. The money I drew in Washington; I
got two months pay from the Government and not knowing
where we might have to go I kept $70 and sent $200. We
expect to receive pay soon when I will send home more and
order what to do with all. As for my working myself out, I
could not do [it] now, just at the time when the Country
calls for 300,000 more men, but I think my friends might

get me a better position in one of these new Regiments now forming.[28] I want you to talk to them and keep talking to them; talk to Critchfield, Leadbetter[29] and Cohn; go and see Joss.[30] If I could get in a new Regiment, I would take Charley Authenrieth along and make him Quartermaster.[31] Many of the officers in the service get positions in the new Regiments who are not as capable as myself nor have as many friends. I know if you will just attend this you may soon have me stationed in some of the Ohio Camps. Resignations are not accepted here under no pretext; only by promotion and transfer can you leave a Regiment or this Army. Everything I took from home I brought here in good order and you may rest assured it dit not come amiss. Lieutenant Childs in a mistake took both of the fruit cakes and before I could reach him, he and the Boys eat both of them. He sends you his compliments and best wishes and thinks you are the greatest woman in the world. The wines and liquors we have been drinking off ever since. I have yet some 3 or 4 Bottles, but so many beg who are sick that it will not last long. The bitters was excellent. I wished since I had all Bitters instead of Joss's fine Brandy and so forth. The only accident I had was with the tongues and dried meat. When we left Alexandria for the Chesapeake I took them all out, ordered them to be packed in a Havresack, and thought of using them when we arrived here, but when we arrived at Newport News and I wanted to cook a

---

28. On July 1, Lincoln had announced a call for 300,000 more men, creating the opportunity for promotion. Long, *Civil War Day by Day*, 236.

29. D. P. Leadbetter was a Democratic politician from Millersburg. Garber, *Holmes County Rebellion*, 11; U.S. Census, 1860, manuscript return, Holmes County, Ohio, 314.

30. N. F. Joss, senior member of a Swiss family which had been among the first settlers of Weinsberg, where he ran a store. In 1860, he had been a Douglas elector. Joss, *Autobiography*, 40; MF, July 19, 1860, July 11, 1861.

31. A private in Spiegel's company, later a sergeant and lieutenant. Roster 5:578. As he was from the Weinsberg vicinity (MF, Sept. 11, 1862), Spiegel's talk of a quartermastership for him may have been intended as an inducement for Joss to seek Spiegel's promotion.

tongue, Henry Adams in whose charge they were, told me "Buy God I forgot them," a sad accident.

I do not know anymore about Colonel B[uerstenbinder] than I dit at home; hope he is gone to the D——L. Of my boys, 47 are with me, some 12 or 15 in the different Hospitals in and about Washington who will be sent here as soon as they get better. Our situation is really a romantic one on the Banks of the James River, along the beach of which are hundreds of nice little fresh water springs. The Country around here was when we came here densely wooded, but has since been leveled and entrenchments thrown up, rifle pits dug and every thing I believe has been done by General McClellan to make our position impregnable, the more so while we are right along side of such kind and friendly protectors as the Monitor, the Galena and twenty other such Monsters.[32]

I have now I think given you an answer to every question in your letter and will therefore give you some generalities.

The late withdrawal or rather repulse of McClellan from before Richmond I look upon as a great disaster to the national cause, though at the same time it can not be denied that the giant Retreat has been conducted by General McClellan in a manner which stamp[s] him at once the greatest as well as gallant, magnificient as well as Scientific General in the World. He is truly a General; the Rebels were worsted at every engagement and their loss is immense, in all probability 75,000; our loss from 15 to 20,000; yet they have the moral triumph of forcing our Army to retreat.[33]

The weather here has been for the last 6 or 8 days almost intolerably hot, perfectly suffocating, but for the last 3 nights we had the severest Thunderstorms and rains which I think Mrs. Southworth has so frequent and yet so truly described. Today it is windy and cloudy, consequently not

---

32. Federal ironclads and other warships.
33. The Confederate casualties were actually about 20,000, to 16,000 casualties for the Union. Hattaway and Jones, *How the North Won*, 199.

very hot. I would love for you to go to Akron to Battles and have him take you and our four childrens likeness on a Card like Mrs. Voris and her children were taken and send it to me. It would be I know an interesting, handsome as well as most welcome picture to me. But I do not want it unless you are on yourself, I know you would make a beautiful photograph; much better than Ambro or daguerreotype. Could you not surprise me?

If I have to stay here much longer I wish you would buy me a good Gold Pen, one that would fit in my large black holder I had and took with me last fall from the Warehouse. Henry [Herzer] knows the size and he can best pick a pen for my taste; tell him to pick one out for me. I forgot it when at home; you can send it by mail. Our Regiment has about 100 sick here who have the Camp diareah but they are getting better as they get acclimated to the Country. Since I have been here I had 7 Boils around my dimensions which generally cover a chair when I sit down but are all open and in good "running order". I had the awfullest sick headache for 2 days I ever had in my life, but now I feel all "bully" in health and spirit. Colonel Voris had a Certificate from the Surgeon stating that he should get a leave of absence in Order to save his life and yet he could not get away, so you see I got my leave just about the right time and I am sure I made tolerable good use of my 15 days leave of absence. I put in as many days as any one could in so short a time; "bully for our side".[34]

I do not look for an immediate advance on Richmond. I think McClellan will have to have Reinforcements and then probably await the cooperation of Burnsides and Pope.[35]

---

34. Spiegel means that he had succeeded in extending his time at home far beyond fifteen days.

35. Earlier in 1862, troops under Ambrose E. Burnside had occupied parts of the North Carolina coast. At the time Spiegel wrote this letter, Major General Burnside was bringing part of his men to reinforce the Union armies on the Peninsula but most would go to northern Virginia. There the Lincoln administration, which had lost confidence in McClellan, was creating a new army under Maj. Gen. John Pope. GB, 57, 376–77; Long, *Civil War Day by Day*, 237, 247.

Whenever General McClellan shows himself to his troops he's received with the greatest testimonials of Joy, I ever witnessed in my life; the air is ringing for miles with cheers; he is fairly worshipped. His old army, who were with him through the 7 days sanguinary Battles, look upon him as their deliverer from almost unavoidable ruin.

Our Brigadier General Ferry is very Gentlemanly but I am fearful of his capacity or desire to see the men comfortable. We have hundreds of men barefooted and bare a———d; for the last ten days we have raised h———l daily and he has not yet succeeded in doing anything for us. Our Division General Peck I have only seen once, a very nice looking man of good reputation.[36] The Genl Commanding our Corps d'Army, General Keys, I have not seen yet. He was to be here to day and inspect us but owing to the inclemency of the weather postponed it until to morrow; he will find a nice looking crew. He is highly spoken of by everybody. I think I have written all that will be of any interest to you and close now, with the assurance that as long as we can have a chance I will write often. Our living for the last 5 days is awful; we can scarcely get anything but Coffee and Crackers and Crackers and Coffee; sometimes the Crackers are fit to eat. The boys however fare better; they get Beans, Rice and Meat, but the officers can not; there are no sutlers near. Some Lemons here sell at 25¢ a piece, oranges 25¢, Cheese 50¢ per pound and not fit to eat, rotten ginger cakes 5¢ a piece. A good sutler could make a fortune in 3 days if he had the goods. . . .

Harrisons Landing Va.<br>July 20/62 Sunday A.M.

My dear Wife and family,

This is Sunday morn; no drill, no extra duty, nothing but company inspection which I will have as soon as I get this letter written.

Since I have written to you on the 18th in answer to your

---

36. John James Peck, a West Pointer, New Yorker, and prewar Democrat, commanded the Second Division, Fourth Corps. GB, 364–65.

very kind and sweet letter of the 13th, nothing of very great importance or notoriety has transpired. It seems as usual that whenever I get a long and real good letter from home, something will take place which invariably turns out well. The afternoon of the 18th when your letter came, we (the Regiment) received Orders from Head Quarters to be ready by 3 o'clock P.M. with one days rations and when so ready, we were ordered to march out about 2 miles in front of our lines and relieve the 83rd New York Volunteers who were on Pickets. I tell you the front of our lines look different from what it dit when we left it after 4 days hard work in skirmishing and so forth. The trees are all felled and our position now is this:

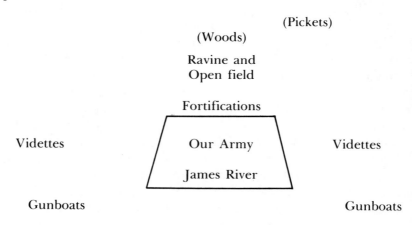

You will see that the army is protected by the James River in the Rear; Gunboats on each side to assist in a most telling manner against any attack; and our Centre by heavy fortifications (and ditches), well mounted by heavy Artillery. You will see that the Pickets are stationed in an open field in front of a piece of Woods and a piece of Woods between them and the front of our lines. The Enemies Pickets are about one half mile distance. You will also see that should the enemy attack our Pickets, the policy would be to fall back in the Woods, draw them on after us, and then fall back in the open field in the immediate front of our lines of fortifications, fighting and drawing them on so as to get them to follow us in the open field when we could get shelter by our Artillery and open fire on the Enemy in such an awful manner as to make it perfectly destructive to the Enemy; having it so fixed at the same time that they could not see our Batteries until they would be on to them. Such were our instructions and of course such our intentions. I got charge with my Company of the right flank Corner of the woods and a route. I posted my Videttes on the different high places, made my Head Quarters and Reserve in the Woods, made a nice bed, fixed my Revolver and after cooking a Cup of Coffee and smoking my pipe sitting with 2 of my videttes in front until about 11 o'clock, I laid down and had a nice, refreshing and comfortable sleep unconscience of any danger. It so happened that nothing disturbed our folks that night. After Breakfast, Orderly Wallick and myself made a Reconoitre in front for about a mile; thought we discovered some Rebels and so forth; sat down by a nice Spring under an apple tree and after refreshing ourselves with Water, we quietly marched back where the boys were laughing and enjoying themselves and where I found Dr. Ebright who had come out all the way out to see whether I got any news from home; he being almost out of his head having received a few lines by a Soldier who passed through Hudson, from that fool Minor T. Ames,[37] stating that when he left Millersburg that Morning, the Doctors little boy, was not expected to live another hour and I have no doubt I shall find him dead when I come home at 4 P.M. The letter was dated the 8th and the doctor had not heard from his folks since and I tell you my dear, that when I showed him your letter of the 13th [that] his little boy was getting better, he felt like a new man. In the afternoon we were relieved and back to our camp without the slightest accident or trophy [sic].

---

37. Ames was baggage master on the branch line railroad from Hudson to Millersburg. MF, Nov. 14, 1861.

Orders are now for officers to have no trunks, men to carry every thing on their backs, and every indications go to show a forward movement of some kind is in contemplation, We had the same Orders last week but as yet no movement. . . .

Camp 67th O.V. July 24 [1862]

My sweet dear Wife
My lovely Children!

In what little time I have to day I would only say I received your good letter written when you had the blues a little on the 17th and part of the 18th. I was happy indeed to hear you were all well and sorry to hear Hamlin and Lizzie were unwell. Since the Scarlet fever is in Millersburg I tremble every time [I] get a letter for fear some of my dear children may be sick. Your letter was as your letters always are a messenger of peace and happiness. God grant you will ever be permitted to be a messenger of happy intelligence to me.

I am to day "Field Officer of the day" and just returned from an Excursion of visiting the pickets and outposts. Everything is quiet in front of our line as a Sunday morning in Millersburg. I feel real good and am of late very contented with my situation; more so than I have been for Months. If I only had about 30 more men in my Company I would consider myself happy. I dit for awhile think I might maybe sing [*sic*] in some of those new Regiments as Colonel or so, but such is not the case. Ohio puts those in who have enjoyed the quietude of a winter behind their stoves with their families, instead of those who have stood the hardships of a mountain Campayne, but I do think now that I will not leave the Service until I have advanced a step or two at all events. . . .

Sunday morning [July] 27/62

My dear and much beloved Wife and Children

I do not know that I ever felt any better since I am in the army than I do this A.M. Though I got up at 5 o'clock with somewhat of a head ache, which after eating my hart crackers and coffee I slept away again, the reason why I feel good are two fold: the 1st and most important of all, the general refregator [refrigerator or refresher?] of my feelings, was your good and kind letter of Sunday last announcing the good health of you and our dear ones; the 2nd reason is, that I yesterday gained the greatest Victory in a military point of view, I ever expected to gain which I will now relate to you and tho it may seem trifling to you, to me it gave as much satisfaction as though I would have received a military promotion.

Yesterday morning we received Orders to get our Companies ready for inspection, Review and Brigade Drill; to appear outside of the Fortifications before Brigadier General Ferry and Acting Major General Peck.

After considerable swearing and confusion, at 8 A.M. we marched out in front of our Streets, formed line-o-Battle and when so formed, the acting Adjutant, Lieutenant Brock, came and told me that I was in command of the Regiment as Major Bond and Senior Captain Commager were both sick.[38] That this piece of intelligence confused me, is scarcely necessary to state here, but when I tell you that I felt nervous and scared I am not exaggerating. Had I known the fact before, I think quite likely I should have been sick but here I was, and could not get out of it. I sent the Adjutant over to Brigadier General Ferry begging of him to excuse our Regiment under the Circumstances but "no go". I labored between hope and fear, but would have been willing to sell out at a very, very low figure. We started and as we arrived at Brigade Head Quarters the Adjutant General told me I must get a horse. I sent back and got Colonel Voris' Horse (of course you know ere this the Colonel is home on leave)[39] and I think as soon as I was mounted I felt "better".

---

38. Sidney G. Brock, formerly of Company H, and Henry S. Commager of Company A. Roster 5:565.

39. Besides trying to improve his health, Voris was seeking recruits and promotion. Urging that he be made colonel, an editor commented, "He has certainly deserved it by his brave deeds and soldierly qualities." *Cleveland Leader*, July 31, 1862, in *Annals of Cleveland* 45:216.

We arrived safely at the place designated where several
Regiments were already drawn up in line and in a little
while I got my Regiment formed on the proper place and
in good shape which gave me some encouragement. Sometime after that the Brigadier and Major Generals arrived
and were received in proper manner, when they got the
troops ready for inspection and review which passed off all
right. After that the Commanders of Regiments were
ordered to appear before General Peck, who received them
very kindly and informed them that he intended to go
through a series of Brigade Drill. I do not believe I felt as
gay as I have felt previous to that time frequently. In the
first place General Peck through some source or other had
the name of being very cross and fierce; in the 2nd place
neither our Regiment nor myself ever dit or saw any drill of
the kind before. However I started, having however by this
time wore off a great deal of my fear and excitement and I
was perfectly cool. I do not intend particularizing the different evolutions and military maneuvering we went through,
as I could not if I would, neither would they be interesting
if I could, but suffice it to say, that I passed through all of
them "without giving one solitary wrong command" and
without one mistake made by my Regiment in the 4 hours
drill. Myself and Regiment were complimented by the
General four times publicly during the drill and since it is
over I received the universal comment by both officers and
men of our Regiment in the most flattering terms, even
Buerstenbinders friends to a man. I tell you it makes me
feel good and yet not dare say so to anybody else but you as
it would feel like blowing, but you my love will rejoice with
me.[40] I gave every command loud, long and plain and the
men acted with an alacrity not often shown in our Regiment. I am still in Command and if I shall stay so for some

40. Spiegel's friend Lieutenant Chapman gave his townsfolk a similar
account of Spiegel's success. He reported that his captain was conspicuous for
"the noble bearing of his person" and "the ability with which he handles the
regiment." Letter of "J.B.C." in the MR, Aug. 14, 1862.

time, I will have chance to learn something. You have never said anything in regard to our fearful night attack; dit you never get my letter giving you a description of it? We are having comparatively speaking easy times; go on Picket once a week and the boys get on guard about twice a week. I get on as regimental officer of the day once a week, Brigade Officer of the day about once a week.

. . . we are having about a dozen Springs dug along the River Banks which gives us good Water except during the "flooding of the tide" at which time we can get no water fit to drink as it overflows our Springs, but it does not stay in long enough to cause any inconvenience to us. Our "grubb" is as variagated in kind as it is in the time. Sometimes we have Potatoes, Onions, Tomatoes, Pickles, fresh Beef, Ham, Cheese, Ginger Cake, Pickled Beef and pork, soft and hard Bread, Corn Meal and flour of which we make Slap Jacks, Corn Cakes and mush, while at other times and very frequently we have nothing but Salt Pork, Beans, Rice, hard Crackers and Coffee.

My appetite has been for a week past exceedingly vicious, perfectly unmanagable at meal times, which I attribute to my excellent state of health and if I hear frequently from home I know of nothing to dampen my spirits or make me feel otherwise but happy.

Colonel Voris will no doubt call on you; if so he can tell you all about me and if you could send me your Photograph and that of the children on one Card, I would be as happy as folks generally are. Do so, you have no Idea what a handsome Photograph you would make.

My boys are getting much better. I have however still nine on the sick list here with me. I learn George Weigand [Weigam] came home discharged. I am truly sorry for that, as I am afraid it will raise a Stampede among my Germans, who will shortly all get sick and all want furloughs or discharges.

I think in two or three days we will get 2 months pay again; if so will send home.

Our usual affairs in Camp are so regular that if you give

a description once you have it at all times. Yet I write to you my dear so that you may have something to read; such as would be of interest to you would unquestionably seem perfectly "stale" to an outsider. Colonel Voris has gone home with the intention not to return unless he gets matters satisfactorily adjusted for the Regiment. I do sincerely hope he may be successful. As things now look I do not apprehend there will be a forward movement for some time unless it would be 8 or 10 miles up the river on Malvern Hill.

The days here are exceedingly hot but the nights pleasant and refreshing so that there is no difficulty in sleeping but should we be compelled to march much in day time, I think it would be "rather unpleasant".

I this week saw the young chieftain McClellan in Company with the Veterans Heintzelman and Sumner, whose Army Corps he reviewed.[41] The General as well as Review was truly a rare sight; the Former a noble looking specimen of humanity; the latter a success of military science. I have not seen but one citizen [civilian] and that one of the female persuasion, since I came here; she I presume the wife of some officer.

The Country bears the marks of a Settlement of Aristocracy, where the masses are led by the inmates of a few grand mansions.

Tell Hamlin that he shall have his $5 anyhow, even if he dit not get most head marks [top grades] as he was "sacking Wool" but he must be a good boy and mind his "ma". Lizzie must have $3 or $5 which ever you think she deserves and also according to her promises of future good conduct.

Mosey must be a good boy at the table, else papa will put him in the parlor all day when he comes home. Hattie, our dear "Pet", you must train as you would have her and all I

---

41. Samuel Peter Heintzelman of the Third Corps and Edwin Vose Sumner of the Second Corps, both participants in the recent Seven Days Battles. GB, 227–28, 489–90.

can do for the present is the promise of my cordial assistance when I get home.

I wished I would know for certain whether Oncle Josey is
in Millersburg yet.[42] I would like to write him a long letter.
I only ask you to keep in good spirit and bear all like a
good true patriotic woman and with the help of God all will
be right. Give my love to Cohn and family and all friends.

Truly your friend and loving<br>
Marcus

July 27–1862

My lovely and good Wife!

Twenty nine years ago you were ushered into existence
and by an Allwise providence and kind parent, raised and
brought up to fill your predestinated function as my wife,
"my joy and comfort". For that, thanks, thanks to the
heavenly father of the universe. I have to day once written
to you and said nothing about this, thinking it might make
you sad, but I can not let the day pass, and for my sake and
those whom we jointly love with all the ardour and candor,
yea fierceness, be joyful when you get this and just make up
your mind that the good Father above, will protect us and
many, many will be the hours of joy and comfort for us yet.

I have written you so much in mine of this A.M. and written so many other letters that I will close this. May God
protect you and the children and grant us happy days after
our unhappy and distracted country may safely be rescued
from the vile hands of traitors and Rebels; a work for which
I am willing to fight, so that my children may enjoy, as we
dit, previous to the breaking out of this accursed Rebellion,
"a happy and united Country". God grant that enough
strong arms and willing hearts may be found in the loyal
States to do this.

Ever your true<br>
Marcus

---

42. Joseph may have accompanied back to Chicago his and Marcus's
mother who had been at Millersburg for the birth of her granddaughter.

July 29/62

My dear Wife!

We are still at the old place and I am still well and hearty, but I have not received a letter from you since the one you wrote the 17th.

What made me exult so much in my last has since proven rather burthensome yet pleasant. Having been so successful at the Review Inspection and so forth made the Major put me in formidable command of the Regiment and I have drilled the Regiment twice since on our own Parade ground and to day I had them out on Division Drill where Acting Major General Peck drilled us again and I must say if anything, my efforts have been crowned with more success than ever, but it is hard work. Lieutenant Chapman is in Command of the Company and I of the Regiment.

The boys of the regiment are awfully pleased with their "new Colonel" as they call me and if I must tell the truth, I must say that I am astonished at myself to see me go through with battalion Drill and the general routine of Commanding a Regiment.

I have nothing new to say to you only we have been getting cabbage and Potatoes and if we only would get soft Bread, we would get along bully.

We get Ice every day which enables us to make Ice cool Lemonade and so forth.

The mail leaves. God bless the Children.

I am your ever true
Marcus

Headquarters 67th OV.
Aug 2/62

My dear Wife and Children!

... The news received in your kind letter of the 27th announcing the death of Dr. Ebrights little son, is dreadful. Oh how I pity the Doctor. I do not know whether he knows it yet or not; I am fearful of seeing him. It will be perfectly "crushing" to him, the more so, since he has been encouraged to hope for better news. Such news to a father is dreadful. He has made every effort to get away for 20 days and had his paper passed all the way through, up to the fountainhead where it failed.—Poor Doctor, good fellow. I pity him in my heart.—

I am still in Command of the Regiment and have plenty to do, but I am pleased to say that I feel perfectly able to perform the task. The boys of the Regiment to a man are perfectly jubilant; they all call me Colonel and when I tell them I am not Colonel, they invariably say, "I wish to God, you were." It makes my boys feel proud of me; when I ride along the front of the Regiment and give a command, it is obeyed with a will that does ones heart good. As to my not feeling disappointed for not getting a Colonelcy in Ohio, you may rest perfectly easy. You know I am none of the kind that feels easy disappointed, besides my chances are very fair here for promotion. Yet if I have to leave the service a Captain, it is no "disgrace" and none of my children need ever be ashamed of [it].

I am sorry to say that Henry Biegle is sick with fever. He occupies my tent and I sleep under a fly. Henry Adams, Chapman and myself attend him and the Doctor comes to see him 3 or 4 times a day. He was taken sick very suddenly 4 days ago, is however doing much better this morning. No Soldier or even Officer ever fared better while sick in the field than he does. I have no doubt he will shortly get well. He is cheerful. I will keep you posted. I received a very kind and encouraging letter from Sister Martha of Michigan,[43] as pleasant a letter as I ever read from her, without a word of complaint in it. She says if she had 10 Husbands she would send them all to War and asks me if she is not liberal. I will answer her to day and send you her letter. Send Martha a Paper of the 17th with my letter of Ship Wreck in.

We have been "so to say" under Arms for 4 days as we expected an attack and I must say I felt as though my day

---

43. Caroline's sister. Barbe, "Memoirs," 5.

of glory was coming, being permitted to lead the Regiment
in Battle. I just think I could have done it up in Style, having had the Regiment on Dress parade, Drill, Review and
Inspection, Brigade and Division Drill. I thought inasmuch
as I had been successful in all the former, I might have
made a decided strike for myself in regard of my ability as
a soldier as well as my willingness, if I could have been permitted to lead the Regiment into the field of Battle, and
never dit the probability seem more likely, than night before
last, when aroused from sleep by terrible cannonading
which at first seemed as though it were immediately to our
left and when we first awoke as though our whole line was
attacked and what is so fearfull "a night attack". I jumped
up and dressed, sword, pistols and all, which I done in a
hurry and started out. When I came out I at once saw that
the firing which by this time was perfectly furious was to
our right and a great part of it on the Rebel side of the
River, who were throwing hot shot and shells over on our
side but in a very short time our "Gunboats" and heavy
"Siege Guns" were brought to bear and in a few minutes
the conflict was fierce as well as grand, horrible as well as
perfectly inspiring, [to] us who stood on the high bluffs on
the River side where we could see every flash just before we
could hear the whizzing and ringing sound through the air
of every cannon fired.

This engagement in all its element of fierceness and
splendour lasted for about one hour, when it slowly grew
less and finally ceased, but ere it ceased we received Orders
to "fall in" and I got my Regiment out in perfect Order in
Line-o-Battle and ready in a very short time and without being the least excited but after staying in line a little while I
ordered my men to "stack Arms" and lay down, keeping
their accoutrements on. After the Cannonading ceased, I
laid down "in full dress", Sword and Pistol as well as spurs,
ready to jump on the Horse which Jacob Grassely had sad-
dled for me but almost satisfied before I laid down we have
nothing to do, as I had made up my mind by that time, that
it was nothing but an attack of the Rebels, who calculated to

destroy our Transports which were laying on the lower
landing but found that our Gunboats and Siege Guns were
too much for them. We had one man killed in a Massachusetts Regiment and one man in a Pennsylvania Regiment
and 7 wounded. Several of the vessels had a few Balls
through them, none seriously damaged.

Major Bond is getting better and I think he will soon take
charge of the Regiment. Our "Grubb" is getting better. The
weather is awful, but I stand it all well.

With my love to Elizabeth, of her I have not heard anything lately, and Gods blessing to the children, you and all,
I am your true

Marcus.

Tell Hamlin he must be a very good boy and learn to
work in the warehouse so I can take him for a clerk.

I have written a letter to the Farmer. My shipwreck letter
is very much admired in the Regiment.

Sunday Aug. 4, 1862[44]

My dear and much beloved Wife
My sweet children!

. . . An hour ago we received notice from the War Department announcing the fact that "Colonel Otto Buerstenbinder has been dismissed from the service of the United States
by Order of the President."[45] This I will look upon as good

---

44. Spiegel wrote this letter on a printed patriotic note sheet prepared for
Shields's Division. On it was a song entitled "Volunteer's Memento." His
willingness proudly to inscribe this to his family suggested that wartime service was beginning to undercut his opposition to abolitionism which colored
the song's content, as in these lines:

> For our FREE LAWS and the CONSTITUTION
> We have enlisted, and THEM we will save.
> If it annuls the whole 'institution'
> That will oppress MAN and make HIM a slave.

45. Buerstenbinder had been dismissed by presidential order on July 29,
1862. File for Otto Buerstenbinder, Compiled Service Records, A.G.O.,
National Archives. Searches of other records revealed no further information
on the particulars of the charges against him.

news as soon as I learn Voris is appointed Colonel, to which the Toledo Folks are making all effort and demonstrations to defeat. Voris once Colonel and I think Everything in due time will be right. . . .

Headquarters 67th Reg't.
August 5, 1862[46]

My Dear Wife and Children:

I have received your several letters almost daily and I can assure you that nothing could give more joy and true happiness than these letters do to me in the field. This morning I had my regiment out on division drill, but was summarily dismissed on account of the battle raging four or five miles from here on Malvern Hill; in which, we have just heard, our folks have whipped the rebels.[47] We are under marching orders, and expect to move in course of an hour.

As we came in we met General McClellan, the gallant and much beloved young chieftain, who was cheered vociforously by every regiment as he passed them to go to the front. Somehow whenever the soldiers of his army see him they seem to feel that all is right.

Lieutenant Chapman is sick with very bad diarrhea. He is not able to go out but when he heard the heavy cannon-

---

46. Published in the MF, Aug. 14, 1862. Unlike other letters in the newspaper, such as one by Spiegel in this same issue telling of the night attack described previously, Spiegel had not intended this one to be printed. But Caroline told someone of its content and in the politically heated atmosphere rumors circulated that Henry Beegle, a young man from the Spiegels' neighborhood, had been left to die unattended and that the letter was designed to discourage enlistments. Hence Caroline asked Democratic editor Estill to publish the letter. Of the rumor mongers Estill snarled, "These contemptible 'slang whangers' congregate at a certain nest in this town to lie about honest men. There is a day of reckoning coming for some of them." He announced that the original letter could be seen at the *Farmer* office.

47. Under pressure from the Lincoln administration, McClellan, who grossly overestimated the numbers of the enemy, was resuming limited forward movements. But his superiors had already so lost confidence in him that on August 3 they had ordered him to move the Army of the Potomac back to Washington to join the forces there. Williams, *Lincoln and His Generals*, 142–46; Long, *Civil War Day by Day*, 246–49.

ading and the report of the impending battle he said: "Gentlemen I shall go into this battle, no matter how I feel."

Henry Beegle is still very sick, and I do not wish to disguise the facts: I am in doubt as to the result, he is in my tent, Dr. Westfall attends him three times a day, and we are doing all we can for him. Let us hope for the best.[48]

If you ever had an idea of how a fair young lady of twenty contemplates, the day previous to her wedding, the happiness of her approaching nuptials you have an idea of how I now feel in the contemplation of the pleasure it will afford me to lead the 67th regiment into battle; which in all probability I will do to day. My dear Wife, I feel serious but proud. I feel adequate for the occasion. I sincerely hope that when you read this you may feel as composed as I do. I know and feel that a kind and all-wise Providence will direct all things for good. I feel as though we shall come out of the contest victorious, and if anything does happen to me, I am only offering a small sacrifice for my beloved country, which always so generous and kind, has opened her arms to receive the down-trodden of other nations.

Give my love to our dear children, and to all friends. I am called to headquarters. Good-by. May God protect you, is the fervent prayer of

Your true and loving Husband<br>M. M. Spiegel

Camp in the field in front<br>of the Breastworks<br>Aug 6/62

My dear dear Wife!
and Children

Instead of being as I presumed yesterday in the midst of hot Battle amid the cracking of Musketry, Clanging of Sword and Bayonet, Roaring of Cannon, we are quietly and peaceably laying in front of our Breast Work mounted by as we call them "our Pets", 12 monster 64 Pounder Siege Guns

---

48. Beegle, who had been eighteen when enlisted, survived this illness and ultimately was mustered out as a corporal after the war's end. Roster 5:579.

patiently awaiting the approach of the Enemy who may probably attack us, as he may think us weak, a great part of our force having been taken to Malvern Hill and other places. If the Enemy attack us here, we will give them fits.

I am still in command of the Regiment, our Major taking suddenly ill at the approach of Battle. The duties of Colonel and commanding a Regiment are by this time as familiar to me as commanding Company and it is not ten times through the day, but I hear them say, "I wish to God Captain Spiegel was our Colonel" and so forth.

This morning and also noon, when I sat down upon the ground to eat my dinner and Breakfast, my legs crossed, eating cold boiled Potatoes, Salt and Crackers which tasted as good to me, as even poached eggs cooked by your mother, I had to laugh when I thought of the Idea of thinking, now if my Cary would all at once just appear here and see it, what would she say? and so strongly and amusingly dit I think of it that I really saw you stand before me laughing. I presume if you would have seen me 9 years ago to day, in such a posture you would have the wedding put off a year instead of one day. Yes my love to morrow we will be married 9 years and thank God as far as I know we feel as one yet. If ever you saw a minute during the past 9 years that you felt sorry for that act, you have experienced more than ever I have. But I am sure if ever you had such moments they were few and far between.

Do you know that there is not another woman so good and so kind and so much appreciated and beloved in the World as you are? I feel to day, as though I had been recreant to my duties when I left you so long, but as the unhappy war was commenced and my country needed my service I think I owed it to you my love and to our four good children to lent a helping hand.

Let us by to morrow sunrise renew our obligations of love and duty; let us though separated in person be united in thought to love and cherish, please and protect each other.

I can not write a very long letter but I thought I had better say a few words as perchance an opportunity offered itself for pencil and Paper and to send to Camp. I get your letters regular and they make me happy and fit for duty. Voris is not yet back. I do not know what success he had. I am satisfied if I live I will be all right. As soon as I can get off honorably, I will resign but I would not like to have the report spread any. Henry Biegel I left pretty sick in care of Henry Adams; most likely he will have to go to the Hospital and be sent North. I hope to god he will get well; he is a good and noble Boy and a faithful standby to me.

Someone in the Regiment received a letter stating that the Military Committee of Cleveland had recommended me to a Lieutenant Colonelship in one of the new Regiments to be raised in Cleveland. I do not believe anything of it as I do not know who in the Committee of Cleveland knows me and also if there was anything of it I should have heard of it.[49]

My dear son Hamlin must continue to work and be good and noble son, mind his ma and be a big boy and little man while his father is gone. My little or rather big daughter Lizzie must be a little Lady and nurse her little sister. She must not rest herself too much; that looks too Lazy and I would not like it.

Mosey I hope will get as many "doosberry" as he can eat and be a good boy. Our Pet I hope will grow and be as good as she is lovely.

When one has established his Householding so well as to have four good sound and lovely children in 9 years he need not be ashamed.

Goodbye my love; god bless and protect you and the children is the wish of your true and ever loving

Marcus

My love to Elizabeth and all.
We had a grand victory at Malvern Hill yesterday, 3 miles from here; took 600 Prisoners, drove the Rebels and killed

---

49. Surviving records of the Cleveland Military Committee at the WRHS do not indicate such a recommendation.

and wounded many, took 6 pieces of Artillery. We had a good many killed and wounded, none of mine.[50]

Harrisons Landing Va.<br>Aug. 7/62

My dear good Wife and children!

I have an opportunity to send a letter by my friend Leroy G. Osborn who with M. J. Lemmon and Wm. Jonston have been discharged from service for disability.[51] Leroy can tell you all about me and as I do not know what he will say I must ask you to let me know. I do not feel very bright to day, having laid out for two days and two nights and nevertheless we have to go this afternoon on outpost duty again. I do however believe that Dr. Westfall and myself are the two healthiest men in the Regiment; I can not say however that the least thing in the world ails me. I am hail, dirty, black and indeed "Lousy". I just caught the first one since I am in the service; the whole Army is in the same fix. I presume Colonel Voris will be back in a few days and I am really sorry he can not bring your pictures.

I perceive with much gratification that our Government is awake to the signs of the times and appreciates the magnitude of its adversary and its attempt in the right way, to bring this war to a successful and speedy termination by calling out 600,000 men and commencing to draft.[52] That will bring out some of those cowards, who set at home [and] ridicule everybody and too cowardly to go themselves. They will have to go as "conscripts", glory enough for one day.

---

50. McClellan claimed only 100 prisoners and far fewer dead and wounded in a battle smaller than Spiegel believed it to have been. OR, vol. 11, pt. 1, 77–78.

51. All men of Spiegel's Company C. Osborn had been corporal; Lemmons was the sergeant whose behavior at Kernstown had offended Spiegel; William H. Johnson was a private. Roster 5:579, 580, 582.

52. On August 4, Lincoln had ordered a draft of 300,000 militia, in addition to the 300,000 recruits for whom he had recently called. Long, *Civil War Day by Day*, 247.

Perhaps they may see fit to appoint me as Colonel in a new Regiment.

This is the anniversary of our "Wedding Day" and I wrote you a long letter yesterday in "pencil writing" about it. I wont take back a word I said yesterday; God bless you. It was "hot" nine years ago, but to day is awful; the scourging Rays, of a meridian Sun, are darting down in all their intensity. Phew it is awful. If it was not for that, I would not care; still I am riding every day since I am in command.

Nothing has happened here since yesterday in a military point. I do not think we will have any fighting here very soon, yet we may. Ask Leroy anything you wish; he ought to know anything you wish. If anybody desires to come in my company, let them come on; if a good fellow will do the best we can for them. How do the patriotic Ladies stand it?

Hamlin can find out of Leroy about his pa. Tell him if I get a field Office I may come to get me a horse and then he can ride it awhile.

You must positively send me your picture as soon as you can, for I have set my head for it and you know how my "dutch head" sits when once firmly planted. . . .

Headquarters 67th Regt.
Aug. 10/62

My dear good Wife and Children!

Your sweet letter of the 3rd instant in answer to mine of the 27th of July in which you announce everything at home in good style and the pleasure felt by you and my friends Cohn and Herzer over my success at my first appearance as "Commander pro tem" of the 67th was handed me yesterday while on Out Post service which since the 7th we have been doing.

I have written to you a good many letters since that time, one of which I send by Leroy who unquestionably ere this has seen you and give you a history of everything.

We are now within two miles of Malvern Hill, which is again in possession of the enemy.

Our Brigade is doing Out Post duty for the Army.

General Ferry, Colonel Osborn of the 39th Illinois, Colonel Forster of the 13th Indiana, Colonel Steel of the 62nd Ohio[53] and myself made a recognoisence up the lines and the different Routes yesterday. With my new field Glass, which I bot since I am in Command, I could plainly see the Enemies line and camps and we heard them play the drums as plainly as our neighboring Brigades. I am delighted with everything and it just seems to me as though everything was delighted with me. Never since I have been in the service have I felt as well as I do now. I will now give you a short sketch of what happened since I last wrote to you. In it I think I said we had Orders to go on "picket" after coming from the entrenchments in the morning.

We started out at precisely 2 P.M. through the boiling hot sun and after marching four miles, the men wore out and overheated, we had a chance to rest and go to the woods to cool off. After my men had cooled off I got them to form line, detached my picket Posts and got the remainder of the Regiment to stack Arms and lay down in the shade. Scarcely had they done so when the enclosed Order [not found] came, calling us back as you will perceive.

I congregated my men, got them in line and started through the sun again, arrived at camp, drew 3 days rations and started, and after a tedious night march of 3 hours, arrived here at 12 o'clock where we have been ever since and after telling you that, after being called in line under Arms 3 or 4 times a day and that often at night, by false alarm or something else, and the regular cooking of the rations with addition of green corn, whordleberries, black berries, green apple and peach sauce, all of which is in an abundance here and I declare the boys make good use in making sauce. We had "Peach sauce" for dinner which was fine. I expect Voris home soon, but I do not expect any promotion as Major Bond and Captain Commager are my superiors (Seniors)

---

53. Thomas Ogden Osborn, Robert Sanford Foster. Boatner, *Civil War Dictionary*, 613, 302, respectively. Clemens F. Steele was a lieutenant colonel. Roster 5:325.

though neither of them worth a d——n. I expect there will be some big demonstrations made by the Officers and men of this Regiment in my behalf and I shall let them go, doing nothing for or against.

I had a mighty good letter from New York and one from Chicago within the last 3 days. Answered New York and will Chicago. Strange why Moses Joseph does not write to me. It is so awful hot here that during the day everybody seeks shade. My boys, one from each Company of the Regiment, fixed me up a very nice House from fence Rail and Bushes which is very comfortable and nice—only there is so many officers laying around. To day I dit not get a letter from you but I hope all is right.

At nights when I lay down and look at the clear beautiful moon, I think of you my dear good wife and of my dear children. In 6 nights I have not had my pants, Boots or Spurs off, ever ready, and if we could only sleep in day time in opposition to the millions of flies, we would be bully.

Give my love to all the children, Cohn and family, Herzer and Family, Elizabeth and all.

Ever your true and loving
Marcus

We have the nicest spring and coolest water, right by our Camp I ever saw or tasted.

Out Post Grand Guard
near Malvern Hill
Aug. 15, 62

My dear, dear Wife and Children,

. . . I had to send 94 men from our Regiment to the General Hospital, though there is but one dangerously sick among them. Henry Biegle was among them; I had word from him this morning saying he was getting along first rate.

I was relieved of the Command yesterday morn by Colonel Voris who brought the good news of your well being [at] the same time that I got your characteristic letter of him. You have drawn a life like Picture of the Colonel. He is a good man but not such as you would fancy; not much heart; made up of Bone, yellow skin and ambition. Nevertheless he thinks there is nobody like himself, but after all he thinks as well of me as he ever can think of anybody. He will do all for me he can. In short, you may rest assured, no matter what he may have said or done about me, I am smart enough to handle him just as I want to and the time I am pretty sure will come very shortly, probably in four or six weeks.

I am all well and in excellent spirits. I eat from 4 to 6 Ears of Corn three times a day and am in as good spirits as I can be and I know that there is not a set of Company officers in active service who live more agreeable and have more sport than those of Company C whatever anybody may say to the contrary notwithstanding. I am now acting Lieutenant Colonel and I do not expect ever to return to the Company, though one does not know. Orders to move immediately,

Good bye, God bless you<br>Marcus

Camp near Yorktown Aug. 22/62

My dear dear Wife! My sweet Children!

Yours of the 12th with the "Terror Strikes"[54] enclosed came to hand this A.M. and I should have set myself answering your good and kind letter and thanking you for the very appropriated present this morning had it not been for the fact that I was detailed on a General Court Martial which sets from 9 to 12 and also for an Order received to make out 3 Muster Rolls, which made it necessary for Lieutenant Chapman and Orderly to occupy my table. I consequently after the Adjournment of Court Martial and after partaking of a dinner of fried Potatoes and Bacon prepared by my own hands, started with Dr. Westfall and Adjutand Brock in the Country some three miles, a ride which

---

54. Perhaps an unidentified novel.

we very much enjoyed inasmuch as we "flickt our Bounce" with as many good sweet Pears and brot home as many as we could get into our Havresack. I only wished you had my Havresackfull at home. I'll bet you could enjoy them; they are truly delicious. Since I have written the other Page, I have read your sweet letter twice, attended dress Parade, eat a very poor supper of strong Bacon, talked and laughed with the Officers who congregated in my tent untill it was as full as it could hold, seen them off and called at Colonel Voris tent, boring him and the Adjutand, and just now returned, assuming the very pleasant and agreeable duty of writing to you my love.

Well in the first place let me give you the good news that I am hearty and well and as cheerful as any man and more so than most of men in the Army, although I have 5 Biles [boils] on me; 1 on the left corner of my Forehead so prominent and conspicuous that General Ferry told me to day, Captain Spiegel that Horn of yours is getting dangerous; 1 on the right leg above the knee, 2 on left below the knee, and one Between and Betwixed a place that troubled me very much in sitting in the sattle for the last week; yet I am getting so that I think it is these Biles that keep me well and hearty.

It is now eleven o'clock and I see that I dare not stop much at Bile description, as I propose finishing this letter this Evening if my Candle holds out.

You have ere this unquestionably heard of the removal of the Grand Army of the Potomac from the James River, which has so far been very successfully and splendidly managed by General McClellan and after 5 days march we arrived on the York River, this place yesterday.[55] I would give you a historic and minute description of Country, Scenery

---

55. Under orders from the Lincoln administration, McClellan was abandoning the base at Harrison's Landing and moving most of the Army of the Potomac to northern Virginia. The Fourth Corps, which included Spiegel's regiment, would be left behind in the vicinity of the Peninsula. Long, *Civil War Day by Day*, 251; GB, 264–65.

and so forth if it were not for the fact, that I will tomorrow write a letter for the press, either for the Farmer or the Cleveland Plain Dealer, which in either Case you can see.[56]

On this march I have been and am yet acting Lieutenant Colonel which is an advantage inasmuch as it gives me a Horse and saves me from marching through the impenetrable dust and gives me a chance to ride sometimes under shade instead of the Hot Sun, besides having the privileges of a Field Officer such as carrying my big Mess Chest while line Officers can only get transportation for a small valise.

I do not know that I have written to you that they took our comfortable Wall tents and made us take what they call Wetch [wedge] tents, a little peeky thing and very small, hot and close, but subsequently they took our wetch Tents and only give us what they call Shelter Tents, 2 square pieces of white drilling about 2 yard square, which is hung over a pole put on a fork on each end, leaving two ends open. Entrance Captains, Lieutenant and men all alike; the only difference that officers get one apiece and men two to a tent, but the Field Officers get a nice large Wall Tent and Fly for each. The consequence of it is that I now have a larger and better Tent than I ever had all alone, for you know that I have not been in command of my Company for a month, though I am with the boys dayly.

Chapman and I board together still. I have however Henry Adams sleep with me in my tent. He is such a good boy but very negligent and forgetful. I am afraid I have to have another Boy, as he can not take care of a Horse and oneselves.

Should I get promoted I would very much like Henry Biegle back as he seems to know my notions best and is careful and sparsam [frugal].

When we left the Peninsula, that is the James River, none knew where we were going to and at present no one knows how long we are going to stay here.

---

56. Neither newspaper published such a letter.

Today we received the first mail for a week. I received one from Chicago and one from Uniontown from Moses. All is well; Josephine lost another child.[57]

Lieutenant Colonel Bond and Major Commager are both sick; the two together would not make a <u>decent old lady</u>: the former a <u>licentious and drunken libertine</u> whose principal avocation is drinking a[nd] wh——g, until he gets too weak for duty; the latter a very fine Gentleman originally cut out for a <u>Hebamme</u> [midwife] but spoiled in the making; he is unquestionably related to Aunt Minah of Chicago.[58] I had intended not to give you any more opportunities for untimely expectations for my promotions, yet as I know everything pleasing to me is gratifying to you, I must relate a little Tete-a-tete which took place this morning between Brigadier General Ferry and your humble servant.

When I was dressed in full uniform this morning for Court Martial, Colonel Voris asked me to go to the Head Quarters to transact some Business. He not being dressed and raining badly, he dit not feel like dressing. As I came up and passed by the Generals Tent in the act of calling on the adjutant general, he called me in his Tent very friendly and asked me to sit down and talk awhile. Among other things he talked of the mail coming and so forth. I told him I had some notion of making applications to the Governor of Ohio for a position in a new Regiment and asked him what he thought about it, "Answer Not my Captain Spiegel; I want you to leave the matter of your promotion in my hands; I will attend to you. A recommendation for your promotion with an urgent solicitation of myself and Major

---

57. Perhaps the wife of Moses Joseph.

58. Despite Spiegel's negative opinions of them, Bond ultimately became colonel of the 111th Ohio and a brigadier general by brevet. Commager became colonel of the 184th Ohio (and the ancestor of a distinguished historian). Boatner, *Civil War Dictionary,* 72; Roster 5:565; Henry Steele Commager, ed., *The Blue and the Gray, The Story of the Civil War as Told by Participants,* 2 vols. (Indianapolis: Bobbs-Merrill, 1950), 1: v. Minah or Minna was the name of Spiegel's sister and also that of an aunt in Germany.

General Peck has already been sent to the War Department and I have no doubt it will come all right, as soon as it can possibly be reached. Your Regiment can not spare you. I had a personal talk with General Peck about you and he thinks you a splendit officer.["]

Ain't that bully and coming as it does from a Connecticut General of high tone, who scarcely ever speaks more than answering questions or giving command to any one. I don't care if I never get promoted; such high praise from a man like General Ferry is honor enough for me. However a Petition will go to morrow signed by every officer in this Regiment to the Governor asking him to put me in Colonel Bonds place. I do not know how much effect it will have, nor do I care. I am well, stout and hearty and mean to do my duty and live for the comfort and happiness of my beloved ones at home. . . .

> Camp near Hampton Va[59]
> Aug. 29, 1862

My dear beloved and good wife!

To day we received the first mail for quite a while and you may be sure it brought me "bliss" when I tell you two sweet letters from you, one from New York and three from my boys who have gone to the different Hospitals, among which is one from Henry Biegle from New York who says he is getting along finely. Your good letters seem to me attempting to conceal a great deal of trouble, anxiety and care which you apparently have and are trying to conceal. This must not be, my good Wife; you must not put yourself to any unnecessary trouble or care. You speak of a very hard letter you wrote me on a certain Sunday which I have not yet received, nor does it make any difference; I shall not think hard of you for it. I think it would have been worth $500 at least had I left Brother Joseph in New York.

---

59. Spiegel's unit had marched to the tip of the Peninsula as part of the movement to Suffolk described below.

Yet I do not feel sorry for it or any thing I done as I have
never yet done anything dishonorable and, as for many mistakes in my former life, I mean to offer amends in the future if God will only spare my life; only try and feel easy
and happy. If you want me to get along well you must be
cheerful; if you want me to be a good Soldier you must rejoice in my little successes as they come; if you want me to
take care of myself you must show me in your letters that
you are as happy and lively as you well can be; then and
then only am I myself. Such knowledge will stimulate me to
be friendly and condescending to my inferiors, courteous
and polite to my superiors, just, equitable and pleasant to all
and mindful to duty, and I am sure success will crown my
efforts; honor and glory for us and our beloved offspring
will await us. I am now fixed in this institution in a fair way
and in my estimation no man can ever be respected or respect himself when his country needs the services of almost
every able bodied man she has. I do not see how I can honorably get out of it now, when in fact everything is going as
well as I could possibly wish, when everybody loves, honors
and respects me. Yet I do intend to come home this Fall in
November on a visit and if anything should transpire so as
to be transferred or promoted I may be home sooner. Be
easy, be happy, be my own dear Wife, loved and worshiped
by your true husband who is making a reputation for you,
the children and himself, that we may all feel proud of,
while in the discharge of the noblest of callings, "serving his
Country". Hampton nearby must at one time have been of
the noblest of Southern towns. The Walls of the Church
built in 1686 and to which the brick were brought from old
England and in which George Washington and many other
distinguished Men of the Country were married, as well as
the walls and chimney of some other 6 or 700 Buildings is
all that is left from that once magnificent City situated on
the mouth of one of the best Harbors in the United States,
namely Hampton Roads. The House of ex-President Tyler
close by here is now occupied by Contrabands as well as the

mansion of the Rebel Colonel Maleroy.[60] We found a Gravestone on a Cemetery close by of 1701 and many are the ancient and interesting sights about here but I can not all give them. By the way, when at Harrisons Landing, across the River from there it is not very far from Sussex County where mother comes from and at one time we expected to go there by way of Petersburg.[61] You have ere this unquestionably seen friend Chapman who has given you all the particulars, I could have gone in his stead but dit not want to leave just now.[62] May take a notion after certain things are accomplished. I bot a new Cap, send my old bugle to my big son; he may wear it on his Cap.

Ever your true and loving husband<br>Marcus

Suffolk Va Sept. 1/62

My dear good wife!

Day before yesterday we arrived here at 6 P.M. after one of the most romantic passage over one of the Strangest and most curious River I ever saw, to wit "the Nanthyman" [Nansemond].

We left Fortress Monroe at 12 o'clock, Companies C, K, D, H on Board Steamer Cecil, Commanded by Colonel Voris and Companies F, A, B, G on Steamer "Sequin" Commanded by me and Companies I and E on Steamer Mary Bell with several companies of the 39th Illinois in Command of Colonel Osborn of the 39th Illinois. The 2 former Vessels left Hampton Roads Saturday at 11 and the North Pier

---

60. The house of John Tyler to which Spiegel refers was his summer residence. Robert Seager II, *And Tyler Too, A Biography of John & Julia Gardner Tyler* (New York, c. 1963), 359. "Contrabands" was the popular term for slaves within the Union lines. Gen. Benjamin F. Butler had termed them "contraband of war" in refusing to return them to their masters. Boatner, *Civil War Dictionary*, 172. Colonel Maleroy is unidentified.

61. Spiegel refers to his wife's mother. One of McClellan's last plans had been for an advance on the south side of the James. Williams, *Lincoln and His Generals*, 142.

62. Lieutenant Chapman had gone home to seek recruits.

at Fort Monroe at 12 A.M. in charge of United States Pilot taken on board at the Fortress.

We started lively up the Chesapeake until we came to the mouth of the Nanthyman when we took for her, the Nanthyman, running through a low region of swamp land which is narrow and at [not completed] Since I wrote the above which was at 8 A.M. I have drilled the Battallion (that is, Regiment) [for] 2 hours this forenoon [of] Company drill and two hours this afternoon [of] Battallion drill, which is no small job these hot days, and I was just quietly laying down on my blanket stretched over the ground, smoking my pipe, when my friend Girty[63] and Adjutant Brock came in and commenced fooling and cutting up, singing "Bull froke jumped from the bottom of the well, swore by God he is just from h——l" and so forth, and got my tea Cup and Plate and accompanied it and finally insisted we must serenade Dr. Westfall and Dr. Forbes, Colonel Voris and Captain Butler[64] which we dit to the great amusement of them and ourselves, and just now returned, 11 P.M. Now my dear Caroline this may appear foolish and simple to you, but yet we amuse ourselves in some way. I do not play Cards, or any other game; I do not drink or spree; I do not run after foreign Gods or strange Women and yet my tent is the rendesvouz of the officers. It is very often that I can scarcely find Room to sit down. I sauce and blaguard [blackguard], then all cut up and make fun; in short when I am well and get my letters regularly from home, I feel lively and must cut up.

I am now writing sitting all alone in my tent, Henry Adams sleeping on the ground to whom I presently will associate myself and my little House with the rough desk made by my boys, who by the way are still with me. Although I am away from the Company, acting Field Officer, and not commanding the Company, yet they will ask

---

63. Captain Alfred P. Girty of Company G. Roster 5:604.

64. Samuel F. Forbes, Surgeon; Lewis Butler of Company I. Roster 5:565, 616.

me for anything and come to complain of every little thing, as though I was still commanding the Company. Since Colonel Voris has returned he has not once commanded (that is to say drilled) the Regiment when I was present. He is very magnanimous to me, saying Captain, if you wish the [to?] drill the Regiment, you may do so; I will give you a chance and so forth, Query, Why?? and so forth.—

I think I am wandering away far from my River description, as it is very late and I do not know as I will resume it tonight. If not, you must charge it to the following facts: 1st 4 hours drill in a hot day is hard work; 2nd My Orderly and Corporal Snydre[65] are and have been for the last day and a half making out payrolls for the Company on my desk; 3rdly the Serenade; 4thly while I write quietly and lonely in my tent it is raining most furiously and while the rain beats down on my tent I feel very much invited to enjoy sleep, 5thly I am almost too tired to sit up. Yet I must say to you Suffolk is one of the most artistocratick looking as well as ancient towns I have yet seen in Virginia, without having any very fine buildings but it looks so ancient and venerable. The folks are most all at home, but I understand there is no sociability between Citizens of either Class or Sex and Officers or Soldiers.

The 4th New York Regiment received our Boys most cheerfully, when they came here. The 4th is a Benbox Regiment, 18 months in the Service and never yet marched or fought, but when our boys came they gave them all they wanted to eat and of the best kind. They say we look rough but they heard we were fighting men. We are now away from all fights and prospects of fights and if you would come here with the children I would try and make arrangements and you could come with Chapman. What say you? Eh? If there is a probability of our staying here, would you come? Tell Chapman we <u>miss him much</u>. You must at any rate make arrangements of sending me your Picture and

---

65. William Snyder of Company C. Roster 5:579.

that of my dear Hamlin, Lizzie, Mosey and Hattie. The news we received from the seat of War this evening is very flattering and if true, will help a great deal to our cause.[66] Would to God It were true. I would really like to see this War to an End and once more be permitted to enjoy the peaceful bliss and happiness of enjoying the Company of my dear Wife and sweet children.

I met to day a Lieutenant Biroker [?], a Yehuday from Alzei,[67] who shed tears when he heard my name. He and his father were great friends of my dear father. He told me that the 25th of this month is Rosh Hashonah and the 4th [of] next month Yom Cipur. He says there is a Synagoge in Norfolk 12 miles from here. I shall go at all events. You and the children must keep both; keep the children out of School the 25 and 26 and 3rd and 4th for my sake and let us pray to the Lord God of Israel for the deliverance of this once happy Country and the Peaceful enjoyment of our family Circle at the End of this unhappy War. God Bless you all.

Ever Your
Marcus

Suffolk Va. Sept. 3/62

My dear Good Wife and Children!

Two days have gone since I wrote to you and two small mails received in the Regiment to gladden the hearts of a few, but unfortunately I have not been one of the few. No Tidings, for me, no mirror of your feelings or plainly pictured, honest and loving heart by your straight-forward words; no word of Hamlin's doings, of Lizzies Smoothbellaship [shmoosbellaship = conversation], of Mosey's KlotzKopfishness [blockheadedness] or of our sweet Babes

---

66. An erroneous report, as the Union army was defeated on August 29 and 30 at Second Bull Run. Long, *Civil War Day by Day*, 257–58.

67. That is, a Jew from Alzey, a German town near Abenheim. Biroker, whose name does not appear on the published roster of the Fourth New York, is unidentified.

buddings and bloomings; tidings, all of which are insep-
arable and each one part and parcel of my soul, my happiness. Is all and everything right? Are they all well? My heart
yearns to know. I feel to night as I have not felt for a long
time, sad and discouraged. Would to God tomorrows mail
would bring me a long, good and encouraging letter; I need
it.

The Month of August has not been a very productive
"Letter Month" for me from home. I think, have only received four from you; hope September may turn out better.

We are now in Camp near Suffolk, a town of some
Notoriety for Aristocracy. The town as I have said to you in
my last is rather handsome and appears retired. The three
rows of Trees in the Streets makes it look shady and
pleasant. There is no kind of Sociability between People and
Soldiers.

I was in town today and had the whiskers of my Chin
shaved, leaving mustache and side whiskers. Everybody says,
I look 15 years younger, except Colonel Voris who does not
like it. Captain Girty make me do it. If I have an opportunity I will send you my picture; they say there is a Gallery
in town. I have not as yet had an opportunity of seeing as
to getting a house here for us and thought best to wait until
I hear from you and also from the effects of the Battles
near Washington.

Things do not look very bright in that quarter. We begin
to feel here as though every effort the loyal men in the
north can make will have to be made ere this Rebellion can
be crushed.

Has Chapman reached Millersburg? I wish he was here as
I sit tonight all alone in my tent, everybody gone to sleep. I
feel lonesome. Colonel Voris is very kind to me; he lets me
drill the Regiment every time of late.

I will have my trunk sent by Chapman. If I get promoted
ere he returns, you can get that Winter blouse of mine
fixed with two Rows of buttons, four on a Side. You can
put four more on the other Side and have Buttonholes but
not until I am promoted.

Spiegel sans beard, autumn 1862

Write me about Hamlin, Lizzie, Mosey, and Hattie and
Elizabeth as well as about everybody else often and a good
deal at a time and then and then only will be happy.

Your ever true and loving
Marcus

Camp near Suffolk Va.
Sept. 7/62

My dear good Wife!

This has been a long, long Sunday; not because I felt any-
ways dissatisfied with the Order suspending all Drill and so
forth except Dress Parade on Sunday; neither could it have
appeared long from the lack of Company, for my tent was
crowded all day with my boys and Officers, but simply I was
so very lazy after being called by my new waiter (a Contraband named David Goliath Smith) to Breakfast. I could
not raise any more ambition than to put on my slippers and
Pants, not even socks, and after washing and eating my
breakfast of roasted Sweet Potatoes and fried Ham, I
walked about camp for about 1/2 hour and returned,
stretching out on my hard Bunk until it, being rather high
near the roof of my tent got untenable from the heat of the
Sun beating against the East side, when I put my blanket on
the ground, drew up the lower part of my tent to [let] the
air go through and stretched out on my back in which position I entertained my numerous visitors, read the tactics and
your old letter over several times, only suffering myself to
be disturbed eating my Roast sweet Potatoes and fried Ham
for Dinner; all the time awaiting the mail, which I felt sure
would bring me some good news.

The mail came while I was eating my supper which for
variety sake consisted of Sweet Potatoes roasted and Ham
fried. I forgot to say we had Tea three times; morn, noon
and supper. As I said the mail came and brought me your
very good and sweet letter of the 3rd in which you confess
a degree of orthodoxy in my old faith the "democratic"
party, by attending a meeting of that time honored and
loyal People of Ohio at Wooster. I am somewhat astonished,

yet I am happy to hear you leaving your nest and flying out a little.

I have nothing new to write to you, nothing of any importance.

I am daily drilling the Regiment and with a great deal of success I think; at least so the boys and everybody else say. I think Colonel Voris will in a few days start for Columbus to make arrangements to fill up our Regiment. If it had not been for a very strong pettifoging Spree [meaning unclear], I should have gone, but really I dit not care as I could have only stayed at home over night, which would not have been a great deal of satisfaction to you or me. The parting after so very short time would unquestionably have been as painful as the arrival pleasant.

I will come some time this Fall or Winter. I somehow took it in my head that the War would not last over winter. Our last defeats will call out spontaneously such a powerful Army and all our resources will at once be opened and used for a quick and successful termination of the struggle and if we should or God forbid should not be successful, the War will have to end this Winter.

The people of Ohio must be awfully excited at the daring onward course of the Rebels in Kentucky but in my opinion they need not be alarmed. The Rebels will never cross the Ohio River.[68]

I will endeavor to get a Horse for Hamlin and also something nice for Lizzie, Mosey and Hattie but they must be very, very good children. I wish you would keep a Book of their behavior and every time they do anything deserving a bad mark give them a Bady [?] Mark and when I come

---

68. Spiegel refers to the fears stimulated by the approach of Confederate forces under Gen. E. Kirby Smith which entered Lexington, Kentucky, on September 1. A hastily raised Millersburg militia company, the "Killbuck Rangers," was among the "Squirrel Hunters" rushed to the defense of Cincinnati. But, as Spiegel expected, the danger soon passed. Roseboom, *Civil War Era,* 398–99; MF, Sept. 18, 1862.

home and they have more than I think they ought to have, I will give all that I brought to them to somebody else. . . .

> Headquarters 67th O.V.
> near Suffolk, Va.
> Sept 11/62

My dear beloved Wife and Children.

My heart was gladdened this morning by the news that Colonel Bond had been promoted to another Regiment and by the prompt and energetic way in which Colonel Voris went to work to recommend me to the Majorship and the very flattering way General O. S. Ferry endorsed it, of all you find copy enclosed.[69]

This afternoon I received your very good letter of the 7th and was very happy to learn of your good welfare and that of our beloved Children. But it seemed that the day which commenced so brightly for me, though powerful rainy for the world at large, dit not remain cloudless for me, for this Evenings mail brought the news that Captain E. S. Platt of our Regiment, who managed since we have been in the field to stay three fourth, yes nine tenth, of his time at home and hang around Columbus, sneaking about the Capitol, managed to get the appointment of Major in our Regiment.[70] It almost drives me crazy, yet what can I, the Colonel or anybody else here do, if true. A junior Captain promoted over a Senior and why? When I fought and led the Boys at Winchester, Mount Jackson, New Market and so forth he was composedly sitting in Cumberland. When I marched blood on my feet in the valley, he was safely and comfortably at home. When I was laying in Command at Goggins

---

69. While the copy is not in the Spiegel Papers, the original letter recommends the promotion of Major Commager to lieutenant colonel and of Spiegel to major. Voris reminded the adjutant general of Ohio of Spiegel's services at the battle of Kernstown and praised him as a superior officer. Col. A. C. Voris to Gen. Charles W. Hill, Sept. 11, 1862, OAGC.

70. Edwin S. Platt of Company E had been promoted to major on Aug. 28 but resigned on Jan. 16, 1863. Roster 5:565.

Point near Malvern Hill in the scorching Rays of a meridian Sun without tents or Shelter, he was safely seated in the Bar Rooms of Toledo and Columbus plotting to cheat me out of my rights.

Why this is done I know not, if it is done for certain I know not, but it comes to me from a clerk of the Adjutants General Office of General Hill. General Hill is from Toledo and a Toledo "Clique" is trying to rule this Regiment as against the boys that are in the field.[71]

Captain Platt knows nothing of military; he can not drill a Company. I am sick at heart to think we should have a Governor of Ohio who would submit a man of a family of a noble wife and four loving innocent children to be disgraced, after having done his duty faithfully, by placing an incompetent old Bachelor over him.[72] Good God, what a shame. There is no use writing to the Governor; he gets so many letters and does not read them that it is throwing labor away. But if you would at once take Chapman, Rex or Cohn or Leadbetter and go down to Columbus;[73] if you can not leave the Baby at home take it with you; the words of a wife and mother are not unheated. If he can not commission me as Major in this Regiment let him appoint me in some other. Show him the recommendations of Voris and Ferry; let him look [at] Brigadier General Ferry, Major General Peck and Keith [Keyes] report of me to the Head of the Army of the Potomac and if he can not give me an appointment in another Regiment, let him give you a recommendation to the War Department to accept my

---

71. Charles W. Hill, adjutant general of Ohio, 1862–63, was a lawyer from Toledo with considerable military experience. Clark Waggoner, ed., *History of the City of Toledo and Lucas County, Ohio* (New York and Toledo: Munsell, 1888), 529–30.

72. Platt was, however, seven years younger than Spiegel. Roster 5:565.

73. Besides his other political and military friends, Spiegel refers to George Rex, a prominent Wooster lawyer, Democratic politician, and Freemason, who was then prosecuting attorney for Wayne County. Ben Douglass, *History of Wayne County, Ohio, from the Days of the Pioneers and First Settlers to the Present Time* (Indianapolis: R. Douglass, 1878), 460–65.

resignation, though I would not by any means resign when my Country needs my services, but I can not stay and be disgraced. Do not think I am excited. I am perfectly cool, only I feel sick at heart and humiliated as I never felt before. I am a Soldier and desire to be treated as such. My friends in the Regiment wanted to press my appointment for Lieutenant Colonel over Commager but I would not stand it and now to be thus treated is outrageous.

I do not believe the Governor knows anything at all of these matters; it all is the action of the Toledo "Clique" who felt sore at Voris success, now venting their wrath at me.[74]

If you can take courage, go to Columbus, see Welker who is a good man and a friend of mine and you should have courage and talk as you can, not get mad, but state the facts, see to my rights. You can have justice done me, I know it. Take a copy of the enclosed (the recommendation) or this copy along; preserve one Copy any how. Do not look lightly on the matter but show true grit, as your husband and the father of your children shows it and is ready to show it daily for his Country and all will be right. I know and feel it will.

I am well and have been Command of the Regiment. Colonel Voris has the "Jantess" [jaundice] and is quite sick; if he could get his leave to go home that he expected, all would be well.[75]

---

74. Spiegel thus associates his rejection with the controversy in the regiment going back to its consolidation.

75. Voris, almost certainly informed by Spiegel of Platt's promotion, made a strong effort on Spiegel's behalf. He wrote to the governor to call his attention to the recommendation already sent to the adjutant general. He urged Spiegel's promotion on grounds of seniority but even more of merit. "Capt S—— is the best man for the place and is well deserving of the place generally—Capt S. is a German Jew by birth—became an American from choice and has indicated his preference for his adopted country by risking his life for its honor—As a military man he has no superior in the Regt.[,] is honest and popular—He belongs to that class of person of all others who should not be slighted." Voris went on to indicate that Spiegel had actually been serving as a field officer and that he had the endorsement of brigade

Do not dear wife wait a moment, but take your babe and some one else, Chapman or Leadbetter or Cohn who I suppose is East,[76] and do not care what folks say but stick up for our rights as I will always do.

My love  
Ever your loving  
Marcus

don't be ashamed to stand up for your husband.

Don't let the Governor put you off; if he wishes to appoint me in the 67th let him give you my Commission. Show him the Copy of the recommendation; the original was sent to Adjutant General Hill, which I suppose he dit not see. Dont tell him I wrote you to go. Good night! God bless you. Send Dispatch from Columbus to me at Suffolk, Virginia, prepaid. God bless you.

Did Caroline Spiegel see the Governor? While she was certainly capable of it, evidence is lacking to prove that she did. Her husband may have decided to take matters into his own hands. On September 13, 1862, he obtained from General Ferry permission to go to Fortress Monroe "on public business." From headquarters there two days later, he received an order to go to Ohio, purportedly on recruiting duty, and within little more than a week he was at home in Millersburg. Meanwhile, Governor Tod formally informed him that the appointment as major had gone to Platt but that this "reflects no want of confidence in you." Whatever his disappointment, Spiegel immediately overcame it by seizing a new opportunity. From the recruits being collected at Camp Mansfield, a new regiment, the 120th Ohio, was being organized. The bulk of its officers and men were from Spiegel's part of the state. He obtained from the officers of his old regiment a recommendation for the lieutenant colonelcy of the 120th

---

and division commanders. In conclusion, he reminded, "As you know we have had too much trouble in our Regt already." He expressed the wish that no cause for further dissatisfaction should "be forced on us by outsiders." A. C. Voris to Gov. David Tod, Sept. 12, 1862, OAGC.

76. Spiegel refers to the periodic buying trips to New York made by Millersburg merchants.

Ohio. Doubtless with the additional help of his political friends, he secured on October 2, 1862 the termination of his captaincy and a fresh commission entitling him at last to wear the coveted oak leaves. Jumping two steps up the military ladder, he had climbed to field rank, with its new problems and almost limitless possibilities.[77]

As to Spiegel's old comrades of the Sixty-seventh Ohio, the regiment fought until the end of the war, most notably at the sieges of Charleston and Petersburg. Colonel Voris was badly wounded at the former, but unlike three of his brothers, he survived the war. Mustered out as a brevet major general, he returned to Akron to become a leader among veterans, an active Republican and ultimately a judge. Spiegel's friend Chapman became a captain in 1862, was wounded a year later and subsequently resigned. Childs served till the end of the war, also being wounded and receiving his captaincy. Sergeant Wallick, whom Spiegel had promoted after Kernstown, became a first lieutenant. Just two months after his marriage in 1864, he was shot and killed at the start of the spring offensive.[78]

77. Pass for Captain Spiegel signed by Gen. O. S. Ferry, Sept. 13, 1862, in the Spiegel Papers, AJA; Smalley and Sturdivant, *The Credit Merchants*, 10; MR, Sept. 25, 1862.

78. Roster 5:563, 578; "General A. C. Voris," *Magazine of Western History* 4(August 1886):507–15; memorial window, Buckley Chapel, and Voris grave marker, Glendale Cemetery, Akron; MF, May 26, 1864.

# CHAPTER SIX

# "The 120th will do to bet on"

In October 1862, Marcus Spiegel found several thousand recruits encamped at Mansfield. During the war's first year, United States Senator John Sherman had organized what he originally called Camp Buckingham as a rendezvous for the brigade he was raising. The field of tents was continued as Camp Mansfield under the command of the senator's older brother, Mansfield attorney Charles Taylor Sherman. Thus Spiegel began a relationship with what was coming to be a prominent Republican family, as well as with his new unit. For the latter, companies from Wayne, Ashland, Richland, and Holmes counties were being organized into an infantry regiment, the 120th Ohio, to serve for three years.[1]

Like Spiegel, the commander of the 120th was a Democrat from Millersburg. Daniel French, who was forty years old in 1862, was a veteran of the Mexican War, having entered as lieutenant and having been promoted for gallantry to a captaincy. A member of a politically prominent family, he had been a prewar deputy United States marshal and railroad mail agent. In 1861, he had helped raise a company at Millersburg and ultimately became lieutenant colonel of the Sixty-fifth Ohio in the Sherman Brigade. After service in the field, he returned to become colonel of the new regiment. The presence of French and Spiegel thus gave a decidedly Democratic cast to the leadership of this regiment being raised in traditionally Democratic counties.[2]

---

1. John J. Patrick, "John Sherman: The Early Years, 1823–1865" (Ph.D. diss., Kent State University, 1982), 140–45; A. A. Graham, *History of Richland County* . . . (Mansfield: A. A. Graham and Co., 1880), 362; Harper, *Ohio Handbook of the Civil War,* 66.

2. Joseph L. Ankeny to Gov. William Dennison, Nov. 28, 1861, in Ohio, Governors' Papers; Roster 8:241; MF, Apr. 18, June 6, July 25, Oct. 10, Dec. 5, 1861. In early September 1862, the original candidate for lieutenant colonel of the 120th had been E. W. Botsford or Butsford. MF, Sept. 11, 1862. For the Democratic character of the four relevant counties, see Cardinal, "Democratic Party of Ohio," 9.

As wartime political partisanship grew more bitter, Spiegel and other Democratic officers found themselves in an increasingly difficult situation. While some Democrats had joined the coalition Union party formed under Republican leadership, many others maintained their own party organization. Most of the latter Democrats supported the war to save the Union but were unwilling to fight to abolish slavery. For a year the Lincoln administration had appeased them. Eventually, however, a combination of political, moral, military, and diplomatic pressures induced the president to turn to abolition. On September 22, 1862, Abraham Lincoln issued his Preliminary Emancipation Proclamation, announcing his intention to free the slaves in areas still in rebellion at the beginning of 1863. As Democrats denounced the national administration, Republicans charged that such criticism undermined the war effort and obstructed the drafting of men into the militia. They called on the military, including Democrats like Spiegel, to arrest certain vocal critics of the conduct of the war, whom they often pejoratively called "Copperheads." On the night of October 11, Spiegel led a detachment of men from the 120th on a special train to Canton. There, by order of the state's Republican Chief Justice, they arrested Archibald McGregor, an editor, and one other Democrat; they took both back with them to Mansfield. Once at the army camp, Colonel French helped ease the Democrats' temporary imprisonment. He, Spiegel, and other Democratic officers also helped to persuade Charles T. Sherman that it was unnecessary to send a similar detachment to Millersburg to overcome draft resistance. Spiegel's home thus escaped military intervention but seething partisanship exemplified by the editorials of his friend Estill boded ill for the future.[3]

---

3. Stephen B. Oates, *With Malice Toward None, The Life of Abraham Lincoln* (New York: Harper, 1977), 307–19; Cardinal, "Democratic Party of Ohio," 1–28 passim; John A. Marshall, *American Bastile, A History of the Arbitrary Arrests and Imprisonment of American Citizens in the Northern and Border States . . .* (Philadelphia: Thomas W. Hartley and Co., 1869, 1885 printing), 121–24; MF, Oct. 16, 23, 1862. The charge against the men arrested at Canton was that they had advised men drafted into the militia to delay in reporting at camp. The local Republican editor said that Spiegel "has many acquaintances here, by whom he is highly esteemed." *Canton Stark County Republican,* Oct. 16, 1862. Canton Democrats assailed the Republican politicians involved in the arrests but made no mention of Spiegel. *Canton Stark County Democrat,* Nov. 5, Dec. 12, 1862.

On October 25, Spiegel and his new regiment left Mansfield by rail for Cincinnati. At the Queen City on the following day, while his men crossed the Ohio River to quarters in Kentucky, Spiegel departed on leave to Chicago. He was escorting his family to spend the winter with his sister Sarah and her husband, Michael Greenebaum, in an apartment over their hardware and plumbing shop. Since the Greenebaums had at least 5 children of their own, the families were crowded but at least the children were happy. Old friends in Chicago, especially in the little Jewish community, were also pleased that one of their own had risen so high in the United States Army. During Spiegel's visit, they presented him with a horse which he called "Charlie." From his Chicago friends also came a sword and ultimately the solid gold eagles that were the insignia of a full colonel. Still glowing with pride, Spiegel rejoined his unit, relieving Colonel French, who had been drilling and disciplining their untried new soldiers.

With these comrades, Spiegel was destined for service in the Western Theater, where the Union had already won significant victories. Earlier in 1862, Federal land and naval forces moving along the rivers that flowed into the Ohio had occupied middle Tennessee. Moreover, similar operations had seized control of the Mississippi River from Kentucky to below Memphis, Tennessee, and had taken possession of New Orleans at the river's mouth. By late summer, the Confederates thus held only the part of the Mississippi between the fortified towns of Port Hudson, Louisiana and Vicksburg, Mississippi. The latter, being bigger, better fortified, and more strongly garrisoned, became the principal Union objective in the West. If it could be taken, its capture would substantially sever the Confederates' communications with their far western states, reopen the Mississippi to Union use, and generally have a great psychological impact. Lieutenant Colonel Spiegel was about to become involved in what many would come to see as a turning point of the Civil War.[4]

Camp near Covington [Ky.]
Nov. 12/62

My dear dear good Wife and Children,

We are ordered to Memphis, Tennessee, to report to the 1st Division, Army of Kentucky, Brigadier General A. J.

---

4. *Akron Summit Beacon,* Nov. 27, 1862; Barbe, "Autobiography," 3; McPherson, *Ordeal by Fire,* 222–34.

Smith Commanding,[5] and I am truly glad of it. That seems like going again to the theater of action instead of loitering around the borders of the Ohio guarding empty forts and defunct Magazines.

It seems I am doomed to see something of the different seats of War; now you may again look with some Interest to my scribblings. I shall try and keep you posted of our trip on the River. We go from here to Louisville, Kentucky, and from there to Memphis. I anticipate a jolly trip, lots of excitement and fun in the sunny clime of the rosy south. Although here only 2- 1/2 days, I have already to day had the pleasure of having Brigadier General Ammon, Commander of the Post of Covington, to dinner with me, a good natured altn Schmoose belah [old gossip?] of the regular Army, who I am satisfied left me with the impression that he was a much more important man than he ever knew before.[6] He is a great friend of my old friend General Kimball. I am as busy as I wish to be. Colonel French left yesterday for Cincinnati with his lady and will not return until tomorrow, so I have to get the Regiment ready, transportation and all, and you have seen and heard when the Regiment left Mansfield, but now it is three times as much. Just imagine of all the questions of a green Regiment going to Dixie, the excitement, and then judge but you know I take it cool. While I write there are 8 standing around both able and willing to ask some very important questions but I have made up my mind to let them wait until after I have said a few words to my sweet ones at home.

My back ache left me and I feel like a young married man in the heighth of glory. Tell Hamlin that if he learns first rate I will take him along down the Mississippi River with me in the Spring. And Lizzie shall have the nicest little

---

5. Andrew Jackson Smith, a graduate of West Point with long service in the Regular Army who became a very capable division and corps commander. GB, 454–55.

6. Jacob Ammen, though Virginia-born, had grown up in Ohio. A West Point graduate, he had taught in several colleges. GB, 6–7.

Bale of raw Cotton there is about Memphis or something nicer and Mosey have a nice a litte He nigger and Theresia, Yettche, Mary, Hannah [?], Mosey and Henry will get something nice if they behave and don't quarrel.[7]

Be easy good girl my dear Wife, all will be right you must read my letters to Mich and Sarah, Henry and Theresa[8] or let Uncle Joseph read them.[9] Direct your letters to my Regt.

Brig. Genl. A. J. Smiths Div.

Memphis Ten

Marcus . . .

Covington Ky. Nov. 16/62

My dear good Wife and Children!

My long absence from the service and the mingling with civilians and receiving their compliments and dainties or the nursing of babies or something else, made me forget my general rule and made me deviate from my adapted custom which, I regret to say, will undoubtedly cause me to be for quite a time without any news from those whom I love as no man loves. You will remember that while in Virginia I never wrote to you that we had marching Orders or that we were about to move, always preferring to await the arrival at a new place and announce it to you. Had I done so this time I would probably ere this have a letter from you, but when we received a preemptory Order, positively directing us to proceed to Memphis, Tennessee, and directing the Quarter Master Department to furnish transportation, I thought myself perfectly safe in telling you to direct your letters to that place. But when about ready to start, the Department Head Quarters under the wise and sage General

---

7. The latter names are those of cousins.

8. Marcus's sister Theresa and her husband Henry Liebenstein of Chicago.

9. Marcus's brother Joseph was also in Chicago which in the end would become his home. But in December 1862, he made what Estill called a "flying visit" to Millersburg. Perhaps referring to his jovial ways, Estill called "Joe Spiegel" an "Irish Dutchman" and said he was "in 'good condition' and 'able to hold his oats.'" MF, Dec. 25, 1862.

Wright[10] (who I believe from what little I saw of him is oftener wrong than right) found out that they had not provided anybody to Guard the 3 or 4 million Dollars worth of property here and consequently ordered us to delay our departure until after 5 Companies now at Maysville, Kentucky, could be brought down, which event we are daily looking for. This Department is in my opinion badly managed, as loose as any I have seen. Oh for a McClellan at the Head of every department, that would be allowed to stay even if he would not pray every hour "God save the African". You have no Idea of the feeling of the Army at the removal of McClellan, no matter what the newspapers say.[11] You know I have generally given you impartial opinion; I say to you now, look out for a Storm. I am hale, hearty and happy and with the exception of one of Job's (big kind) comforters [i.e., boils] in the neighborhood where it materially interferes with my comfortable sitting I have not reason to complain. Charley has the nicest loping canter or any other kind of step that any man could wish for; in short he is all I could wish for. He is the pet Horse in the Regiment. Colonel French returned yesterday from Millersburg where he accompanied his Wife. He has now taken charge of the Regiment again and I have easy times. He is a perfect Gentleman. I think more of him every day; he uses me like a Brother. When you write you must say something pleasant about him that I can show him. . . .

Covington Ky. Nov. 19/62

My dear dear good Wife and Children!

I am happy to announce that I am again able to sit up and feel all right after laying for two days and a half on my

---

10. Horatio Gouverneur Wright. GB, 575.

11. On Nov. 7, 1862, because of his slowness in taking the offensive after Antietam, McClellan had been replaced as commander of the Army of the Potomac. He had not hidden his opposition to the adoption of the emancipation of slaves as a war aim. Williams, *Lincoln and His Generals*, 170–78.

back suffering most unmercifully with an awful Bealing [boil] which I had cut upon last night about 11 o'clock after which I rested perfectly easy and awoke this morning feeling as gay as a Lark, and if I should perchance to day have received a letter from you, my dear good wife, written in good spirit and announcing the happy fact of our dear Children and friends all well, I should have been perfectly happy. . . .

At last the five Companies of the 115th Regiment which were to relieve us here arrived this afternoon and we shall probably leave tomorrow Eve or Friday Morning for Memphis. I am truly glad of it. This staying here dit not suit me; it is neither Citizen nor Soldier. I do not like the Idea of Shoulderstraps and blue cloth in a peaceful Country, more especially so near Ohio, where every little depritation [depredation] committed (and some always will be) hits our true and loyal People of Ohio, more the pity since the noble State has so very lately gone democratic.

This being a very rainy day and the horizon looking so very much like rain for some time to come very forcibly reminded me of the fact that neither I nor my Charley were perfectly equipped for a "down South" Winter Campaigne. I therefore started with Colonel French to Cincinnati where we purchased each a large Gum [rubber] Coat, Gum Cap, Gum Gloves for us and a very large Gum Blanket and Gum Horse Hood for our Horses. Myself as well as Charley are now fixed so as to stand the Cold as well as the rain. I never was equipped as well before and yet it may come to pass that an unpleasant little affair may happen to me before I leave and that is, my John gave the two Red Shirts and one pair of the Green drawers that you made for me, one gray Shirt (that striped one I bought of Cohn last Winter), 3 Handkerchiefs and one pair of my heavy knit drawers to the Wash Woman yesterday and she agreed to bring them in day after tomorrow and most likely we leave tomorrow. He does not know her name, neither does he know where she lives, yet we may find out tomorrow.

My evening companion is Dean.[12] He is the pleasantest
and most accomplished man I most ever saw; he is a good
man. The only thing I have against him is he talks and
brags so much of his wife and Children and family and so
forth that I can scarcely get a chance; still I force it in edge-
ways. Last night while I lay suffering we talked until 1/2
past ten and I had almost forgotten my boil until after he
left, when my pains were so severe I had to send for the
doctor to open it. While Dean was here among other things
we talked of our Childrens prayers and when I told him
our Children's morning prayer he was so taken with it, he
wrote it down at once and sent it to his "Charlotte" to learn
it to his children. Dont let my Hamlin, Lizzie and Mosey
forget it. When I repeated it to Dean last night and thought
of my dear dear Children and you my love, I had to shed
tears. Good bye my dear Hamlin and Lizzie, be good Children so our dear Mosey and Hattie will learn only good of
you, and so that when your father with the help of Almighty God returns, he will only hear good of you. God
bless you my dear wife and Children

Marcus . . .

On Board St. Ft. Wayne<br>Nov 22/62

My dear good wife!

This afternoon (about 20 minutes ago) our Post Master
brought me a letter from you dated 19th. Oh such a good
sweet dear letter, such a kind letter; it seemed like old
times, when after a long absence I used to get one good
sweet letter describing Hamlin, Lizzie, Mosey, Hattie and all.

We are still laying on board Steamer near Covington
shore getting ready to start; shall probably do so to night. I
spend this forenoon (Shabbath) [Sabbath] by being in Dr.

---

12. Ezra V. Dean, regimental quartermaster. At thirty-eight when mustered, he was one of the unit's older men. Roster 8:241. Dean was a lawyer
and the son of Ezra Dean, a prominent lawyer and Democratic politician from
Wooster. Douglass, *History of Wayne County,* 365–66.

Wise's[13] School [Shul = Synagogue] and hearing a very good
Sermon by the Doctor. I think I was a devout Israelite; a
beauty full service, good singing and good service and fine
Sermon. After Synagogue I haunted up Ezra and Lewis,[14]
spent forenoon [afternoon] with them. Their folks have an
awful time at home, Grandpa Sebrell [?] and one of their
oncles died and several aunts dying. I am shure of getting
Ezra discharged without doubt. My Charley is now pronounced the gayest and finest horse in the service. Every
body says he is fine English blood. I was offered $300 in
green backs for him. He has the proudest and gayest gate
(lope and canter) you ever saw. I asked the Colonel $500
(Colonel Ingels U. S. Regulars)[15] and if he had taken me
up, I would have backed out. He is a perfect Angel and follows me like a Pet. Just think: your Liege Lord in Command of Steamer Fort Wayne, one of the finest Steamers
ever floated [on the] Mississippi River; 500 as good men
and 21 officers under him who look upon him as <u>the man</u>;
every accomodation you could imagine and everybody his
friend and think for one moment, <u>is he not bully? Eh?
Say?</u> . . .

On Board Steamer Fort Wayne off Port Covington Ky.
Nov. 23/62

My dear dear Wife!
    You will see by the above that we have not travelled very
far since I last wrote to you, which I think was written on

---

13. Bohemian-born Rabbi Isaac M. Wise was a Democrat relatively un-
enthusiastic about the war and silent on the issue of slavery. He became one of
the founders of Reform Judaism in America and of Hebrew Union College in
Cincinnati. Korn, *American Jewry and the Civil War,* 7, 40–44. From Covington,
Spiegel had crossed the Ohio River to Cincinnati to attend Rabbi Wise's synagogue.
    14. Probably Ezra L. and Lewis C. Sebrell, Company F, 115th Ohio. Ezra
was discharged for disability at Cincinnati on Jan. 8, 1863. Roster 8:165.
    15. Name crossed out and corrected, possibly erroneous. Rufus Ingalls,
the only Regular Army colonel whose name was close, was quartermaster of
the Army of the Potomac. Heitman, *Historical Register* 1:562; GB, 246.

Board Steamer Dunleath, a small Steamer which was found too small and therefore unloaded and the large and roomy Steamer Fort Wayne was furnished us.

Colonel French is on Steamer Silverwave with five Companies, the right wing; Major, Adjutand and Chaplain and Dr. Hammond[16] and myself on Steamer Fort Wayne with 5 Companies, the left wing, Quarter Master Dean, Sergeant Major and Doctor Stover,[17] 90 mules, 12 Wagons and 2 Ambulances, any amount of Quartermaster Stores and Sutler Goods and so forth.

The River having been so very low, causes almost every Boat to be out of fix and consequently a great deal of repair is necessary to complete them in a manner for running Order; besides the thing of loading Rations, Baggage and so forth of 900 men is not a very pleasant job, besides being one which can [not] be done in a short time. But of all contrary and stubborn as well as novel occurrences that I ever saw, the putting a board a Boat [of] ninety mulish Mules beats them all. We have them however this (Sunday) Eve all loaded but 16, and are now sure of starting by about noon to morrow. We board with the Captain at the cost of $1–25/00 per day, State room included; we get good "Grubb". This Evening Quarter Master and myself were invited to a Supper, Mr. Banning at Covington, a wholesale Merchant in Cincinnati, formerly from Trumbull County, Ohio,[18] and both Dean and myself left the House strongly wishing for the dear ones at Home. Such a nice man, such a splendit woman, such a fine lot of four children and such an exquisite Supper, such a warm and cordial treatment, such a well regulated family. Everything, everything and yes more than all, the friendly pottling of the little boy when father came in and the sweet sounding, Pa, all, all drew and

---

16. John W. Hammond, assistant surgeon. Roster 8:241.

17. Christopher C. Stouffer, assistant surgeon. Roster 8:241.

18. David or Jeremiah W. Banning, partners in a firm of commission and forwarding merchants, both of whom lived in Covington. *Williams' Cincinnati Directory . . . for 1861* (Cincinnati: Williams Directory Co., 1861), 51.

reminded me of my sweet Children and good good Caroline, but such is life. Mr. Banning lives in a perfect Pallace on the Banks of the Ohio where when on the top of Magnificent Mansion they can overlook the Country around. I have been invited a dozen times since we stayed here, often by Major Beakmans[19] Brother and Sister-in-law and their friends at Newport, Kentucky, for Dinner and Tea and parties, yet I never went, though the Major and many of the Officers went and coaxed me to go. Last Friday Afternoon 4 Ladies from Newport (right across the River) came on Board the Boat and told me they had got up a "farewell party" [on] purpose for me and I must be sure and come. I very politely accepted the invitation "if possible" but when Evening came I sent a very polite note of "impossibility" and stayed at Home. Last night after spending as I told you Forenoon in Synagogue [and] afternoon with Ezra and Lewis, I spent the evening with the Colonel and Lieutenant Colonel of the 115th Ohio Volunteers and I am now satisfied it is all right and Ezra will be discharged. To day the Colonel, Lieutenant Colonel and Major of the Regiment took dinner with me and tomorrow morning I feel satisfied I can get him discharged. I write you this Eve just to spend my Eve with you my love, not that I have anything interesting to write. . . .

On Board Steamer Fort Wayne off Port Evansville Ind.
Nov. 30/62

My dear dear Wife and Children!

I have just time to say to you that I am again well and hearty. I have been sick in bed for almost 3 days with a terrible cold which had settled in my Breast and threw me in a fever and was as sick as I have been since I am in this Country. I thought at once I had to lay by and send for you, but thanks to the Doctors and many many kind friends, I am again up and all right. You know if I say so it is so; only a little weak and compelled to take care of myself

---

19. John W. Beekman. Roster 8:241.

which I do. They tell me I talked all the time in my fever of my dear, dear, good and lovely Wife and Children. I will commence a good long letter for you and mail as we pass Cairo, Illinois.

God Bless you all<br>Ever your Marcus

I am so weak that it makes the sweat come, to write. Give my love to Sarah, Theresa, Henry, Mich and all.

Only so far after 8 days travel, very slow.

Head Quarters (left wing)<br>120th O.V. Board Steamer<br>Fort Wayne off Port,<br>Island Number 10, Dec. 5/62

My dear dear Wife and Children!

It is just now 10 o'clock in the Evening and I have only a few minutes ago dismissed the Officers School which by the way is getting very interesting[20] and our Steamers have just landed for the night and the Officer of the day has reported the Pickets out through the woods (a precaution necessary in these parts to prevent being surprised by Guerillas) and as I slept about 3 hours to day I thought best to go to work and give you a little history of our journey.

In doing this I might as well tell you at once that as far as Sceneries and Landscapes are concerned I can say but little, having spent but very little time on deck.

We left Covington Barracks the 21st and Covington Shore the 24th ultimo and have ever since with but very little exception been confined to the narrow limits of a Steamboat crowded with 475 living "men" with all their "exhume" of impure and foul air, 31 of that number sick, twelve of the thirty one very sick. You know that I never feel very well while traveling either on the Cars or Steamer and on this

---

20. The 120th's officers studied Silas Casey's *System of Infantry Tactics* (1861), adopted by the army in 1862. Spiegel required them to demonstrate familiarity with twenty pages each day. Letter of Capt. W. G. Myers, Dec. 9, 1862, in *Wooster Republican*, Dec. 25, 1862.

long and tedious journey I have not enjoyed as much comfort as usual.

The continuous noise of the Steamboat Machinery, with the yells, the disputes, the songs, the coughs and the gruntings, and even some moaning of the soldiers, the Ho Eh Oh of the crew, and gay and festive little laughs and otherwise produced merriment of the Officers and the diarehea which has run me pretty well; all these together have made me wish frequently that we were at Memphis.

When we left Covington the Water was very low but a rise was expected to come from Pittsburg, which however dit not reach us until after we were four days [out] and during the four days stuck on numerous Sandbanks. While sticking on one of those Sandbanks, our Captain who has been working hard all night came to the Cabin in the morning about 5 A.M. out of humor on account of this slow progress in getting his "vessel" off the ground, tried to "vent his rath" on the many boys who on account of being sick were laying on the floor in the Cabin. He came to my room and commenced swearing and cussing about the d——n men filling up the Cabin and so forth and he was not going to live like a hog and so forth. I rubbed my eyes and did not feel very kind to him for so unceremoniously waking me, besides many of the boys gathered around and by their countenance I perceived that they expected me to say something not too kind to my friend the Captain. I therefore told him, "the boys in the Cabin are sick boys and must lay in there nights and if you do not like it I am sorry for it, and just let me caution you, never to come so early again and making such an infernal mess and noise; if you do I think I shall find boys enough on board this boat to throw you over board about as quick as any double quick maneuver was ever performed" and from the "thats so Colonel," "just give the word" and so forth and the gestures of the boys, I believe he concluded to let well enough alone and from that day to this he has never tried to interfere with my own domestic affairs on board the boat, and I have to day no better friend than old Captain Bob Whitney of the Fort Wayne.

On our way here we stopped at Matison [Madison], Evansville and Candletown [Cannelton], Indiana; the latter place has a very large Cotton Factory which however at present is working only half time. We also stopped at Louisville, Kentucky, at Cairo, Illinois, and at Columbus, Kentucky; at all these latter places we have to report to the commanding Generals. At the first General Boyle, the next General Tuttle, at the latter General Davies, Commands. Of the three, General Tuttle suited me best; him and I got quite familiar.[21] I made the acquaintance of Captain David Heiner[22] who fought and beat the Rebel Ram Arkansas. He was wounded seven times, is an old cuss and quite an original Character, is an awful Democrat and can drink as much Whiskey as most any other man without getting "beastly drunk". Besides him I made the acquaintance of many Gunboat fellows who have been in all the fights on the Mississippi, but they expect Vicksburg will beat them all and if I mistake not, I think to be able to give you a description of that as an Eye Witness and participater.

We had some fears of being ordered off from Columbus and take the Cars but we are now permitted to go on to Memphis for which I am glad as that will give us an opportunity to take our land transportation with us. We have with us 16 Six mule teams, our Mules in good order, and 2 two horse Ambulances, which makes quite a respectable transportation for one Regiment. If we will only be permitted to keep it, we will be as well fixed and equipped as most any Regiment that ever took the field.

You have frequently asked me what became of our

---

21. Jeremiah Tilford Boyle, James Madison Tuttle, Thomas Alfred Davies. GB, 40, 513, 114, respectively.

22. David A. Hiner was pilot of the gunboat *Tyler* when it fought the *Arkansas* near Vicksburg on July 14, 1862. U.S. Navy Department. *Official Records of the Union and Confederate Navies in the War of the Rebellion*, 30 vols. (Washington D.C.: Government Printing Office, 1894–1927), ser. 1, vol. 19, 38.

Women.[23] Well, the youngest one of the two went home;
the oldest one, the "matron" is on Colonel French's Boat.
She left the Hospital and talks of cooking for some of the
officers; I do not know what they will do. She does not
speak to me because I said that wherever there is woman in
the field she generally does not amount to much and her
husband is not worth a d——n for the service. We have two
Women on board of our boat; one in Conyers Company,[24] a
Mrs. Steel and looks for all the world like Mary Lawson,
and the other a Mrs. Haggard in Braytons Company[25] who
everybody would swear her to be the sister of Mrs. Weaver
of Uniontown if one dit not know that that sister was married and lived at the "old forge". They are however both of
them I think very kind and good women and are going to
cook; the Mary Lawson looking one was very kind to me
when I was sick and had it not been for the Idea that she
looked so very much like my old friend I could have enjoyed the little dainties and Tea she cooked but as it was I
really dit not. Ezra had not had his discharge when I left
but was promised it and if he has not got it yet will get it, as
I mean to write to the Colonel and Lieutenant Colonel this
evening yet. . . .

Camp Oliver near Memphis Ten.
Dec. 14/1862

Dear Friend yea Brother![26]
  Your very kind and congenial letter English and German
I found here Monday the 8th after arriving on the 7th. You
may ask then why not answer it immediately? Answer: for

--------

23. Women accompanied a number of Civil War units. Some were wives of
officers and men; others like those mentioned by Spiegel intended to act as
nurses. Most soon gave up, as did those with the 120th, whom Spiegel does
not mention later. Mary Elizabeth Massey, *Bonnet Brigades* (New York: Knopf,
1966), 65–86 passim.
24. George W. Conyer, Company K. Roster 8:269.
25. Rufus M. Brayton, Company B. Roster 8:245.
26. Probably to his cousin Moses Joseph of Uniontown, Ohio.

the first time since I have been in the service I have been taken with the diarehea on Board the Boat and dit not get entirely over it until a few days ago. It run me down in flesh and spirit so much that I dit not feel like writing and with all this I dit not dare to report unfit for duty on account of disembarking for the first time with a new and green Regiment, when one does not wish to have it appear green, requires the united unflinching and unceasing efforts of every officer in it that had any experience, more especially when there are but two who can boast of anything in that line. Disembarkation, joining the unjointed Wagons, unloading Mules and Horses, Stores and Subsistance, Men and officers, fix everything in order so as to move through a City like Memphis. After a weary journey of two weeks on Government Transports over two Rivers in a low stage of water, and selecting Camp, lay it out, pitch Tent, see to the ditching, cleaning, wood, watering and feeding a Regiment of 950 men. [This] takes labor and when one has to do a full share of that sick, weak and weary at that, [it] is truly not a trifling affair and a little rest is like a precious Jewel. Such was my fix, yet I stood it and am happy to announce to you my true and trusty friend I am to day hale and hearty and only a little the worse in flesh, say 12 pounds.

We were two weeks and one day coming here. I commanded the left wing of the Regiment on the Fort Wayne, a large and spacious Transport Steamer, and Colonel French commanded the right wing on Steamer "Silver Wave", a boat of same Size. Though both were boats of good size, yet when loaded with 475 men, Mules, Horses, Wagons and so forth, they were well crowded. Our progress on the River was slow and tedious owing to the low water; we had to lay by nights and dit not travel overly fast in day time. When about 30 miles above Cairo, the Steamer Silver Wave ran a rock and sank; we took off men and stock and landed them on the beach, proceeded to Cairo where I procured another boat the J. L. Prinkle and upon these boats without any further accidents we arrived safely at Memphis the 7th instant. Memphis is a beautiful City, full at the present of trading Yehudim [Jews], Women and Contrabands [escaped slaves]; the Cotton buying attracts many men here and often large fortunes are made in a short time. Men from St. Louis, Cincinnati, Baltimore and so forth are here with large Stocks of Goods and making money fast.

We were assigned to General Smith's Division but when we arrived here, General Morgan of Ohio (of Cumberland Gap notoriety)[27] ascertained that Colonel French was commanding the Regiment and, Colonel French having been a Lieutenant under him in Mexico, insisted upon having us transferred to his Division, to which General Sherman consented.[28] We are now in Morgans Division and yesterday in the reorganization the General gave us the position of honor as the 1st Regiment in the 1st (advance) Brigade. We had two Brigade Drills and I am proud to say our Regiment done splendit and [I] certainly feel good since I done nearly all the Battalion Drilling our Regiment had.

I find myself very well known among our Ohio Officers and have already many good friends. The noble animal presented to me in Chicago and beautiful rigging and mounting from you are attracting attention and I am as well mounted as any officer in this Army, no General excepted. Our Brigade consists of 120th Ohio Volunteers, 118th Illinois, 69th Indiana, and 22nd Kentucky, and Brigade Commander is Colonel Sheldon of 42nd Ohio (Garfield's Regiment), a very amiable Gentleman and represented as a fine

---

27. George Washington Morgan attended but did not graduate from West Point. He served in the Texas and Mexican Wars. A strong Democrat, he practiced law in the 1850s at Mount Vernon, Ohio. Earlier in the Civil War, he commanded at both the capture and the evacuation of Cumberland Gap, Tennessee. GB, 333–35; Boatner, *Civil War Dictionary*, 213.

28. William Tecumseh Sherman (1820–91), a graduate of West Point and an able but often controversial leader. He was the brother of Sen. John Sherman and of Col. Charles Taylor Sherman, mentioned previously. Under Ulysses S. Grant, he commanded the troops then being collected at Memphis as part of the Thirteenth Corps for the expedition against Vicksburg. Boatner, *Civil War Dictionary*, 194, 750–51.

officer.[29] He called on me this morning and we had a very pleasant talk. General Morgan is from Mount Vernon, Knox County, Ohio, a good man and feels very much interested in our good opinion of him as he comes so near our neighborhood. It doesn't hurt.[30] We are ordered to be ready for land or water by the very latest at the 17th instant, 3 days yet, cutting us down in tents and transportation which means I think an expedition on Vicksburg. Well, we are ready for it; our boys are keen for a fight. As for myself I dont care; if it comes I am ready, if not I shant make a fuss about it. A. Ruhman is well; he sleeps in my tent every night. He is doing duty regular, makes a good soldier but he will "not fight". He says, "I don't mind being a soldier but I don't want to fight."[31] When the time comes I shall manage to have him out of the fight. I will fix it so as to send him honorably to the rear on an errant for me; that is, if really any fight appears imminent; if only prospective I will let him sweat a little; he is a very good boy. The relation between me and my fellow officers is most happy. Colo-

---

29. Lionel A. Sheldon, born in New York, was raised in Lorain County, Ohio, where he became a lawyer. Having been active in the prewar militia, he helped raise troops for the Civil War and finally became second in command in the Forty-second Ohio, the regiment in which Col. James A. Garfield first began to win national repute. An effective administrator, Colonel Sheldon was brevetted brigadier general in 1865 and subsequently was a Republican office-holder in Louisiana and New Mexico. F. H. Mason, *The Forty-Second Ohio Infantry, A History of the Organization and Service of That Regiment in the War of the Rebellion with Biographical Sketches of Its Field Officers and a Full Roster of the Regiment* (Cleveland: Cobb, Andrews and Co., 1876), 21–27; Boatner, *Civil War Dictionary*, 738.

30. Sentence originally in German.

31. Quoted words originally in German. Abraham Ruhman was an eighteen-year-old private in Company K. Roster 8:271. He was probably the Prussian-born son of Rebecca Ruhman of Canton, Ohio. U.S. Census, 1860, manuscript returns for Stark County, Ohio, 149. He was Jewish. Simon Wolf, *The American Jew as Patriot, Soldier and Citizen* (Philadelphia: Levy-type Co., 1895), 336.

nel French is a Gentleman of the first Water, a true and trusty friend and a splendit officer. Major Beekman a very clever fellow, the Adjutand gay and happy and the Quarter Master who is already promoted to Brigade Quarter Master like a Brother to me. All the Company officers are vying with each other to please me and the men I could not wish any better.[32] I would very much like to see Esther and her little daughter; give them my love. I am expecting to come to Ohio in May if I live and then will see you all and if we wont have a gay time its because we dont know how. . . .

As Spiegel indicated in the previous letter, Memphis was a center for cotton buying. Wartime shortages of this Southern product had driven up both its price and the profits to be made on it. Since much of the supply came from across the enemy lines, those Union officers who were not personally profiting from the trade grew bitter as they saw the return flow of supplies into the Confederacy. Despite the involvement of many native Americans in cotton buying, some critics influenced by the antiforeignism which had mounted in the previous decade singled out the Jews as the main malefactors. The most conspicuous manifestation of such anti-Semitism was General Order Number 11 issued on December 17, 1862 by Gen. Ulysses S. Grant. In it, Grant ordered Jews "as a class" expelled from his department, which included parts of Tennessee, Kentucky, and Mississippi. The order resulted in hardship to several Jews and in protests from the Jewish community in the North. Under Lincoln's orders, Grant on January 4, 1863 hastily revoked the order, which he had occasion to regret in his post war political career. The order had not been enforced in Memphis and, as the following letters reveal, Spiegel was afloat on the Mississippi during most of its effective period. Nothing in Spiegel's letters indicates knowledge of the order by their writer, who was at that time probably the highest-ranking Jewish officer in

---

32. One of the 120th's captains said Spiegel was "a gentleman in the social circle, and as a military officer has the universal admiration of the whole regiment." Letter of G. P. Emrich, dated Dec. 17, 1862, in *Wooster Republican*, Jan. 1, 1863.

the Department of the Tennessee. Indeed, he expressed growing admiration for his general. His cousin Simon Wolf later helped defend Grant against charges of anti-Semitism.[33]

Camp Oliver near Memphis Ten.
Dec 17/62

My dear dear Wife!

I just returned with my Regiment from the Brigade Drill Ground, a beautiful level piece of ground and one of the most loveliest of days, the sunrays just warm enough to make one feel comfortable without even a Coat on and in short one felt like the tropical clime was just the clime for one to be happy. Everything went off so pleasantly; my boys performed so beautiful. Colonel French, who is so very kind

---

33. For a description of trading at Memphis at this time, see Jeffrey N. Lash, "Stephen Augustus Hurlbut, A Military and Diplomatic Politician, 1815–1882" (Ph.D. diss., Kent State University, 1980), 162–72. Grant's General Order 11 read as follows: "The Jews, as a class violating every regulation of trade established by the Treasury Department and also department orders, are hereby expelled from the department within twenty-four hours from the receipt of this order. Post commanders will see that all of this class of people be furnished passes and required to leave, and any one returning after such notification will be arrested and held in confinement until an opportunity occurs of sending them out as prisoners, unless furnished with permit from headquarters. No passes will be given these people to visit headquarters for the purpose of making personal application for trade permits." OR, vol. 17, pt. 2, 424. Various hypotheses have been proposed to explain Grant's issuance of Order 11. One is that Grant's father, Jesse, had made a deal with some cotton dealers from Cincinnati who happened to be Jewish. For a share of the potential profits, Jesse Grant purportedly brought these men to his son's headquarters and sought to obtain permits to trade in cotton. General Grant, who had felt for some time that the cotton traders were interfering with the war effort, wrongly believed that all such were Jews and used "Jew" as a synonym for "cotton trader." Incensed when he learned that traders were manipulating his father, Ulysses S. Grant expelled his father's associates and then issued his infamous order. Bruce Catton, *Grant Moves South* (Boston: Little, Brown, 1960), 352–54. For more on this order, see John Y. Simon, ed., *The Papers of Ulysses S. Grant* (Carbondale: Southern Illinois Univ. Press, 1967– ), 7:50–56. For its enforcement and reactions to it, see Korn, *American Jewry and the Civil War*, 121–55 passim.

to me, has now for the last three days given me the chance to take out the Regiment, an opportunity for which I would not take a great deal, from the fact that I can take my boys right among 5 or 6 old Regiments, among them the bully 16th Ohio who drilled for the last 15 months under the great English Drillmaster Colonel De Courcy[34] and my boys say, "with Colonel Spiegel to drill us, we dont care a d——n for any of them," and really I dont. My boys are doing bully and I think when mounted on my "English Grayson" and everybody says "Charley" is full blooded, I am putting on "more than airs". Well well when everything went so nice, I told the Adjutand (the only one who assisted me today on drill), now if I can find a letter from home when we return and find all well, I shall be gay and happy, and as expected so I found it. Your sweet good letter of the 14th was waiting for me, after interval of 21 days, the one last before that was dated November 23.

Although your letter was not quite as cheerful as many a one that I have received from you, yet it was you out and out: the care, the love, the uneasiness, the scolder, the Comforter, the [illegible—possibly a variant of balebosteh = homemaker] and last but [not] least, the reassurance that I have a woman who is best, kindest and most loving of all women living. God bless you.

Now to your questions. When at Cairo I would gladly have come home but could not, without running the risk of being left behind and that I dit not dare to risk as I was in Command of the left Wing of the Regiment. How it came that I had the diareah I can only explain by the fact that I am a great water drinker and not being used to the River

---

34. Part of the Sixteenth Ohio was from Holmes County, hence Spiegel's mention of it. MF, Dec. 25, 1862. John Fitzroy de Courcy had been an English major and commanded a Turkish régiment in the Crimean War. Ella Lonn, *Foreigners in the Union Army and Navy* (New York: Greenwood, 1969, orig. pub. 1951), 283. Many American volunteers viewed him as an overly strict disciplinarian—according to one "a brave but not always judicious soldier of fortune." Mason, *Forty-Second Ohio,* 143.

Water I had to get used to it. As to my state of health now
I am better than ever, feel real well and can eat like a
Horse; the only trouble is that we have not got anything
very good and not a very good Cook even if we have anything. As for coming home before I get real sick, I intend
to do by all means whenever necessary. Your advice to quit
soldiering I know you do not mean, as I never before had
half so good a chance and I do really mean to rise to some
distinction in this Campayne if God spares my health and
there is nobody in this World who would feel prouder of it,
than my own dear Wife.

I am extremely sorry to know you all have suffered with
bad colds as it is very unpleasant in the winter and I am uneasy until I hear you announced all well again inasmuch as
cold always sits so hard on you. You must take the best of
care of yourself. How is dear Mosey now? Hope he is better. I knew there was something wrong when I had to wait
so long for a letter. Poor boy, he must have suffered much;
I am glad you give him Codliver Oil, as it is the best thing a
child can take; how does he like to take it? Hattie is commencing early with her teeth; she must be a fine child; God
bless her.

I am glad to hear Hamlin and Lizzie are good children.
I knew they would be as you always say, "they took after
me", "umbeshreea" [knock on wood]. I am happy to learn
you are satisfied; take things easy and I do not want you to
work very hard of course. I know Sarah dont want you to,
yet I know your disposition. Goodman wrote to me he gave
you a standing invitation to go to the Lectures this winter
and you had accepted like a good old friend. I want you to
go and also to the Theatre at least once a week, so that
when I come home I talk war and its incidents and you
Theatre and Lectures and then both of us about the children. I think it as little as Oncle Josey can do to take you to
theatre every once a week; he ought to feel proud to take a
Lieutenant Colonel's Wife and if he can not afford it, he
knows I will cheerfully refund. I want Elizabeth to go once
in a while. If she is a good girl and I know she is, I want

her to see something too. I hope my dear mother has ere
this returned; she will be a good deal of company; give her
my love and kiss her for me. I also had a very kind letter
from Chapman to day; he and the boys are well, but awfully
down on Colonel Voris as you see out of the letter of
Girty[35] I send you.

Colonel French is as true and kind to me as any man can
be. He does not do the least thing without consultation. If
all officers would feel that way to each other, the War
would soon be at an end. Major Beekman is the kindest of
men; he would kiss my big toe if I would let him at least
three times a day; it almost makes me sick of him. Quarter
Master Dean is now Brigade Quarter Master; I have no better friend in the World. You must not get tired of my long
long letters, when I commence I can scarcely quit. I could
write you almost a quire of complimentary acts and notices
our Regiment, myself and Horse, and Colonel received since
we came here. In doing this I might however appear a little
on the "bragerdocia Order" and I would rather wait until I
see you but suffice it to say it is as unexpected as it is agreeable. Only one thing I must say: when General Morgan and
Major General Sherman reviewed our Division, General
Morgan said to French and myself, "Gentlemen I heard
more compliments on your Regiment to day than on any
other in the Division" and General Sherman said before all
his staff and Officers "this 120th Regiment is the best new
Regiment I have yet seen in the field in regard to appearance, drill and discipline."

After several interruptions I quit there last night; my tent
is as usual the place to come, to ask questions, advice and sit
down. The consequence is this morning that I dit not get
my letter finished last night and in all probability it will
have to be cut short. Why? As usual and as it used to be on
the peninsula and all through my campayne that whenever I
get a letter from you after I had none for several days or

---

35. Capt. Alfred P. Girty, Company G, Sixty-seventh Ohio. Roster 5:604.

quite a while, that the arrival of such a letter is indicative of something will happen; so this time.

Though we had been ordered to leave on the 17th for the embarcation of an expedition for the Capture of Vicksburg yet the 17th past and we thought perhaps we go and perhaps we dont but with your letter came the Order to move this morning and now while I write, the Bustle of striking tents, packing and hurrah generally at this time 6 o'clock A.M. would at once convince any passer by that a busy day is expected. Now my dear Wife as to my going to Vicksburg, the Order of General Morgan and so forth, I will describe in a letter which I commenced and intend to finish on board the boat to Henry Greenebaum, but I mean simply to say, feel easy; this trip will do me good and good will come from it. The Tent comes down over my head; I must close.

God bless you and the children. Remember that I am engaged in an undertaking that if successful will do more to close the War than anything yet done.

Ever your
Loving
Marcus

As Spiegel indicated, Vicksburg in Mississippi was indeed an important target. The Lincoln administration had already instructed the army in Louisiana under Nathaniel P. Banks to operate against Port Hudson, Louisiana. As for Vicksburg, Lincoln had authorized a Democratic politician from Illinois, Maj. Gen. John A. McClernand, to recruit a force in the Old Northwest and lead a water-borne drive to take the rebel stronghold. Many of the troops sent to Memphis had originally been intended for McClernand's force. Grant would have preferred not to have had McClernand, whom he viewed as inept and a possible rival for command, but the administration instructed Grant to give McClernand immediate command of the force on the river. Because of broken communications, however, the expedition left Memphis under Sherman before McClernand arrived. With Spiegel aboard, it steamed downriver while McClernand tried to catch up. Meanwhile, Grant was commanding a coordinated thrust down the railroad through the center of Mississippi, threatening Vicksburg from the rear. Either his force or Sherman's would outnumber any army that the Confederates were likely to bring against them; between them they might easily force the evacuation of Vicksburg. Prospects seemed bright for sundering the Confederacy and reopening the Mississippi to Union navigation.[36]

> Head Quarters left Wing 120 O.V.I. on Board
> U.S.S. Key West No. 2 afloat on the Mis. River
> between Helena and Gaines Landing
> Dec. 21/1862

My dear Brother Moses![37]

I have just returned from the Hurricane Deck where I witnessed the getting loose from the Shore at Helena [Arkansas], and superintented the falling in the Column of the Fleet at Regular Order of my gay little Steamer Key West No. 2 which with five Companies of the gallant 120th comfortably quartered on her, I have the honor to command. When I arrived in my State Room and commenced taking off my boots I looked at my watch and found it to be only half past eight P.M., too early to go to sleep, so I concluded to put on my slippers and enjoy my hour between this and bed time by writing to you, my true and trusty friend, thinking that perhaps this being Sunday Evening and out of business you might perchance be sitting in your happy family circle and forsooth talk about me and if so our thoughts might meet and embrace each other; a comfort which we may perhaps be deprived of for some time to come, but let us trust in our heavenly father and hope for the best. While I write the boat shakes awful but if we do not get a shell or two through our Ladies Cabin I think my writing may be with a little care intelligible, but if that little accident should happen it might make me <u>rather</u> nervous and spoil my handsome stenography.

---

36. Hattaway and Jones, *How the North Won*, 293–94, 300–301; Catton, *Grant Moves South*, 324–40.

37. To his cousin Moses Joseph, Uniontown, Ohio.

I have, if my memory serves me right, in my last letter from Memphis given you a graphic description of my situation which if I have told you at all, I am satisfied that [I] have said, so far as Colonel, Brigadier and Division General is concerned, I could not be situated better. They are truly all my friends and any of them will go as far to please me as any superior officer ever dit for an inferior, in fact it seems to be their constant studdey to do something that I would like. Colonel French is in command of the right wing on board Steamer Jesse K. Bell and our Brigadier with his staff are on board of her. They sent for me this afternoon while we lay coaling and I had to take supper and, amid negro singing and dancing, guitar playing, smoking and dancing, joking and laughing, we whiled away a merry time until the signal gun rang through the air, which reminded us that the Flagship was leaving and we were to follow and then they coaxed me the hardest kind to stay over night and join my command in the morning. But they didn't know that I left my Major behind very drunk, and he was totally incompetent to issue even the simplest order; a serious problem of our dear Major which is very harmful to him since he unfortunately understands very little in his most beautiful sobriety, "à la militaire", but he is a rather pleasant, nice fellow who would kiss my big toe three times a day if I gave him the opportunity.[38]

As for this Department, I must say that I am not much impressed with its order, discipline, nor soldiery bearing of the Soldier. I am sorry to say we find many Regiments out here utterly demoralized, who, instead of being able to pride themselves of being Soldiers in the Great and glorious cause of the Union and for the Constitution, can boast of being a debauched set of ruffians and many of them might be termed a perfectly lawless set of robbers and thieves. My God, what will become of such men after the War is over? Oh for a McClellan in every Department that could go on

---

38. Entire sentence, except "à la militaire," originally in German.

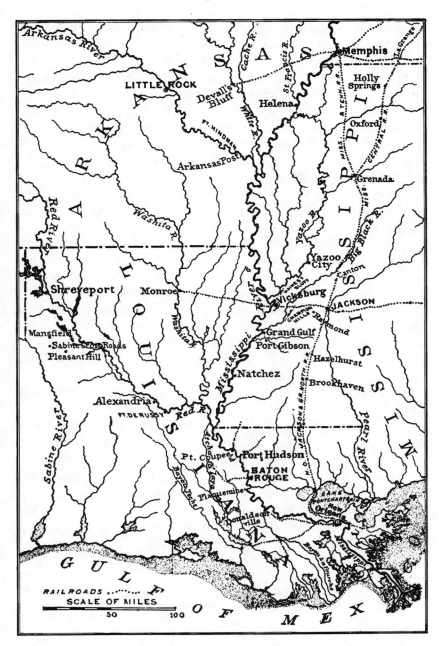

Mississippi Valley Region (from *Battles and Leaders of the Civil War*)

undisturbed by a jealous set of abolitionists and while he would soon end the war we could after it is over boast of having had a civilized mode of war fare.

Speaking of McClellan reminds me of the facts that the last news we had was that Burnsides was agoing to have a fight and somehow, I do not know why, but knowing as I think I do that part of the army I am ever since apprehensive.[39] I am almost affeared to say it, but it just seems to me that Burnsides or any other General in Command of that Army would get whipped, except McClellan. May be you will laugh at me, but Moses I think I have sufficient knowledge of military to justify me in saying that McClellan is the only man for that Army and ere this War is over I think the whole Country will have to acknowledge it, in spite of all evil and malignant opposition of a jealous and rodden hearted abolition crew, who are using all their efforts to influence the President who I really think is an honest man if let alone. Enough of this dark picture and let us hope Burnsides may be successful or may ere this have driven the Rebels from the Rappahannock and Mattaponie and every other Anie[40] and may ere this have Richmond; he made a good General under McClellan.

Now Mosey you must allow me to run a little tonight as I am all alone in the Ladies Cabin and nothing but the regular puffs of the steam out of the pipe and the regular working up and down and back and forth of the Machinery of the boat is all I have for Company. Officers and men are in the Arms of Morphis and I feel like letting my thoughts run as they will, knowing they go to a friend, where the foolish part will be overlooked. By the way, they may be the last I ever will have an opportunity to send to you. I trust and pray they may not, but the fortunes of War are as

---

39. Ambrose E. Burnside had replaced McClellan in command of the Army of the Potomac. Spiegel's fears were justified. Even before this letter was written, Burnside had in fact already been defeated at Fredericksburg. GB, 57–58.

40. Spiegel refers to the rivers generally of northern Virginia.

[those] of the outside world, very uncertain only a little more so, but let us hope, pray and trust that God in his infinite Mercy may, as He has often before, protect and deliver me from all harm, for I have really much to live for. Yet I mean to do my duty and my whole duty and if my poor life will be any benefit and assistance in ending this long and unfortunate Struggle in favor of our glorious Union, God knows I will gladly give it. Oh my dear Moses it would do your Soul good to see a fleet of over 100 Vessels besides the Gunboats on the father of waters. The Vessels filled with Uncle Sams boys, gay, happy and cheerful, all ready to meet danger and do battle for the good old Flag. Oh yes, by the way, I have not yet told you where we are going to and what for, but I enclose you a copy of General Order 13 issued by our brave Division General which will explain itself.[41] By the heading you will see where we belong and by reading you will see where we are going and what we mean to do. And I will only say that the 120th and your humble servant, mean to do their full share if we get a chance. It will no doubt be hot and bloody work. The expedition consists of about 40,000 men under General Sherman (a Brother to Senator John Sherman and also [to] Colonel Sherman of Mansfield)[42] and a fleet of Gunboats in command of Rear Admiral Porter.[43] I think that force should take Vicksburg and clear the Mississippi River to New Orleans and I think they will. About an hour before I left Memphis I made the acquaintance of a Son of Loeb Herrnsheim, a brother to the one that married "Cheuley"

41. This order of Gen. George W. Morgan dated Dec. 19, 1862, announced that the expedition's mission was the reopening of the Mississippi and "planting the Stars and Stripes upon the stubborn rebel fortress of Vicksburg." Morgan exhorted his men to bravery. Copy in Soman Coll.

42. Besides William Tecumseh and John Sherman, he refers to Col. Charles Taylor Sherman, who commanded Camp Mansfield. The size of Sherman's expedition was actually about 32,000 men. Boatner, *Civil War Dictionary*, 153.

43. David Dixon Porter commanded the Mississippi Squadron as an acting Rear Admiral. Boatner, *Civil War Dictionary*, 661.

von Gundersheim and also Charley Schloss, a brother in law
to Esther.[44] They as well as myself felt most d——n sorry
that we dit not meet before. We met under singular circumstances.

After I had my people in the boat, I walked along the
riverbank and saw a Yehudah and his wife. I remembered
the Sabbath and decided to have a kosher lunch. So, as my
friend and his wife came closer, I said, "Happy Sabbath,
dear people," frightening the gentleman and probably his
wife, being offered "Happy Sabbath" by a man in uniform
with sword, spurs, and so forth and so forth. I asked where
one could eat a kosher lunch. The gentleman said I could
go with him, or to Mr. Levy who was holding a Jewish
Boarding house. I went to Levy and found him and about
30 Jews very surprised when I asked if I could have a Chanukah lunch (my friend at the river bank told me Sabbath
Chanukah). But when I sat at the table and Levy took a
good look at me he said, "I think the face looks familiar"
and when I told him my name he said, "Dear God, a son of
Rabbi Mosche of Abenheim, a Lieutenant Colonel." I was
surprised and discovered soon that he was a son of Loeb
Herrnsheim. Carl Schloss is married to Levy's niece. We
went to visit him and he was very busy and I promised to
return in the evening and stay overnight but unfortunately
the departure signal was given an hour earlier and I had to
miss a pleasure I would have very much enjoyed and I am
convinced it would have been very stimulating for both of
us.[45]

Just now the Signal of danger sounded. I must go and see
what it meant. Supposed Guerillas in the Woods on shore

44. Spiegel originally wrote "they as" to begin the next sentence before
deciding to add the words after "Schloss."

45. The preceding paragraph was originally in German and Yiddish. The
Memphis Jews mentioned have not been identified. There are several Levys
listed in the United States Census of Memphis in 1860. References elsewhere
in the Spiegel letters make it likely that "Esther" lived in the vicinity of
Uniontown, Ohio.

and the whole fleet anchored. It is awful dark and I do not believe we will make any demonstrations to night. The Gunboats are plying up and down and I think they can attend to any thing ordinary for to night.

With this interruption it is getting late and I must bring my long Epistle to a close. Now Moses let me tell you write often and do not wait for me, for many times weeks may pass in a campayne like this that I may not have a chance to write to you, but at any time will it give me undescribable happiness to hear from you, my more than Brother. . . .

> On board U.S.S. Key West
> afloat 220 miles below Memphis
> Dec. 22 1862

My dear dear good wife and children!

. . . Nothing of any importance has occurred, except the burning of 2 plantations which is a daily occurrence. Whenever any boat is fired into from shore by Guerillas they land, take what they find fit to use, and burn the neighborhood. This is my Order "Should you be fired into by any person on shore, land, clean out all opposition, take such property as you think of any value to the Government of the United States and burn the neighboring houses, barns and so forth." Now this may be necessary and may be just but I declare I can not see it; for instance many good and true Union men may live along the River and some malicious Guerillas happening to know of the Fleet coming may congregate on this or that ones property and fire into the boat. The man, the widow or the orphans who may perchance live in that neighborhood will have to suffer, while the guilty Guerillas long before the boat lands will be safe out of reach, miles away on their Horses, laughing at the mischief they have done. Such is the justice of War and such may be necessary but such would surely not be my mode of warfare; yet if I get fired into I shall do as directed. But my opinion is that such acts of violence in my humble opinion, have a great tendency of demoralizing the Army and creating an ungovernable spirit of violence, while on the other hand it scarcely if ever strikes "the guilty".

We are hailed by darkies in the most cheering spirit and great manifestation of joy. The poor devils frequently by signs, gestures and so forth imploringly ask to be taken out of bondage. That seems hard to see and not to comply; yet if all the agitation had never been and those poor and unfortunate men been left in their once happy state of carelessness, there is no question but they would have been more benefit to humanity in a social, philanthropic and humane Auspice but as it is, it seems hard to deny a privilege to <u>be free</u>. Yet when on the other hand you see thousands of the Contrabands pulled away in the same manner from their masters, in a miserable and starving and filthy condition, then in a spirit of philantrophy you will say, better be in slavery than such freedom as I can give you. . . .

On the same, boat, wooding at Millikens Landing
20 miles from Vicksburg on
Christmas Morning

My dear!

They say we have a few moments time to finish a letter and mail it. I would say to you that I am getting better and heartier every day, I never felt better. The weather is splendit, I enclose you a flower plucked in the woods this morning; every thing is growing nicely.

I was this morning shown the plan of operation; I will give it to you in short. We are to land somewheres near the Yazoo River, reduce Fort Haines in the Yazoo.[46] Grant will join us somewhere between the Yazoo and Black Rivers. General Banks will come up from New Orleans with his expedition and Grant, Sherman, Banks and Admiral Porter with the Gunboats will jointly operate together.

I saw the maps and everything and think there can be no doubt of success. It is a gigantic movement and if only the

---

46. By "Fort Haines," Spiegel means Confederate fortifications at Haynes Bluff on the Yazoo. From the Yazoo it might be possible to take Vicksburg from the north or east. For a map of these operations, see OR Atlas, pl. 37, no. 4.

junctions are properly and successfully made, we must be victorious. Dont say nothing about this. In 32 days I had one letter from you. How do you think I am to stand it? Are you well?

I wish I knew it.

The weather is like June and July at home; everything growing delightfully.

Good Bye. God bless You and the Children and all the friends.

Your true and loving,
Marcus

Hd. Qrs. left Wing 120th O.V.I. Str. Key West No. 2
Dec 26/62
9 miles up Yazzoo River Mis.[47]

My dear dear Wife!

It is with much pleasure and gratification that I again sit in my Cabin after a day of unusual Excitement and have the pleasure of writing to you my love. This morning we left the Mis. River right at the mouth of the Yazzoo and slowly & cautiously made our way up this River for 9 miles   We are now I believe some 10 miles from Vicksburg. To day after we landed a small Rebel force attempted to trouble us and we were ordered out & if ever I felt proud in my life I do this night. Everything turned out during the Excitement just to please me. When I recieved the Order to get out the Regt. & form a line-o-Battle right in front of a piece of Woods where heavy firing was going on, I thought I would let Col French who was quite unwell and in bed, have all the rest I could and get the Regiment out before I would call him.

While I told the Adjutand to have the Captains bring out the Companies, I told Johny[48] to bring Charley from the boat and I wish you could have seen him come up the Bank Snorting dancing & pawing a fair representative of a "War

---

47. This letter is reproduced verbatim.
48. An unidentified servant.

Horse" and as soon as I had him out & got on him I felt as
easy and safe as I never dit before at times of battle. By this
time the Comp came & the gunboats & Batteries comenced
playing furiously Infantry was going it at a very rapid rate
in front of us and the Boys came out & formed like Veterans not a bit Excited   Every man to his place & perfectly
cool. Well well the Rebels retired and our Regt dit not get a
shot, Enough is known to Everybody that the 120th will do
to bet on.

Col French is just what I Expected as cool where the Bullets whistle as he is in a parlor he can not be scared nor excited

But to morrow is the great day, to morrow Vicksburg is
to be taken and we are to perform a great part I just saw
the plan.

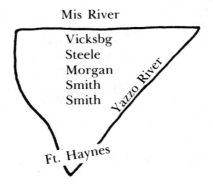

Steeles Division is to march directly on Vicksburg, our Divi-
sion to his imediate Right to engage the forces & forts,
Smiths to our Right, while A. J. Smiths as a faint is to try
and reduce Fort Haynes about 5 miles from here on the
Yazzoo River.[49] The Original Plan was for us to wait untill
Banks comes from New Orleans & Grant from Grenada
[Mississippi], but Sherman wants the Glory alone, I hope to
God we may be successfull. Whatever my part may be I am
satisfied it will [be] performed that neither you nor any of

---

49. Sherman's division commanders, in addition to Morgan and A. J.
Smith, were Morgan L. Smith and Frederick Steele. Boatner, *Civil War Dictionary*, 153.

my Children will ever have to be ashamed off (it is to hot in here to write) and I trust and pray to my heavenly father that in his infinite mercy he may grant me the privilege in telling you of this important event for many days & Years to come.

God bless you and the Children. Remember me to all the friends and since to morrow bids fair to be a bussy day let me go to Bed & have sweet dreams of my dear once at home and I feel that all will be right with me, in fact I know it. Your ever true & loving husband

Marcus

As Spiegel surmised in the preceding letter, Sherman's ambition and possibly his desire to take Vicksburg before the arrival of McClernand might have influenced his decision to attack at once. On the other hand, an attack was in line with his original instructions from Grant and might be successful if Vicksburg were as lightly held as he and Grant had expected. What Sherman did not fully comprehend— and it made the crucial difference—was that the Confederates had forced Grant to retreat by destroying his main supply base. Thus, far from having to draw troops from Vicksburg to oppose Grant, the Confederates were able continually to strengthen the force facing Sherman. Even at the end, Sherman's army still outnumbered them but the terrain wiped out the advantage. As Spiegel explains in the following letters, the Union army had to advance through swamps and woods obstructed by bayous and a lake. The Northerners could approach the fortified bluffs at only a few points commanded by the Confederates' increasingly numerous cannons. In such circumstances, this battle of Chickasaw Bluffs, the first for Spiegel and the 120th, might well have been their last.[50]

---

50. Hattaway and Jones, *How the North Won*, 311–13; Catton, *Grant Moves South*, 342–43. To oppose Sherman's 30,720 troops, the Confederates had about 6,000 when he landed, 13,792 by the conclusion of the major fighting, and 25,000 before Sherman finally withdrew. Boatner, *Civil War Dictionary*, 153–54. In his own justification for his actions, Sherman claimed that Grant's orders were to attack as soon as practicable and that he had done so, expecting every minute to hear the guns of Grant and Banks. "Remarks" in Rachel Sherman Thorndike, ed., *The Sherman Letters, Correspondence Between General and Senator Sherman from 1837 to 1891* (New York: Scribner's, 1894), 172–73. For another account with maps of the battle of Chickasaw Bluffs, see Earl J. Hess, ed., *A German in the Yankee Fatherland: The Civil War Letters of Henry A. Kircher* (Kent, Oh.: Kent State Univ. Press, 1983), 40–52.

Str. J.K. Bell opposite Millikens Bend La.
Jan. 3/63

My dear dear good Wife!

May the year 63 be of at least as happy a turn to you as 62 and as much happier as God in his infinite mercy may bestow in answer to the sincere and warm prayers to Him offered for your welfare by your true and devoted Husband.  M. M.

By the dispensations of kind providence I am again permitted to sit in my little State Room and write to you my good Wife and speak of my dear Children and kind friends even after going through a week of fearful dangers, hardships and privations more fearful than I ever dit before. Yea where death, danger and destruction raged at a furious Rate, good God permitted me to come out with out a scratch and with none greater loss than the one Spur off my Boot, my Rubber overcoat, my Pants and Coat tore to pieces in the Woods and by the Rabbid advance and excitement.

However before I go any further I would simply say if your duties in Chicago are so important or Paper, Pen and Ink so scarce that you can write so few letters and so very short ones to me, I think you had better go to Ohio, for to night our Regiment received 1100 letters and but one from you to me and that written on half sheet, and half of that only from you. Although it was short and sweet, yet I am selfish; I want longer ones and more of it. I have written [i.e., read] that one three times and will now stop and read it again. I have done so and God bless you; it is good but I want more of it. Yet I feel happy, whereas had I not received that I would to night feel miserable.

Before I commence with a description of the Siege of Vicksburg, I will say I am happy and glad to hear of my Hamlin being such a good Son and learning so well and looking so hearty. I hope by the time I come home he can read the newspaper for his Pa in German and English. I heard to day Lizzie dit not speak out very loud in school; she must speak out well and be a very good young Lady so

her Pa can feel proud of her. I am glad Mosey takes his
Hair [*sic*] Oil so good, that is just the thing he wants. Oh
but it would do my soul good to see little Hattie sit on the
floor. Sarah's short Letters do me much pleasure; I hope
she will continue. Why dont Michael write?

We calculate as soon as we are settled again to elect
Brother Joseph as Sutler of our Regiment.[51] Has he gone
in the Oyster Business for good? While I am writing, the
Ladies Cabin is occupied by the Steamboat Officers playing
Poker, by our Officers reading the Papers of the 22nd in
which we got the news of Burnsides defeat;[52] just as I always said, nobody but McClellan can lead that Army and every other General will get whipped. A Heavy Thunder
Storm is raging outside, the shocks of Thunder fairly shake
the earth and more especially our boat and the rain is
furious. Oh how I pity the poor boys who have to stand
picket. While I write I can hear the moaning of the sick
which grieves me much. We have about 50 on my boat and
about 200 in the whole regiment; 3 or 4 on my boat are
dangerous, 15 very sick and the balance unfit for duty, but
such is soldiering and such is the contract we entered into.
Now for the fight. I have already given you a short sketch
of what happened Friday the 26th and if I am not mistaken
I think I said in that letter that the conduct of the boys of
the 120th would do to bet on and I can now say I was perfectly right and their conduct for a new Regiment was never
surpassed. Now my dear, if in this short description the all
important I comes frequent and as also what I done, you
must not think me egotistical for I know that that very par-

---

51. By act of Congress, one sutler for each volunteer regiment was "to be
selected by the commissioned officers of such regiment." The sutler was
allowed to sell specified articles at fixed prices to the troops, receiving in
return a lien on up to one sixth of their pay. No officer was to "be interested
in any way" in the sutler's business. As Spiegel's letters suggest, all of these
provisions were often loosely construed: OR, ser. 3, vol. 1, 938–40.

52. Battle of Fredericksburg, Dec. 13, 1862. Boatner, *Civil War Dictionary*,
313.

ticular part of it is as much interest to you than anything else done and as it is not considered for publication it can matter but little to anybody else.

Saturday [December 27] at 10 o'clock A.M. we were ordered to form close Column of Division and advance through a thicket. After throwing out skirmishers to cover our front and flanks, we done so and advanced. (I should here say, that in my last I have told you that I had seen the Plan of Battle and that it was a gigantic movement. In that plan it was intended that not much of anything would be done before some kind of a junction with Banks and Grant could be quite or nearly made but in the meantime it is reported that the news came that General McClernand of Illinois was coming here to take Command, when General Sherman shall have said, "he would go to H——l or Vicksburg before McClernand came." Whether this be so or not, that much I do know; in less than 48 hours from the time the first plan of operation was shown, a second one was ordered changing into an immediate attack by our Army all along the line from Gaines [Haynes] Bluffs, a high fort on the Yazoo River, to Vicksburg, a distance I think of 7 miles.) Very well, as I said we advanced through the thicket and, while there to our right and somewhat in advance cannonading was briskly going on. We steadily advanced until we emerged into an open field when we deployed from close Column to battle line. By this time fighting on our right of both Musketry and Artillery was briskly and lively progressing, but only occasionally a stray shell or wandering musket ball would whizz apast our lines. We were ordered to halt and lay flat on the ground. After laying thus for about 1/2 to 3/4 of an hour our folks (Lindsays Brigade[53] of Morgans Division) succeeded to drive the Enemy and we had to follow up as reserve to Lindsays Brigade. Another stand was made and fighting commenced livelier than be-

---

53. Col. Daniel W. Lindsey's Second Brigade, Third Division. OR, vol. 17, pt. 1, 646.

fore. This continued until about an hour before night when it ceased for a short time. Then and then only dit I do anything that I would not repeat now nor hereafter. I invited several brother Officers to go up with me and see the battle field. Two of them accepted and we started to see the dead and wounded. When we came to the left of our lines we inquired for the dead and wounded, and learned they had all been carried to a white house beyond the Line. Now to get there we had to cross a high Levee or Road. Along side, (that is) behind its right Bank, lay our Soldiers with their Muskets on the Levee; on the left of it was a kind of narrow Sloughs and opposite the slough, brush and that brush full of Rebel Soldiers and if anybody has an idea that going along a Road which is probably as long as from Henry Liebensteins Store to the Sherman House,[54] on each side loaded Muskets (though the Rebels you could not see), now if anybody thinks there is any fun in this let him try it. As I gave the invitation I dit not want to back out. I tipped my hat, gave Charley the full depth of my spurs and galloped through, ran the Gauntlet safe though a many honestly meant bullet came whizzing past me and my friends, who came along way behind as they could not catch up with Charley. After seeing and learning our loss was about 60 in killed and wounded, we galloped back and arrived safely with our boys. I almost wished I had stayed out, for when I came out I found out that I was detailed as Brigade Officer of the day. I took a piece of cold meat and bread, all I had since morning, jumped on my horse to post my pickets; a job which took me until after 11 o'clock to post them and carry the countersign to them. When I returned I took my Blanket, wrapped myself up and laid myself besides my horse and slept like a prince until 3 o'clock A.M. [on December 28] when we were called up and stand to Arms. At about 5 A.M. the ball opened by heavy Artillery fire, where I was the night before looking at the wounded, as well as to

---

54. Locations in Chicago.

our left (by Steele's Division), on our right by A. J. Smiths Division, and on our extreme right by Morgan L. Smith Division.

. . . the day advanced and the Sun seemed plowing its way through a dense fog which prevented anyone of seeing his neighbor two feet from him which of course led me to the conclusion that the awful and terrific Cannonading and Musketry not far from us on our right must be a great deal of it at random. As the fog cleared away we could plainly see the smoke of the Enemies Cannons along the Hill Side and across the Bayou, playing away with a rapidity as though they meant to annihilate us but were as vigorously answered by our own. Our forces on our right slowly advanced, driving the Enemy by inches who in turn contested every inch of ground with a valor worthy of a better cause, which from the advantage of their position made it hot work for us. As our advance slowly gained Ground we followed, being the 2nd Brigade from the reserve, and when by 9 o'clock we were just in front of a Gap coming from the Hills where the Enemies Guns played furiously, we were Ordered (our Regiment) to return and file left along the bayou, take a position on the 2nd Slough from which General Morgan said, I expect a flank attack; hold that position at all hazard until relieved or reinforced. We started and as we came out of Range of the Shells and out of immediate danger, I am not ashamed to own it, I felt for the time relieved. We made our point, deployed the Regiment and laid down on the ground. Just then our boys came with a dinner of which we heartily participated, not having had any breakfast.

We had scarcely done dinner when an Aid galloped up, ordering us to the right where the ground had been stubbornly contested and the fight severely raging.

The Bugle sounded the Assembly and my boys came in. We threw them into close column by Companies and marched to Scene of Action.

As we came near, the roaring of cannon and the crackling of small Arms was furious yea terrific. The Shells busted all

around us and many times they came within a very near
space of Charley and myself.

General Morgan ordered us to advance to the Battery and
when ordered to advance, dash furiously forward. As we
came to our Battery it was perfectly awful; there were 20 of
our Cannons playing with all the velocity they could and at
the same time drawing all the artillery fire of the Enemy.

Our Regiment was in an awful place, and for a new Regiment behaved like Veterans and just then I became perfectly enraptured. I could talk to every one, knew the danger, but the fear of death had perfectly left me. I dashed
back and forward, felt proud and was admired and ap-
plauded. Just then General Morgan came; he had talked to
Colonel French and came and shook hands with me and
said, "Colonel Spiegel, I am proud of you as an Ohioan; I
feel doubly proud of so gallant an officer. One more charge
for the good Flag and the day is ours." By that time he told
me shortly to go back a little piece, cross the Bayou and get
up the Hill in the Woods and charge on the Rebel Battery,
while De Courcys Brigade should charge to the right. We
started and when we got across the Bayou we had to go up
a straight Bank, very high, which Charley made handsomely
until he got almost up the Bank to where the top bended
outward and he could not make it. I jumped off, got a root,
swang myself around it, taking Charley by the rein; he
made a leap and cleared the Thicket when on top and as
soon as our Regiment reached up we formed in line, advanced our Skirmishers and cautiously felt our way, not
knowing how soon we were to meet the hordes of the
Enemy. The 49th Indiana had in the meantime come up
and formed on our right. After advancing some 300 yards
we halted and Colonel French and I advanced by ourself to
ascertain their position using my glass. We probably only
crept 100 yards when we discovered the Rebel flag, proudly
waving on their rampart; we returned and advanced our
Command. When our skirmishers came to the point probably where Colonel and I had previously been, they saw the
Rebels and commenced firing; the Rebels answered with

vigor. We then promptly advanced our whole line as also the 49th Indiana. The stray Bullets then came thick and as soon as we felt the Bullets we called in the Skirmishers and went at them, Oh the noise [of] that firing I remember as long as I live. Our boys stood bully and I soon saw the Rebs were shooting too high. We fired and loaded and fired and yelled until we drove them into their Rifle pits and kept them there, thinking every minute DeCourcy would charge from below and we would have to from above but thank God he dit not charge and we dit not have to.[55] After a fire of two hours and a half, we were relieved by General Frank Blair and his Brigade and we retired with the loss of 1 Officer and 11 men killed and 61 wounded in the 2 Regiments. Nothing particular during the night, only cold and nothing to eat and very tired. Thus ends Sunday.

Monday Morning [December 29] opened like Sunday with heavy Cannonading; the Rebels having planted many new Batteries during the night shelled us vehemently and it became necessary to change our position. At 9 O'clock A.M. we were ordered to advance our Regiment to the main Bayou and support our folks laying a Pontoon Bridge across the Bayou. Our Boys advanced steadily though under a fearful fire and a many shell as well as Bullet whizzed apast me that day. We knew that, by a signal from our Division which was the firing of 12 Guns in rapid succession, a crossing or attack should be made along our whole line. The Signal was given and all the Batteries opened. Such a firing I never be-

---

55. Spiegel if anything understates the difficulties of the situation. His brigade commander, Col. Lionel A. Sheldon, reported that the 120th, advancing amid obstacles, became crowded in the center. He continued, "receiving a sharp fire from the enemy for the first time (it being a new regiment) some confusion occurred; but through the aid of the faithful and well-directed efforts of Colonel French and Lieutenant-Colonel Spiegel order was soon restored and the regiment put into position." He concluded with praise of the unit and its officers. OR, vol. 17, pt. 1, 644. According to one of Spiegel's officers, Capt. Benjamin Eason of Company E, "Just before we opened our fire, I heard Lieut. Col. Speigel [sic] command 'Give em h——l, boys! aim right at 'em; G—d d—— em!'" *Wooster Democrat*, Jan. 29, 1863.

fore heard; it was awful, terrific, grand and fearful and from where we was engaged we could see DeCourcy's Brigade make the charge they were to make the day before, assisted by Blairs brigade which were to do the day before, but in vain. Such were the preparations that in less than an hour both were repulsed with a loss of killed wounded and missing of no less than 2500 men.[56] We were kept under fire until 9 P.M. At 4 P.M. it commenced raining in consequence of the heavy artillery fire; when at 9 P.M. all but 100 men of our Regiment were relieved, we found our wet Beds about half mile in the rear. The boys had scarcely laid an hour when the Rebels commenced shelling us and having the Range of our Camp, we had to change Quarters; a thing we had to do twice after that, having three men wounded by two shells. The rain poured down all night; at about 3 o'clock A.M. I took sick and was very sick all night.

Tuesday [December 30], nothing of importance. The Rebels gave us privilege to come over to their line and bury or take out our dead. I went over too and I only wished I had not. Oh such horrid sights; they had stripped all our dead of everything but their Shirt and Drawyers. Tuesday night we were ordered to take possession of the rifle Pits in front and protect a Battery by throwing 5 Companies in the Breastworks which our men threw up during the night; very little firing. Wednesday occasional shelling but everybody asked, how can we ever do anything with our force against their Gibraltar, as every morning showed us new Batteries which they had been planting. Before I close I must relate a little incident that happened to me on Wednesday [Decem-

---

56. In ordering the attack by the brigades of De Courcy and Blair, Sherman reportedly said, "Tell Morgan to give the signal for the assault, we will lose 5,000 men before we take Vicksburg, and may as well lose them here as anywhere else." Hattaway and Jones, *How the Union Won*, 313. Casualties in the two brigades actually totaled 1,327. Boatner, *Civil War Dictionary*, 154. For a graphic account of the assault parallel to Spiegel's but from the viewpoint of those involved (and with a useful map), see Mason, *Forty-Second Ohio*, 160–65.

ber 31]. I was sitting greasing my Boots which through the rain and mud had got stiff. I sat on a log where I slept the night before, when a shell came and buried itself within three feet of me but fortunately did not explode; had it exploded I [*sic*] would have made bad work of me. Wednesday night 4 Companies were of our Regiment ordered as advance Picket. Our Pickets was out and it was about 8 o'clock when we received Orders to "evacuate". Then came the tug of War, the Anxiety of mind was awful. Our Regiment was to be the last Regiment to leave and our Pickets the last of all. I was fearful that if the Rebels would hear our Artillery move, they would make an awful attack on us by shell and otherwise and then we to be the last. But they were not wide awake and without relating the whole, let it be enough to know that when [our] detachment of 4 Companies of Picket arrived safely on the other Side of the slough my heart expanded and my praises went fleuently to the Everliving God. We were the last to leave the field but arrived safe at our Boat.

Our Expedition is a grand failure. It is said we are now going up the Arkansas River; if we do I hope we are more successful.

You must be satisfied with this imperfect description.

Our Regiment and Colonel French and myself earned a name of which we and our children can be proud.

I have such a bad place to write.

God bless you,
Your loving and ever true
Marcus

finished Jany 6/63
Charley is not very well.

As Spiegel indicates, the Union repulse had been complete. The embarrassed Sherman had contemplated an attempt to outflank the Confederate entrenchments but, failing to achieve surprise, abandoned the effort. When he withdrew his forces, he had suffered 1,776 casualties, almost nine to one compared to the enemy. Yet Spiegel's regiment had escaped with relatively minor losses. Because the 120th

Ohio had not participated in the major assault, none of its men had died and only twenty were wounded.[57] On January 2, 1863, as the expedition returned to the mouth of the Yazoo, Gen. John A. McClernand finally caught up with what he still considered to be his independent Army of the Mississippi. While he continued to hope to capture Vicksburg, he felt the need for cooperation by Grant's army. Until that could be obtained, he accepted a suggestion by Sherman that they attempt to capture Fort Hindman on the Arkansas River. From this Confederate fort on the site of the old Arkansas Post, gunboats could descend to menace Union transports on the Mississippi.[58]

Steamer Key West No. 2<br>January 8, 1863

Landed at the mouth of White River, Ark.

My dear dear Wife and Children!

Your very kind, loving and encouraging Letter of the 27th December with several others enclosed came to hand last night and I really think it done me more good than all the medicine on the Boat could have done; it was a good old letter and gave me much comfort. I have written you a long letter giving you a partial history of the fights at Vicksburg. They were awful terrific but I suppose that ere this you have it in the Papers. It may be that the Papers will be very careful about it but whatever they say it was an awful defeat and with sick, wounded, killed and missing, I doubt not but that to day we have 8000 men less for duty than the day we left Memphis and Helena. The only successful part of the operation was the evacuation of our forces and whether the success can be attributed to the skill of our Generals or the neglect of the Rebels is a matter to be decided by the historian hereafter. I forgot to say to you that Charley in consequence of hard riding and exposure [was sick] but is better now. I also forgot to say to you, that in the morning after the evacuation, the Rebels left their forts

---

57. Boatner, *Civil War Dictionary*, 154; OR, vol. 17, pt. 1, 625.
58. Catton, *Grant Moves South*, 344; Thorndike, ed., *Sherman Letters*, 183.

and in mass came marching down on us and I stood in the
Pilot House of the boat and must say as they advanced
stately and determined they looked well; their skirmishers in
advance who, as an Officer on a Horse raised his sword, all
fired and fell flat on the ground. Their Column advanced
within 150 yards of our boats and fired; our boys fired
[back]. The bullets came as thick as hail around me as I
walked over the hurricane deck making my boys lay down
and fire; one entered the Chimney just by my head, but
they got the worst of the bargain, for our Gunboats quietly
went up the River a piece and got to the Rear of them and
opened a destructive fire on them and their loss must have
been awful. We are now to go up White River to make an
attack on some fortifications they have up the River; I hope
we will be more successful this time.

General McClernand commands now our forces called
"The Army of the Mississippi". General Sherman commands
the right Wing and our old Division Commander General
Morgan the left Wing, both under McClernand.

General Osterhouse, a German, commands our Division; I
hope he is as good a man as Morgan.[59] Our Division belongs to the left Wing and Ranks as 2nd Division, 1st Army
Corps, Army of the Mississippi.

Men, Officers, who 60 days ago were in favor of fighting
till the last man and the last Dollar is gone, are now in
favor of Compromise strongly on most any terms; I never

59. Peter Joseph Osterhaus was born in 1823 in Rhenish Prussia. After
some military education, he became involved in the Revolution of 1848 and
had to flee to the United States, eventually settling in St. Louis. Earlier in the
Civil War, he had fought at the battles of Wilson's Creek and Pea Ridge. In
1862, he was a brigadier general but his subsequent services in Sherman's
Georgia and Carolina campaigns won him a major general's commission.
After the war, he served in the consular service and died in Germany in 1917
just before his native and adopted countries went to war with each other. He
was clearly one of the more able and distinguished foreign-born Union officers. That Spiegel was able to win his respect, as indicated below, is strong
evidence of Spiegel's military ability. GB, 352–53; Lonn, *Foreigners in the
Union Army and Navy*, 182–84.

in my life saw such a change in an Army in two weeks. Why we had 11 Resignations offered in our Regiment in one day and in every Regiment it is the same. Every body is getting tired of the War. As for me my feelings have not changed. I can stand prosperity and also adversity. [No conclusion.]

> Steamer Key West No. 2
> Landed on the Arkansas Shore
> January 9/63

My dear dear good wife and children!

As I intend to keep you posted on the military movements of the "Army of the Mississippi" of which your "Liedge Lord" is an humble member I will again write to you a few lines. We left the Mississippi River this morning about 10 o'clock, started up White River until we came up to what is called the "Cut off" about 8 miles up. We left White River, turned into the "Cut off" and came from that into the Arkansas River, traveled up Arkansas River some 50 [miles] from the mouth where we landed for the night. A few miles from here is a Rebel fort called Arkansas Post, renowned as one of the oldest Indian trading Posts in the Union, also a great [place] for Emmerson Bennetts "Bar [Bear] Hunting" Stories.[60] Coming up the River we received more friendly demonstrations from Arkansan Gals and Women than we received since we left Covington. At one place, there had about 10 Girls congregated on Horseback with Huge Dogs and Hounds with them, waving their Red and White Hankerchiefs and screaming "hurrah for the Yankees". From their appearance as near as [I] could judge them as they stood on the River bank, I think they were out hunting.

About one hour ago I was shown the "plan of operation" for to morrow in taking the Rebel fort. I think the plan is a good one, but I am <u>very slightly</u> thinking the Rebels have a

---

60. Emerson Bennett (1822–1905) was a prolific writer of frontier adventure tales published in popular periodicals and dime novels. Ralph L. Rush, "Bennett, Emerson," in DAB, 2:193–94.

"plan of operations" also and it may in many instances not precisely agree with that of our commanding General.

Now as I always like to be on record with you about these matters, I would now like to give you my opinion about to morrows operations. In the first place let me say to you that although I know but little of the new Commander of this Army, General McClernand, I have nevertheless most implicit confidence in him, while for our old Commander [Sherman] I had nothing but contempt and detestation and looked upon him as utterly unfit to lead an Army. Now our folks judge the Rebel force at Arkansas Post 8000 men, pretty well fortified with many guns, among them two of 120 pounds Caliber, and the plan is to surround them. Now my opinion is that if the Rebs have but 8000 men, they will not stand fight to 25,000 or 30,000 men with a fleet of Gunboats to the front of them but they will evacuate to night and if they stand fight it is evident to me that our General has been wrongly informed and he will not surround them as easy as he thought he would, but we will find another Vicksburg but at the same time I feel almost certain we take this point. So far as I am concerned, I feel gay and cheerful to night and am ready for another fight, but for the sake of the 250 sick and wounded boys and daily increasing and crowded on the floor of the Cabins of our two Boats, I would wish this Expedition would soon settle down somewhere and let the poor boys off.

This thing of being crowded up on a boat for 3 weeks and only being taking off for the purpose of exposure of a fight is not a very enviable situation.

I expect to give you a long and elaborate history of our operations at Arkansas Post. To night it rains; the climate is not near as warm as Vicksburg; the air more refreshing. Out of our 860 men we took from Memphis 3 weeks ago, we can not take over 350 in the fight tomorrow; yet most of them would be all right in a few days on "dry Land" to gather strength. My love to the children and all. God bless you all.

Marcus

Ark. Post Jan 12/63

The flag of the 120th was the first planted on the Rebel Fort.

My dear dear Wife!

Yesterday was a glorious day. We met the enemy and fought them terribly and took them beautifully; some 7000 of them with every thing.

I am too excited to say much. Our Regiment was the first to charge and we charged up to the ditch of the powerful fort and then fought them under the most terrific fire for an hour and half.

I presume I have no 2 inches on my whole body where the bullets dit not whizz apass me; Oh, my God, such perfect hailing of bullets and busting of shells, Cannon balls tearing up the ground big enough to use the holes for graves of its unfortunate Victims. Oh it is perfectly awe inspiring, terrific, yet most delightfully glorious to get out unhurt.

For the first time my dear Wife let me say to you I believe I am a Soldier, every inch; no fear, perfectly cool, yet snap enough to encourage my men. I will only say, I have a good Horse (a perfect match to Barcrofts Horse); I call him Linny. Have a good saddle and bridle and a splendid Colts Revolver.

Our boys had 68 horses which we turned over.

You have no Idea of the amount of wagons, horses, mules, ammunition, clothing, commissary stores, cannons and rifles our folks took.

It is decidedly the most glorious and complete victory of the War, with out much loss.

Everything came out perfectly as planned by General McClernand.

We can not be too thankful to God for his kind preservation; my heart is too full.

Ever your true and loving husband,
Marcus

Our loss is 6 killed, 27 wounded and 9 missing
My love to my dear children and all.

The Union forces had indeed captured a formidable position. The fortification on the site of Arkansas Post was a massive earthwork built on thirty-foot bluffs commanding an ox-bow bend of the Arkansas River. But with nearly 30,000 men, McClernand's attackers greatly outnumbered some 5,000 defenders. While Federal troops which had been landed on the night of January 9 invested the fort on the land side, the Union fleet prepared for a simultaneous attack from the river. In the decisive operation on January 11, General Osterhaus and Colonel Sheldon shared Spiegel's satisfaction over the charge of the 120th. As Spiegel suggests, French, Spiegel, and their men were pinned down under enemy fire just under the fort's wall. Not until firing ceased as the Confederates began to surrender to landing parties from the fleet was it possible for the 120th's color bearer to reach the wall. Other units also claimed to have been first on the fort but their brigade commander, Sheldon, publicly proclaimed that the honor belonged to the 120th Ohio. Union losses were about 1,061; Confederate about 4,900, mostly captured. The official return for the 120th's casualties on January 11 showed 2 killed, 9 wounded and 11 captured or missing.[61]

Ark. Post Jany 15/63

My dear dear Wife!

Today I had set apart for doing some tall corresponding, but alas for the ruined anticipations, we have marching Orders. On the 13th we pitched tents and scarcely were they up when it commenced raining and rained and stormed like fury until [unfinished]

Board Jesse K. Bell Jan 16/63

Yesterday in all the Storm we had to strike tents and get on board the boats. We are much more crowded than we have ever been from the fact that we had to take all the stuff and so forth of the Rebs as well as themselves and yet there will probably be $200,000.00 worth of Goods our folks can not take.

Whenever a mail comes, everybody gets letters except I and I often could shed tears that I get so few letters from

---

61. Boatner, *Civil War Dictionary*, 24–25; Mason, *Forty-Second Ohio*, 171; OR, vol. 17, pt. 1, 717, 745–48, 750; *Wooster Democrat*, Mar. 5, 1863.

you, but I have said so much about it that I will say no more.

I expect we go to Vicksburg again. The mail leaves and I <u>must</u> close.

My love to all. I feel much better than I have for two weeks past and if it were not for a thundering big bile on my leg I would feel bully.

Could you not write, say one letter every week?

Ever, ever your true and sincerely
loving husband,
Marcus

I expect Joseph here soon.[62]

---

62. His brother was coming to become regimental sutler.

CHAPTER SEVEN

# "No Peace Democrat"

Spiegel and his regiment confronted a crisis in the peaceful weeks which followed Chickasaw Bluffs and Arkansas Post. Returning to the vicinity of Vicksburg, they settled into what amounted to winter quarters in a swamp. Inability to take Vicksburg and defeats elsewhere frustrated all of them; political acts of the national administration angered many of them; illnesses weakened and killed a large number of them. Diarrhea and dysentery, those great, ignoble butchers, took a heavy toll of the unseasoned troops. On many days the 120th Ohio buried four or five dead. The living, still eating the regular army ration without fresh vegetables, deteriorated in condition. Enlisted men grumbled, officers tried to resign, and all became increasingly demoralized.

Democrats among them often blamed leaders and their policies for the dire situation. Like Spiegel, many bemoaned the removal of McClellan. Even more resented President Lincoln's Emancipation Proclamation of January 1, 1863.[1] They had enlisted to save the Union, not to free a race which many of them viewed as inferior and unfit for liberty. In letters and newspapers, they had read the Ohio Democrats' charges that emancipation would result in the "Africanization" of the state through an influx of ex-slaves, charges which had helped the Democrats to carry the 1862 Ohio election. By early 1863, Estill, editor of Millersburg's Democratic organ, was opposing the "further prosecution" of "this war, as now conducted" which he termed "a JOHN BROWN raid on an extended scale."[2]

------

1. One of the better descriptions of the ill health and poor morale in the 120th Ohio is a letter by an unnamed writer dated Young's Point, Louisiana, Feb. 27, 1863, in the *Wooster Democrat*, Mar. 26, 1863. See also ibid., Mar. 5, 19, 1863; *Ashland Times*, Feb. 19, 1863; MR, Mar. 12, 1863. The winter of 1862–63 was the low point for morale throughout the Union army. Bell Irvin Wiley, *The Life of Billy Yank*, book one of *The Commom Soldier in the Civil War* (New York: Grosset and Dunlap, n.d.; orig. pub. 1951), 277–82.

2. Cardinal, "Democratic Party of Ohio and the Civil War," 107, 118–21; MF, Feb. 5, 1863.

Among the prewar Republicans in the 120th Ohio, some joined in the opposition to emancipation and even wrote complaints to Ohio Democratic newspapers. Republican editors, unwilling to publish such letters, claimed that they were the result of Democratic propaganda. They blamed Democratic civilians for writing and publishing "all manner of falsehoods," telling the soldiers "this is a *negro war*, a *damned Abolition war*, a *disgrace for a white man to be in*, & c." And they blamed Democratic officers for permitting the circulation of such propaganda. The Republicans did not neglect to remind their readers that both French and Spiegel were Democrats.[3]

As for Spiegel, he surely continued to be a Democrat and a friend of Democrats. One of his intimates in the Regiment, Q.M. Ezra V. Dean, was a particularly outspoken defender of the Democracy and critic of President Lincoln. On the steamboat between Ohio and Memphis, Spiegel had presided over an officers' meeting to discuss proposals to end the war, a meeting in which most Democrats voiced continued support for Stephen A. Douglas's popular sovereignty plan to let the territories decide whether they would have slavery while Republicans opposed its spread. Spiegel also maintained ties with the even more extreme Democrat who edited the *Farmer* of Millersburg. On December 14, 1862, having learned that James A. Estill's brother, junior editor, and fellow Mason, Eliphaz, had died as a result of a buggy accident, Spiegel sent his condolences. "The ways of kind Providence," he philosophized, "though apparently hard on many occasions, are always just, and we must teach our hearts to humble submission." He then went on to give his usual flattering references to Holmes County soldiers serving in the vicinity. However, this was his last letter published in his old friend's newspaper.[4]

One reason that Spiegel's letters no longer appeared in the *Farmer* may have been a growing difference in attitude. As the following letters show, Spiegel still favored McClellan and opposed abolitionism. But he also quickly indicated that he did not share Estill's opposition to continuing the war, even if it became one against slavery. Like many in the armies of both sides, he was coming to share a sort of

---

3. *Wooster Republican*, Feb. 19, 1863; *Wooster Democrat*, Mar. 5, 19, 1863; the quotation is from the *Ashland Times*, Mar. 12, 1863.

4. *Wooster Democrat*, Mar. 5, 1863; MF, Nov. 27, Dec. 25, 1862, with Spiegel's letter in the latter issue; MR, Nov. 20, 1862.

soldier culture which subordinated issues to victory. This simple approach would help him and the 120th Ohio to survive the morale crises of the late winter of 1862–63.


                                              Youngs Point La Jany 25/63
My dear dear much beloved and kind Wife, never, I think, dit man love and increase in love towards his good and kind wife more than I do.

To day I received your letter of the 8th instant in which you trembled in suspense and fear to learn of my fate but thank God ere this you have learned of my welfare. Since that day I have passed through dangers, perils, privations and hardships, and yet with the help of kind Providence I am still hale, whole and hearty and though I have seen many of my comrades deposited in the soil of Mississippi, Arkansas and Louisiana, many others down with raging and fearful diseases, many of them mutilated and amputated, yet the Almighty has kindly preserved me and let us pray that he may bless and preserve me so that I can after I am through with war, live in happiness and peace and con-sumate the happiness and peace for those whom I love so much. May God bless and preserve you for me and grant me the happiness to assist you, my lovely wife, in raising our dear Children in the fear of God and estimation of the world. I do want to see you all, my dear, and I am sick of the war and I do want to get out; I do not fight or want to fight for Lincoln's Negro proclamation one day longer than I can help, yet I do not [wish] after having undergone all the hardship, danger and privation of 15 months campayne and then leave it in disgrace. As soon as I can get out hon-orable I will and that may be in the Spring or before or not until after. The great trouble is to get a resignation accepted. I can not get the Doctors certificate of disability, for I am too well, and such a certificate is the only thing that discharges a man. I must await a favorable opportunity and do not expect to get out much before summer. Colonel French having the bloody Flux [dysentery] is making prepa-

rations to get out of the service and if so I think I will have
to be Colonel a little while before I get out. Keep up courage, trust in God and all will be right. I think very much of
getting out before the wool season, yet I am not certain
whether it will do me any good.

Well, I feel good and am in good spirits, though camped
in a muddy cornfield a half mile from the great Mississippi
River which is raising 3 feet every 24 hours and almost up
to the levee; yet I feel gay and well for I got a letter from
home assuring me all is well at home and that is all I need
to make me feel well. My diareheah is all cured and I can
eat like a horse. Let me first explain to you, what a fine
Supper we had this evening and you will agree with me,
that for men 1600 miles from home and dead broke we
fare fine. Bill of fare: Coffee and Tea. Buiskuits and soft
Bread, Chicken Pot Pie (rather heavy), fried Pork, Irish
Potatoes boiled and sweet Potatoes baked, Apple pie, stewed
Apples and canned Peaches and so forth; is that not grand?
A Yehudah from Memphis whose name I do not know sent
me yesterday by Captain Conyer a Box full of things and
we live fine. Now about the situation. We are situated on
the Louisiana side of the Mississippi River, 3 miles above
Vicksburg; our forces extending down about 2 miles below
Vicksburg. Our folks are endeavoring to finish the Canal
which General Butler commenced last summer in order to
change the direction of the Mississippi River so as to Leave
Vicksburg in the dry.[5] Whether they succeed or not I am
unable to say, but I think that for the present there will be
no immediate fight; how soon it commences I know not.
Our Regiment, which left Memphis with about 850 men and

---

5. Brig. Gen. Thomas Williams actually had begun the attempt to dig a
ditch across the narrow peninsula or bend opposite Vicksburg. Gen. Ulysses
S. Grant, who was superceding McClernand in command of the operations
against Vicksburg, adopted the canal and several other experiments at
bypassing the Confederate fortress. High water and local flooding defeated
the canal project—though after the war the river did cut through the bend.
Catton, *Grant Moves South*, 376–78, 380, 527.

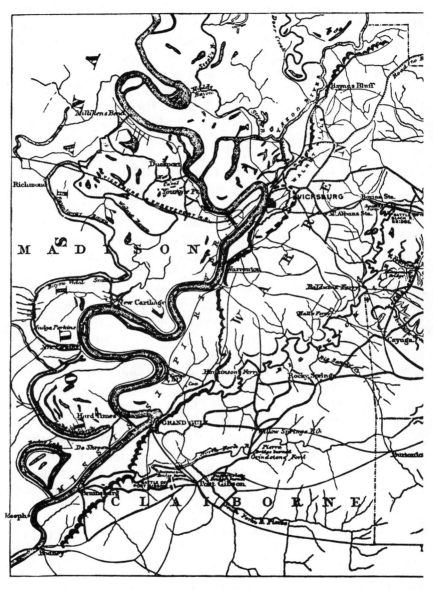

Vicksburg Campaign (from *Battles and Leaders of the Civil War*)

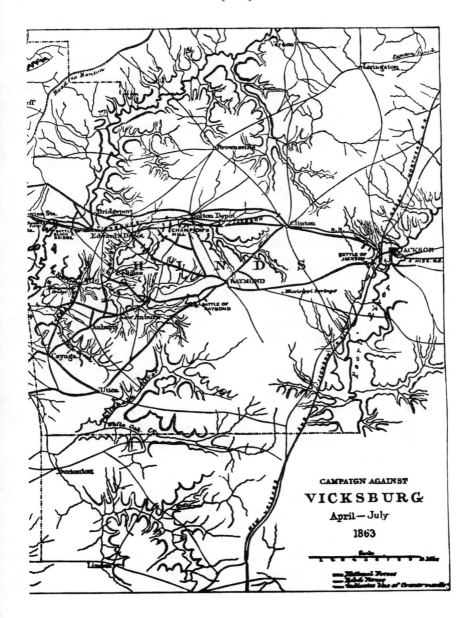

CAMPAIGN AGAINST
VICKSBURG
April—July
1863

33 officers 5 weeks ago, has now about 350 men and 11
officers for duty and they disheartened and discouraged. In
fact the whole Army is discouraged and very much dissatisfied in consequence of Lincoln's Proclamation which fell
like a thunderbolt among the troops. I am sorry the old
man forgot himself and took such bad advice.

Michael, I wish you could be here and see the workings
and hear the Soldiers talk.[6]

My new Horse is improving; he is not as gay as Charley
which is all right again, but he is a very good and stout
horse and I think he will make a splendid horse for family
use. If God spares my health I mean to bring Charley and
Linnah home with me and they will make us a gay team
and let us trust that many may be the happy rides you and
I will take with my gay and furious War Horses and they
are so gentle that you can handle either. . . .

To Michael and Sarah I can not be too thankful for the
many acts of kindness shown daily to my dear family, may
God bless them. To day I got A. Ruhman a place as Clerk
on General Osterhauses Staff; he feels bully. I am looking
daily for Joseph or a letter from him. I hope he will come;
if he does it will pay. If he has not started yet and intends
to come, tell him not to bring over $1000 worth of stock
and after that is sold, he will have made enough to buy
from the profit. My love to all the friends. If we stay here
and have a little time I will write to all. Good night, God
bless and preserve you.

Ever your true and loving husband
Marcus

Youngs Point La January 29/63

My dear kind and good wife!

. . . Your kind letters always give me new life and it always
seems to me shortly after I get a letter from you "soldiering
is not so hart after all". We are still camped at the same

---

6. Michael Greenebaum, Spiegel's cousin and brother-in-law, was an ardent Republican.

place described to you in my letter a few days ago, but a
great change has taken place since; the rainy and disagreeable weather changed day before yesterday in a cold afternoon and a clear cold night and yesterday morn the sun
came out bright and clear and we had a splendit day and to
day likewise, most magnificent weather, delightful indeed.
The mud is fast drying off and the boys are beginning to
feel better and many of those who have not been too far
gone are beginning to feel the benificent and wholesome influence of a warm Southern Sun in January.

The greatest enemy we have at present to content with is
the Mississippi River. It is rising fast and in many places is
overflowing its banks; should it continue to rise and soften
or break any part of the Levee, we would have to skedadle
or swim. The Canal built for the purpose of changing the
Mississippi River is filling up but not washing very fast and
I doubt very much it will ever change the course of the
"Father of Waters".

There have been several changes of late in our Army.
Our Brigade is now commanded by Brigadier General
Vandever of Iowa[7] in place of Colonel Sheldon relieved.
Our new Brigadier seems a very clever fellow; I am not
much acquainted with him yet. Our old Brigadier Colonel
Sheldon, was a very clever fellow, would do anything and
everything for me but in a fight he was the very man to
select as an associate, for you would be sure of being out of
reach of the bullets, and yet not in all the Army could you
find a man bolder and more daring before and after a
fight, than our old Brigadier. He has gone back in honor to
his old Regiment the 42nd Ohio.

Our division is commanded by Brigadier General P. J.
Osterhaus, a German who is a Soldier and a Gentleman and
treats me with marked kindness and respect. Our Corps was
until to day commanded by acting Major General G. W.
Morgan of Knox County, Ohio, a splendid man and brave

---

7. William Vandever. GB, 523.

Soldier. He was a warm friend of mine and I am truly sorry
he asked to be relieved from command which was done to
day and Brigadier General A. J. Smith succeeds him in the
Comand. Morgan is quite unwell, but I think it is General
Sherman's fault that he leaves; he never could get justice
either for himself or his command.[8] Brigadier General A. J.
Smith is said to be a good Officer and a very clever fellow,
but to me the loss of Morgan is more unpleasant than anything I had since in the service; he was a true friend to me
and the whole Regiment and I could have had him do anything for me. When I called on him, he showed me as
much kindness as a brother and no matter who was with
him, he would take hold of me. . . .

Youngs Point La. Feby 2/63

My dear dear little Wife!

Your very good and encouraging favors of 24 and 25
mailed in same envelope with Joseph's letter came at noon
and I found them this evening. They gave me undescribable
happiness; I feel gay and happy and I would if I had an
appreciative audience cut up to night like in days of yore. I
am hale and hearty; everybody is complimenting me on my
returning good hearty look and with it the buyoncy of Spirit, for I was like many somewhat reduced by the awful exposure and indisposition but unlike most of men in the
Army I always keep cheerful and the consequence is that I
do not get down very low and [am] soon all right with a little rest. But as I have no one in my little lonely Tent except
Abraham Ruhman who is sick and I nurse him, I can not
cut up much. Abraham Ruhman, I had about a week ago
got him a very nice position as Clerk at General Osterhauses
Head Quarters, but he took sick two days after he was there
and three days ago I had him brought to my tent and since

---

8. Sherman blamed Morgan for alleged mishandling of his division at
Chickasaw Bluffs but Morgan's specific reason for resigning was his opposition to the use of black troops. He was a postwar Democratic congressman
from Ohio. GB, 334.

that he (of course being at my quarters) gets regular medical attendance and is improving. He has always been so
good and kind to me and being an old acquaintance I could
not see him among strangers while sick. Is that not right my
dear? He is doing well and I think in the course of a week
can return to duty. I think I have written to you that Johny
took sick at Arkansas Post and one or two days after the
fight I had to send him to Memphis Hospital, I do not
know how he is doing. We have a colored man who cooks
for our mess; he is a good cook and we live well, such as we
can get, and yet our boarding does not cost us $10 per
month each, while at the boats it cost $10.50 per week and
then we had very poor board.

You wanted to know how I got the new horse. Why my
boys captured 68 horses and I took one of them. It was after night and I dit not get as handsome a one as I would in
day time. He is a mate to Barcrofts horse, very gentle and a
splendit goer. Charley I told you has been very much under
the weather but is getting all right. He is the Horse of the
Army, as proud as Peacock and as safe as an old Family
Horse, and I can ride him right into the cannons mouth.

I also took a very good colored boy with me from Arkansas, about 15 years old, to wait on me but he is sick. I have
a great big fellow named Hiram attending my horses and
blacking my boots and I do the balance of my chores.

Many of the boys are getting better but it seems that
those who have been very weak, many of them are dying;
we buried 12 within the last three days. We have now nearly
500 men for duty and yet 300 sick. Since the 1st of January
we lost in killed, died and discharged 62, add to that the
losses of the month before in which the battle of Vicksburg
occurred and you will find our Regiment suffered very
much within the last 60 days, but I am in hopes we are getting better.

There is one Item of news I must give you but you need
not say anything in your letter to me about; that is you
need not mention of the part concerning Colonel French.

You know I told you in Mansfield if I could only succeed

in keeping from creating any jealousy I was all right. I have succeeded admirably. I have often kept Officers from sending letters to Papers in which they would insist in praising me very highly and have done all I could to prevent any feeling of that kind and I must truly say that Colonel French used me as well as ever I was used by any body in the world. Now to my Story. You know we have a German General commanding our Division consisting of three Brigades of Infantry, three Batteries of Artillery and a Squadron of Cavelery. That is General Osterhaus and you also know that generally I am not very much prepossessed in favor of any high Officials because they are Germans as I invariably look upon them as impracticable or big Reshoim [wicked ones] but contrary to my expectations in General Osterhaus I found a man free from any of those prejudices usual almost with German Officers and besides all this a Gentleman and an Officer who from the very first had treated me with much cordiality and Preferment. French often said to me "you are the Generals man"; "I am nowhere" and so forth and so forth, and I thought I could see something that he dit not like it much and I really avoided Osterhaus as much as I could.

The day General Morgan (of whom I spoke to you) left us, Colonel French went to see him and there met General Osterhaus. When he came home, he told me he would resign, he was sick of the war and so forth and so forth.

As we had both frequently spoke that way, I thought it was only talk and would blow over, but it seemed he insisted and told me I could assist him in getting it through, by talking to General Osterhaus. I told him I could do him no good with the General, he says "yes, you can I know it now; he thinks you are all the man in this Regiment, Brigade or Division". I told him I thought the General had treated me as he dit every Officer, but French said he knew better. He said: "As soon as I met him, he asked about you, said he knew the first time he met you at the Field before the Fort at Arkansas, you were a splendid Officer. In fact, says he, any man that sees you, would know at once you were a man

of military education and General Morgan said, yes indeed I
have noticed Colonel Spiegel often on the Field and he is a
gallant and noble Officer and Osterhaus talked all the time
about you and so forth and so forth."

Well, you see I was and am yet very sorry to see the Colonel resign but he would insist and I wrote his Resignation
for him. I saw the General and spoke to him about it and
he said, "Oh my dear Spiegel, that pleases me, very much. I
never liked him and still don't like him."[9] Now his resignation is in; whether it will pass or not I can not say, but one
thing I do know; Osterhaus will approve it; yet I doubt very
much that it will pass as it is not easy to get out of the service. I am pretty well satisfied it will not be accepted. The
Colonel was in about a half hour ago and he is sorry now
that it is in and I am really sorry too. He has been so very
kind to me, I would hate to loose him but I am pretty sure
we will not. I want you to stay in Chicago until Spring, say
1st of April or until after Pesach [Passover], and then you
go home. I hope ere this and am pretty sure Uncle Sam will
have paid us some money, so that I can furnish you. If I
can come all right; if not you go home and fix everything.
Build our arbor and so forth; fix the Grape vine, have a
supporter build in Arbor Style for the Grapes and fix
things, just as you want them so that when I come home
everything looks well, when the old weather beaten Warrior
returns to his friendly home. I am just of your Opinion that
if it from now on does not pay me I will leave it, as I have
done my duty fully. It pays me now clear of expense $160
to 170 per month and that is not so bad.[10]

I have written you my views in regard to getting out. It is
now nearly midnight and I must start on my rounds to the
Pickets. Wish you were here to take a ride with me if it
were not too awful stormy to night. Two of our Rams ran

---

9. This quotation was originally in German.

10. A lieutenant colonel's basic monthly pay and allowances totaled $170,
plus forage for two horses. Eaton, *Army Paymaster's Manual*, 127.

the Blockade at Vicksburg to day. They fired 76 shots at
one with their heavy guns, hit one of them eleven times but
hurt nothing nor no one.[11]

My love to my children, mother and all,

Ever your true and loving husband,
Marcus

Youngs Point La. Feby 9/63

My dear dear Wife!

I am in good Spirits, good health and good hopes. I can
not thank kind providence enough for the preservation of
my health and if only I would get more frequent assurances
of your good health and that of my dear good children I
would feel perfectly happy until I could feel happier and
that is at home with my little family. The water drove us
out of our nasty swampy place where we were camped before and we had to move a half mile up the river and fortunately got a much nicer and dryer Camp Ground.

We are still in "Status quo" before Vicksburg; the running
of the blockade occasionally by a Gunboat and the heavy
cannonading during the performance is all that changes the
daily routine of a dull camplife. News I can say but little;
only that my little darkie Jimmy died last night. He has
been sick a week and I had him well nursed which is different from what is generally done in this Army; when a nigger takes sick he is turned out to die and they do die by
scores and in all corners. I am all in ecstasy with the Idea of
seeing Brother Joseph and can scarcely wait for him; he will
make it pay and like it.

If he has not left send me some white Shirts and Paper
Collars to stand up. Did you ever receive the $5 I sent you?
I think the Paymaster will be here in a few days and then I
will send you some money.

---

11. The Union ironclad ram *Queen of the West* ran past the defenses of
Vicksburg in broad daylight. Unharmed, it proceeded to attack Confederate
shipping below Vicksburg. Long, *Civil War Day by Day,* 318.

I sent a nice double Barrel Shot Gun for Hamlin to Millersburg, sent it to Cohn. When Hamlin gets big he can go hunting.

Give my love to mother, Michael, Sarah, the children, Henry, Theresa and children and all the friends and kiss all my beloved children.

Ever your true and loving husband,<br>Marcus

To day I build me a nice fireplace in my tent and it draws splendid: it looks so much like ones home to see a fireplace. Weather warm; no rain for two days.

Youngs Point La. Feb. 17/63

My dear dear good Wife!

Yesterdays mail brought me your kind and rather in an offendedly rude [?] written letter in answer to one I wrote to Oncle Josey sometime ago complaining of you not writing enough.

If ever ever I said anything unpleasant or offensive to you, my kind wife, I most humbly ask your forgiveness and pardon.

It does make me feel so bad and so uneasy and cross, when the mail comes and brings everybody letters but me, that I say something very unkind but you know I can not mean anything unkind or unpleasant to you my good wife. After the battle of Arkansas Post when I felt in the highest glee we received three mails in one week and not one word or letter dit I get. Can you wonder at me being uneasy? I got so down in spirits that I was almost mad that I was so much complimented on my behavior and success but as soon as I heard from you I felt proud of it. Now my sweet wife you must forgive me and think that if I say anything at all not just right, it is in consequence of my jealous and undying love for you and my dear family. I am well and hearty and not for three years have I had so bully an appetite as for three weeks past.

The health of our Regiment is not improving any I am

sorry to say. We have only 350 men for duty; many of the "unfit for duty" would soon be all right if they only had a change of diet. Many die every day in this Army. The levee for three miles is almost one continual Graveyard of new Graves. Last night Captain Phelan of our Regiment died, a poor man, leaves a Wife and seven small children.[12] He as well as many other ones die simply because as soon as they get sick a little, they give way, become despondent and sure to die. Poor Phelan was one of my most ardent and warmest friends; he was a devout irish Catholic.

For the last 4 days it rained here continually day and night and it makes it very disagreeable but I have a new rubber overcoat and leggins presented to me by Captain Myers of our Regiment who resigned and gone home,[13] so that I can go out in the rain. I have thank God no complaint at present, neither Rhumatism nor Phthysic [throat or lung infection]. I never was better.

I have a very pleasant little house and here I describe it. I have two tents; one a Wall Tent and in the Rear closed on it a common or Wedge tent and, having opened the centre seam in the Rear wall of my Tent, it answers for folding doors to my common Tent. As you enter my tent, in the Corner stands a large table made out of Store Box, by taking out 3 sides and leaving three, ⊏▭⊐ then nailing a board right under the top which makes a shelve. On that table I am now writing to you. After passing the table on the right hand side, you would see a very nice big fireplace which I helped to build, I just took out one breadth of my Tent, about a yard wide and a yard and a quarter high, in which I keep a very good fire; although it is not cold, yet the inceassant rains make everything damp. After passing the fire place is a corner in which stands a Box containing my clothing and so forth and on which Abraham Ruhman is sitting, who is well again but still stops with me and in a

---

12. Patrick Phelan, the forty-two-year-old commander of Company H. Roster 8:263.

13. William G. Myers, Company G. Roster 8:260.

manner waits on me. He is a very good boy; I am trying to get him discharged. Then, comes the opening in my common tent. On the left hand side stands my cot, on which I rest my weary and virtuous body. Lately an old friend of mine and a warm one at that, Charles B. Flood the former editor of the "national Democrat" came down with a Steamer load of Sanitary Goods for the sick.[14] As soon as he found out I was here, he sent me a nice bed tick which I have filled with hay, two sheets, pillow slips, 1 pair Mittins, 2 woolen Shirts, Pin cushion, dried Apples and Peaches and Codfish and many other little things with his compliments, also a "schlafrock" [dressing gown], and since that he is continually trying to do me good by everybody; the same man you know that was so anxious I should be Census Agent.

I also have in my tent a nice arm chair and cane bottom chair and camp stool which make a very comfortable little Tent. I wish to God you could see it; I know you would enjoy it. In my little tent we have a keg of ale bought by our mess, my saddles, water bucket and so forth.

This week Captain Gordon,[15] General Osterhauses Adjutant General, called on me and brought Colonel Garrard commanding 1st Brigade[16] and his Aid de Camp, also Colonel A. Schwarz, Inspector General of 13th U.S. Army Corps, Lieutenant Caldwell Aid de Camp[17] and they spend

---

14. Flood's Democratic newspaper, published in Cleveland with patronage from the Buchanan administration, had opposed Stephen A. Douglas and supported John C. Breckinridge in 1860. Societies in several Ohio cities, including Cleveland, collected and forwarded supplies for soldiers. Roseboom, *Civil War Era*, 366, 441–42.

15. Probably William Augustus Gordon, who had served under Osterhaus in the Twelfth Missouri. Heitman, *Historical Register* 1:465.

16. Col. Theophilus Toulmin Garrard became brigadier general to rank from Nov. 29, 1862. GB, 168.

17. Probably Adolph Schwartz, formerly major of the Second Illinois Light Artillery and originally commander of a Missouri independent battery. Heitman, *Historical Register* 2:45; Amann, *Personnel of the Civil War* 2:157. Caldwell is unidentified.

quite a nice time at my quarters. This Colonel Schwarz is a splendid officer and a Son of General Schwarz in Baden.

That same day Major General McClernand rode through our Camp for inspection.[18] I made his acquaintance, asked him to alight which he did and came in and stopped with me quite a while, so you see I have very important visitors. Now you must not think that I am going round enjoying myself and acting fancy, but on the other hand if my conduct as an Officer and Gentlemen suits these men and they feel like seeking my acquaintance and use me very kind, I know you would not want me to refuse it. I forgot to say that I have a floor in my tent. I am daily waiting for Josey and everybody else is waiting. We will make it pay with the help of God and as soon as it has paid pretty well we will "leave the service". Now my dear girl I do not want you to worry yourself about me any more than you can help; our sweet baby will soon be a big Girl and then you can go round with Colonel Spiegel, you know.

You know you always was as handsome as any of them; you must try and keep so, keep up for my sake. You know how happy and proud it makes me feel to see my wife, the mother of my dear four children, look well. If you could only set on the saddle in my little tent and hear me tell the folks of my dear wife, I know you would smile if not laugh out hearty. There never was a man as proud of his wife and four children as Colonel Spiegel, in the world.

Hamlin's letter pleased me very much. I hope he can talk German well when I come home; I will write to him soon. My Lizzie ought soon to be able to write to her pa a few lines. I would very much like to see Moses in his new pants; he must not forget his pa. Little Hattie must be quite an institution with her two teeth. Oh but I would like to see her. Elizabeth must not feel discouraged. There are just as good

---

18. After Grant absorbed McClernand's forces into his Army of the Tennessee, McClernand remained at the head of what became the Thirteenth Corps, to which Spiegel's regiment belonged. Catton, *Grant Moves South* 376.

a Mac arells in the sea as ever have been caught and if it
isnt this Mac it will be another one, even if I have to throw
out the bait to catch one. . . .[19]

Young's Point La. Feb. 19/63.

My dear dear Wife,

So much excitement in camp this morning that I scarcely
know what to say. Colonel French and four other Officers
and a number of men leaving for their happy homes.
Though I would be a happy man indeed were I permitted
to leave for my Home, yet to leave as some do I would
rather wait awhile.

My lovely wife, Abraham Ruhman who I got discharged[20]
will call on you and tell you all all that I could write. He is a
good boy indeed and can give you much of interest. God
Bless you, my love and stand by you. I am hale and hearty
and will soon see you.

Your loving and true husband,<br>Marcus.

Head Quarters 120th O.V.I.<br>Youngs Point La Feby. 20/63

My dear dear lovely Wife!

Most likely ere this reaches you Abraham Ruhman, who
left here to day has been to see you and told you many
things concerning me which I am satisfied have interested
you. Yet though he has only left this morning with many
verbal messages of love to you from [me], yet I feel so happy and rather lonesome that I can not go to sleep without
conversing with you by means of paper and so forth. I miss
Colonel French this Evening; he has always been very kind
to me, in fact extremely so.

---

19. Apparently a play on the name of McCormick in whom Elizabeth had
been interested.

20. The surgeon's certificate of disability for Ruhman was dated Feb. 20,
1863. Roster 5: 271.

I have this day issued three long General Orders in relation to matters in the Regiment and two Special Orders.[21] I am determined to renovate and regenerate the Regiment; I can not stand to see men die from sheer inactivity and neglect. We had this morning 315 sick men reported and I am willing almost to bet my existence that in one week from to day there will not be 200 reported.

This Evening the Officers forwarded to the Governor a recommendation for my promotion endorsed by the Brigade Commander, General Osterhaus, General McClernand and Colonel Schwarz, the Inspector General of this Army.

I send you a copy of it.[22] I feel proud of such a document; it will be a fine piece of Literature for our family. I want you to show it to all my friends in Chicago; every one of my friends who had an Interest in the fine Horse they presented me I would more particularly like to see it. Ah old girl, dont you feel proud of your Soldier husband. . . .

---

21. Spiegel summarizes these orders in his next letter. His General Order 1, brief and to the point, stated that his first object would be "to reduce the sick list, and re-establish the health, efficiency and cheerfulness of the regiment." He concluded, "I know we can do it, and I am satisfied we will do it." MR, Apr. 2, 1863.

22. The copy, made "expressly for Mrs. Spiegel" by Sgt. Maj. Benjamin T. Jones, is in the Chicago Jewish Archives, photocopy in Soman Coll. In it, twenty-two staff and line officers of the 120th petitioned for Spiegel's promotion, citing his service and his "bravery, coolness and courage." Colonel Garrard, his brigade commander, characterized him as "a most excellent and worthy officer," with which General Osterhaus concurred, adding that Spiegel was "faithful & energetic" and "thoroughly acquainted with all the duties devolving upon a Regimental commander. . . ." McClernand strongly recommended immediate promotion and Inspector General Schwartz thought Spiegel "to be exactly the officer required to restore better discipline to that Regiment. . . ." An unnamed writer of a letter from the 120th dated Feb. 27, 1863, in reporting the officers' recommendation of Spiegel for promotion, called him "a true soldier and well worthy the position." Clearly suggesting attributes admired in Civil War officers, the writer noted Spiegel's attentiveness to the soldiers' wants and concluded, "one thing is certain he will never ask the men to go where he is not willing to lead." *Wooster Democrat,* Mar. 26, 1863.

As soon as the Regiment three days ago fell in my hands, I issued the most stringent Order for meals, diet, cleanliness and so forth that could be and I gave notice to the Officers that whatever Company was not by the 1st day of March perfectly free of lousyness and filth, the Tents, arms and accoutrements in good condition, such Company Officers I should report to the Head quarters of the Army to be dismissed the service for incompetency and I assure you, every one can see the effect; everything looks encouraging, live, and cheerfulness is returning and I am satisfied in less than one month a decided improvement will be visible.

Many of the Officers have resigned in our Regiment and I hope about 8 more will resign; they are good men but just as fit for military Officers as I am fit for a "Hebamme [Midwife] Fabermann". With good young and energetic Officers such as I will select, I will soon have a regiment second to none in the service in discipline as we now already are second to none in fighting.

I could almost see Hamlin open his large blue eyes and straighten himself when he told you about his puff he received from his teacher. He is all right; you know you always said he was Spiegel all over. Dont you think the Spiegels all right? My Lizzie must take good care while she has the chickenpocks so she wont catch cold and so that she can go to School soon and learn in order that she will be smart enough to wear that pretty dress I bring for her. She is perfectly right, it will be a Union Dress. Mosey's blue Pony will be forthcoming whenever he gets big enough. I would very much like to see the two pretty little teeth of my sweet little Hattie. As to her having black eyes and being able to say Pa, I do not feel like discouraging you, but ones wishes are frequently father to ones thoughts and believes.

My Horses and Horse fixings are all right, clothes with the exception of Handkerchiefs are all right, and I am all right. God bless you and all. Write often to your true and loving

Marcus

I am awaiting Josey with the greatest anxiety.

Dear esteemed Mother:

Don't worry about me. With God's help and your blessing everything will be alright. I hope your Jewish son [illegible] will give you much much joy and you don't have to worry about Brother Joseph when he comes. The Sutlers are in no danger at all, not more than if they were at home, and if it is God's will he will soon make enough money to visit you again very soon.

With greetings and kisses from your ever-loving son, Marcus.

Dear Brother-in-Law and Sister—

Today I was wishing from the bottom of my heart that Mich. were here so he could see his brother-in-law command his regiment as a colonel.

Good night, your Marcus.[24]

Youngs Point La. Feby 24/63

My dear good wife!

Your very kind and lovely letter of the 17th came to night and that it was congenial and pleasant as the "Sun of a lovely day in June" need not to be said. To hear that you are well, a description of my good and lovely children and the assurance of the well being of my dear Mother and friends is all it needs to make me feel a gay, bold and happy "Sodger boy".

I am really disappointed at the failure of being able to obtain the group of the faces of you and the children. I had secretly flattered myself to be surprised with just that very pleasure and I feel reluctant and chagrined to give it up. The conduct of little Hattie, so very unlady like, however convinces me that I ought to be at home, for it is really "shocking" for people of our standing: you an expectant Colonel's Wife spending the Winter by enjoying the pleasures and amusements of a large City and I an Officer in the United States Army, to have a daughter most nine months

---

24. The postscripts to other family members were originally in German.

old that acts so very unlike a "Young Lady" of Education and Accomplishment. The only consolation left me is that when I come home I must take Hattie especially in my care. Yet aside from all sport, I feel very much annoyed for I had made all calculations to have it.

I have written so much of late that there is scarcely anything left for me to say, for besides digging on the Canal, Breakfast, Dinner and Supper, Drill, Inspection and dress parade, there is nothing new, with the exception of my unceasing efforts to reduce the sicklist by encouraging the boys and making them clean and wash, and I am happy to say I am succeeding very well. I have it down from 315 to 255 in five days. Of the worst cases about 4 are dying in our Regiment every day; the Doctors think to night the balance will most all get well.[25]

I would just like if you could see the General and Special Orders I issued since taking command. I have to be strict in order to save the Regiment. I discharged all my darkies; they stole more from us than they earned. There is not a negro in our Regiment. Though thousands are idling about here, none of the Soldiers will have anything to do with them any more.[26] Do you remember a bright little drummer boy by the name of Lewis at Camp Mansfield?[27] If you dont, I bet Hamlin does. Well, he is a very handsome boy, a very genteel and smart boy, and looks and talks for all the world like Hamlin will at his age (12 years). He was always a

---

25. Others also noted the decreasing sick list. Spiegel's sergeant major associated it at least in part with the men's improving spirits. "Homesickness kills more than all diseases in the army," he maintained. "The homesick soldier neglects the cleanliness of his person, disease of course sets in, and there being no spirits to keep him up—death ensues." [Benjamin T. Jones] to Grand Mother and Aunt, Mar. 3, 1863, in Benjamin T. Jones Papers, WRHS.

26. Grant had recently issued orders designed to discourage additional blacks from gathering in his camps but by the Lincoln administration's order this policy would soon be superceded by one of welcoming runaway slaves and enlisting many in the Union army. Catton, Grant Moves South, 401–4.

27. Lewis O. Hull, Company A, had been mustered in at thirteen years old on Aug. 10, 1862. Roster 8:245.

great favorite of mine and I kept my eye on him. Some two weeks ago he took sick and looked bad and, belonging to a Company where 16 had died, I was afeard my little pet would die. I had him brought to my quarters and saw to him, attended and encouraged him and as soon as he got better, had him a good bed made in my cook tent and I have now the pleasure of seeing him hale and hearty; his red cheeks and bright eyes returning. He now tends to drumming all the calls, 15 a day, and is assisting our white cook. He is as happy and gay and good looking that I know you would love him if you would see him. My expenses since we are in the field are about 20 Dollars per month and for that I live fine.

My little friend Henry the Sergeant Major[28] was promoted a Lieutenant for his bravery on the field and is now on his Uncle Major General Sherman's Staff; he comes to see me once or twice a week. The weather is very warm and since it ceased raining incessantly, the health of the men is improving and they are getting more cheerful. My horses are doing tolerably well, but not as well as they would if they could be covered.

I have not shaved since I left Memphis. The Major [John W. Beekman] has been very sick for the last month past, but is now about fit for duty. The Adjutand[29] is very well. The Quarter Master [Ezra V. Dean] has also been very much under the weather but he too has recovered. He is a great friend of mine. Dr. Stanton our new Surgeon[30] is very much of a Gentleman and a warm friend of mine. Drs. Hammon and Stouffer, our assistant Surgeons, you saw on the Cars; the former is very much of a Gentleman and so is

---

28. Henry Stoddard Sherman. Roster 8:241. The son of Charles Taylor Sherman of Mansfield, he was the nephew of John and William Tecumseh Sherman. Thomas Townsend Sherman, *Sherman Genealogy.* . . . (New York: T. A. Wright, 1920).

29. Williard Slocum. Roster 8:241.

30. Byron Stanton. Roster 8:241. He was a cousin to Secretary of War Edwin M. Stanton. See following.

the latter, only I do not have much faith in him as a Doctor. I believe I can truly say all the Officers in the Regiment are my friends. Eleven of the old Officers have resigned and gone home and 6 more ought to do so, as they are too old and sickly to stand service. It takes young, energetic and active men who have always been used to hardships and hard labor, like me, for instance, to be able to stand campaigning. I believe I answered all your questions. I am daily looking for Josey to come, am anxious to see him and hear what he has to say about my Hamlin, Lizzie, Mosey and that bad girl Hattie. Ever your true and loving

Marcus

My love to Elizabeth.
You must try and keep well and hearty and good looking; dont trouble yourself so as to get old looking. I want you to be as lovely and handsome as ever, to enjoy a many many happy year in each others "Youthful Company".

Dear Mother:
    Although I wrote to you just yesterday, I cannot let this letter leave without assuring you, dear Mother, of the child-like love and devotion of a loving son for the best mother who has yet lived. I am well and healthy, thank God and if I had a piece of stuffed stomach or about 10 yard fresh lungsausage, which you prepared, I could then, if you were here, offer you a hearty snack.
    I long very very much to embrace you, dear Mother and I hope to have that pleasure very soon.
    I am expecting brother Joseph daily and believe that, if he comes, he can sell five hundred dollars worth a day. I am convinced.
    Many regards to the dear sisters, brothers-in-law, brother and friends, your devoted Marcus[31]

Without his having planned it, Spiegel's measures to restore his regiment's health and discipline stood him in good stead in the politi-

---

31. This note to his mother was in German.

cal controversies of Ohio. On February 19, 1863 the *Republican* of Wooster in Wayne County, home of many of Spiegel's men, had published an editorial blaming the Democratic officers of the Sixteenth and 120th Ohio for those regiments' demoralized and unhealthy condition. The editor had ranked French and Spiegel among "political demagogues and rebel sympathizers in disguise" who were preventing the 120th from winning glory. Four days later, William G. Myers, former captain of Company G, he who had left his rain gear for Spiegel, thrust another dagger. Myers made public to his neighbors, also in Wayne County, a letter written in December 1862, in which he had charged his regiment's staff officers with hostility to the Lincoln administration. While especially attacking Q.M. Ezra V. Dean, he had also criticized French and Spiegel.[32]

The subsequent controversy went beyond the predictable rebuttal by the Ohio Democratic press. On March 6, the company officers of the 120th, among them two Republicans from Wayne County, adopted resolutions denouncing the *Wooster Republican*'s editorial as "an infamous falsehood" written by a "vile slanderer, a base and malignant falsifier, and a traitor to his country and her soldiery." They praised their regiment, the resigned French, and their new commander, Spiegel. Significantly, the Republican organ in Millersburg was among the newspapers which reprinted the resolutions.[33] The editor of the *Wooster Republican* replied that he had not meant to criticize the whole regiment, while for a time still indicting Spiegel, among others, for Democratic politicking. Myers, whom Democrats charged had helped inspire the original *Republican* editorial, then went even further in his attack. As part of a critique of Democratic officers of the 120th, he sneered that Spiegel was "not a particular friend of Father Abraham on account of his Proclamation of Freedom, nor of Gen. Grant for his proclamation *excluding all Jews* from his army corps. . . ." Whether or not Myers accurately described Spiegel's feelings toward Grant, he had made the only recorded clearly anti-Semitic reference to his former superior.[34]

Spiegel soon had a chance to strike back. On April 6, Myers wrote to a sergeant in his former company a letter in which he urged all Republicans in the unit to stand by him against Quartermaster Dean

---

32. *Wooster Republican*, Feb. 19, 1863; *Wooster Democrat*, Mar. 5, 26, 1863.

33. *Wooster Democrat*, Mar. 26, 1863; MR, Apr. 2, 1863.

34. Myers denied responsibility for the original editorial. Letter of W. G. Myers, Mar. 13, 1863, and editorial, *Wooster Republican*, Apr. 2, 1863.

and Colonel Spiegel, whom he accused of "treachery and disloyal motives." Unfortunately for Myers, the sergeant was, like Spiegel, subordinating his old political loyalty to his allegiance to the soldier community within his regiment. Myers's correspondent gave Spiegel access to the letter and thus armed him for a mortal counterblow. Spiegel sent to the Wayne County Military Committee and to Ohio newspapers copies of Myers's letter. "As long as that man Myers contented himself by showing his personal hatred to me, in slandering me in the most vilifying, malignant and unscrupulous manner through the public press," Spiegel informed the editor of the *Wooster Republican,* "I felt it beneath my dignity to notice him." Spiegel went on to charge that his former subordinate had gone beyond personal attacks to "secretly trying to alienate the faith of my boys in their commander, and that at a time when daily advancing expecting to meet the enemy. . . ." The *Republican* editor published Spiegel's letter together with a copy of his patriotic speech on taking command of the 120th. While continuing to cast blame on Dean and the departed French, the editor who had begun the controversy closed it by opining, "Colonel Spiegle [*sic*] has infused renewed energy and determination throughout the ranks of his Regiment, and from all that we can learn, he has the full confidence of his men. . . ." Henceforth, Spiegel would be praised and sought after by Republicans as well as by Democrats.[35]

Millikens Bend La<br>March 18/63

My dear dear good Wife!

This I am satisfied is the longest interval of my writing to you since I am a Soldier and if you will only forgive me and listen to my excuse, I will agree never to do so again.

On the 27th [of February] I received a letter from you and Uncle Josey stating (dated the 17th) that Josey would start in a few days. I had then written you three long letters for three successive days and according to that letter I

---

35. *Wooster Republican,* May 7, 1863. See also *Wooster Democrat,* May 7, 1863. Writing to another Republican newspaper, a civilian who had brought supplies to the 120th called Spiegel "an excellent officer, and a kind hearted brave man" and credited him with the unit's improvement in health and discipline. Letter of T. C. Bushnell, undated, *Ashland Times,* Apr. 16, 1863.

looked for Josey in a few days, waiting with patience. On the first [of March], I received orders to change my camp on account of being surrounded by water and when moved and fixed, I had two of the most severe boils coming on me that I have had for years, one awful one in front right on the abdoman and one on my seat, and for one whole week I was laid up, not even able to get off of my cot. They were so severe that they threw me into a fever; there I lay almost swearing and sweating with anxiety and fever about Josey and just a day after my boils opened and I was able to go round, I received Orders to move my Regiment to this place called Millikens Bend, 15 miles above Youngs Point.

The day before we moved the Regiment was paid up to the last day of October but I dit not get any pay but we are promised to get paid off to the last of December and then I will get pay for three months. You can easy imagine that I dit not feel very gay when our Regiment was paid and Joseph was not here.

Well, we moved up here and every day dit I look for Jo and postponed writing to you inasmuch as I heard that Joseph was seen in Memphis. Finally on the 14th he arrived at Youngs Point and I had a Lieutenant stationed there for three days, examining boats that arrived. The Lieutenant brought him up on the first Dispatch and thank God I saw him and heard such loving news from you and the dear Children and Mother and all the friends. Night before last he opened; Yesterday and to day he had opened. In the two days he took in thirteen hundred Dollars in Cash and sold two hundred Dollars for Credit as good as cash in a few days. Such a rush you never saw. Three of my Lieutenants sold for him all day; the seven hands were as busy as they could be. At night they had to work opening and fixing up. Joseph and Sinsheimer[36] and Jim dit not get their breakfast yesterday till three o'clock in the afternoon. I am in their tent all I can but you know of course it would not

---

36. Aaron Sinsheimer, Joseph Spiegel's associate as sutler.

A sutler's store, Harpers Ferry, Virginia, from an engraving in *Leslie's*

do for me to sell anything; yet I think I am doing him a little good anyhow. He sold every Hat and every pair of Shoes he had and at a good profit. If he had known as much as he knows now what was and brought down the Goods, he could have taken $1000 a day for the next two weeks.

You have no Idea how popular he is already. Everybody likes him except the other Sutlers.

He has the Trade of four Regiments. In a few days he will go after a new Stock. Sinsheimer said to me to night "when one has such a Brother as an Officer with such a reputation, the Sutlership is a pleasure."

I am as happy as any Soldier in the Army can be. If the Boys only keep their health and have no bad luck, they cant help making lots of money and to me it is a great comfort to have Josey with me. I will now commence writing about other matters. Uncle Josey cant tell enough about the dear children, one and all of them and my little Hattie more especially, Mosey more particularly, Mosey [Lizzie?] more emphatically and Hamlin more specifically. He brings me gladdening tidings indeed.

I must tell you now but you must not feel jealous that I had calls from 5 very nice Sesesh Ladies, and they were all very much taken with me. You may ask how comes that; well, while at Youngs Point my Regiment was the first Regiment to the Picket lines and all who came inside the lines were conducted to my Head Quarters. Many Sesesh Ladies came inside the lines to see about their runaway Niggers; among them were 5 who came just at dinner times which of course I invited and they accepted. Since then they send me nice bouquets and so forth.

When we came up here we came within four miles of one, a Widow Lady Mrs. Nutt.[37] As soon as she heard it, she came and give a pressing invitation for me to come and see her. A few days ago I took the Quarter Master with me

---

37. Probably a connection of Dr. Haller Nutt, builder of "Longwood" at Natchez, whose family owned several plantations. William L. Whitwell, *The Heritage of Longwood* (Jackson: Univ. Press of Mississippi, 1975), 19, 22.

and went out and we were princely entertained. She has 3 grown daughters, is very aristocratic and lives in a very aristocratic Style. Since then she send me a very nice lot of Sausage, three large Rolls of Butter and a lot of Peaches and better than all a nice fresh Cow and Calf, all with her compliments. What do you think now? Aint your old man popular with the Ladies? And dont you suppose I enjoy my glass fresh milk and Bread just about right?

It is now 11 o'clock and at 7 to morrow I have battalion Drill and having been up last night late to help Josey, I must close.

Will write now often again and give you all the news. Josey intents starting up the River in a few days. Dont forget the picture.

Ever ever your true and loving husband<br>Marcus. . . .

Millikens Bend La<br>Mch 18/63

My dear Wife

I have written to you last evening and have nothing new to say, only that this is a very hot day; the weather here is awful hot of late.

I had a very good Battalion Drill this morning; the Boys begin to feel young again.

Sinsheimer [it] seems can not stand the hart work as well as Josey; he was nearly worn out last night. I left him sleep in my bed; he is very lame this morning. I think that he will probably start North to morrow for new Goods instead of Josey.

I have nothing new this morning. Captain Eason and Captain Emmerich[38] who have resigned on account of ill health, they are both very warm friends of mine and I am satisfied that they will do me honor wherever they go.

I am fearful my friend Captain Conyer is dead before this. He was on a hospital Boat and last Evening I heard he

---

38. Benjamin Eason, Company E, George P. Emerick, Company D. Roster 8:254, 251.

was dying. I am very sorry I could not have seen him; he wanted to see me very bad. Poor man, how I pity his good Wife and 5 handsome and good children. I wanted him to resign a good while ago but he would not do it.[39]

This morning I send recommendations for 16 Sergeants to be Comissioned Officers in my Regiment. Among them I recommended my friends Sergeant Major Sherman and Ben Jones as first Lieutenants.[40] If I get them all commissioned, I will have as good a set of Line Officers as are in the field. I recommend the Major to be Lieutenant Colonel and the Adjutand to be Major and that Lieutenant Taylor that was so clever to you at Orrville as Adjutand, so you see I remember your friends.[41] As soon as I get my Commission as Colonel I will inform you, though I get all my O.B. [Official Business] from the different Headquarters addressed to me as Colonel Spiegel.

The men are leaving.

Good bye
ever your
Marcus

Millikens Bend March 22/63

My dear dear good Wife!

One year ago to day about this time (4 P.M.) as we were fixing for Dress Parade and just when the boys brought a good Soup, we were ordered to report South of Winchester to General Shields on the field. Well do I remember how much I deplored, when we had [to] go on double quick

---

39. George W. Conyer, Company K, died on Apr. 11, 1863, at St. Louis. Roster 8:269.

40. Both Sherman, who was acting as a lieutenant, and Benjamin T. Jones, who had replaced him as sergeant major, were in fact promoted to first lieutenant. Roster 8:241.

41. Maj. John W. Beekman became lieutenant colonel and Adj. Williard Slocum became major. But James B. Taylor became first lieutenant of Company H while Henry S. Sherman eventually became Spiegel's adjutant. Roster 8:241, 263.

through the mud knee deep, the loss of my soup; well do I remember the first shell that whizzed through my company in the Rear of that little Ladyboy Corporal LeRoy Osborn; well do I remember the consternation depicted on his countenance, as though it were but an hour ago. The anxiety I felt in deploying my company as skirmishers for the first time under fire, is still vividly and lively before me.

That night, the getting up next morning, the commencement of the serenading in the morning by the heavy artillery is all plain to me and the events of the day; it seems to me as though it were but shortly and that I could yet hear the whizz of that Shell that took off the head of the Cannonier to my right, but the time from noon till night is still to me as it always was a terrible dream, every part of which I knew after I awoke.

The loss I sustained of my noble Company, the gallant boys that fell by my side are still as then warmly lamented and ever will be cherished green in my memory until life ceases.

Since that time, my love, I have seen and learned much. I have seen men dying of disease and mangled by the weapons of death; I have seen them wounded and seen their wounds being dressed, limbs amputated and bullets extracted. I have seen and experienced hunger, hardships and privations; I have with delight and honor welcomed the deafening roar of the Cannons by Land and Water as a signal of the commencement of hostilities. I have witnessed hostile Armies arraigned again each other, the charge of Infantry at the death-outpouring Artillery, the Bayonet charge and repel, Cavelery hunting men down like beasts, forts fall and towns refuse, the ferociousness of Gunboats and the sturdy resistance of Forts. I have learned to see all of it cooly and with ready presence of mind and yet through all this the Grand Architeck of the Universe has preserved me, the good father and God of Israel has favored me with his gracious kindness of being a loving husband to a good wife and a kind father to my beloved children and a trusty Son and Brother to the best mother and kindest of Sisters and

Brothers and an appreciative recipient of the many acts of kindness by my host of truest of friends. Have we, my dear, not all reasons to be ever thankful to that allwise and kind providence.

While seeing all this I have been steadily gaining in friends, influence and position. Thank God I can leave my children a legacy which will inspire them to hold up their heads and walk uprightly through the world and that is "a reputation as a Soldier and Patriot". I have always done my duty and if God spares my health I always will and I know my love you will feel satisfied with me. It is only within the last day or two that I have an opportunity to get any chances to talk to Josey about you and I must confess the news he brings from all of you is such as will only inspire the heart of a Soldier to good. He tells me you look as well and hearty as you dit 10 years ago and says that you are in good Spirits, thank God for that. I was afeard you would trouble yourself about me so much as to leave symptoms on your countenance or your lovely features but he assures me that you indeed look well and hearty and pretty. Hamlin, my dear Son, Uncle Josey tells me that you are a fine and good boy, that you behave yourself like a young Gentleman. My dear Son, if you would only know how good it makes me feel to hear such good news from you, you would be the best boy in the world. Now I will tell you some good news; this afternoon I got a nice little bay pony mare for you. She is a very smart little pony mare; she has a nice little white spot on her forehead and very nice little legs. I think she will have a little new Colty in the Spring; if so you must give the little Colty to your little Brother Mosey. I am not sure whether she will have a Colt but she looks very much like it, and everybody says so. Sam [?] French brought the pony from the Country for you and Tom Orr gave me a nice little Saddle for you, one that he captured at Arkansas Post.[42] I send out Skouting Parties twice before, to bring in

---

42. Thomas Orr was a private in the 120th. Roster 12:713. French's name does not appear on that regiment's roster. Roster 8:241–72.

a Pony for you but they failed; now I got it, but you must give it a name. When I come home in May I will bring it; what shall I call it?

Now my dear Lizzy, Uncle Josey also tells me very good news of you. He says that you are a regular little Lady and behave very well, that you are growing fine and doing well; that is right my dear. Of course you know that I will bring you something handsome when I come home; be a good child and mind your ma and all will be right.—My dear Mosey, Uncle Josey says that you are a very good boy and that you look so well and like a little man in your pantys; you must be pa's good sonny so that pa can put you on the little pony and kiss you; you are pa's good sonny. My dear little Hattie, I would very much like to see her indeed; she must be a sweet one from the picture Josey gives of her. Oh how much I long to see them all.

I think now I have treated on all the subjects as to the family and now I must talk about business. In the first place I would like to have you return to Millersburg after Pesach [Passover] by way of Lima[ville] and Uniontown, enjoy yourself and see your friends with the whole Mishpacha [clan].[43] I will send you money as soon as we get our pay which I think will be shortly. I do not exactly know when Pesach is but expect to find out. I have sent home a double Barrel Shot Gun for Hamlin and a marble slab for a nice little stand which some of the boys gave me; the Shotgun I sent to Cohn and the Marble in Care of Rex of Wooster. The marble is not of so much intrinsic value as it is for a relic; I will have a little stand made for it.

I intend to go home in May and stay 30 days, providing there are no active operations going on here and I can get away. I think I can for I have a great many friends above but to day I lost one of my best friends. Lieutenant Colonel Schwarz, Inspector General and Chief of Staff, had to go home on account of his wounds; they were healed up but

---

43. Spiegel evidently refers in part to the Hamlin family.

commenced putrification on the bone and he had to go home and have it opened again. He was a warm friend of mine and of great Influence, but still I still got General Osterhaus and he is a warm friend of mine indeed. I was invited to dinner at his place yesterday and I tell you we had a fine German Dinner indeed. As to other business I can only say to you that if God spares my health I intend to stay in the Army until the Rebs are brought to terms; I am as good a democrat as ever I was, but no peace Democrat.

When I see you in May, I will "open up my heart"[44] to you. Good night, God bless and preserve you.

Ever your true and loving
Marcus

## A DEMOCRATIC SOLDIER.[45]

A colonel of one of the Ohio regiments, a Democrat of the most uncompromising order in a private letter to his brother-in-law, of this city, a Democrat who never faltered in his life, speaks of the political aspect of the war and the times, He says:

Headquarters O.V.I.
Camp McClernand
Millikens Bend La.
March 23, 1863

My dear M:

Your good and encouraging words though but few of them are nevertheless ever welcome and cherished; they always express the true metal and are such that will always gladden the heart of a soldier.

I often wish this unfortunate war were over, and I permitted to enjoy the comfort and happiness of a comfortable home and blessings of peace in the cozy circle of my little

---

44. The quoted words were in German.

45. Clipping from an unknown [Chicago] newspaper in AJA. The letter was probably written to Spiegel's Republican brother-in-law, Michael Greenebaum, hence all of the editor's references to Democrats apply to Spiegel.

family, but nevertheless, as much as I wish it, I do not want to see it close until the enemies of my beloved country are conquered and brought to terms. Men who are so contemptibly mean and unprincipled as to wage war against the best government in the world and trample under foot the flag that was ever ready to protect you and me and every one who sought its protection from oppression, must be taught that, although a noble country to live in peaceably, yet it is a powerful government to rebel against. I want to hear the first cry for peace commence at Richmond, sound through the air from thence to Charleston, S.C., and reach from there to Vicksburg, Miss., accompanied with a proposal to lay down their arms and acknowledge the supremacy of the government. Then and not until then, will I say peace. I have been in the service eighteen months and will stay as long as necessary (health permitting), until that end is accomplished.

That is my Democracy. In my estimation the administration had made two great errors: 1st the removal of McClellan; 2nd the Emancipation Proclamation. The first weakened us, the second strengthened the enemy, yet what matters that—errors or not, the government must be sustained by every loyal citizen and the d——d rebels whipped. I am well, hearty and in good spirits. We expect to commence active operations against Vicksburg; if so, I hope you will hear a good account of me.

Millikens Bend La.
March 24/63

My dear good wife!

I have only yesterday mailed a great big long letter for you, Michael and one in German for mother; yet as some of the boys who are discharged are going home, I thought [I] would send a short letter to you and perhaps if they would mail it at Cairo it might reach you in advance of the one sent yesterday by mail.

Yesterday I received your very kind letter of the 14th in which you in consequence of A. Ruhman's not coming to see you, I could see a little of the "blues" sticking out, but what of that? I am satisfied to receive one or two letters from you every month in which you have a little the blues and urge me to "resign"; that is quite natural and then it shows me that you have not changed any, that you are the same plain and honest woman, "as you feel so you say."

Then I know that on the other hand that when you think that I am hale and hearty and just in the act of rising by staying in the Army, while coming home without an earthly excuse for forsaking my post in the face of the enemy would be disgrace, I know then by thinking over it you come to the conclusion, I want him whole, I want him honorable, I want him so that his children, I, or him can readily answer when asked, how long dit your father or husband stay in the Army "Until his country had no further use for his services," or Until he had performed his whole duty.

What could I say now? Nothing that would clear me from a stain!

Should Governor Tod refuse to commission me or should I receive any indignity from any other source or should my health demand it, or the condition of my family imperatively demand it, then I would leave the service at once. But while I am honored and fairly used from everybody, in the best of health thank God, my dear little ones in charge of the best woman in the world, and in face of an enemy, I can not nor would you have me resign.

I sent you $50 a few days ago; as soon as we get paid will send the balance. It may be that I will get 5 months pay in a few days. The pay of a Lieutenant Colonel is 167 Dollars per month, the pay of Colonel is 193 Dollars per month and forage for three horses.[46] My expense now is not over twenty Dollars per month; while in the field expenses are small, while in a City they are large. You need have no fears as to the Government going Bankrupt; she will pay and her pay will pay debts.

---

46. A colonel's monthly pay and allowances totaled $194. Eaton, *Army Paymaster's Manual*, 127.

How would you like to buy the lot next to our House where Atkins now lives. This Idea has been so prominent in my mind within the last three months that I could scarcely get it away for an hour. I think it would make us a magnificent home. What do you think? I will try and get a leave of Absence in May to come home for thirty days and if we are not in active engagements, I think I will have no trouble in getting it; Osterhaus will help me and then wont you be glad with me because I have to go again? I think you will a little.

Josey is doing very nice trade, though for two days it rained incessantly and he is out of a great many things, yet he still takes in from 150 to 200 Dollars Cash per day. He is looking for Sinsheimer. He will be in Chicago before you go home and then he will tell you everything. I have no particular plan for the future, anymore than to live for you, my love and the children only, to live so as to make you happy and be a good boy.

God will not, I feel it, forsake us, for He has ever been kind and gracious to us.

In Abraham Ruhman I am disappointed; I thought him more of a man, but you know I never feel troubled over people's ingratitude. I got him discharged, without examination or anything; he never knew anything of it until I handed him his Papers; he is very ungratified.

The little drummer boy is still under my care and doing well; his father came here to take him home but he would not go. Many of the Ohio folks come here after bodies of the deceased Soldiers and looking after the sick; they bring plenty of fruit and every thing else. Yesterday I was presented with 16 cans of all kind of fruit, a lot of Apple butter, Peaches dried, onions and everything else. Whenever the boys get anything from home they bring me in a good share. We have now a Chicken coop right by my tent with 20 chickens in; in day time I let them out. They lay eggs enough for Custard and pumpkin pies which our Cook backes and with our two Milch Cows we live as good as any family in Ohio. I never lived as well and half as cheap in camp; they (boys) never disturb the Chickens or Cows since they belong to me. My love to the children, Mother, Mich, Sarah, Elizabeth, oncle Gumpel and all.

Ever your true and loving
Marcus

CHAPTER EIGHT

# "My boys will follow me anywheres"

Through his vigorous support of the war, Spiegel put himself at variance with many in his strongly Democratic home district of Ohio. There opposition to fighting in order to free slaves was strengthened by opposition to the arrest of vocal opponents of the Lincoln administration—arrests like that in which Spiegel had participated while at Camp Mansfield. His old friend Lyman Critchfield, who had been elected state attorney general, had denounced military arrests at a meeting in January 1863 at Columbus. Critchfield had stirred statewide controversy when he advocated "armed resistance" to such usurpations and found little to choose between Lincoln and Confederate President Jefferson Davis. Another of Spiegel's friends, James A. Estill, edited what the Republicans branded as one of Ohio's most extreme "Copperhead" publications. Estill's *Millersburg Farmer* defended its right to undermine the tyranny of the "Congo Dynasty," as it termed the now antislavery government in Washington.[1] After his wife's return to Millersburg, Spiegel would learn of increasingly violent words and deeds in his county.

His attention to political wars necessarily was peripheral to his concentration on the real war on the Mississippi. After a winter of experimenting with a variety of ways to bypass Vicksburg, General Grant had decided to try a bold new approach. He would open a land and water route through the swamps below Milliken's Bend and down it move the bulk of his force. Gunboats and transports would run downriver past the defenses of Vicksburg. These would ferry the army to the east bank below the Confederate fortress city. There they would be free to maneuver in several possible directions. Grant designated McClernand's Thirteenth Corps to begin the movement down the west bank. When Spiegel wrote the following letters, he did not yet know that his regiment was in the vanguard of what could be Grant's military masterpiece.[2]

---

1. Cardinal, "Democratic Party of Ohio and the Civil War," 139–43; MF, Feb. 26, 1863.

2. Catton, *Grant Moves South*, 407–21. For a good map of the whole campaign, see 427. See also, OR Atlas, 36, pl. 1.

Spiegel did indicate, however, that he knew his personal prospects were steadily improving. As revealed by his letters, his expectation of promotion was fulfilled; commissioned on March 30, 1863, he became entitled to wear the silver eagles of a full colonel in the army. Moreover, he began to have golden hopes for his postwar career. His younger brother, Joseph, for whom he had secured the position of sutler to his regiment, was prospering greatly. Marcus Spiegel thus had not only the comfort of his brother's companionship but also the expectation of sharing in Joseph Spiegel's success. In the following communications, Spiegel tells his wife of the two brothers' dream of establishing a dry goods store in Chicago, and pictures for her a brighter future.

Holmes Plantation, Madison Parish La.
April 6 1863

My Dearest Caroline, my sweet wife!

I received your very kind and encouraging letter of the 25th and your "blue one" of the 21st and can assure you that I am happy indeed to know "all is right among mine own."

Uncle Josey has unquestionably ere this told you everything about my situation at Millikens Bend so that I need only say to you how I am fixed and what happened since we left the "Bend".

Two days after Uncle Josey left us, I received marching Orders, whereupon we pulled up stakes and put for Richmond, a march of 15 miles; really the first march my Regiment made since in the service and they performed it as they do everything else and that is "very well". We halted close by a town called Richmond, the County or Parish seat of Madison Parish on Roundaway Bouyou, pitched tents and made ourselves comfortable. The afternoon after we landed there, General Osterhaus with 4 Companies of the 6th Missouri Cavelery and the 69th Indiana Infantry left to advance on Burdell [Vidal] Bouyou. Next morning at nine he ordered General Gerard [Garrard] our Brigadier to advance 1 Regiment of Infantry and one Company of Cavelery near the junction of Burdell and Roundaway Bouyou and if possible let the 120th Ohio Volunteers be the Infantry. Dont you suppose I felt proud when the Order came? I was asked by the General Gerard how soon I could start; I told him in a half hour. I called my Officers together and told them that in 30 minutes the Tents must be stroke and everything packed and Wagons loaded and the men with knapsacks and accoutrements and guns in line for march.

And so it was in thirty minutes we started. At Richmond the Cavelery reported to me and we advanced in the usual precautionary manner. We heard on the Road the Rebs. were near the place. When within 2 miles of the destination I placed the Regiment in command of the Major and dashed on and dont you suppose I felt important when at the head of my Cavelery Escort I swept along the Road, encouraged by the nicest weather and most magnificent country I ever saw? I felt as though I could do anything. When we came near the Rebs. landed on the other side the Bouyou, I took possession of Holmes Plantation, one of the nicest, grandest and most tasty plantations I ever saw. I wish I could describe it to you. My boys arrived in due time; I put out my pickets and then the boys pitched in.

The plantation is deserted by the white owner and a good many of the slaves, but it was and is still yet full of Chickens, Turkeys, Geese, ducks, Pitchens, Sheep, Cattle, Sugar, Molasses, Salt Hams and in short, everything you could think of. My boys live in clover; they all eat off of china dishes, gild striped, and have their tents carpeted.

I occupy a Parlor and Bedroom furnished in 5th Avenue style, have my office in the Library and Staff and field Officers all have very nice quarters. I am in command of the Post. The Cavelery that I have with me belongs to the 2nd Illinois; they are fine fellows and brave. As soon as we arrived here I sent a courier to General Osterhaus and announced the fact; he sent back a congratulatory Order to the Regiment. This morning he was here and stayed all forenoon. He was awful well pleased and after consultation he concluded that in the morning I will have to move again, taking along Lanpheres four Gun battery of Artillery.[3] I am sorry to have to leave so nice a place but glad to take the advance; the boys feel so good when they can have everything and they feel proud of their position, getting the advance, more expecially since the 16th Regiment of their own Neighborhood that blowed so much has to stay behind.

I am well and hearty and feel as though if I could only see you, the children, and mother, sisters, and Brothers and their children, I would be situated as well as any body need to.

As to business, Jo will tell you all. Sinsheimer is back at the Bend. They will have to get a team now. We will be paid in three days, when I will send the money home for you.

Send you some abstracts of Wayne County Papers.[4] Give my love to all all all and remember that I will come to see you as soon as possible.

God bless you.
Your ever true and loving
Marcus. . . .

Perkins Plantation La.[5]
April 27/63

My dear dear Wife!

Thank God I am rewarded after a long and continual waiting with anxiety to get a letter from you, and that lovely Picture which looks so well. Oh my girl it done me good to see your faces; I feel proud of that lovely Group.

There is not a Major General in this Army that can show so noble looking a family.

You, dear Wife, look magnificent; you never had half so

---

3. Capt. Charles H. Lanphere's Seventh Michigan Battery. OR, vol. 24, 591.

4. Probably concerning the controversies referred to in the previous chapter.

5. Spiegel had moved by way of Smith's Plantation down Bayou Vidal and was again near the Mississippi well below Vicksburg.

good a picture taken before in your life; Hamlin, my heart rejoices to look at him; he is truly a perfect Picture. Lizzie looks as sober as Preacher, yet with all she could scarcely contain her imputance. Mosey, dear soul, looks as round, plumb and lovely as I never known him before. I want Hatty dear.

I hope the Lord may not judge me vain as I regard my beloved family, for I am proud of them in love. God bless you all and preserve you all for me, is my constant prayer.

I have not seen Brother Joseph yet; he stopped 8 miles back here at my old Camp at Smiths Plantation and they say he is selling at the rate of two thousand Dollars per day. I know nothing of your design, know not where you are, but shall send this letter to Millersburg.

I send three hundred Dollars to Enos Brown and Company and three hundred and Sixty Dollars I left with Sinsheimer to send to you as soon as we found out where you are. Please tell Cohn that I can not be a Candidate for Probate Judge under any circumstances.[6] I can not come home in time and I understand they are against the War, for hasty peace and that I can not go. If the Democrats are not in favor of whipping these Aristocratic Rebels until they consider they are whipped, I am not with the democrats and I will just wait until they get right again. I will say nothing but keep thinking; you need not say anything. The more I see of them, the more I get convinced that the only way we can ever have a peaceful and happy country is by fighting them until we whip them. I am glad to learn that Martha[7] is so patriotic and of course you, the noble wife of a (full) Colonel[8] are also. Just speak out to them; dont be afraid while you are right. General Osterhaus is one of natures

---

6. Democratic nomination in Holmes County meant all but certain election. In the end the Democrats nominated and elected James A. Estill as probate judge. MR, Oct. 29, 1863.

7. Probably Caroline's sister.

8. Spiegel had been promoted on Mar. 30, to rank from Feb. 18, 1863. Commission in Soman Coll.

Noblemen and the best and most active Generals I yet met
in America; he is also a true and warm friend. He is with
me or I with him every day; we ride together. He is about
45 years old, has a family in St. Louis.

He is a good man, intelligent and a splendid Scholar.

Dr. Stanton is our Surgeon; he is from Salem, Ohio, a son
of old Dr. Stanton,[9] a Cousin to the Secretary of War. Beekman is the Lieutenant Colonel, Slocum Major and my little
friend Sherman is my Adjutand. We all mess together, the
three field officers, Adjutand, Quarter Master and the three
Doctors. It does not cost us $2 a week and we live in good
style.

I wrote to you my commission dated back to February
18/1863 and I have now, no doubt but what I can draw my
pay from that date.

I am so anxious to see Joseph and hear from you, you
can't imagine; he sent me the Picture.

As for my coming home, I know you can not possibly be
as anxious to see me as I am to see all of you, yet the time
for my coming is very uncertain as no one can get off during this time of active operation.

We are ordered to move at once. God bless you. Ever
your loving and true Husband
Marcus. . . .

Within the next few days, Spiegel and his regiment boarded boats
which took them across the Mississippi and landed them at Bruins-
burg on the east bank. From there, McClernand's corps and other
Union troops already totaling over 23,000 men marched inland. If
not stopped, they would first take from the rear the Confederate
batteries at Grand Gulf below Vicksburg and then threaten Vicksburg
itself. To oppose them the Confederates had only about 6,000 men
but did have a defensible position based on ridges, with the
approaches made difficult by wooded ravines. The battle on May 1,
1863, of which Spiegel describes his part, was then called Thompson's

9. Benjamin Stanton, pioneer physician of Salem and father of Byron
Stanton. George D. Hunt, *History of Salem and the Immediate Vicinity, Columbi-
ana County, Ohio* (Salem, 1898), 147–48.

Hill but went into history as the Battle of Port Gibson, named after the pretty little village just behind the Confederate lines.[10]

## Report of Col. Marcus M. Spiegel,
### One hundred and twentieth Ohio Infantry[11]

In The Field, May 4, 1863.

GENERAL: I have the honor to herewith transmit the following report of the part taken by the One hundred and twentieth Regiment Ohio Volunteer Infantry in the action of Thompson's Hill, on the 1st instant.

About 5 o'clock in the morning, we were ordered to advance and take a position on the right of Lanphere's battery, which was accordingly done, under a severe fire of the enemy's shell, in which position we remained about half an hour, when we advanced to the edge of the ravine, and from there were ordered to advance and form a line of battle in a ravine to the extreme left of the division. Soon after, in conjunction with the One hundred and eighteenth Illinois Infantry, we advanced briskly across the open field, taking a position behind a fence fronting the enemy, and in support of the Forty-ninth Indiana, who were deployed as skirmishers on the edge of the woods. Soon thereafter Colonel Keigwin,[12] of the Forty-ninth Indiana, informed me that he had been ordered to the right on a line with his position, and at the same time I received orders to cover the front with my skirmishers, and relieve him. I then advanced Companies A, F, and K as skirmishers, and D, I, and B in support.

At 7:30 I was ordered to recall all but one of my companies. I moved, as ordered, to the right, in advance of our line, to relieve the Forty-second Ohio.[13] While passing be-

---

10. Catton, *Grant Moves South*, 424–28.

11. OR, vol. 24, pt. 1, 588–89.

12. Col. James Keigwin. For his report of this battle, see OR, vol. 24, pt. 1, 586–87.

13. The historian of the Forty-second Ohio blamed the 120th for firing too low at the enemy at one point in the battle, killing five or six of the Forty-second. Mason, *Forty-second Ohio*, 193–95. See 194 for a useful map.

tween our batteries and the position of the Forty-second
Ohio, the enemy's shell, grape shot, and bullets flew thick
and fast around us, but the brave and gallant boys moved
briskly and bravely on, until we arrived in front of the
Forty-second Ohio, close to a ravine running parallel with
the enemy's strongest position. I then engaged the enemy
about twenty minutes, without being able to do him much
harm, he being completely under cover on the opposite
bank of the ravine. I then advanced as skirmishers some of
the best shots from all the companies down into the ravine,
with orders to advance, closely supporting them with the remainder of the regiment, and keeping up a constant fire
toward the top of the opposite bank. When nearly down
into the ravine, I discovered the exact position of the
enemy's advance, toward the left, on the opposite bank. I
then charged upon them with the regiment, and quickly
drove them from the bank to the knoll, where they rallied
and made a stand, which only increased the determination
of my brave boys. Rushing up the bank, we drove them
pell-mell from behind the knoll, taking 8 prisoners.

When I had obtained possession of the knoll, I did not
deem it prudent to pursue them farther, being at least 300
yards in advance of any of our troops, and in danger of
meeting the enemy's entire right wing massed behind a
number of old buildings directly in front of me. I deployed
my regiment on the knoll, in order to punish the retiring
force and hold the position against a more formidable
attack. As soon as the retiring enemy had rejoined the main
body, the attack was renewed with redoubled fierceness and
energy, but meeting with such continued and well-directed
volleys from us, he fell back under the cover of the houses
again. I then continued to fight the enemy, who was con-
cealed behind logs, fences, and houses, and some perched
upon the tops of trees, until my ammunition was beginning
to give out and many of the guns were becoming unfit for
use, when I was relieved by Col. T. W. Bennett, of the
Sixty-ninth Indiana, and ordered to retire. I then fell back
to the second ravine in my rear, replenishing the empty car-
tridge boxes with ammunition from the boxes of the com-

rades who were killed and wounded. I remained in that position until late in the afternoon, when, seeing the charge made on the left, I quickly formed my regiment, marching them toward the charging column, in order to support them, if necessary. When, however, the enemy fled in confusion, a glorious victory won, the One hundred and twentieth had nothing more to do than to exult, cheer and be merry, and that I assure you was done.

I cannot close this report, general, without saying that the men of the One hundred and twentieth Ohio have not only justified their former reputation, but have even excelled it. They displayed a gallantry and bravery on that day which will never be forgotten by their country. To the line officers, all of whom stood bravely up to the work, I am indebted much for their aid and courage in carrying out every order given. Lieutenant-Colonel Beekman has shown himself an officer worthy of the position he holds. While promptly assisting in maneuvering the regiment, his encouraging and cheering words were always heard along the line.

Major Slocum, while with me in the morning, showed that coolness and courage for which he is well known in the army, and while detailed to take charge of the skirmishers of the left flank of the division, did his whole duty to the entire satisfaction of the general commanding the division.

Adjutant Sherman, though young in years, has truly shown himself a veteran in the field. He possesses all the elements necessary to qualify him for the position he holds; brave and cool, he becomes courageous and dashing when the occasion requires it.

Both officers and men have my sincerest thanks for their cheerful cooperation on the field of Thompson's Hill.

M. M. SPIEGEL<br>Colonel Commanding

Near Big Sandy May 7,/63

My dear dear and sweet wife!

I have but little Paper, no Pen nor Ink, but enough to say to you that I am still alive, again well and love you more than ever. You must not feel uneasy if you do not get letters very frequent, for we are moving every day; no paper, no chance to send, neither have we received a mail for nearly two weeks. Yet I am in hopes that as soon as it comes it will bring me a long, good and sweet letter from you.

I have sent you a letter written on Coloured Paper about the Battle[14] and I am satisfied you will feel happy and not a little proud of your "homely man" when you see my report and learn how fearlessly I stood up. Here many speak of me in the highest praise and my boys most all worship me and you ought to hear how proudly they speak of their "brave Colonel".

God bless you and my sweet Children. As soon as I have an opportunity I will come to see you and, Oh God, such a sweet and happy time I anticipate in seeing you and the dear children, you cant imagine. We may have a Battle to morrow; if so I will with the help of God do my duty. Kiss the children. God bless you.

Your<br>Marcus

In the last Battle I had only 3 killed, 3 mortally, 8 severely and 6 slightly wounded. May God bless you, my love.

After their defeat at the battle of Port Gibson, the Confederates evacuated that village and the river batteries at Grand Gulf. Spiegel, together with the remainder of the Thirteenth Corps, moved northeast, following the Big Black River which separated them from the Confederate army garrisoning Vicksburg. Meanwhile, Grant had additional troops marched down the opposite bank of the Mississippi and ferried over to strengthen his army. While he also had more rations brought down, he intended to travel light and live largely off the country. Thus, as Spiegel makes clear, the army would move rapidly.[15]

---

14. Perhaps a copy of his official report; no other letter is in the Spiegel Papers, AJA.

15. Catton, *Grant Moves South*, 428–36.

In the field near Big Black River Mis.<br>
May 9/63

My dear Wife, my lovely Cary!

Here I am laying crowded under a little Rail hut covered with green brushes to shield us from the burning Sun and I have just heard that there was an opportunity of sending of a letter and so I have been successful in getting a little paper of one [of] the Boys, Ink and pen of another, and by these means I can say to you "that Richard is himself again." Since the Bealing in my Ear and my Boil behinded busted, I feel all well again. It is now about three weeks since I have not seen or heard anything from you except that lovely picture for which I would not take $1000. I have written you two notes since the Battle which if you can read [them] will give you an outline of the fearful but gloriously Victorious Battle.

For eleven days past we have had continual marching and Bivouacing. I have not seen my tent for 13 days, neither have I slept any wheres but out doors nor had my clothes off since that time. Some nights we marched till one and two o'clock, yet I feel all right and in excellent Spirits.

We are to day stopping and resting and I therefore took off my Drawyers, Undershirt and shirt and have my negro Boy washing it; I sit in the Shade until it tries [dries]. I have not seen Joseph yet; I think it is real mean in him, not even to come after the Battle. How dit he know but what I am wounded? Yet I hear of him often; he is doing a Splendid Business. I suppose he has cleared two thousand Dollars since he is back and perhaps they have made four thousand Dollars since they came to the Regiment and all in cash. You need not be alarmed; I mean to get my share in due time. Cary my love, just feel perfectly easy about me; I am doing well. I am establishing myself a reputation which will stand for life and I know you feel proud of it. Besides my expenses are not $10 per month, I live very saving, and if God spares me I mean to have three or four thousand Dollars in Money in hand before I leave the Army, so that whatever I start I can start without having so much uneasiness of mind, so that I can sit and talk to you, honour and love you undisturbed and unmolested, and treat you, my angelic and heroic wife, in a manner you deserve. Caroline, I know and appreciate the Heroism it requires for you to lead the life you have been compelled to live, since I am in the Army and many times since I first took you from your quite happy and girlish Home; a many pang I feel when I think of all, but rest assured, my love, that if kind providence spares me my life and health, it shall be my object to atone for all. Loving as I do you, I feel that I shall be able to do it.

It was my design to give you a description of the beautiful engagement between our Gunboats and the Landbatteries at Grand Gulf by day and night but I think I will have to defer it until I come home, when I can tell you more than I ever dit before, for I do think that in the last 6 months of my life I saw more of life than I ever did before and trust I may have benefited thereby. A few days ago a man was here from Wooster and I gave him two hundred and fifty Dollars to send to you. Sometime ago I got $800; I send $300 to Enos Brown and Company and paid Debts with some and had $400 which I wanted to send to you but I knew not where you was, as Joseph had not yet returned. So as soon as I found we had to move I sent my money to Joseph or rather Sinsheimer. The next day while on march I took in over $200 belonging to the Regiment which I had in my Pocket and so I thought I would send it to you. I do not know whether Joseph sent you any or not; neither do I know whether you are at Chicago or Millersburg, but hope soon to be able to find out. As soon as this active campaign is over which will have to be in the course of a month or less, I will come home and stay home a Month at least and then we will talk it all over. My love and Respect to Hamlin, Lizzie, Mosey and Hattie. I will bring two nice Bay Ponies, 1 for Hamlin and 1 for Lizzie and Mosey. I shall also bring my Charley Horse along and leave him at home till fall; he looks so very thin and poor. I must now close. Last night I was on a recognoitering expedition with General Osterhaus and we had a lively time with the Rebs. Charley although thin is full of life.

Your true and loving<br>Marcus

My love to Cohn and Family.

During the next few days, Grant moved his army northeast between Vicksburg and Jackson, the Mississippi state capital, through which ran the only railroad linking Vicksburg to the rest of the Confederacy. There Gen. Joseph E. Johnston, the newly appointed commander of all Southern troops in Mississippi, was desperately attempting to collect reinforcements. To prevent Johnston from consolidating his force with that then at Vicksburg, Grant struck first at Jackson while Spiegel's regiment remained with the troops guarding the army's ill-defined flank and rear against any sally from Vicksburg. After driving Johnston from Jackson, Grant turned toward Vicksburg. The change of front put the Thirteenth Corps in the advance but not the 120th Ohio which General Osterhaus left behind with another regiment to hold the village of Raymond. Thus Spiegel did not participate in the major battle of Champion's Hill on May 16, in which Grant prevented the Vicksburg garrison from moving north to link with Johnston, nor in the subsequent engagement at Big Black River bridge which drove the garrison back into the defenses of Vicksburg. Grant then invested the fortress city and summoned all available troops for an assault. Spiegel's official report, which summarizes in sequence his participation in the attack on Vicksburg, precedes his personal letters on the assaults.[16]

Headquarters 120th O. V. I.[17]<br>Black River Bridge, May 27th, 1863

Col. James Kegwin, Commanding First Brigade, Ninth Division, 13th A.C.:

Colonel:—I have the honor to submit herewith the following report of the part taken by the 120th regiment in the engagement on the 19th, 20th, 21st, 22d and 23d instants. On Monday morning, 18th May, I received orders from Ma-

---

16. Catton, *Grant Moves South*, 436–49; OR, vol. 24, pt. 2, 12.
17. Published in MR, June 25, 1863.

jor General Grant, commanding department, to move forward with my command from Raymond with all possible dispatch and join my division in the field near Vicksburg. I accordingly started from Raymond at daylight on the morning of the 18th, having in charge about 300 prisoners of war, which I was instructed to turn over at Edward's station. On my arrival at Edward's station I turned over the prisoners and pushed on rapidly until about 11 P.M., when I rested my command til 3 A.M.; roused my men and pushed forward, joining the division just on the eve of engaging the enemy on the fortifications in the rear of Vicksburg, about 9 A.M. on the 19th. On my arrival, reported to Brig. Gen. Lee,[18] then commanding the 1st brigade, and was by him assigned to take position on the left of the 118th Illinois and right of 7th Kentucky. About 10 o'clock I received orders to advance.—When, after moving forward about half a mile, crossing a series of very difficult ravines or gullies, we received the fire of the enemy. Seeing our exposed position on the crest of a ridge, Gen. Lee ordered me to deploy my regiment in a ravine [a] short distance in front. The regiments on my right and left receiving the same orders. In this position we remained until ordered to charge on the enemy's works, early in the afternoon. When this order was received, although my men were nearly worn out by forced marches of the day and night before from Raymond, they nevertheless formed quickly, and seemingly their extreme weariness was forgotten, and when the command 'charge' was given, they moved off as though well rested, charging over hills and ravines for more than a mile, all this time exposed to the fire of the enemy's well-placed batteries, under scorching rays of the sun, all striving to excel each other, truly showed the bravery and gallantry of the boys. Arriving on the hill opposite the fortifications, we were ordered to halt and rest; just then Gen. Lee was severely wounded, and by evening we were by you ordered to fall back to the

18. Albert Lindley Lee, a twenty-nine-year-old lawyer from Kansas, had acted as McClernand's chief of staff in the recent battles. GB, 278.

ravine from which we started on the charge.—About 10
o'clock A.M. on the 20th I received orders to move forward
and occupy a ravine running in front of the enemy's works
on the left; from that position I threw out two companies as
skirmishers to cover my front, keeping up a brisk fire continually drawing the attention of the enemy, while our folks
were planting a battery on the hill to my right and rear.—
After we retired, as per your order, to the old position,
leaving one company as a picket. At the break of day on the
21st, again moving forward to the position held on the 20th,
taking three companies to cover the left flank, and one the
front. Skirmishing was unceasing during the day, changing
the companies when out of ammunition and their guns too
hot to handle. At night was ordered to withdraw to [the]
position occupied [the] night before. The 22d, at daybreak,
assumed position as day before. At 9 o'clock A.M. I was
ordered to form my regiment in double column closed in
mass and support [the] 7th Kentucky and 118th Illinois in a
charge, at the same time being informed that a simultaneous
charge of the army along the whole line would be made.
About 10 o'clock the order to advance was given, and the
column, 7th Kentucky in advance, moved on. When we arrived at the crest of the hill above the ravine, a terrible and
withering fire from the enemy met us, from which the advance suffered greatly. Finding that crossing the hill under
such a fire would be destructive, while even after crossing
the hill an impassable ravine and abettis [sic] had to be confronted, and our forces would be at the mercy of the
enemy, the column was halted and the charge abandoned. I
here received orders to advance three companies of my
command through a ravine to the left and occupy a position
close by one of the enemy's forts, and the boys, by vigorous
and close shooting, kept the enemy from using his cannon.
I remained all night in the ravine. The 23d I was ordered
to fall back to our first position, being relieved by Gen.
Hovey's forces,[19] leaving two companies as skirmishers who

---

19. Alvin Peterson Hovey's Twelfth Division, Thirteenth Corps. Boatner,
*Civil War Dictionary*, 412.

were relieved by Gen. Hovey's on the eve of the same day. The same eve I received orders to prepare for a march by daylight to Black river bridge.

I cannot close this report, Colonel, without expressing my gratification and just pride at the gallantry and good behavior of the officers and men during the five days of peril, hardship and privation. They have my heartfelt thanks, and richly deserve the thanks of their country for the cheerful and prompt manner in which they performed every duty assigned them.—While all have done so well, it is useless to particularize.

Respectfully your obed't servant,
M. M. Speigel [sic]
Colonel 120th O. V. I.

Spiegel had participated in both of Grant's unsuccessful attempts to take Vicksburg by assault. The first on May 19 had been a hasty try at overwhelming the Confederates before they could arrange themselves for a siege. In it Spiegel's regiment lost only three wounded out of total Union casualties of a thousand. The regiment was even more fortunate in the second assault on May 22, in which Grant threw his maximum strength against the rebel-held ravines and earthworks. The 120th charged gallantly. According to an observer in another unit, "It is a good regiment, and Col. Speigle [sic] is just the man to lead his 'iron-clads,' with his ever-waving sword, cheering and calling to 'Come on my bullies.'" But, perhaps because General Osterhaus assigned the 120th to a diversionary role on one wing, the regiment did not receive the brunt of the enemy fire and suffered much less than the rest of the division. While Spiegel reported only one man wounded, Grant's combined casualties were 3,199. There would not be another general assault; instead, Grant relied on siege tactics to starve out the Confederates. To protect his rear against any attack by Johnston's army outside the city, Grant dispatched troops, including Spiegel's regiment. In the following letters, Spiegel gives a less formal account of the assaults and subsequent movements.[20]

---

20. Long, *Civil War Day by Day,* 355, 356; Catton, *Grant Moves South,* 450–55; OR, vol. 24, pt. 2, 20, 159, 160. The quotation is from MR, June 11, 1863.

In the field before Vicksburg

May 23/63

My dear dear good wife

After five days of the hardest kind of fighting in the front we were about a half an hour ago relieved to fall back here about a mile to the Rear and rest. The fighting so far has been terrific and as yet we have not taken Vicksburg; we have taken two forts and were driven out of them again.

My Regiment made two charges, the first one perfectly terrific awful; I never saw shot, shell, crape [grape] and Bullets fly thicker in my life and yet I had but four men wounded and my men stood and kept their line as on dress parade while on the charge and during the hottest Brigadier General Lee (who had taken charge of our Brigade in the morning) came up to me and said, "Spiegel by God you are a man after my own heart; you are doing bully and your men are the bravest I ever saw." The Regiment was at least 20 yards in front of any of the 10 charging Regiments.

The loss so far has been in my Regiment miraculously light, only 8 wounded and I am struck by a piece of shell on my left knee which knocked the skin off, bruised it some and makes it a little painful. I did not suffer it to be published for fear you would see it and be uneasy.

General Lee was wounded by the same shell badly; he had to leave the field. I am sorry; he is a brave and gallant Officer and a Gentleman.

We have Vicksburg already surrounded and it must fall. From our position we can see the Church steeples but they have a heavy line of fortifications clear around.

The greatest consolation I have during the last two weeks of continual fighting, marching and hardship, is that lovely picture of you and the dear children. I sent one of my men 34 miles to the Rear for it where I had left it in my trunk. I am looking at it about 5 times an hour and I fear that some times I am talking to it. As soon as Vicksburg falls I will come home and stay at least <u>one month</u>.

My Adjutand Sherman is one of the gayest and bravest

young men that ever lived. He sticks to me through thick and thin, always by my side no matter how much the danger.

I think Vicksburg will fall within a week and let us pray to God that I may get out as safe as I have so far and then I will come home and tell you more news than you <u>ever heard.</u>

I mean to buy wool in June and have a bully time [illegible word].

I must close as the man who agrees to carry this to Helena, Arkansas, is leaving. God bless you and the children and all friends.

Your
Marcus

In the field near R.R. Bridge Big Black River Mis.
May 25/63

My dear good and kind Wife!

You will see by the above that the whereabouts and plans of a soldier are frequently as uncertain as his life is insecure. When last (two days ago) I wrote to you a few hasty penciled lines from the front in the Battlefield of Vicksburg, I surely thought that my next one would more apt to be written in Vicksburg, than 15 mile back here to the rear. But such is war. Now for the facts.

After fighting for five days and nights with but two days rations before Vicksburg; after skirmishing, charging, deploying in line and again in mass, standing picket, supporting batteries, building Breastworks for ourselves and charging at those of the enemy; in short after five days of the most laborious, hazardous and terrible hardship and privations, when we expected relieve, we received an Order to get ready to march in an hour.

How is that? Well, Osterhaus who is known as a careful, brave and discreed General who is always sent with his fighting Division to the most difficult places, was Ordered out here in consequence of news being received that the Rebel General Joe Johnston was advancing on our Rear with

a force of fifteen thousand. Well, here we are eleven miles
from the Battle field and in fact I feel relieved; I was
almost tired of hearing the incessant roar of the hundreds
of Cannons and Mortars, the rattling of musketry, which latter never ceased for a minute the five days and the former
never stopped any for the last five days or nights. You are
perhaps anxious to know how it stands with Vicksburg. Well
we have it perfectly surrounded; we are close up to their
works on every side, but their works are almost impregnable
besides being so situated that you can not approach one of
their numerous forts without going over ravines, abattis, fallen timber and every hindrance possible.

We have charged every fort and were repulsed with fearful losses every time; we had possession of two forts but
could not hold them. The Idea of charging flesh and blood
against all the ennumerated obstacles and heaps of dirt and
a concealed enemy is about played out and in fact as need-
less as it is unpropitious. We are so situated that Vicksburg
must fall shortly with all the force therein contained, providing our Government will keep its forces elsewhere engaging
the Enemy in such shape that he can not take away one of
his Armies from the front of Rosencranz, Hooker, Hunter
or otherwise.[21] Vicksburg and its powerful Army captured
and Secessia in the South West is gone up. General Grant
has shown in this campayne more true, gay, dashing, bold
and strategic military skill than has been displayed by all the
Generals combined since the Rebellion broke out. He de-
ceived the Enemy all the time; they as well as many of the
Generals in his Army knew not what he was agoing to do
until he whipped the Enemy at five different points and
had his whole Army surrounding Vicksburg and, if no un-
forseen event [occurs], Vicksburg will soon be ours.

It seems like Sunday to us, to be without the continual
whizzing of bullets and bursting of shells but how long we

---

21. Spiegel refers to the Union armies of William Starke Rosecrans in
eastern Tennessee, Joseph Hooker in Virginia, and David Hunter in South
Carolina. Boatner, *Civil War Dictionary,* 708, 409, 411, respectively.

may be permitted to enjoy this pleasant quietude, God only knows. If Johnston advances as he has for two days past, he will be on us by to morrow noon. My Regiment has been extremely fortunate thank God. Since we landed on the Mississippi Shore and in all the fights, I have only lost 33 in killed and wounded and perhaps 10 as prisoners, among the latter two of my best Officers, Captain Eberhart and Lieutenant Wallace.[22]

As for myself I feel in good spirits. I have already wrote to you that I was struck by a piece of shell on my kneecap. It knocked the skin and bruised the flesh and bone a little but I never left the field and have not been off duty on [its] account. In a few days I will be all right, scarcely feel it in walking now.

My Regiment was in two charges. In the first one General Lee lead us and kept on my immediate right; it was a fearful charge and never in my life did I see shell, crape [grape] and so forth fly thicker but I was in front of my Regiment and the Regiment [was in front of] the whole charging column. General Lee on the field and in the hottest came to me and said, "by G——d Spiegel, you are a man after my own heart and your Regiment stands like a Rock; Aye the line is as straight as on Dress parade; take a drink with me."

Dont you think I felt bully? My boys will follow me anywheres. I have it so now that I can go in as cool as on Battalion Drill; everything must be learned and I really think I had a good School. It is no Science in my estimation to send a lot of men in a hot place where they will get mixed up and frequently slaughtered and then have a big list of killed and wounded and make a big fuss while the Commander is admiring the bravery of his men at a distance, but it is a pretty and difficult study to lead your men carefully into dangerous places and do the most damage to the Enemy

---

22. Henry H. Eberhart, Company A; Robert P. Wallace, Company C. Roster 8:242, 248.

and least to yourself; the latter I am endeavoring to study
and I believe that at least I am favored with a little consolation in knowing that in this Army I have the reputation of
being somewhat of an apt Scholar.

My Sergeant Major, a very nice young man by the name
of McCay, had his shoulder badly shaddered by a shell;
Sergeant Waters of Company D, a splendid young man, had
the socket of his shoulder knocked and afterwards taken out
by the Surgeon.[23]

By the way Dr. Pomerene of our County is our Medical
Director and by the way with the exception of Ebright the
best man I ever saw for the place; he is a great friend of
mine.[24] My three Surgeons are excellent men; the Surgeons
name is Stanton, a Son of old Doctor Stanton of Salem; he
is a splendid man; he is one of the Division operating Surgeons. The two assistants, Hammond and Stouffer, are very
good men. As soon as Vicksburg falls I mean to go home
and I do not believe you can imagine how much I long to
see you all; if it were not for your likenesses I do not know
what to do.

As for resigning dear Caroline, I do not feel that I can as
long as my Country needs my services for the suppression
of this unholy and wicked rebellion. I am not in favor of
settling this until the miserable cusses that would ruin our
beloved Country are thoroughly convinced of their error
and completely whipped. It makes but little difference to me
whether the Holmes County Republican or democratic party
give me credit for anything; you can feel perfectly easy on
that score, for I do also. One thing is certain, that my fighting in this War will leave an inheritance to my beloved children of more value then all the Gold in India. I hope to
live to see the day when my boys will point with pride to
their father's history during his country's trouble. If this
War should come to a close soon and the Rebs whipped,

---

23. John D. Mackey, John W. Waters. Roster 8:241, 251.
24. Dr. Joel Pomerene was Medical Director of Osterhaus's Division. OR,
vol. 24, pt. 2, 21.

God knows I would love it, for I long for home with all its blessings and I think I ought to be at home and assist in raising my children. If they consolidate Regiments into companies in charge of the Lieutenant Colonel as per Order of the War Department, then they will muster Colonels out of service. Then I could go home honorable, for my Country would not need my services any longer. I understand that will be done and I think it would be a good plan and would save the government a great deal of money. For many of the Regiments have not over four Companies in it and there is no use of having so many Officers and paying them. . . .

My boys alone have fired off in the five days before Vicksburg (48,000) forty-eight thousand cartridges, so you can think the whole Army must make a great deal of noise.[25]

Hd qrs 120th O.V.I. near R.R. Bridge
Big Black River Mis. May 25/63

My dear dear Wife

This morning I unexpectedly yet nevertheless with great joy received your kind letter of May 9th which I will first answer in detail, though I have but this morning written to you. In the first place you say you have not received a letter from me since April 6th and that I write to everybody else except to you. Now my dear, let me tell you that I have written regular to you except in the week when I expected Uncle Josey home daily and [to] learn from him whether you left Chicago, whether he gave you money, whether he paid Guthman and so forth, but without seeing him we

---

25. As indicated by Spiegel's later comment, Caroline proudly permitted a Millersburg newspaper to publish parts of this letter. Its publication in the Republican organ, whose editor appreciated Spiegel's "opinion of traitors and the war," suggested the Spiegels' growing estrangement from the Democrats. Estill may well have been pained. Only a few weeks earlier, in attempting to refute letters from the army critical of Democratic views of the war, Estill had listed Spiegel first among Holmes County "men of talent and education" in the army who did not write "any bombastic slang effusions" for his rival newspaper, the *Republican*. MR, June 18, 1863; MF, May 14, 1863.

were ordered to march and I addressed your letters to Chicago.

About the sending of the money to Enos, is simply like this: I received some money from the boys to send to Enos; Enos knew then we received 4 months pay and not knowing where you was and whether you had received any money from Josey or not, I could not send money to Mr. Enos without paying him that old debt. I then sent him $300. I had nearly $375 left which I gave to Sinsheimer when we were ordered to march, expecting shortly to hear from you through Josey, not knowing where you was. Since then I have not seen Josey. In the meantime some one paid me $250 belonging to the Regiment and in time when we were daily in battle, a Gentleman from Wayne County came here and I sent the $250 to Rex to give to you without a letter or anything else, expecting to refund the money to the Regiment as soon as I meet Sinsheimer or Jo. You may give it to Cohn or anybody else you please. The Government now owes me $575, most of which I expect soon. As for me making much, I am now getting $192 per month; my expenses are now twelve Dollars per month. I can assure you that I am living as saving as I possibly can, any doubts expressed by you to the contrary notwithstanding. I am spending no money for anything. While on the River and in Covington and Memphis our expenses were heavy, but for the last 4 months I do not believe I spent $75 altogether.

As for Uncle Josey, I expect they have cleared four thousand Dollars in Cash since they commenced. I think that is almost as well as he might have done at home.

I mean to make Uncle Josey and his partner pay the $500 to Henry Liebenstein and the $500 to Weimer and Steinbacher.[26]

---

26. As indicated in chapter 2, Spiegel owed a prewar debt to the Millersburg banking firm of Enos, Brown and Company and apparently also to his brother-in-law Henry Liebenstein. Weimer and Steinbacher, evidently also creditors, had been among the original owners from whom Spiegel and Herzer had bought the "Red Warehouse" (see MF, May 17, 1860).

As for my coming home, as I told you this morning, as soon as Vicksburg falls I will apply for a leave and no man in God Allmighty's World can be more anxious to see his dear family than I, even if you do scold me every time you have the blues. During all the hardships we are living well; our mess fares better I think than any mess in this Corps. It consists of [the] Lieutenant Colonel, Major, Adjutand, Quarter Master, Surgeon and two Assistant Surgeons, and myself. We have two of the best boys to cook and forage for us in the whole Army and during a Battle, no matter how dangerous our position, one of them will hunt us at meal time and bring us something to eat.

I am really glad you have a fresh cow, for of late I am nearly crazy for Bread and milk; we still have one good cow, but too many in the mess to get much milk. I send you an abstract of a paper that (the only paper) used to pitch into me. Dont you think he comes under nice? I do not see what produced the change.[27] Every thing is quiet to day. We have a large tent in which we all stop. The boys have a lot of Tents we got from the Rebs that we drove out. . . .

In the field Big Black Bridge Mis.<br>May 31, 63

My dear dear Wife!

. . . We are still in the same place as when I last wrote to you, a very quiet place where we hear the cannonading of our folks at Vicksburg Day and night. I am hale and hearty and in Excellent spirits, have nothing to wish for if it were not that I feel as though I must some times just run off [to] see you and the dear children, and then I get [out] that dear picture and feel as well as I can. You may feel perfectly easy as far as my dear little Hattie is concerned, as I feel just as well towards her as I do towards any of them; I often picture her sweet face before my imagination and I do really wish I had her profile.

---

27. Probably the *Wooster Republican*, May 7, 1863, discussed in the preceding chapter.

I would very much wish, if you would write me a little more incoraging as to my military career, but I know you write as you feel at the time you write and although you say in every letter resign and so forth, I am nevertheless satisfied that you feel as proud in my achievements and as I do and I am satisfied that in your heart you do not now want me to resign, when you know that resignation is "disgrace" unless a man is sick, which thank God I am not.

Cary my love, my heart and soul are in the cause, though I make no blow, though I write no letters for popularity, though I say it but to you, yet I am satisfied as I am that "God liveth" that our cause is just and that as an honorable man I must stay in the service as long as my Country needs me and while I can serve my dear family more by an honest and honorable name then by leaving a stain on my name in forsaking my Country and her flag, just then when she needs me and when by my experience and influence I can do her some service.

There is a balance due me by Enos Brown and Company of forty Six Dollars and forty three cents, $46,43/100, which I ordered them to pay over to you whenever you call for it. I sent you $250 by a Mr. Caufman of Wooster without a letter, expect you have received it.[28] I have not yet seen Joseph and do not know where he is but expect he is doing bully business along the river. I received a letter from Henry Herzer and Colonel French; they would like to go into business here. As soon as Vicksburg falls, I expect to start for home and expect to stay with you quite awhile, go to Uniontown, Lima and so forth with you. My Charley is quite sick; he has the "scowess" [scours]. If he lives till I go home I will bring him along and leave him till fall.

I sent you a Copy of my reports of the late Battles which is a very correct history of my doings; hope you will find them interesting enough to read them. Let Cohn and

---

28. H. K. Kauffman had brought sanitary supplies to the Sixteenth and 120th Ohio. *Wooster Republican*, May 28, 1863.

Ebright read them and if Estill will not publish them, tell Ebright to have them published in the Republican. . . .[29]

Private!

My dear dear Cary!

When you see Enos and talk about the money tell him if he wants to read part of my letter he may, you know it would please him. I really dit not think of writing for anybody's eyes but yours. I just now looked over it and am satisfied that 2nd sheet would do Dr. Enos a great deal of good.[30] Tell him he need not say much about as I do not want you troubled though I mean to come out public when I come home. Also show him Banks General Order No. 23.[31]

I love you my dear my sweet Wife and have a chance to show it some time I hope.

Ever yours
Marcus . . .

[Undated note without heading]

My dear, dear good Wife!

I thought it would please you to say a few words to you private, though I really know of nothing but the world may know. Every body may know that I have the best wife in the world; every body ought to know that she deserves to be and that I do love [her] more every minute of my live;

---

29. Democrats charged that Spiegel's friend Dr. Ebright was now a member of the semisecret and pro-Republican Union League. MF, June 18, 1863. An indication of the growing difference of opinion between Spiegel and Estill was the fact that Spiegel's reports in fact did appear in the MR, June 25, 1863.

30. Dr. Robert K. Enos, whom Spiegel expected to share his view of the war as expressed in this letter, was one of Holmes County's better-known Republicans. See chapter 2.

31. Gen. Nathaniel P. Banks's General Order 23, Department of the Gulf, Mar. 23, 1863, forbade his army and its followers to buy and sell Southern products or take property for private use. It declared, however, that "the legitimate right of an army to obtain its supplies from the country it occupies" would "be exercised to its fullest extent." OR, vol. 15, 1115–16.

every body may know that our past life has been one of un-interrupted comfort and pleasure; though frequently have I had my troubles, yet never I think have I forgot that I have the best Wife in the world, and endeavored to use her as such.

I now willingly subscribe to your doctrine that the more a man gets of certain things, the more he wants, and on the other hand if he has none and feels satisfied.

In the field near Big Black Mis. June 3/63

My dear good wife!

I have just heard that a mail was to leave here at 6 o'clock this Evening for the River and from there North.

In a half an hour we are ordered to have Brigade Inspection of Arms so you will know I have but little time to write. Yet if I merely say to you that I am at the same place I wrote you from last and that I am well and anxiously waiting for Vicksburg to fall in order that I can start home, say that as yet [I] am as hearty as ever, say to you that I love you more than ever and say to you that I am longing for the time to see and embrace you and see my beloved children, I think it will at least be some satisfaction.

We are just near enough to hear the terrific cannonading of our folks at Vicksburg day and night without being in any danger from that source. Yet we do not know how soon we may expect some fun here of our own inasmuch as General Johnston is this afternoon positively reported to come this way. If we can only prevent reinforcements from reaching the Rebels at Vicksburg, we can take the town with all its Garrison. This Army has had the most brilliant chain of Successes of any Army since the beginning of the War, yet the crowning Victory would only then be won if Vicksburg is taken. I have to day heard Joseph was in St. Louis, I have not seen him for over two months; hope to see him soon.

The assembly sounds.

Adjeu . . .

In the field near Big Black Miss. June 7/63
My dear dear wife!

It is nearly one year since I was called upon to witness the fourth birth of our beloved and blooming offspring. Well do I remember your sufferings; as if it were but a moment ago, do I remember the heroic and womanly like demeanor and the loving and confiding looks I received from you, during all your labor and the joy we both felt when the lovely and pretty Hattie was presented by my dear mother, who at once pronounced her "the prettiest child that she has ever seen."[32]

Allow me to congratulate you on her first "birth day". May God our heavenly Father grant that we may live to see many many of them in peace, love and happiness. May it please God to give us many happy days with our Children, so that we may raise them an ornament to Him and an emulation to His teachings.

I would love to be with you to night; I know and feel you are just now thinking of me, but we will have to wait awhile, trusting that Vicksburg will soon fall.

With hearty prayers for your welfare and that of our beloved Children, I remain to the best and loveliest Wife in the world

A true and loving husband
Marcus

You dont know how much I love you . . .

Clear Creek Miss June 10/63
My dear dear Wife!

We have again moved about two miles from our camping place at Black Creek [to] a very pretty place in the woods near Clear Creek. As yet no other Regiment but the 120th is there but I understand several others are to come here and I am to get command of the Brigade.

Thomas Orr will leave for home and I thought best to

---

32. Quotation originally in German.

write a few lines to you. There is nothing new; while I write to you the cannons at Vicksburg, 5 miles from here, are thundering powerful and I still hope that we will get the town in a very few days. I am well and hearty. For three nights past our Regiment lay on its Arms every night and several times during each night drawn up in Battle line, but turned out only small Rebel scouting parties.

Captain Moffit[33] of my Regiment started for home to day; he lives near Orrville, is a very nice Gentleman, one of my warmest friends. He promised me he would pay you a visit as soon as he came home with his wife; use him well for my sake. You will like him I am sure; he will tell you all about me.

I still intend to come home as soon as Vicksburg is taken and calculate to spend as happy a time, God willing, with my dear wife and children as any man could have.

My health is very good though I do not like this hot weather here quite as well as I might. The heat is never under 88 degrees and often as high as 92 in the shade; to day we had a very good rain. You must remember that I have to come on a sick leave and of course I do not feel quite as well. I have a great deal of trouble with those boils, one about every two weeks and some times every week.

Thomas Orr and Captain Moffitt will tell you all the news.

I am so anxious to see you that I can scarcely write anything; it seems like ten years since I saw you. I expect to see you look like a young girl. Good bye. God bless you all.

Your true and loving husband,
Marcus . . .

Big Black Miss, June 29/63

My dear dear Wife!

Your very good letter of the 9th instant I received three days hence and the pleasure of hearing of your and the

---

33. Valentine Moffitt, Company D. Roster 8:251.

dear Childrens health and of receiving sweet little Hattie's picture is indescribable. She is lovely indeed, and of course you will not deem me vain in saying so, more especially when I tell you that General Osterhaus and everybody else that sees her says that she is the only "Pa Pa Child" I have. Do you too think she looks like me? God bless her, I am proud of her as I am of all my family; everybody that knows me sees the picture and woe unto him, that speaks not in inspiration and praise of all. The reason why I have not written for several days was simply owing to the fact that I had expected "Vicksburg to fall" and go home, but yesterday I was to the front and looked at all the positions and I must confess that the place looks no nearer taken than it dit when we left 5 weeks ago. Although our folks are nearer, the only advantage I see is that we are fixed to hold them easy and can use most of our force against Johnston, should he attack us. Everything here looks at least satisfactorily for the Government; not so I fear with the Eastern Army and the people at home.

Looking to Virginia, where we have dates to the 23rd, I fear Lee is too much for Hooker; all our Generals, Officers and men feel so.[34] McClellan should have that Army. Major General Sherman, an Army Officer and perhaps the most accomplished General in this Army, told me a week ago, "McClellan is the only man that can successfully cope with Lee" he knows them both from West Point and understands their Calibre.[35]

Not only that it looks bad in that Army, but judging from the Reports of Holmes County in the Papers (and also other places), there seems to be a spirit to resist the Government

---

34. Robert E. Lee had begun the offensive campaign which would culminate in the invasion of Pennsylvania and the Union victory at Gettysburg. His opponent at the start was Gen. Joseph Hooker. Boatner, *Civil War Dictionary*, 332–33.

35. Not literally correct, as Lee's class at the Military Academy was 1829, McClellan's was 1846, and Sherman's was 1840. Boatner, *Civil War Dictionary*, 476, 524, 750.

and bring on a Collision, resulting in Civil War at home; I
tremble when I think of it. Though I fear nothing from
"Camp Napoleon" as it is called, yet the signs are bad and I
wish you were out of the County. If you can sell the house
for $1200, do so and I will agree to clear off all Mortgages
and when I come home you can move away. They may have
difficulty in Millersburg and I could not bear the Idea of
you living in a town where you would be in danger of suffering the trials of War. You need not say anything about
me saying that, yet still I do not care. It is a shame. I can
scarcely think of anything else. I think it wrong to arrest
Citizens in the loyal States for Civil offences and try them
by Court Martials but it is ten times as bad to resist the laws
of the Government.[36]

---

36. As indicated above, Democrats in Ohio opposed the arrest of certain
civilian opponents of the Lincoln administration and "Peace Democrats"
among them opposed the further conduct of the war, especially to free slaves.
In May 1863, the United States military arrested former congressman Clement L. Vallandigham for his allegedly treasonable utterances and convicted
him before a military commission. After being sent into exile by President
Lincoln, Vallandigham became a martyr to many Ohio Democrats, who
nominated him for governor. The partisan bitterness concerning the war
encouraged opposition to conscription. Near the village of Napoleon (later
named Glenmount) in southwestern Holmes County, several civilians being
arrested for a minor attack on an enrolling officer were released by a crowd
or mob. Rumors spread that draft opponents had established a fortified
camp. On June 17, 1863, some 420 troops sent from Columbus seized the
campsite. While there was some shooting, there were no fatalities. A "Peace
Commission" from Millersburg including several of Spiegel's old friends and
acquaintances arranged for the surrender of several men and settled the
affair. The Ohio Republicans used the "war" in Holmes County to discredit
the Democrats. Roseboom, *Civil War Era*, 405–16; Garber, *Holmes County
Rebellion*, pp. iii, 2–11. MF, June 25, 1863. Spiegel was like many field soldiers
in his rejection of the Ohio Democrats' position. The first sergeant of Company I of the 120th, professedly a Democrat, told his mother that Vallandigham and his running mate "must be a set of <u>fools</u> to think that the
voters of that party will support such <u>men</u> as they are." In words about the
Civil War not unlike Spiegel's, he avowed, "I believe it to be our duty to
uphold the Administration in measures it may take to put down the Rebellion
for our country's sake." Letter of James R. Pollock, June 23, 1863, in *Mansfield Herald*, July 15, 1863; Roster 8:266.

Since I wrote to you last, we moved again; we are again near Big Black Bridge, close to the Rifle Pits. We are daily looking for Johnston to attack and if he does he will get a warm reception. I consider Grant's situation perfectly safe as against all the forces the Confederates can bring in this Section of Country against him.

It is awfully hot here, but we stand it; we have not much to do except standing Pickets and that is much easier in the Summer than in Winter. We are at present more excited about Hookers Army and the Raids into Maryland and Pennsylvania than we are about Vicksburg, because the latter is sure to fall, while Hooker seems in a precarious position. Let us trust to God for the best.

As for myself I am hale and hearty, never was better, sweating like a good fellow, though trying to take it as cool as anybody dare.

My boys are tolerably well off, yet over fifty are having chills and fever. Joseph has his tent at General Osterhauses Head Quarters about 300 yards from here.

Sinsheimer has a Tent about two miles from here with the 2nd Brigade of our Division; they are doing bully business. They have taken in seven thousand Dollars since Josey came with his new Stock; they sell every day from five hundred to a thousand Dollars for Cash; they will clear four thousand Dollars on this last Stock if Johnston stays away three days longer.

The Paymaster is here and will pay us two months pay in a few days and then I will send you about three hundred Dollars again; if he pays us 4 months I will send you seven hundred.

If God only spares my health I think I begin to see bottom. I do hope my love that we may soon see the time that we can live as people like us should and raise our beloved Children, becoming to them and us who love them as we do. I have about made up my mind never to commence business without sufficient means to carry on whatever I do without a dead weight hanging around my neck; if I can not do it big, I will do it small, but on my own Capital.

Josey hopes to make about twenty thousand Dollars for him and Sinsheimer and then start a fine Dry Goods business in Chicago and have me go in as Partner.

How would you like to live in Chicago at these prospects? . . .

Big Black Miss. July 1/63

My dear dear Wife:

. . . Our situation is as it was when last I wrote; we are fortifying and expecting the Rebels to attack us, which may happen in a few days; the latest reports say, that Johnstons Advance is within five miles of us. His Army is reported fifty thousand strong, yet I feel confident if he attacks us we can whip him. Vicksburg is not yet taken, very little firing to day. If we whip Johnston, Vicksburg will surrender; the only hope Pemberton has, is to be relieved by Johnston.[37] We have St. Louis and Chicago Papers of the 26th and I must confess everything looks gloomy in Pennsylvania; it seems Lee is bound to go to Philadelphia, My God, what is our Potomac Army doing. Would to God, President Lincoln would recall McClellan; he would make Lee pay dearly for his impudence. McClellan is the only man in America that can do it, so says Grant, Sherman and nearly every General here and I, though a much, much lesser light, would bet my life upon it.

I am still saying if Vicksburg falls I shall come home, and am still in great hopes that it will soon fall, and I might here say even if that event transpires, dont look for me home at once, for it takes some time to get a leave of absence through and more particularly will it be a little more trouble for me now, since General McClernand, who was a friend of mine, had been removed. Our new General I do not as yet know; he is said to be a very strict disciplinarian;

---

37. Johnston, who assembled little more than half the force reported by Spiegel, was unable to rescue the Vicksburg garrison led by General John Pemberton from the ever larger force besieging the town. Catton, *Grant Moves South*, 460–61.

his name is Ord.[38] For the last three weeks we are having
Peaches and Cream, Peach Pie, Blackberries and Cream,
three times a day; Oh how often have I wished for you and
the children. Two weeks ago I saw an Orchard of two hundred and fifty acres, nothing in but Peach trees of a dwarf
nature and just as full as they could hang. It done my Eyes
good to see such a sight; the trees were loaded with the
golden fruit. Blackberries are here by the million; you can
ride for miles at a time and the Bushes look perfectly black.

Joseph boards with us, though he has a cook and Sinsheimer often comes riding almost starved to get a good
meal. To day we settled our Bill for the months of June
and living as we do and paying $18 per month to our two
cooks, our Bill was only Six Dollars per month for each.
Aint that cheap? I have not heard from you since the 9th
but hope to get 2 or 3 tomorrow. I have not seen a Paper
from Holmes County since the 28th of December. I am sorry too; I would like to read the local news. I do wish you
would put up one of each every week, put two "one cent"
Stamps on the Bundle and send them to me. Oh by the
way, Desilva[39] showed me to day a slip out of the Holmes
County Republican of the 18th with part of a letter from
me to you; how dit that come in the Paper? I am sorry to
see it; not that I take back one word I said in it, only that
part which Lee said to me and so forth looks too much like
Bragadocia, when in print and repeated by ones self. To
you my love, you know I can say anything that happened to
me, whether complimentary or otherwise for if bad, you
would sympathize and if good enjoy it equally with me, but
never mind it is done and let her up.[40]

38. Grant removed McClernand, whose ability he had long distrusted, for
publication without submission through channels of an order congratulating
the Thirteenth Corps for its part in the assault of May 22. Catton, *Grant Moves
South,* 457, 466–67. Unlike McClernand, Maj. Gen. Edward O. C. Ord was a
West Pointer and Regular Army officer. GB, 350.

39. 1st Lt. Manuel B. DeSilva, Company E, Sixteenth Ohio. Roster 2:519.

40. Patriotic statements from his first letter of May 25, 1863, appeared in
MR, June 18, 1863.

How do you live? I hope good. Don't live stinchy. Don't be hankering for any thing and too "geitzig" [stingy] to buy it. I want you and the dear ones to live as well as anybody, for if I come home and find out you have lived stinching along, I shall not be pleased. My friend Dean told me to night that he wrote to his Wife two weeks ago to go to Millersburg and make your acquaintance; perhaps she has been there and perhaps she may soon come; use her well and let me hear your opinion of her. These very pretty moonlight nights I sit before my tent most every night and look at the moon wondering whether you think of me, what you might be doing and really I do sometimes forget myself and feel at home, I think sometimes our Spirits (Thoughts) in their wanderings meet. Dont you think so dear? After I get through I get up, go in my tent, take a long long look at the "dear faces", then go to sleep and often dream of you. I will look at the pictures now and see how you all look.—

Good, good, all look so pleasant except Lizzies appears a kind [of] cross to night. Would to God you were here or I there to night. Oh that this accursed Rebellion might be crushed, peace restored to our unhappy Country so that the many good and true men and noble woman, husbands and wifes, Parents and Children might be united again and live in peace. I do not believe that ever a greater sin was perpetrated in the Eyes of the Lord, than was by those, who brought about this State of affairs.

I hope the Holmes County War is successfully ended and no lives lost, though there might have been serious Results followed from so crazy undertakings. I hope that when I come home you will have some good "H[L?]andcaese" [cottage or pot cheese?] for me. I think I could enjoy some. My love to my Hamlin, Lizzie, Mosey and Hattie. I want all of them to give you a good kiss for me and promise to be good children till Papa comes home, when they may all cut up and Papa will cut up with them. My love to Elizabeth, when will she be Mrs. Mc? My love to Cohn and family, Dr. Ebright and all. Dit Ebright get my letter?

Ever ever your true,
Marcus.

Big Black Miss. July 4/63

My dear dear Wife!

This is a glorious day for our noble boys here; all of us feel wild with enthusiasm; our forces entered Vicksburg this A.M. We took 27,000 prisoners and 227 pieces of Artillery.[41] The grandest Victory of modern history. We raised a Liberty Pole in my Regiment, made Speeches and hurrah and so forth.

My God, such a happy set of boys; this splits the Confederacy. I am only sorry we have to go further right off; it seems Jackson is our next place, Grant is determined to follow up his Victory. He is the greatest Chieftain of the Age; the boys worship him. I will have to postpone my going home until we get to some place where we stop awhile.

Such a fourth of July I never saw, without anything to drink and yet everybody wild.

God bless you
Your loving
Marcus

Just before the surrender of Vicksburg, Grant had put Sherman in charge of a subsequent blow against the Confederate force that Johnston had been collecting. Sherman's orders were to cripple Johnston's army if possible, destroy the Mississippi Central Railroad, and generally remove any threat to a Union-held Vicksburg. On July 11, the Union attackers put Jackson under partial siege. A day later, Spiegel and his regiment were outside the Confederate earthworks while Lanphere's Seventh Michigan Battery fired at the enemy. A considerable part of the artillery ammunition was defective—General Osterhaus had complained that at certain times at Vicksburg, "our deficient missiles were more dangerous to our own men than to the enemy." One of Lanphere's faulty shells accidently exploded near Spiegel, wounding him in the upper thigh of his left leg.[42] Having

---

41. Closer figures are nearly 31,000 prisoners and 172 cannon captured. Boatner, *Civil War Dictionary*, 479.

42. Johnston evacuated Jackson on July 16. Hattaway and Jones, *How the North Won*, 432–34; Long, *Civil War Day by Day*, 383, 386; OR, vol. 24, pt. 2, 588, with quote from Osterhaus on 21; certificate of B. Stanton, Sept. 3, 1863, copy in Soman Coll.

played a daring role in the campaign that split the Confederacy, Marcus Spiegel unfortunately was wounded at its conclusion.

Hd. qrs. Division Hospital
in the rear of Jackson Miss.
Sunday 12th 63

My dear dear Wife,

This morning I was very severely but not in the least dangerously wounded in my left leg, by a shell, a large flesh wound, in the groin. Dont be scared by reports; I am doing as well as I could. I sent for Brother Josey and will start home as soon as he comes and I am satisfied that under your kind care I will be able for duty in two months.

The enemy charged on me yesterday but I drove them splendidly and fearfully. Day before yesterday I opened the Ball. My wound is doing well, but from our own shell. I lost so far here 4 officers wounded and 14 men.[43]

Good bye my love; I will see you soon, God willing. God bless you and the children.

Ever yours
Marcus

Hd qrs Division Hospital
before Jackson Miss.
May [July] 15/63

My dear dear Wife!

This is the fourth day of my wound and thank God I am doing exceedingly well. I expect to be able to be moved in an ambulance to the River in the course of two weeks and when at the River I can easy get home. You must feel easy my good wife, dont be discouraged; if I only were at home and had you attend to me I am satisfied I would be well shortly.

With Gods help I mean to be home soon and will have much, much to tell you. I think I had better have a bed in the big Room below, dont you?

---

43. Official casualties for the 120th at the siege of Jackson included four officers and nine men wounded. OR, vol. 24, pt. 2, 545.

The worst thing is that I am compelled to lay on my back all the time and can not move; it makes me very tired.

Brother Joseph is with me. Drs. Pomerine, Stanton, Bern, Steveson and Ritter are with me most all day, besides the Medical Director of the Corps comes every day.[44] I am satisfied no man could be taken care [of] better under the circumstances than I.

God bless you and the children; hope soon to see you. Am too tired to write much.

Ever your true     Marcus

Vicksburg July 24/63

Here I am lying since arriving at the Railroad Depot, suffering mental agony. I can not get any word from my papers. I want to go home. Home oh, sweet word, oh lovely sounding word.

Home, where I know my dear wife and children are awaiting me with terrible anxiety and throbbing hearts. Home with all its blessings; there will I soon recover from my fearful wound. The kind caresses of a loving wife, the sympathizing smile and the pleasing words of my lovely Cary will help me more than all medical assistance.

Then you Generals and so forth, why in the name of God do you not hurry up my paper?

From Vicksburg, Spiegel was sent by boat up the Mississippi and by rail to Chicago. Still on a stretcher, he was carried to the home of Michael Greenebaum where a doctor required him to rest without speaking until it was time to take him to the train to Ohio. At a junction en route, the mother of his adjutant saw him and candidly reported that he looked "terrible." On August 1, 1863, lying in a freight car, he finally reached Millersburg and a crowd of friends carried his cot up the hill near the tracks to his home. Three nights later, a serenade by the Democratic Band capped the hero's welcome.[45]

---

44. For Drs. Pomerene and Stanton, see above. Drs. Bern, Steveson and Ritter are unidentified.

45. Hannah (Greenebaum) Solomon, *Fabric of My Life, the Autobiography of Hannah G. Solomon* (New York: Bloch Pub., 1946), 17; Harry Sherman to Colonel Spiegel, Aug. 17, 1863, copies in Chicago Jewish Archives and Soman

As Spiegel's wound gradually healed, he found himself in a community where war heroes were a factor in the increasing political strife. Local Democrats continued to denounce the Lincoln administration's war policies and stepped up their efforts to elect Clement L. Vallandigham governor. Expressive of the tone of their campaign was a wagonload of Millersburg girls in the great Vallandigham procession, clad in white dresses with one beauty depicting the Goddess of Liberty, riding under a banner inscribed "Fathers Protect Us From Negro Equality." Though Spiegel had made evident his differences with his party, he nonetheless remained acceptable to its partisans. In part, this was because leading local Democrats, including Cohn, Estill, and Henry Herzer, were his intimate friends. Moreover, the Democrats found it valuable to claim such a heroic veteran in order to rebut Republican charges that the Democrats were Copperhead traitors. Thus when the Millersburg Democrats on August 13 held a supper to honor Lieutenant De Silva, who had been dismissed from the Sixteenth Ohio for writing published letters critical of the national administration, Spiegel's house was among those at which a procession stopped to cheer. After the Republican rally on October 6 for John Brough, their successful gubernatorial candidate, Estill felt safe in calling upon Spiegel for confirmation of his account of Republican provocations, including the importation of armed militia from Akron.[46]

Yet Spiegel also was sought after by Republicans. To lend credibility to the Union ticket with which they appealed for the support of "War Democrats," they needed to attract prominent soldiers who were undoubted Democrats. Thus, unlike such friends as Cohn and Colonel French, Spiegel was not pilloried in the *Millersburg Republican*. And, on August 3, when with the aid of crutches he was able to travel up to Akron, that city's Republican editor welcomed his visit with praise of his war record. "Col. Spiegel," the editor pointedly continued, "though a thorough-going Democrat, is no Copperhead, and believes in whipping the rebels into submission to the lawful authority of the Government they have so wantonly attempted to destroy." Spiegel was in the happy position of receiving support from both of the political parties.[47]

---

Coll.; Barbe, "Memoirs," 5; MF, Aug. 6, 1863. In the same week Spiegel's old friend John B. Chapman, who had been promoted to captain of Company C, Sixty-seventh Ohio, arrived home with an arm wound received at the assault on Fort Wagner, Charleston, South Carolina. MR, Aug. 6, 1863.

46. MF, Aug. 20, 27, Sept. 17, Oct. 8, 1863.

47. Roseboom, *Civil War Era*, 409, 418–21; MF, Oct. 29, 1863, *Akron Summit Beacon*, Sept. 3, 1863.

Nor was he forgotten in the world outside Millersburg. From his cousin Simon Wolf he received a letter beginning, "Hero of twenty battles I greet thee! honor to the brave." Wolf was practicing law in Washington, D.C., and running an agency for collecting claims against the government. As Wolf was beginning to form the political relationships which would make him a powerful lobbyist, Spiegel might well take seriously his cousin's pride in "the honor of your friendship" and Wolf's invitation, "anything I can do for you, command me."[48] From Harry Sherman, his former adjutant who was then at home in Mansfield, he learned that General Osterhaus at a large reception in St. Louis had given to friends, including two generals, "a very glowing account of your [Spiegel's] bravery and heroism and also your splendid qualifications as an officer & soldier in the last compaign just ended." Almost simultaneously Harry's father, Col. Charles T. Sherman, wrote a letter crediting Spiegel with much of the success of the 120th Ohio and recommending his promotion. Clearly Spiegel had the political backing as well as the professional record necessary to win a general's stars.[49]

Thus, conflicting forces pulled Spiegel. On the one hand, patriotism and ambition called him to the field. Indeed, his obvious paternal interest in his men strengthened the call. In late September, a close friend in the 120th reported that "'I wish Colonel would come back' is muttered as many times in one day as there are soldiers with it." If Spiegel heard that his regiment was in battle, the friend inquired, "how can you help saying to yourself 'my boys wanted me there'" and added, "Yes we will look in vain for someone to say 'boys, come on.'" Yet to answer that call would mean again leaving Cary and his beloved children, who had been growing up in his absence. Even the infant Hattie was over a year old that autumn while "Mosey" was three, Lizzie seven, and Hamlin nine. The older children were big enough to play in the nearby woods and watch the frequent drilling by the

---

48. S. Wolf to cousin, Aug. 13, 1863, in Spiegel Papers, AJA. Simon Wolf (1836–1923) had been born in Bavaria. A Washington lawyer, Spiegel's cousin became unofficial advisor to presidents from Grant through Harding. For Wolf's career, see Simon Wolf, *The Presidents I Have Known from 1860 to 1918* (Washington, D.C.: Press of B. S. Adams, 1918).

49. Harry Sherman to Colonel Spiegel, Aug. 17, 1863; Chas. T. Sherman, Aug. 18, 1863, statement without addressee, both copies in Soman Coll. The presence of the latter document suggests that Spiegel was beginning to assemble the recommendations necessary to support his promotion.

militia. Despite his ties to his children and despite his wife's frequently expressed disapproval, Spiegel responded to the attraction of the military, and his desire to fight to preserve the Union. After obtaining several extensions of his leave, he eventually decided to return to the field.[50]

---

50. Ben Jones to Colonel [Spiegel], Sept. 26, 1863, Spiegel Papers, AJA; Barbe, "Memoirs," 4.

CHAPTER NINE

# "I will be 'Starred'"

As early as October 22, 1863, Spiegel made his by-then customary announcement of his willingness to carry letters with him to men in his regiment. Continuing problems with his wound delayed his departure, however, and meanwhile he drilled the local militia, from which he tried to get recruits for the 120th Ohio. Because the unit had been organized under the Union state administration and included few if any Democrats, editor Estill jibed at his friend's effort to induce what he called the "Featherbed Volunteers" to go to war. Nonetheless, Estill showed obvious sympathy for Spiegel, whom he thought "still unfit for active duty." Estill remarked, "In the opinion of many of his friends, he has stood about all the soldiering he can do." Despite such warnings, and against doctor's orders, Spiegel left Millersburg on about November 13. He may well have travelled with his friend Benjamin Cohn, who was on a business trip to New York at the same time. While in New York, Spiegel had a photograph taken and sent a copy to his wife, for whom he also bought a piece of muslin. About November 25 with the help of crutch and cane, the wounded warrior boarded the steamer *Creole* for New Orleans.

Spiegel was headed for what superficially seemed to be a backwater of the Civil War. For over a year and a half, Federal forces had held much of southern Louisiana. Under Gen. Nathaniel P. Banks, with whom Spiegel had served in the Shenandoah Valley, the Union soldiers spent much time at fortified points along the Mississippi. Meanwhile, the politically appointed Banks was preoccupied with attempting to reconstruct the state's civil government. Yet even in this seemingly quiet theater, Spiegel could encounter danger. Confederate forces lurking nearby might raid at any time. More significant, Banks might take the offensive. He had originally come with instructions to use Louisiana as a base to invade Texas; the Lincoln administration was anxious to begin reconstructing the latter state, too. Perhaps of greater importance, the United States wished to demonstrate its authority over Texas to the French, who had intervened in Mexico and were about to bring Emperor Maximilian to a

Mexican throne under their protection. Should Banks respond by moving into western Louisiana and Texas, Spiegel would again face mortal peril.[1]

Plaquemine La. Dec. 7/1863

My dear dear Wife and children!

I am satisfied you are uneasy and think it is not as it ought to be or perhaps think me derelict. It is true I might have written to you from New Orleans three days ago on my immediate arrival but when I tell you it would have been such an one as I do not like to send, for when I came to New Orleans I had the severest Head Ache I have had for many years and as soon as I could stand up I started for the different Hospitals and then joined my boys, from which place I now write.

The trip from New York to New Orleans would have been and unquestionably is a grand and sublime one for most of people, especially for those who are not light headed enough to be Sea Sick, but for me it was anything but pleasant; for five days out of the eight I was as sick as I could well afford to be. The fare was fine and grant [grand] but I could not enjoy it. I intended you know to give you an elaborate description of my journey but being below and sick most of my time I have not much to say.

In New Orleans I stayed a day and a half, mostly in the Hospitals looking after my men. I there learned that my Boys were in Plaquemine, Louisiana, about 100 miles above New Orleans on my old friend the Mississippi River. I left New Orleans at 5 o'clock in the evening and arrived in camp about 5 o'clock in the morning where I met one or two of the boys up. One of them [said], "helloh Colonel

---

1. MF, Oct. 22, 29, Nov. 5, 12, 1863, with quotation in last issue; MR, Nov. 12, 1863; Spiegel to Caroline and children, Nov. 24, 1863, in Spiegel Papers, AJA. McPherson, *Ordeal by Fire*, 308, 404–5, 412; Hattaway and Jones, *How the North Won*, 293, 345, 432, 476.

Spiegel, oh but I am glad to see you" and in less than no time you could hear a trementeous commotion all along the Tents, such as "say, the old Colonel has come back"; "Colonel Spiegel arrived"; "I tell you by God he has come back," "where is he"; "Aint I glad though"; and in less than no time I was surrounded by my whole command, everybody eager to shake hands and look at me; most of them in their Drawyers, some of them naked, none of them with a Hat or Cap; when someone proposed, "Three cheers for the old Colonel," which were given with a yell so as to alarm the slumbering neighbors. It was a Scene long to be remembered; everybody felt good and I felt better. I truly feel proud of it.

The boat leaves. Plaquemine is a beautiful town on the Mississippi. The boys feel fine, better than I ever saw them and if we are permitted to stay here this winter I shall say, glory.

Charley Herzer was here and will leave on the first boat. If he gets a Permit from the Custom House Officer in New Orleans, he will start business here.[2] How are the children? My love to Hamlin, Lizzy, Mosey and Hattie. My love to Elizabeth; is she married?

Your true and loving<br>Marcus

Joe and Sinsheimer are well.[3]

Not all the familiar faces of Spiegel's friends and acquaintances in the regiment were there to greet him. Lieutenant Colonel Beekman,

---

2. As further explained in the following, Charles Herzer, brother of Spiegel's former partner Henry Herzer, had come to Louisiana to set up as a merchant.

3. Spiegel's brother, with Sinsheimer's help, was still sutler of the 120th. His stock included such eatables as Ohio butter and apple butter, green apples, and oranges. *Plaquemine Picket Post*, Dec. 24, 1863, a soldier weekly quoted in Otto F. Bond, ed., *Under the Flag of the Nation: Diaries and Letters of a Yankee Volunteer in the Civil War* (Columbus: Ohio State Univ. Press for the Ohio Historical Society, 1961), 91.

once the heavy-drinking major, had died at home in Ohio. During the summer Adj. Henry S. Sherman had resigned and in the fall Spiegel's intimate, Q.M. Ezra Dean, had followed suit. But such close friends as Surgeon Byron Stanton were still with the 120th Ohio's staff and Benjamin T. Jones, whom Spiegel had liked while sergeant major, was now first lieutenant of Company G. And among the privates there were many who thought warmly of what one called their "brave and gallant" colonel. "He is so kind and good to all the boys that they not only respect him as an officer, but reverence him as a father." Such was the colonel's popularity that within a few weeks some would refer to the regiment's camp east of Plaquemine as "Spiegelville."[4]

New Orleans La.[5]
Dec. 13/63

My dear dear Cary & Children!

I just recd. your short Note written after the return of Cohns journey from New York it was very short but sweet— The few words "Hattie knew your Picture" was as much as a whole history of Glory to me. I came here this A.M. from Plaquemine to assist Charley & Joseph in getting a Permit through to start a Store in Plaquemine I know not yet with what success. I somehow or other do not feel as well at home in the Army any more as I used to, many hours of night I lay & think of home, I frequently think I can hear you cry as you dit a certain night & say I know you dont care any thing about me, it startels me. Caroline my love, I want some positive assurance of you, that you are not mad at me any more and if I ever done or said any thing to injure your feelings forgive me, forgive me, for God knows I love you as no man loves his wife. Write to me a long letter & say it is all right. If Charley & Josey succeeds they will make a nice thing.

I have written to New York for some more of those pictures most all my officers want them.

---

4. Roster 8:241; letter of Thomas J. Dague, Dec. 10, 1863, in *Wooster Democrat*, Jan. 7, 1864; Bond, *Under the Flag*, 90.

5. This letter is reproduced verbatim.

I am glad to hear the Children doing so well. The mail leaves at 3 o'clock and it is half past two now.

God bless you. Ever your true & ever dearly loving husband,

Marcus

Strictly                                Plaquemine La January 3/64
Private                                                   (Private)

My dear dear Wife and Children!

Sunday morning, everything quiet; most of the boys are in Church listening to a Cermon on the New Year delivered by the Chaplain of the 22nd Kentucky and I thought I would treat myself with the pleasure of conversing with you my love, inasmuch as I have an opportunity of sending my letter to New Orleans and from there letters are more apt to go, while from here there is very much complain of letters being lost.

I received your very kind letter of the 13th ultimo yesterday and was very much delighted in hearing of your and our beloved childrens welfare, though I must confess I could see a little dolefulness, considerable of the "blues" through it and Cary my love it grieves me, grieves me deeply inasmuch as I am the sole cause of it. My dear Caroline keep up Spirits for my sake, for my love sake, and trust to Almighty God and the poor efforts of your doting husband that all will be well. Our Star is brightening, our destiny looks hopeful and encouraging. My Hamlin wrote me a very good little Note and I am happy to know his Arm is getting better. I was fearful he would not get along well, thank God for that much. I would be very very much pleased if [I] could be at home and hear Hamlin and Lizzie's dialogue; they must say it pretty and remember it until I come home.

Mosey must be a good boy and his Papa will bring him something very nice and he may go along to War with his Pa when warm "weazer" [comes] and my dear little Hattie must not forget her Pa Pa who loves her very much. I am very glad to hear that that boy suits you so well; if he is a good boy I will do well by him. I expect Elizabeth is married by this time; I wish her much Joy. You must not over-do yourself; get a Girl; don't work too hard. We are able to have a Girl and I shall feel a great deal more satisfied than to think you are over working yourself. If the forth coming heir appearant be a prince he shall be named William Tecumseh Sherman Spiegel after my friend General Sherman; how do you like W. T. Sherman Spiegel, Eh? If a lady, Caroline Frances. What do you think of my Choice? You see I am looking ahead. God bless it whatever it be. If you can only keep up Spirit, and your health, all will be right; if you could only know how I love you and how much time I spend thinking of you and ours and how I am calculating and bound to have things, you would surely feel better; I know your wants.

I hereby after deliberate and calm consideration for many days, yea weeks, declare and promise to you that I will make due and full reparation for the past; never never shall you shed a tear over any thing I hereafter say or ever [have] a sad feeling over any action of mine. Your wishes shall be my law and your desires my guide for my actions.

Now it is out.

In as much as this is a strictly private letter, I will write another one which you can and in fact I would rather you would show to Henry Herzer.

I am well; my leg pains me and whenever the proper time comes I will come home. In the meantime be patriotic to every body and be assured my patriotism has not diminished since I came here.

Adjeu Adjeu Your true love,<br>Marcus

Plaquemine La. Jan. 3/64

My dear dear Wife!

... I have but very little news to write inasmuch as our little town of Plaquemine presents but very little news. We have about 2000 Soldiers here, Infantry, Cavelery, and Artillery; we have one Fort here and are now building another very large one. This town is 105 miles from New

Orleans on the Mississippi River, named after Bayou Plaquemine which starts from here and connects with several
Bayous until it leads into Texas or the Gulf of Mexico; the
Bayou is navigable in the winter on high water only. Back
of us is a very rich Country, plenty of Cotton. Close by here
the Planters raise nothing but Sugar and Molasses of which
this year they had a very excellent crop; of course they had
not as many acres as usual but the yield and quality is fine.

The most of the slaves here consider themselves and are
in reality free[6] and all the sugar raised right around here
was raised by the Compensated labor System and many of
the haughty and overbearing Slaveowners who one year ago
declared they would sooner starve then employ a freed
negro now are mighty glad to get them. I shall when Charley goes back send some Sugar and Molasses for our use;
enough to do us a year at least.

As far as Charley's Business is concerned, I am sorry to
say that it has not been very successful, though I have him
fixed now so that I think it will pay all right. The Market in
New Orleans was so terribly over stocked when Charley
came with his Goods that had he sold it in New Orleans the
losses would be severe. I therefore went to work and got
him some papers to start into the Country, but Charley is
too bashful; it takes a man here in this Country who can
talk and has gaf [gaff = glib words]. I wished a thousand
times Henry [Herzer] had been here instead of Charley; he
would have carried the Paint 3 weeks ago with such Papers
as I got for Charley. Charley is a very good and safe businessman and will do all right when things are all fixed and
he can be behind the Counter or in the Warehouse but here
it takes a man that can talk and turn himself to get the Permits.

---

6. Plaquemine, seat of Iberville Parish, was in the part of Louisiana in
which Lincoln's Emancipation Proclamation had declared all slaves free. Roy
P. Basler, ed., *The Collected Works of Abraham Lincoln*, 9 vols. (New Brunswick:
Rutgers Univ. Press, 1953–55), 6:29.

I have now a new set of the very best Papers for him again to get a permit to start a Trade Store here in this Place, He goes to New Orleans on the first Boat and I feel almost satisfied he will succeed in getting the Permit and then he will be all right. If Henry would have the Papers and leave here with them to night, I am satisfied he would get through all right.

I think this is an excellent Place for business; if one can get the Permit to start, one can buy Cotton, Sugar, Molasses and Rice.

In a few days I can tell you more. If Charley had to sell things in New Orleans he would lose one thousand Dollars; if he gets his permit he can clear ten thousand between this and Spring.

I only wish Henry had sold out and gone with me, but it cannot be helped now.

Charley however is an honest, upright and worthy man.

[End of page]

Plaquemine, La. Jan. 15/64

My dear dear Wife!

The very latest from home is a long and very agreeable letter dated July, 15th 1863, four days after I was wounded before Jackson, which came to me yesterday; it was a good lovely and agreeable letter. I have read it over twice and find it more pleasant than ever; that was written when you expected me home after the fall of Vicksburg. Oh such a return; yet if [I] think of the sufferings, I find it pleasing when intermingled with your angelic like care and patient nursing I received from you. Then I have to involunteerily ask myself, dit I use the author of so much goodness, kindness, patience with the proper respect and loving kindness. Ah my love, I am afraid when weight in the scale I may be found wanting, but never mind; it will all be right yet, I feel; I know I will, and am bound to have it right. Now my love, you keep these letters and see whether I will be as good as my word.

Charley has as yet not succeeded; he is again starting for

New Orleans to day and if he does not succeed he will go home after buying a lot of Sugar and Molasses. I have given you my opinion about it; he is a good man but he is too easy in this Country.

I thought I would stay here until the first of May when I mean to resign and go home. If you can sell our house you may; if not I have some trading in Millersburg until Fall or move away as you wish it. The Sutler business is very slow here too.

. . . When we get pay which will be soon, I will send you $11 or $1200 Dollars to straighten everything. I hope Cohn is not any ways "uneasy". If Charley comes home he can pay for the Warehouse and stable; if he does not soon go we will send it.[7]

I am not doing much now. The boys are generally very well, not much sickness of any kind. The weather is very nice again. We had five cold days for this Country; one day it snowed a little. . . .

Plaquemine La Jan 22/64

My dear Wife, my sweet Cary!

. . . You must not expect any news inasmuch as this [is] as monotonous a place as ever Millersburg can be. We are living here right on the Mississippi River and with exception of three or four Steamboats landing here every day which are called Coast Packets and travel from Baton Rouge to New Orleans and back, we have no news. When I first came here we had 4 Regiments of Infantry, 3 Batteries of Artillery and one Company of Cavelery. Since then two Regiments of Infantry, the 22nd and 7th Kentucky and two Batteries have been moved to Baton Rouge where they got up a big scare the other day.

This leaves us the 42nd Ohio and the 120th Ohio, 1 Battery and 1 Company of Cavelery, sufficient to hold this

---

7. Evidently Spiegel and perhaps Charles Herzer had borrowed from Cohn to pay for obligations connected with the warehouse. As indicated below, Spiegel also was having a stable built.

place against all marauding forces they can bring; we are
building a very large and formidable Fort here. The weather here is beautiful, just like our June; it is very warm and
the air is mild, wholesome and refreshing. I wish to God
you could be here. Colonel L. A. Sheldon of the 42nd Ohio
is in command here; you know if you remember what I
think of him; he commanded our Brigade last year at
Chickasaw and Arkansas Post. Yet he is a very clever man
and extremely kind to me. He has his wife here; she is from
Lorain County; a regular build Western Reserve Yankee
Girl. I do not see her often, though very much pressed to
call. I saw her twice in four weeks.

Dr. Stanton, Adjutand,[8] Uncle Josey, Sinsheimer and myself spend most of our time together. There was a report
yesterday that there were a lot of Rebels twelve miles from
here, so I started out with a Company of Cavelery. Uncle
Josey and Doctor Stanton and my friend Lieutenant Miller[9]
(whom you saw at home) acted as volunteer Aids, but we
found "nary Reb" after a hard ride. I managed to get four
dozen Eggs and we came home. We are living in a House
all together (i.e. field and Staff); our boy does the cooking
for our Mess. Uncle Josey's business does not go very well
just now; there are so very few troops here and they have
no money and the lines are closed.

I have at present 12 Sergeants in Ohio on the recruiting
Service; I do not know how well or whether at all, they suc-
ceed. It takes so long somehow to hear from Ohio and the
North generally that we do not know what is going on. In
New Orleans they have news once a week at least but here
it is very irregular.

Captain Moffit sent in his resignation Papers about three
months ago and a few days ago they came back accepted. I
am very sorry for them indeed. Since I am here I have
learned and seen more of what the horrors of Slavery was
than I ever knew before and I am glad indeed that the

8. Elias Fraunfelter. Roster 8:241.
9. Benjamin F. Miller, first lieutenant, Company D. Roster 8:251.

signs of the times show, towards closing out the accursed institution. You know it takes me long to say anything that
sounds antidemocratic[10] and it goes hard, but whether I stay
in the Army or come home, I am [in] favor of doing away
with the institution of Slavery. I am willing for the Planters
to hire them and in favor of making the negro work at all
events, inasmuch as he is naturally lazy and indolent, but
never hereafter will I either speak or vote in favor of Slavery; this is no hasty conclusion but a deep conviction. Yet I
never mean hereafter to be a politician, but quietly as a
good citizen doing duty to my God, my family, my Country
and myself.

Charley has left here about a week ago; I think however
he is yet in New Orleans. You must write me a long, long
letter and many of them and ask me ten thousand questions
in every one and I will take them up one by one and answer them. This is the tirest place I ever was at, during my
Soldier life, but the boys are so comfortable and feel so very
well that I am not at all anxious to leave here. We had a
negro woman cooking for us when Uncle Josey, Charley
and Sinsheimer messed with us, but it is so far for them
and they left us and we discharged our Cook and have only
our boy. One of my men who deserted in Covington and
was brought up by the Provost Marshal was tried by a Court
Marshal and sentenced to forfeit all his pay and condemned
for six months hard labor on Fort Espararox [Esperanza],
Texas, with a Ball and Chain on his right leg, a very very
hard sentence indeed; I would rather they would have shot
him, for death is not so hard as degradation.

I am well and hearty and if I had my dear, dear little
family here I would not wish anything better, but as it is my
heart is ever yearning for home, home with all its blessings.
I hope you are comfortable during this extreme awful cold
weather, such as I see by the Papers you must have had; it

---

10. That is, opposed to the policies of the Democratic party.

makes me tremble to think you had to be there without me; God grant all was right.

Hamlin must continue to be a good and obedient boy. He is about getting to be a youth and he must endeavor to learn well and make a man so he can aid and assist his father and mother when they get old. I hope soon to be at home when I can teach him and help him along. . . .

My leg still hurts me most all the time and I come to the conclusion it always will, yet not enough to hurt me in the common avocation of life.

I expect the Paymaster here every day and whenever he comes I want to send about $1200.00. If you can sell the House after the stable is up, you may do so; if not I will try it awhile in Millersburg next Summer. . . .

Plaquemine La Jan. 30/64

My dear dear good Wife!

In the midst of plenty I feel want; surrounded by lively scenes and activity I feel dull; in perfect health I feel sick and lonesome and why?

The last news I received from you was dated December 23, 5 weeks ago, just think of it, and what makes it so much the worse we have news of northern dates as late as January 18, 26 days later than from my dear family, and worse than all is the news I heard this day; namely: Charley Herzer left here about two weeks ago and promised me if he could find a letter for me in New Orleans he would send it here the first opportunity and to day I heard, he took a letter out of the office for me and lost it. If I had received a stun by a shell I could not have been shocked more and worse; it made me mad and worried; I can scarcely talk to anyone and scarcely look at anyone.

It would certainly not be very pleasant for Charley to come under my mild observation just now.

I do not know what to say. The weather is delightful, only at noon or about noon it is too warm to go out; you never saw a June pleasanter or warmer as January is here.

We have very little to do here; it is awful dull. I do nothing scarcely but read; I am now reading Charles Levers Tom Burk of ours,[11] a very pleasant work. I am homesick and tired.

You must write often and write direct to the Regiment.

Write me everything no matter how trifling it appears, all about the children and all, all, every little thing about your dear self. . . .

Are you well? Do you want me as bad as I want you?

God bless you. Your ever loving and true husband.

Marcus

Plaquemine La Feby 12/64

My dear good and kind Cary!

Yesterday I received your very good and loving letter of the 22nd ultimo and I have been joyous ever since; I say like you this is the first real good and lovely letter I received since I left home; the others all were as blue that they made everything look black to me, but thank God "Richard is himself again."[12]

The weather here is as lovely and nice as any climate could possibly be. We can walk around for weeks past, yea for the last five weeks, with our coats off; feel pretty comfortable.

I will first try and answer your every question you ask in yours and then give you the news which is very slim. Of course the time will come when we will have a fine Horse, Carriage and sleigh and drive ourselves and enjoy it and let me assure you my love that time is not very far distant.

As for moving and leaving Millersburg, I am perfectly willing. If you can sell the House you may; it ought to bring

11. Charles Lever, *Tom Burk of "Ours"* (1844), a novel of the Napoleonic era by a popular Anglo-Irish author. Gordon Goodwin, "Lever," in Sidney Lee, ed., *Dictionary of National Biography*, 22 vols. (London: Smith, Elder, 1908–9), 11:1017–19.

12. Colley Cibber, *Richard III, altered,* act 5, scene 3, reprinted in *The Oxford Dictionary of Quotations*, 2d ed. (London: Oxford Univ. Press, 1959), 144.

$1400.00 or at least $1300 with the new stable. The New Orleans business is a failure for various reasons, yet I think there will not be anything lost. I think and of course you will let the Children continue at Mrs. Lowmans, more especially if they made any progress.[13]

I have not received your letter relating to the warehouse matter but I received the one you referred to; I suppose your business letter is the one Charley lost. Well we are looking for the Paymaster every day, yet if he does not soon come I am thinking he may stay away until the 10th of March when I will receive eight (8) months pay and if so will send you ($1500) fifteen hundred Dollars. If Charley comes home before I send any money, he can let you have $4 or five hundred Dollars; it seems to me you ought to be able to manage that with friend Cohn, for a little while.

Uncle Josey is well and hearty. Business has not been very profitable for some time.

Taking his sickness, their journey in New York, their stay in New Orleans and the late business into consideration, I doubt whether they are worth as much to day as they were on the 4th of July last. I wish Mr. Benjamin much joy; he certainly married a fine looking female and I think his bridal time amply repaid him for the extraordinary trouble and inconvenience he had in obtaining the necessary "Yivutoolicks"; I sincerely hope he stood it well.[14] As for our "Affair" you may rest perfectly easy; I will be home if God spares my health whenever it comes off and long enough before hand so as to be sure of not missing it, though really in your last you do not seem very certain whether is agoing

---

13. Probably a teacher of some kind but not specifically identified.

14. Spiegel probably refers to the marriage at Millersburg on Jan. 2, 1864, of George T. Benjamin and Lizzie K. Cameron. They were married by the Reverend Joseph W. Swick, an Evangelical Lutheran minister. MF, Jan. 7, 1864; Nellie M. Raber, "The Marrying Parsons of Holmes County, Ohio, 1825–1875," a typescript in WRHS. The word "Yivutoolicks" or "Yivritoolicks" is difficult to read and obscure in meaning. Possibly it is a derivative from "yarishe," meaning an inheritance or dowry. Or perhaps it is "yomtov-dicks" and refers to holiday or festival paraphernalia.

to be an "Affair" at all or whether it is all "wind". I suppose
though ere long the matter will be positively decided and
you must not omit to inform me as I think I have a very
large share of interest in the matter. Your "Kindbett" [child-
bed] present shall not be very slovenly you may bet; it must
be O.K. . . . .

We have but very little news. Two of my Companies, A
and I, are stationed 18 miles down the river on the opposite
side superintending the building of a broken levee. Josey
and his clerk Louis Burger of Chicago, a son of the Widow
Burger, are down there and two nights ago they came near
being captured by the Rebels. Their outpost picket of 15
men of Cavelery, 4th Wisconsin Regiment, were surrounded
at 12 o'clock at night and all captured but one who was fortunate enough to get away and inform and alarm Captain
Au[15] Commanding the two companies of my Regiment, who
got them out in time, to prevent being captured; it was a
pretty narrow chance. They say Josey behaved like a true
Soldier. He came up to day with his stock. I think though
he rather prefers staying with the big crowd.

I have been to see several large Planters and find them
very hospitable; they live like princes, are proud and
aristocratic, but exceedingly pleasant and agreeable to the
Federal Officers. Slavery has been abolished in Louisiana[16]
and they are just as keen to get the negro to work for pay
as they used to while slaves, and I am satisfied in twenty
five years from now, the negro will be an educated, well to
do laborer and the white man none the worse. This you
know I see from my own experience; I am now a strong
abolitionist, but I want laws and regulations by which the
negro must be made to work and educated and the present

---

15. Christopher Au, Company I. Roster 8:266.
16. Though Lincoln had excluded then Union-occupied parishes of
Louisiana from the Emancipation Proclamation, General Banks had effec-
tively ended slavery in January 1864 in the entire area under his control. Joe
Gray Taylor, *Louisiana Reconstructed, 1863–1877* (Baton Rouge: Louisiana
State Univ. Press, 1974), 33.

Master be compelled to do it. Slavery is gone up whether the War ends to day or in a year and there is no use crying over it; it has been an awful institution. I will send you the "black code" of Louisiana[17] some of these days and I am satisfied it will make you shudder.

Now understand me when I say I am a strong abolitionist, I mean that I am not so for party purposes but for humanity sake only, out of my own conviction, for the best Interest of the white man in the south and the black man anywheres. I find some few large slaveholders concur in my opinion; of course the major part of them would prefer the old System. The poor white man, the mechanic and laborer in this country however, find that a new era is dawning for them in this Country (South); herethefore they were almost worse [off] then the negro slave here. I have not had the pleasure of meeting but very few of the fair sex down here; what few I meet I find overbearing, haughty and stubborn, powdered over with flour or white paste to make them look ridiculous; they are much worse than the southern man. I think a married lady of a large Planter is really a secondary Institution.

General Banks I think manages the political Department excellent. I think he will have the State in the Union a free State in a very short time; he is decidedly one of the smartest Statesmen of the Age; I wish he would be our next President.

I send you a few Pictures; I doubt not you will get one from nearly all my boys in the Regiment; they are getting them taken here.

As to my plan I can not tell you; we will I am satisfied agree upon some plan when I come home. As long as the war looks so important and call after call for men, it seems as though a soldier and Patriot could have no rest except in

---

17. The prewar Slave Code, derived from the French *Code Noir*. Ulrich Bonnell Phillips, *American Negro Slavery: A Survey of the Supply, Employment and Control of Negro Labor as Determined by the Plantation Regime* (Baton Rouge: Louisiana State Univ. Press, 1966, orig. pub. 1918), 493–94.

the Army. I have an excellent Regiment, my men almost worship me, and if I were to resign to day, one half of my officers would also and perhaps demoralize the Regiment which could be doing the Government more harm then my humble efforts perhaps ever done it good; but never mind, I do not believe you really want me to resign. I think you are really proud of your Soldier man, only you do not like to let on.

Good bye. God bless you, my love to the children and all friends.

Ever your true<br>Marcus

Perhaps because of his concern over "our 'Affair,'" his wife's pregnancy, Spiegel took advantage of the opportunity to join the men whom he had already sent home on recruiting duty. He arrived at Millersburg about February 27, looking "fine" according to Estill. "'Fall in' to the 120th," urged the rival editor of the *Republican,* citing Spiegel's reputation as an experienced officer. Other recruiters used more tangible lures. In Ashland, Lt. Col. Williard Slocum advertised bounties ranging from $400 to $652. Since Texas was a probable objective of the Union force in Louisiana, Slocum touted it in words reminiscent of a real estate salesman, urging young men to go "where you will find a pure climate and the richest country in the world." By mid-March, Spiegel was confident that the combined effect of such appeals would attract 150 to 200 recruits for his regiment.[18] He then returned to the field.

Cairo Ills. March 31/64

My dear dear Wife and children

I will be careful not to write too "forhayist" [excited] this time so that you can not scold me again and yet I can not help right here in telling you that I am convinced, mind you convinced, that I have the best and truest little wife and sweetest and best behaved children in the world; dont get "prochis" [angry] now for such are my conclusions and the more I see of others, the more I am convinced.—When I

---

18. MF, Mar. 3, 1864; MR, Mar. 3, 17, 1864; *Ashland Times,* Jan. 21, 1864.

came to Columbus I found I was detailed on the very disagreeable duty of assisting in conducting recruits and deserters to their different Regiments. I at once asked to be relieved but Colonel Burbank, full of red tape, could not or would not do it.[19]

I called on the Governor and he telegraphed to the Secretary of War on Thursday; I was relieved Friday.[20] I left in company with my recruiting Sergeant [illegible name] who asked me to accompany him to Lima, Allen County, and get the Provost Marshal Assistance for him. By the way I must say here that I managed to get transportation to Cairo by way of Chicago via Crestline [Ohio].

At Lima we stopped 5 hours but could not do him any good. . . .

On the Cars I met Isaac Greenebaum on his way home.[21] I arrived in Chicago Friday night, found them all well and all living together at Theresa's. Michael rented a house close by Theresa. Mother is well and looks well. She is very much down about me staying in the Army and is also bound she wants to be "Gefattern" [Godmother] next time.

Henry Hart just arrived from Germany, looks well. I wrote a long letter to Aunt in Worms; Henry says I am her pet and she says she would give half of her fortune to see you and the children. . . .[22]

---

19. Col. S. Burbank commanded the Draft Rendezvous at Columbus. *Poland's Columbus Directory and Classified Business Mirror for 1864* (Columbus: O. R. Nevins, 1864), 48. He was probably Sidney Burbank who had attended West Point from Massachusetts and been colonel of the Second United States Infantry. Heitman, *Historical Register,* 1:262.

20. The Union party's John Brough was now governor while Edwin M. Stanton was secretary of war. Roseboom, *Civil War Era,* 426–27.

21. A brother of the Greenebaums to whom Spiegel was related by both blood and marriage.

22. Henry Hart was a cousin of Spiegel's. Marcus's family in Germany was generally proud of his accomplishments. Jews in Germany having been forbidden to become officers, he was the first to be such in his family's history. Informing him of this distinction, his Aunt Mina in Mainz wrote that his photograph occupied the most prominent place in her home. Letter dated May 10, 1864, in the Spiegel Papers, AJA.

On the cars here I saw a German woman nurse a baby and every ones in a while she would take up a little Girl about five years old and throw the shawl over it and let her nurse. . . .

Baton Rouge La. April 10/64

My dear dear Wife and good Children,

You have ere this unquestionably received my letter from Cairo in which I stated all of Interest that had occurred since my departure from home as well as the fact that I would leave on the Steamer Hannibal for the Regiment. You will see by the above that my Regiment moved from Plaquemine to this City Baton Rouge, the Capital of the State of Louisiana.

Here I arrived safe day before yesterday after a long monotonous and tedious trip; long because it was a very slow Boat, monotonous because the weather was so very unseasonable as to prevent any one almost from going outside of the Cabin, and tedious because I had heard at Memphis that my Regiment had been moved from Plaquemine, Louisiana, and gone up Red River but which subsequently proved false. The passengers on Board were generally a set of men who seemed interested by nothing except cards, which entertainment you know I dont practice and perhaps never dit. Eh?[23]

Yet with all that I saw and got acquainted with four professional Gamblers, two and two in a set.

The first set were from Freeport, Illinois, a smart low cunning set who would stoop to most any kind of meanness and the dirtiest kind of tricks even for five dollars and one of them I believe would cut a mans throat for $10, if he could do it sneakingly; these two traveled from Cairo to Memphis.

---

23. Spiegel may have made a promise to cease playing cards, at least for a time. Among the unpublished personal messages in his letter to Moses Joseph of Dec. 14, 1862, was "tell Marx that the time is still coming close when according to my oath I dare play Solo again and then I will take him."

The two latter were from New Orleans at present, got a Board at Memphis. I saw them fleece a fellow out of nine hundred ($900) Dollars in about two hours. They are fine looking fellows, good countenances; indeed one had a large blue eye, an open face and splendid smile, but a perfect Master of the Art. His name is Eagle and he was raised in Wayne County. Although I dit not play and told him I could see him do it, he took quite a fancy to me, was very kind and said he honored and respected a Gentleman who would not play any Cards at all. In Natchez we stopped a few hours; we walked up town, Dr. Gill, my new assistant Surgeon who came with me,[24] a Mr. Wentworth and that man. Coming by a show window in which stood some very nice toys, among them some Ladies Toilet Boxes being an imitation of a bowl full of Gold Coin, I remarked "that is very pretty;" he went in, asked the price, $8.50, pulled out his Pocket Book and paid for it, handed it to me. I at first refused but he insisted and wanted me to select anything else I liked but of course I would not take anything else. I will bring the Box home if I do not lose it.

He went to New Orleans and I suppose will "cheat" some poor devil out of one hundred times that amount. I mentioned these things as a matter of "news" and "experience".

We stopped and wooded at "Youngs Point" nearly opposite the place and within one hundred yards of where I was stationed in February, 1863, and when I looked over the many, many graves and thought of the brave and noble fellows whose ambition ended there by becoming victims of the malarious "Swamp", I felt sad.

At Vicksburg I looked over the many ravines and Hills, the rifle pits, forts and abatises and felt proud that I also done my might in aiding to rescue that "Gibraldar" from the hands of the Enemy. At Bruins Landing I saw the very spot where my Regiment disembarked the day before the Battle of "Thompson's Hill".

---

24. John C. Gill. Roster 8:241.

I landed here and found my [regiment] pleasantly situated here at the West End of the City by the penitentiary, a powerful and commodious Building. My Boys were happy indeed and I received a cordial and warm reception such as King could feel proud of. The first night at about 12 o'clock I was serenaded by a new and excellent "String Band" formed in my Regiment since my absence, "<u>Auch so good nice die Elizabeth</u>". Though I am sorry to say the Regiment is not as healthy as it was at Plaquemine; though nothing serious yet, we have flux and fever.

This certainly was a beautiful and thriving City before this Cruel War. The State House, a magnificent as well as Gigantic structure, is situated on as lovely and romantic a spot as you could wish to see, on an eminent slope on the Banks of the Mississippi surrounded by an ornamented yard, of all the tropical flowers and shrubbery; I can not describe it to you, only let me say it is really grant, though the inside of that once beautiful building is all burnt out. The Arsenal, the blind and deaf and dumb asylums and the United States Hospital are all monuments of Beauty and former Prosperity.

The City in itself is nothing very grant. The Stores and places of Business are but indifferent; would not [compare] for style and beauty with those in Wooster; they would perhaps with Millersburg.

The Dwelling houses are generally the plain true Southern style; square, large and high Room, and very wide Porches on each story and on every side of the house. People I know but few as Yet. Brother Joseph and Sinsheimer are in New Orleans; I have not seen them yet. . . .

Baton Rouge La. April 20/64

My dear dear Wife

. . . Since my arrival here I have been busier than I had previously been for a year; am working very hard with my Regiment and I am happy to say the fruits show worthy of the labor—For a week past we had to rise at the early "<u>peep of dawn</u>" about half past 3 o'clock A.M. and are ordered to remain under arms until after "Sunrise" owing to a big "scare" they get up in this town about twice a month, lasting from the morning of the 1st to the Evening of the 15th and the 2nd scare from the morn of the 15th to the Eve of the last of the month.[25]

It being very damp from dawn till Sunup and unpleasant to let the men stand still, I drill them till after "Sunrise"; at 7 o'clock Breakfast, at half past 7 Guard Mounting. At nine I drill till eleven; at one I have Inspection, from three to five Battalion drill, at 6 Dress parade, from 7 to 9 in the evening I have Officers School, so you see I am hard to work. I feel well on it, only I have a very severe rheumatic pain in the small of my back, which troubles me to rise when I am sitting down.

My Regiment never looked better than it does now, everybody compliments me on them. I have scarcely been out of Camp since I am here; only after Dress parade we ride a half hour, Dr. Stanton, Dr. Gill and myself.

Dr. Gill is my new assistant, an excellent young man, and we all like him well. A very pleasant little affair took place night before last. As I was quietly laying on my couch, preparing my lesson for the next day School, my door was opened and in came Captains Jones, Frowenfelder and Miller; Jones commencing to make a speech presenting me with a beautiful "Meershamm pipe" worth about $50, a beautiful Present indeed. I was taken by surprise truly, yet I rallied and made (they say) a very good reply. It is just what I always wanted. I shall send it home to have it taken care of, and let us hope that when in after years I sit by my own fireside surrounded by my true and loving wife, my good children, smoking my "meersham", I may be able to enjoy with you, my love, the comforts of life due to us and tell you many a little tale of my military campayne, and may the days be many and happy ones for all of us.

---

25. Baton Rouge had, however, been the target of an unsuccessful surprise attack by the Confederates in 1862. Boatner, *Civil War Dictionary*, 50.

Uncle Josey and Sinsheimer are here but not doing much.

Uncle Josey attends every drill and parade and watches it with as much interest and joy as though it was a family affair.

How are all our dear children? Are they doing as well as they were? Do they study well? and behave as good as when I was at home? Does Hatty know me yet? And how is Henry Sherman Spiegel? Fine I hope. You must write often and write me everything and tell me how everything is going. I bought a horse here, a black fine horse, for $250; I am offered $350 for him. If Charley was here I think I would sell him (that is the black). Is Charley Herzer at home? Are my new clothing done? I would very much like to have them.[26]

We suffered a very severe defeat at Red River, lost 22 Guns, 250 Wagons and 3500 men. I should not be surprised if our Brigade would be moved.[27] I send this letter by a young man going to Ohio. Good bye my love. God Bless you.

Your true and loving
Marcus

Baton Rouge La. April 23/64

My dear dear Cary!

I got your very good and kind letter (full of troubles) yesterday and must say I had to take a good and hearty laugh over it; poor Girl, so much trouble. It seems then that Elizabeth and the cistern both "caved in" at once, only the remedies are different: while the former unquestionably will

---

26. As indicated below, he was having clothes made by his friend Benjamin Cohn of Millersburg.

27. At the behest of the Lincoln administration, Banks had undertaken an expedition up the Red River to conquer most of Louisiana and perhaps enter Texas. Though he had great numerical superiority, he handled his troops poorly and was defeated at Sabine Crossoads, Louisiana, on April 8. While avoiding disaster on the next day at Pleasant Hill, he decided to retreat. Union losses at the two battles were over 3,600. Hattaway and Jones, *How the North Won,* 519–21.

receive further "excavation", the latter will have to be filled up; so it goes in life, like maladies to different parties need frequently quite different cure. Well, well, the reason I laughed was because I could see you in all your troubles so natural in your letter. I am really glad the cistern caved without an accident for I never liked it where it was and, as you request, I agree to be saving enough to make up for the "unexpected expense". I am indeed glad Elizabeth is married; it certainly takes a heavy responsibility from us and we can truly congratulate us inasmuch as we married her off well.[28] I will write her a maseltof [congratulatory] letter. You must not do the work yourself, by no means. Get a Girl and I promise upon my honor that I will save two Dollars per week which I can easy do. I will never forgive you or myself if you should get sick on account of working too hard; do get a Girl and a good one and do not look to a half Dollar more or less per week. Now do this at once, I order it Himmell [? = heaven].

. . . Shall be very glad to get my new Clothes, as mine are beginning to look very shabby; yet inasmuch as we have marching Orders for Red River I am not so very particular as I would have been if we stayed here.

I would really have liked could we have been permitted to stay here awhile longer, not but in fact my force [?] is in the field, yet for reasons of the health of my recruits I should have preferred staying here, but the Eastern troops got whipped up Red River and we Western boys will be relieved here from Garrison duty by them and go and perhaps retrieve the defeat they sustained.

We may not however start for a week or so. I understand McClernand is to take Command of the Expedition; if so I look to the result as a Success, as almost foregone conclusions.

---

28. On April 7 at the Spiegels' home Elizabeth Foust had been married by the Reverend Swick, to Adam Petry. Her husband had succeeded Spiegel as Henry Herzer's partner at the "Red Warehouse." MF, Apr. 14, 1864.

Here we expected an attack; were up early, two hours before day every morning and under Arms, but I never felt there was any use for it, but our old General "Philip St. George Cooke, Brigadier General, United States Army", is an Alarmist and a regular old Granny but a very clever Gentleman.[29]

When we leave here we go to Alexandria and should not be surprised, if we were successful, but I might someday or other write you a letter from Texas, that is Galveston.

I would really like to get there. In the meantime will keep you posted of all our maneuvres, fads, prospects and doings and you must not be uneasy on account of me for I feel almost assured "all will go well" and that with the favors of a kind providence our mutual happiness and bliss will be furthered by it. God grant all for the best.

My prayers, wishes, hopes, fears, all center in you my love; I think I know and appreciate you and I feel and know that ere long we can enjoy the comforts of marriage life and respectable and well to do folks, together in the circle of our dear good children and be happy.

I received a very kind and encouraging letter from Simon Wolf giving me positive assurance that I will be "Starred" though it takes time, perseverance, money and pluck, but he says it shall be done. I will send you the letter as soon as I answered it. Petitions will flow into Washington on my behalf, I think, and all will be right; then you will be "Generalin" [a General's wife].[30] News I have but little if any to communicate to you. I am to work harter than ever I have for a year past, studying and drilling and I can see the

---

29. Cooke, who was then fifty-four, was indeed a West Pointer with long service in the prewar army. He was the father-in-law of Confederate Gen. J. E. B. Stuart. GB, 89–90.

30. It was common knowledge among Spiegel's officers that prominent generals had recommended this promotion to brigadier general of volunteers. Capt. James B. Taylor to Mrs. Caroline Spiegel, June 28, 1864, in the Soman Coll.

effects. Would to God you could see it; I am satisfied you would feel proud, even if you would not say it.

This is Shabbath and I am invited to a regular Shabbath Dinner at Mrs. Baer, a Jewish Widow here; a place that would seem very pleasant to go to if it were not for 6 as mean children as I ever saw.[31] The woman is as near Harriet (of Michael) Joseph only about 10 years older in looks, as any two persons I ever saw in looks and appearance, only this Lady is [as] thoroughly educated in French, German as [in] English, but for all the world like Yette. She has a Store, is making money. It is a place of resort for Dinner and so forth for the Union Officers and of course she is smart enough to get permits and so forth for them to send Goods out. That finishes all my acquaintances here. Roselles is making a fine Soldier; he is learning to drill. He is no drummer but a Soldier; he is well liked and in a good Company. I prefer letting him learn to drill and make Soldier than a Servant.[32] Uncle Josey is very well, but Sinsheimer is quite unwell. Uncle Josey goes up Red River with me when I go. . . .

Baton Rouge La April 27/64[33]

My dear good Caroline!

Your very good kind sweet and long letter came together with yours of the 2nd packed up in the Clothing and I must say it made me feel full of love and admiration and were it not that I feared a lecture from [you] I would write you a real as you call it "ferhayist" [excited] letter, but you would give me a lecture on it again.—Well to begin I had to day

---

31. This may have been the Bavarian-born woman who in 1860 was listed as Susan "Bear," then thirty-five years old and the mother of seven American-born children. Her husband Simon, a prosperous merchant, was then living. U.S. Census, manuscript returns, 1860, East Baton Rouge Parish, Louisiana, 495.

32. This name does not appear on the roster of the 120th. Roster 8:241–72. Perhaps he was never formally mustered.

33. This letter is reproduced verbatim.

one of those surgical operations performed which I have so
often to undergo, which before it was cut open prevented
me from sitting down, I could walk, ride Horseback, but not
sit. I had to take my meals standing.

The new suit is the best fit I ever had of Cohn or anyone
else. I wore it once on Dressparade, but as you desire, take
very good care of it, and I will promise you that when you
and the Children come down here this fall to spent the winter, the suit shall be in good condition yet to act "the cheva-
lier" with my lovely & good Wife. You say in your letter
reading of "men whose absence from home loose the
charms of home" setts you thinking sometimes I do not
think my dear Wife, that it should or ought, if I would
think that my sweet home with all its to me lovely sur-
roundings, with the many loving hearts could ever loose its
charms I would wish to cease to live.

Would to God you could hear me on all occasions and
under all circumstances speak of my Wife and my Children
and my home or know the feelings of my heart and thought
would never never entertain room in your heart. It made
me feel sad when I read it, but I know you ment not to
hurt me.

Tell the children that I feel very happy indeed to know
they are doing so well, tell Hamlin not to feel discouraged
even if Lizzie beats him in a Headmark or two spelling is
only one Branch of Bussiness and he may excell in many
other things and Branches and tell him that Captain Ben
Jones and all those who saw and know him say that he is
the nicest little Gentleman Boy they ever saw and if we live
and stay in this Department till Fall he may come down with
you and we spent the whole winter together. There are
Officers here who have their Wifes and eight Children here.
I do not think we shall have quite as many this winter. Tell
Lizzie that I have not yet been in New Orleans for her
piano, I am much pleased with her keeping head, that is the
way to do she is the Girl for me.

Mosey must be a good boy and stay in the House and
mind his ma, if he does I will bring him something real
nice, if not I will not bring him anything.

You must not let my dearest Hatty forget her Pa Pa I remember her well.

It is so pleasing to hear & be able to talk only good of his children, Poor Lieut. Col. Slocum who only lately came here, his Son stole a five hundred Dollar Check and sold it in Columbus and ran off & if they catch him, he will be put in the Penitentiary, the boy is only 12 years old, the Lt Col who sleeps in the next tent to me laments and crys most all night, if any of my Children would do so disgraceful a trick or act mean whereby their Pa and Ma would come to shame, I would pray to God to be killed in the first Battle rather then live to see them again, but thank God I fear not, my children are good children and honest and they will not tell any lie or take even the least little thing that does not belong to them.

You need not fear of mother coming if I do not come for her she will not come so you can be easy on that score.

I do not know yet wether I can come or not I know one-thing however and that is "if I can, I will, cost what may."

Uncle Josey has gone to Vicksburg to get permission to start a Store, I will fix the Ancony matter all right.[34]

In one thing I have changed and that is it used to make me feel bad when you lectured me about being saving and careful, but now it pleases me and I hope you will do so "lightly" in all your letters, I am sure it has a good influence and I promise you to be as saving as I can consistently with my station if you agree to get a good Girl and [not?] "stinch" for yourself, I will save all you spend in getting just what you want.

I send you again a few Pictures and I hope you will by and by get familiar with every face in the Regiment, they are truly good boys I love them and I believe the feeling is mutual.

---

34. Perhaps a reference to the Ankeny Family of Millersburg. The Spiegels were acquainted with several of them and one young woman had been especially friendly with Joseph Spiegel. Hallie Ankeny to Mr. Spiegel, Jan. 11, 1863, copy in the Soman Coll.

Our new asst. Surgeon Dr. Gill is a real fine fellow, we could not have found one any place to do the Regt. & our "mess" better, he is as all of us "Gentleman born".

General McClernand & Staff passed here the other day to go up Red River and if possible retrieve the great disaster we sustained up there, by the utter & gross inefficiency of Genl. Banks, perhaps since the first Bull Run fight we have not sustained so disgraceful a defeat as we dit up Red River, Our Army is demoralized and disheartened up there & if Banks is not removed I know not what will follow. He pays more attention to Secesh and Cotton Speculators to please them then he does military, the former he can do the latter he is utterly incompetent to fill, he is a good politician but not worth a pinch of snuff as a Soldier.—[35]

We are ordered up Red River and are awaiting transportation, I hope by the time we get up there we may have Genl. Jno. A. McClernand command the Dept. I have no doubt the next letter you get from me will be written on board of the Transport on our way up the River.

In this City there is nothing new, I marched the Regt. on Parade through the City day before yesterday and we were highly complimented by everybody.

I wish I had Charley here, I believe I could get a thousand Dollars for him here, as soon as one of my Officers goes home I shall send for him. I hope Lemmon has him again.

Has Charley Herzer got home yet, tell them to write to me, how things stand, I am anxious to know[36] Roselles is making a fine Soldier he is with Miller[37] & doing fine, he drills well and likes it well.

The weather here is very hot, as hot as it is in Ohio in July, everything is in full growth & we get beans new Pota-

---

35. Then and later, charges that cotton traders accompanied Banks's force—indeed that the whole operation was a "cotton speculation"—tainted the Red River campaign. Hattaway and Jones, *How the North Won*, 522.

36. He arrived at home on April 19. MF, Apr. 21, 1864.

37. Probably then Capt. Benjamin F. Miller, Company D. Roster 8:251.

toes & any kind of Vegetables our living is very good but not near as good as it was some time
[The letter stops in mid-page]

On April 30, 1864, at Baton Rouge, Spiegel and almost four hundred men of his regiment boarded the steamboat *City Belle*. Their destination was Alexandria, Louisiana, where Banks's defeated army was delaying its retreat until the Union fleet could pass the rapids of the Red River. Stopping en route at Port Hudson, the *City Belle* picked up a hundred more troops belonging to other units before beginning to ascend the Red River on May 2. On this journey, Spiegel was not his usual cheerful self, having just received a letter from Caroline telling him of an accident to his beloved son, Hamlin. On April 14, the boy had been playing with a friend in the shop of the *Millersburg Farmer*. Somehow he put his left hand in the printing press, which took off his forefinger. According to Estill, "The little fellow stood the sawing off of the bone and the dressing of the finger with a courage that but few men would show under similar circumstances." This was small comfort to his father; for the first time Capt. Ben Jones saw his good friend give way to despondency. "'Ben, I am not doing justice to my family,'" Spiegel said, "'I ought to be at home but I cannot leave the boys.'" Spiegel continued, "'I fear this Regiment will be the death of me yet.'"[38] Still he continued upriver and on May 3 the *City Belle* passed Fort De Russy.

Realizing that this captured fort near Marksville was the last Union strong point before Alexandria, Spiegel took precautions against attack. He placed some two hundred of his men on guard with loaded weapons and instructed his officers to be alert. He was ready for a guerrilla attack but was not ready—on his unarmored transport he could not have been ready—for the large force which the Confederates were able to insert below Alexandria because of the chaotic situation produced by Banks's retreat. At Davide's Ferry near Snaggy Point, a position about thirty river miles from Fort De Russy, some thousand dismounted cavalry with four or five cannons waited be-

---

38. W. Slocum to Mrs. M. M. Spiegel, May 23, 1864, Spiegel Papers, AJA; Boatner, *Civil War Dictionary*, 688. MF, Apr. 21, 1864, does not mention Hamlin's first name but Moses was too young to have been playing thus and Capt. Ben Jones to Mrs. C. F. Spiegel, Jan. 2, 1865, Spiegel Papers, AJA, source for the second quotation, speaks of "Hamlin's misfortune."

hind the levee. Two days earlier they had captured a Union steam-boat and the unconvoyed *City Belle* was their next target. About 4 P.M. on May 3, after Spiegel's transport had unwittingly passed one con-cealed battery, the Confederate guns opened fire from above and below the hapless *City Belle,* with volleys from rebel cavalrymen's mus-kets completing the ambush. According to one of Spiegel's captains, "such a torrent of shot and shell as was poured into the boat I never saw before and never want to witness again."[39]

Spiegel was in or near the cabin, which the first shell traversed, doing great damage. Uninjured, he rallied his men and encouraged them to maintain a steady counterfire—to no avail. The second shell hit the pilothouse and killed the pilot. Almost immediately thereafter, a shell cut the steam pipe and entered the boiler. While the boat drifted helplessly, about a hundred panicky soldiers jumped over-board. In this hopeless plight, according to some of the confused accounts, Spiegel may have exposed himself on the hurricane deck to wave a white flag. In any event, he was on the upper deck when a rifle ball struck him in the abdomen. He was carried below to the shat-tered, bloodstained cabin. Lt. Col. Williard Slocum then sent a man with a line to the bank opposite the Confederates and, having fas-tened the boat, escaped with about 150 men. The remaining 250 members of the 120th were lost; most, like Spiegel, becoming prison-ers. The whole engagement had lasted only thirty to forty minutes.

Spiegel, who had survived major battles, knew as soon as he was hit that in this obscure clash his luck had finally run out. A gunshot wound to the intestines was almost invariably mortal because of infec-tion. Still, he had no wish to die in agony and expressed great concern when the Confederates prepared to set fire to the *City Belle.* Several of his "boys" waded through four feet of water to carry him ashore. In a nearby house, he was cared for by his regimental surgeons. His be-loved brother Joseph, who had received a flesh wound in the arm, was also at his side and was of great comfort to him. To them, Spiegel spoke mainly of those at home. "This is the last of the husband and father, what will become of my poor family?" he cried out to Surgeon Stanton. He still had the presence of mind to ask the physician to take his new meerschaum pipe to Hamlin as an heirloom. During the

39. Jones to Mrs. Spiegel, Jan. 2, 1865; Lieutenant Colonel Slocum to his wife, May 12, 1864, in *Ashland Times,* June 4, 1864; Boatner, *Civil War Dic-tionary,* 7, 688; letter of Capt. Christopher Au, May 23, 1864, in *Mansfield Herald,* June 22, 1864; MF, May 26, 1864.

night, Spiegel suffered intense pain but next morning he felt better and dared to hope that he might recover. Conscious almost to the end, he sank into death about 4 P.M. on May 4. The following morning, the odyssey that had begun thirty-fours years earlier on the Rhine ended in a muddy grave on the bank of the Red River.[40]

No longer would he share his regiment's triumphs and tribulations. The captured majority of the 120th Ohio were marched through several Confederate bases in Louisiana. In accordance with Civil War practice, the surgeons were quickly released but, though Joseph Spiegel accompanied them to the mouth of Red River, he was retained because of a dispute involving certain Confederate civilians in Union hands. Like most of the 120th, he was marched to Camp Ford near Tyler, Texas. Lacking good shoes, he suffered much on the way but once in Camp Ford, one of the less severe war prisons, he and his two assistants lived relatively comfortably until their release in 1865. As to the part of the regiment that escaped, the disaster and the death of their popular colonel spread a pall of gloom which shrouded the demise of their organization. The remnant of the 120th became part of the 114th Ohio even as its surviving officers adopted resolutions praising Spiegel and wrote letters of condolence to his widow.[41]

In Millersburg, Caroline Spiegel, then thirty years old, shared grief aggravated by uncertainty with the many relatives of men in the 120th Ohio. Because of poor communications and the capture of so many of the witnesses, confusing reports circulated as to what had happened. So intense was political partisanship that Democrats and Republicans were inclined to interpret the reports differently. While some Democrats saw the event as a tragic military defeat, some Republicans charged that the rebels had engaged in "a cold Blooded murder raid."

---

40. At least two other Union colonels were killed in the attack on the *City Belle*. Two days later, the same Confederate force captured a transport carrying the Fifty-sixth Ohio and also a Union "tin-clad," while destroying another of the latter. Boatner, *Civil War Dictionary*, 7–8; *Ashland Times*, June 4, 1864; *Mansfield Herald*, June 8, 22, 1864; W. Slocum to Mrs. M. M. Spiegel, May 23, 1864, B. Stanton to Mrs. C. F. Spiegel, May 8, 1865, Capt. James B. Taylor to Mrs. Caroline Spiegel, June 28, 1864, all in Spiegel Papers, AJA; OR, vol. 34, pt. 1, 474–75; MF, May 26, 1864.

41. Stanton to Mrs. Spiegel, July 19, 1864, Ben Jones to Mrs. Spiegel, July 19, 1864, Jan. 2, 1865, "Resolutions on the Death of Marcus M. Spiegel," all in the Spiegel Papers, AJA; letter of "Aaron," May 7, 1864, *Akron Summit Beacon*, May 26, 1864; Smalley and Sturdivant, *The Credit Merchants*, 12.

For Caroline, the most difficult moment may have come in late May when a false rumor circulated that her husband was still alive. Frantically she induced his friends Cohn and Enos to write to the military in search of reliable information, including the location of his grave.[42] As she became sure that Marcus Spiegel was dead, the widespread praise for her late husband may have helped her to bear up—even possibly the conclusion of Estill's warm obituary, which read, "To the bereaved widow the quotation is eminently applicable: 'The Lord loveth whom He chasteneth.'"[43]

Bringing more tangible comfort, Caroline's mother came to assist at the birth of the Spiegels' child on July 6, 1864. Instead of the namesake of General Sherman about whom Spiegel had joked, the child was a girl whom Caroline named Clara Marcus, the first name being that of one of her husband's sisters, who had died as an infant. While Benjamin Cohn administered Spiegel's small estate, Simon Wolf secured for his widow a military pension.

Preparing to raise her children, Caroline Spiegel remained true to their father's religious tradition which she had made her own. In February 1865, she and her children moved to Chicago. While thereafter she occasionally visited her mother in Ohio and her sister in Michigan, her life was mainly with her Jewish relatives. The Spiegels, kind and generous, bought for her a double house. She lived by supplementing her pension with the rental of half the house and with income from sewing. In the early 1870s, after the Chicago Fire had damaged her home there, she and the children returned to Ohio where she ran a small boardinghouse in Akron. This woman who had once perforce learned German Jewish cookery reported with satisfaction that she did all the cooking and that her half dozen boarders ("all Yehutan but one, he is German") spoke German at meals. But, as she informed her late husband's relative, Rabbi Felsenthal of Chicago, "we have no [religious] servis here[; I] was only in the Shule [synagogue] once and that was on the occasion of a weding." At it, "the

---

42. MR, June 2, 1864; MF, June 2, 1864; quotation from A. Franks to D. H. Jones, May 27, 1864, Jones Papers, WRHS, Cleveland; copies of Benjamin Cohn to Major General Canby, May 26, 1864, R. K. Enos to General Canby, June 13, 1864, both in the Soman Coll. Many of the letters cited here refer to Mrs. Spiegel's concern about the body and to the unsuccessful effort by several of his officers to recover it during Banks's retreat. According to family traditions, the shifting of the Red River later obscured its location and possibly swept it away. Barbe, "Memoirs," 3.

43. MF, May 26, 1864.

poor teacher" [one of her boarders] "was allmost scared to death it being the first marriage ceremony he had ever preformed." Caroline Spiegel soon rejoined the Chicago Jewish community, whose religious life centered on the reform Temple Sinai and whose social circle included many of Marcus Spiegel's relations. Among them were relatives of her mother-in-law, Regina Herz Spiegel, who thrived in business. Having anglicized their name, they became members of the clothing firm of Hart, Schaffner and Marx. Caroline also saw her niece, Hannah Greenebaum Solomon, become a leading member of the community, a cofounder of the National Council of Jewish Women.[44]

Joseph Spiegel returned to Chicago shortly after the war was over, having been released from prison camp. The family was jubilant because they had feared that he, too, had perished. Joseph eventually opened the small dry goods store that he and Marcus had so often discussed. After many years of hard work and ingenuity this thriving business evolved into the well-known Spiegel Catalogue Company. Unfortunately, Marcus did not live to participate in the founding of this successful American enterprise.

Of the children of Caroline and Marcus Spiegel, one also became a cofounder of the National Council of Jewish Women, and a very active member of the Chicago Jewish community. Lizzie, who married Martin Barbe, was also first president of the Jewish Manual Training School of Chicago and longest-lived member of the family, dying in 1943. She was the great-grandmother of Jean Soman. The others who remained in Chicago died relatively young; Moses, who never married, died in 1884, and ten years later Clara, who had married Isaac Woolf, died. The other two children moved to the Pacific coast. Hamlin, the oldest and husband of Hattie Goldstein, died in San Francisco in 1935. Hattie Spiegel, who had married Thomas Nerney, lived in San Diego and was killed in an automobile accident in 1919. Her mother had lived with her for a few years and Caroline's near-foster child, Elizabeth Foust Petry, by then a widow, had joined her. Elizabeth died in California but Caroline returned to Chicago. There she died on November 19, 1901, and was buried at Hebrew Benevolent Cemetery.[45]

---

44. C. F. Spiegel to Mrs. and Mr. Felsenthal, Jan.[?] 1872, in Jeanette Freiler album in possession of Elizabeth Stein.

45. Marcus Spiegel's mother, Regina, died at Chicago on Oct. 7, 1870, and Caroline's mother, Lizzie Hamlin, died near Limaville, Ohio, on Nov. 14, 1873. MF, July 28, 1864; Spiegel Pension File, National Archives; Barbe, "Memoirs," 5, AJA; Solomon, *Fabric of My Life*, passim; family memoranda, Soman Coll.

Monument erected at Vicksburg by survivors of the 120th Ohio

By then, the world had all but forgotten Marcus Spiegel. He had not lived to see his new daughter nor to enjoy living in a united country with his beloved family. His death had also blocked his strongly recommended promotion to brigadier general and had eliminated the possibility of a successful postwar career, which might have kept his name alive. Some of the aging "boys" of the 120th Ohio did remember him as "one of the noblest of men" and saw to it that his name was given the most prominent place on the monument to their charge at Vicksburg.[46] Occasionally Jews attempting to refute anti-Semitic slurs on their patriotism also recalled the memory of Marcus Spiegel's wartime service. Descendants, too, would rediscover him. Indeed, the true Marcus survives only in the great body of letters which Caroline and her descendants so carefully preserved. In them lives the heroic warrior who experienced so many aspects of the Civil War; here also is the immigrant successfully adapting to America; the student absorbing a new culture; the effective politician; the struggling businessman ambitious to do better; the loving son, husband, and father. Most moving, here is what Estill remembered as "a genial companion, a man of noble impulses; a kind and affectionate husband, a warm and sincere friend."[47] Over a century later, Marcus Spiegel is still a true patriot who left his family a proud legacy; a fascinating man with truths to tell.

---

46. *Picturesque Wayne: A History in Text and Engraving* . . . (Akron, Oh.: Werner, n.d.), 154; monument to 120th Ohio at Vicksburg National Military Park.

47. MF, May 26, 1864.

# Selective Bibliographic Essay

Unpublished Material

The most important source of information on Marcus M. Spiegel certainly is the Spiegel Papers deposited by Jean Soman at the American Jewish Archives, Hebrew Union College, Cincinnati, Ohio. The collection includes all of his extant wartime letters to his family. While these are written mostly in English, there are a few passages in German and occasional words in Hebrew and Yiddish. In the Spiegel Papers are a few other items, one of the more useful being the typed "Memoirs" of his daughter, Lizzie T. Barbe, which provides information on her girlhood. The Jean Soman Collection at Miami, Florida contains additional manuscripts, photographs, and photocopies. Several of the latter are taken from originals in the Jeanette Freiler Papers, Chicago Jewish Archives. A manuscript collection with a few references to the 120th Ohio Regiment is the Benjamin T. Jones Papers, Western Reserve Historical Society, Cleveland, Ohio (WRHS).

A significantly distinctive treatment of the political background of Spiegel's period is Eric J. Cardinal, "The Democratic Party of Ohio and the Civil War: An Analysis of a Wartime Political Minority" (Ph.D. diss., Kent State University, 1981).

U.S. Census, 1860, manuscript returns for Holmes and other relevant counties, provides identifying information on Spiegel and on even his more obscure associates. Microfilm copies are at WRHS and elsewhere. Spiegel's own compiled military service record is available from U.S., Adjutant General, National Archives, Washington, D.C. More useful as a source of family information is Spiegel's pension file at the same agency. Ohio, Adjutant General, Correspondence to the Adjutant General, and Ohio, Governors' Papers, contain a few items related to Spiegel's military service. Both collections are at the Ohio Historical Society, Columbus.

Government Documents

For published summaries of the military records of Spiegel and his comrades, see Ohio, Roster Commission, *Official Roster of the Soldiers of the State of Ohio in the War of the Rebellion, 1861–1866,* 12 vols. (Akron:

Werner Co., 1886–95). One of Spiegel's military reports and many documents pertinent to his campaigns are in U.S., War Department, *The War of the Rebellion: A Compilation of the Official Records of the Union and Confederate Armies,* 70 vols. in 128 (Washington: Government Printing Office, 1880–1901). Maps are in the accompanying atlas which has been reprinted as U.S., War Department, *The Official Atlas of the Civil War.* Introduction by Henry Steele Commager (New York: T. Yoseloff, 1958).

## NEWSPAPERS

The press of Millersburg, Ohio is the richest source on the community in which Spiegel lived just before and during the Civil War. Especially important is the Democratic *Holmes County Farmer,* whose editor, James A. Estill, was Spiegel's close friend. In it are several Spiegel letters no longer surviving in manuscript. The *Millersburg Republican* offers contrasting views and contains Spiegel's military reports. The *Daily Toledo Blade* includes much of the extant data on the controversial career of Colonel Otto Buerstenbinder. For the political combat involving Spiegel and the 120th Ohio, the *Democrat* and the *Republican,* both of Wooster, are indispensable.

## BOOKS AND ARTICLES

Orange A. Smalley and Frederick D. Sturdivant, *The Credit Merchants: A History of Spiegel, Inc.* (Carbondale: Southern Illinois Univ. Press, 1973) is useful for Spiegel's family and its subsequent activities but contains several factual errors on Marcus Spiegel. For some of Spiegel's associates, see Jacob Rader Marcus, *Memoirs of American Jews, 1775–1865,* 3 vols. (Philadelphia: Jewish Publication Society of America, 1955). A few reminiscences of Spiegel are in Hannah G. Solomon, *Fabric of My Life: The Autobiography of Hannah G. Solomon* (Philadelphia: Bloch Publishers, 1946).

For Spiegel's prewar home area, a good source is Fred W. Almendinger, *An Historical Study of Holmes County, Ohio,* M.A. thesis, University of Southern California, 1938 ([Millersburg]: Library Archives of Holmes County, Ohio, 1962). Also helpful is D. P. Garber, *The Holmes County Rebellion* (n.p., 1967). While the following works have the laudatory quality characteristic of their genre, they provide information on several of Spiegel's contemporaries: *Commemorative Biographical Record of the Counties of Wayne and Holmes, Ohio, Containing Biographical Sketches of Prominent and Representative Citizens, and of Many of the Early Settled Families* (Chicago: J. H. Beers, 1889); Ben Douglass, *History of Wayne County, Ohio, from the Days of the Pioneers and First Settlers to the Present Time* (Indianapolis: R. Douglass, 1878); William Henry Perrin, ed., *History of Summit County, with an Outline Sketch of Ohio* (Chicago: Baskin and Battey, 1881); Andrew Jackson Stiffler, *The Standard Atlas of Holmes County Ohio, to Which Is Added an Authentic History of the County, Historical Sketches of Each Township and Village, Biographies and Portraits of Representative Men and Valuable Statistics, etc., Together with a Map of Ohio and a Map of the United States* (Cincinnati: Standard Atlas Publishing Co., 1907). For pictures of Spiegel's warehouse and other Millersburg scenes, see Joseph A. Caldwell, *Caldwell's Atlas of Holmes Co. Ohio from Actual Surveys by and under the Direction of Henry Cring C.E.* (Condit, Ohio: J. A. Caldwell, 1875).

A fine modern summary history of the Civil War is James M. McPherson, *Ordeal by Fire: The Civil War and Reconstruction* (New York: Alfred A. Knopf, 1982). Also fine, especially for military strategy, is Herman Hattaway and Archer Jones, *How the North Won: A Military History of the Civil War* (Urbana: Univ. of Illinois Press, 1983). Still useful for information on many topics is Mark Mayo Boatner III, *The Civil War Dictionary* (New York: David McKay, 1959). For higher officers, see Ezra J. Warner, *Generals in Blue: Lives of the Union Commanders* (Baton Rouge: Louisiana State Univ. Press, 1964), and for a wider range of officers see Francis B. Heitman, *Historical Register and Dictionary of the United States Army from Its Organization, September 29, 1789, to March 2, 1903*, 2 vols. (Washington: Government Printing Office, 1903).

Valuable for background on Spiegel's own ethnic group is Bertram Wallace Korn, *American Jewry and the Civil War* (Philadelphia: Jewish Publication Society of America, 1951). See also Simon Wolf, *The American Jew As Patriot, Soldier and Citizen* (Philadelphia: The Levy-type Company, 1895; reprinted Boston: Gregg Press, 1972). Although both of the following are dated, they treat the role of Spiegel's state: Whitelaw Reid, *Ohio in the War: Her Statesmen, Her Generals, and Soldiers*, 2 vols. (Cincinnati: Moore, Wilstach and Baldwin, 1868); Eugene H. Roseboom, *The Civil War Era, 1850–1873*, vol. 6 of Carl Wittke, ed., *The History of the State of Ohio* (Columbus: Ohio Historical Society, 1944).

Spiegel's first regiment and its second commander are dealt with in *The Sixty-Seventh Ohio Veteran Volunteer Infantry: A Brief Record of Its Four Years of Service in the Civil War, 1861–1865* ([Massillon, Ohio, 1922]) and in "General A. C. Voris," in *Magazine of Western History*,

4(August 1886):507–15. On the Battle of Kernstown: A. C. Voris, "The Battle of the Boys," in Military Order of the Loyal Legion of the United States, Ohio Commandery, *Sketches of War History, 1861–1865; Papers Read before the Ohio Commandery of the Military Order of the Loyal Legion of the United States, 1890–1896* (Cincinnati: R. Clarke and Co., 1896), 4:87–100; Franklin Sawyer, *A Military History of the 8th Regiment Ohio Vol. Inf'y: Its Battles, Marches and Army Movements* (Cleveland: Fairbanks and Co., 1881); Frank E. Vandiver, *Mighty Stonewall* (New York: McGraw-Hill, 1957).

Helpful in understanding Spiegel's campaign in the western theater is Bruce Catton, *Grant Moves South* (Boston: Little, Brown, 1960). For another account of the battle of Chickasaw Bluffs, see Earl J. Hess, ed., *A German in the Yankee Fatherland: The Civil War Letters of Henry A. Kircher* (Kent, Oh.: Kent State Univ. Press, 1983). Other useful sources are Frank H. Mason, *The Forty-Second Ohio Infantry: A History of the Organization and Services of That Regiment in the War of the Rebellion with Biographical Sketches of Its Field Officers and a Full Roster of the Regiment* (Cleveland: Cobb, Andrews and Co., 1876) and Otto F. Bond, ed., *Under the Flag of the Nation: Diaries and Letters of a Yankee Volunteer in the Civil War* (Columbus: Ohio State Univ. Press for the Ohio Historical Society, 1961).

# Index

Adams, Henry, pvt.: 92, 100, 131, 143, 149, 156, 161
Akron, Ohio: Spiegel lives in, 9; and Spiegel's business, 10; militia at, 14n; Spiegel visits, 303; Spiegel's widow lives in, 338–39
*Akron Summit Beacon,* 91
Alexandria, Va.: described, 117–18
Ames, Minor T., 135
Amish, 11, 15, 106
Ammen, Jacob, gen., 176
Anisansel, Henry, col., 34n, 44
Ankeny Family of Millersburg, 333n
Anti-Semitism, 13, 191–92, 250
Arkansas: unionists in, 219
Arkansas Post, battle of, 219–22
Au, Christopher, capt., 320
Authenrieth, Charles, pvt., 130

Baer, Mrs., Baton Rouge widow, 331
Baltimore, Md.: described, 113
Baltimore and Ohio Railroad: destruction along, 61–62, 65
Banks, Nathaniel P., gen.: praises Sixty-seventh Ohio, 87; Spiegel praises, 321; Spiegel criticizes, 334; mentioned, 65, 71, 75, 82, 97, 196, 204, 206, 207, 210, 290, 306, 307, 320n, 328n, 335, 338n
Banning, David or Jeremiah W., 182–83
Barbe, Lizzie. *See* Spiegel, Lizzie
Barbe, Martin, 339
Baton Rouge, La.: described, 326
Bear, Simon, 331n
Bear, Susan, 331n
Beegle, Henry, pvt., 122, 143, 146n, 147, 149, 153, 156, 158
Beekman, John W., maj.: drinking by, 198; promoted, 256; Spiegel praises, 273; dies, 308–9; mentioned, 183, 191, 195, 248, 270
Benjamin, George T., 319
Benjamin, Judah P., 114

Bennett, Emerson, 219
Bennett, Thomas W., col., 272
Berm, surgeon, 302
Bierce, Lucius V., 16
Biroker, lt., Jew from Alzey, 163
Blacks: as army servants, 166; as political issue, 303. *See also* Slavery and Slaves
Blair, Frank, gen., 214, 215
Bloomery Gap, Va.: operation against, 40–44
Bond, John R., maj.: Spiegel likes, 44; Spiegel criticizes, 152–53, 157; mentioned, 137, 145, 148, 158, 168
Botsford, E. W., 173n
Bowman, Andrew J., sgt., 89
Boyle, Jeremiah T., gen., 186
Brayton, Rufus M., capt., 187
Brock, Sidney G., lt., 137, 154, 161
Brongh, John, gov., 303, 323
Brown, John, 65
Browning, Orville Hickman, 115
Bruce, James E., sgt., 86, 87, 89
Buel & Taylor, 10
Buerstenbinder, Otto, col.: background, 16–17; Spiegel meets, 21, 22; charges against, 28n, 31, 34; Spiegel criticizes, 60–61, 65; arrests Spiegel, 67, 70; investigation of, 50, 73, 98; dismissal, 145; mentioned, 24, 35, 38, 44, 49, 54, 58, 72, 90, 131, 138
Burbank, Sidney, col., 323
Burger, Louis, 320
Burnside, Ambrose E., gen., 132, 200, 209
Butler, Benjamin F., gen., 227
Butler, Lewis, capt., 104, 161
Butsford, E. W., 173n

Caldwell, lt., aide-de-camp, 239
Cameron, Lizzie K., 319n
Camp Buckingham, Ohio, 173
Camp Chase, Ohio, 17, 20

Camp Ford, Tex., 337
Camp Mansfield, Ohio. *See* Mansfield, Camp, Ohio
Canton, Ohio: arrests at, 174
Carroll, Samuel S., col., 101
Casey, Silas, 184n
Chapman, John B., lt.: characterized, 48; combativeness of, 146–47; promoted, 172; wounded, 303n; mentioned, 20, 21, 25, 29, 34, 38, 42, 51, 55, 64, 66, 69, 77, 92, 103, 104, 106, 138n, 142, 143, 154, 156, 160, 162, 164, 169, 171, 195
Chase, Salmon P., gov., 14
Cherryholmes, Jacob, 73
Chicago, Ill.: Spiegel lives in, 3–7 passim; his widow lives in, 338–39. *See also* Jews
Chickasaw Bluffs, battle of, 204–18
Childs, George L., lt.: characterized, 48; promoted, 172; mentioned, 43, 44, 51, 64, 92, 99, 103, 106, 130
*City Belle*, attack on, 335–36
Clark, Francis, 6
Cleveland, Ohio: camp at, 16, 20
Cleveland, Military Committee of, 149
*Cleveland National Democrat*, 239
*Cleveland Plain Dealer*, 156
Cline, William, pvt., 21
Cohn, Benjamin: background, 11, 12; Spiegel's debts to, 14, 129, 130, 287, 314, 319; mentioned, 32, 46, 72, 98, 99, 125, 126, 130, 141, 151, 153, 169, 171, 179, 259, 269, 289, 303, 306, 309, 328n, 332, 338
Commager, Henry S., capt., 137, 152–53, 157, 168n, 170,
Conyer, George W., capt., 187, 227, 255–56
Cooke, Philip St. George, gen., 330
"Copperheads": arrested, 174. *See also* Democrats
Corps: First, 218; Second, 140; Third, 140; Fourth, 123, 133, 155n; Thirteenth, 189n, 239, 240n, 265, 274, 277, 298n
Cotton trading: at Memphis, 188–89, 191–92
Critchfield, Lyman R., 126, 130, 265
Curtis, Samuel R., gen., 113
Custer, George Armstrong, gen., vii

Daum, Philip, 84
Davenport, Jean. *See* Lander, Jean Davenport
Davide's Ferry, battle at, 335
Davies, Thomas A., gen., 186
Davis, Jefferson, 114, 265
Dean, Ezra V., q.m.: political attacks on, 250–51; mentioned, 180, 182, 191, 195, 225, 248, 254, 270, 299, 309
DeCourcy, John F., col., 193, 213, 214, 215
*Delaware*: sinking of, 118–20
Democrats: in Holmes County, 11, 12; attitudes on war, 12–13, 15n, 174, 295n, 303; oppose emancipation, 224–25, 265; praise Spiegel, 250, 251. *See also* Holmes County War
Dennison, William, gov., 15, 16
DeSilva, Manuel B., lt., 298, 303
Dobbs, Millersburg civilian, 97, 101
Douglas, Stephen A., 8, 11, 12, 114, 225
Draft: Spiegel favors, 150
Durbin, Greene, capt., 119

Eagle, gambler, 325
Eason, Benjamin, capt., 214n, 255
East Liberty, Ohio: Spiegel store at, 8; men from, 21; spring at, 41
Eberhart, Henry H., capt., 284
Ebright, Thomas McBride, surgeon: son dies, 135, 142–43; Republican, 290; mentioned, 32, 40, 51, 54, 77, 80, 101, 285
Edgerton, Sidney, 115
Ellis, Calvin A., Mrs., 113
Ellsworth, E. Elmer, 117–18
Emancipation, ix, 4n, 5, 174, 312, 320n. *See also* Spiegel, Marcus M.; Slavery and Slaves
Emanu-El, Temple, N.Y., 3n
Emerick, George P., capt., 191n, 255
Enk, Henry, pvt., 121
Enos, Robert K., Dr., 12, 13n, 287, 290, 338
Enos, Brown Co., 14, 98, 269, 276, 287n
Estill, Eliphaz, 225
Estill, James A.: background, 10, 11; opposes Lincoln administration, 224, 265; differs with Spiegel, 286n, 290, 303;

obituary for Spiegel, 338; mentioned, 12, 13, 31n, 59n, 91, 100, 108, 109, 112, 121, 146n, 174, 177n, 225, 269n, 322, 335

Fahrion, Gustav W., lt., 92, 98
Faulkner, Charles J., 63
Felsenthal, Bernard, Rabbi, 4, 338
Felts, Elizabeth (Lizzie). See Hamlin, Lizzie
Ferry, Orris S., gen.: praises Spiegel, 157–58; mentioned, 118, 119, 133, 137, 152, 155, 168, 169, 171
Flood, Charles B., 239
Forbes, Samuel F., surgeon, 161
Ford, Hyatt G., capt., 24, 89
Fort Donelson, Tenn.: capture announced, 43
Fort Hindman. See Arkansas Post, battle of
Foster, Robert S., col., 152
Foust, Elizabeth: background, 9; seeks husband, 45–46, 56, 73, 240–41, 299, 308, 310–11; marriage, 328–29; postwar life, 339
Foust, George, pvt., 21
Foust, Sarah, 9
Francis Clark's Dry Goods Emporium, 6, 7
Fraunfelter, Elias, lt., 315n, 327
Freemasons. See Masons
Fremont, John C., gen., 113, 116
French, Daniel, col.: background, 173; Spiegel's friend, 178, 179, 191, 192–93, 195; at Vicksburg, 205, 206, 213, 214, 216; at Arkansas Post, 222; political attacks on, 225, 250–51, 303; resignation, 233–35, 241; mentioned, 174, 176, 182, 187, 188, 189, 198, 226–27, 244, 289
French, Sam, 258

Garfield, James A., col., 189, 190
Garrard, Theophilus T., col., 239, 242n, 266, 267
German-Americans: in politics, 8; in Holmes County, 11
Gettysburg Campaign, 294, 296, 297
Gill, John C., surgeon, 325, 327, 334

Girty, Alfred P., capt., 161, 195
Goldstein, Hattie, 339
Gordon, William A., capt., 239
Grant, Jesse, 192n
Grant, Ulysses S., gen.: order against Jews, viii, 191–92, 250; Spiegel praises, 283, 300; mentioned, 196, 197, 204, 206, 207, 210, 217, 227n, 240n, 265, 274, 277, 278, 280, 296, 297
Grassly, Jacob, pvt., 21, 23, 25–26, 54, 71, 144
Gratz, Louis A., vii
Greeley, Horace, 59n
Green Township, Ohio: Spiegel store in, 8
Greenebaum, Elias, 3
Greenebaum, Henry, 3, 5, 68
Greenebaum, Isaac, 323
Greenebaum, Michael, 3, 8, 175, 230, 302, 323
Greenebaum, Sarah, 1, 3, 175
Greenebaum Brothers, bank, 4n
Guerillas, 202–3
Gundersheim, "Cheuley" von, 202

Haggard, Mrs., 187
Hale, John P., 114
Hamlin, Caroline Frances. See Spiegel, Caroline F.
Hamlin, Lizzie, 5, 338, 339n
Hamlin, Stephen, 4, 9n
Hamlin family, 4–5
Hammond, John W., surgeon, 182, 248–49
Hampton, Va.: described, 159–60
Harrington, Eli, pvt., 21, 21n
Harrington, Theodore N., pvt., 21, 21n
Harrington, William F., pvt., 21, 21n
Harrison, William Henry, 122
Harrison's Landing, Va.: described, 122–23; entrenched camp at, 125–26, 134
Hart, Henry, 323
Hart, Schaffner and Marx, 339
Hebrew Benevolent Cemetery, Chicago, 339
Hebrew Benevolent Society, Chicago, 3, 6
Heintzelman, Samuel P., gen., 140
Heller, Adolph, 106, 106n
Heller, Meahala, 106n

Herrnsheim, Loeb, 201

Herzer, Charles: merchant in La., 308, 309, 312–14, 316, 319; mentioned, 55n, 317, 319, 328, 334

Herzer, Henry: background, 11, 12; Spiegel's partner, 13, 287; q.m. ship for, 22, 32, 45; mentioned, 55, 97, 132, 151, 153, 289, 303, 308n, 311, 312, 313, 329n

Hill, Charles W., AG, 169, 170, 171

Hiner, David A., pilot, 186

Holmes County, Ohio: people of, 11–12

Holmes County War: 265, 294–95, 299

Holmes Plantation, La.: described, 267

Hooker, Joseph, gen., 283, 294, 296

Hovey, Alvin P., gen., 279, 280

Hull, Lewis O., drummer, 247–48, 263

Hunter, David, gen., 283

Hunter, M. T., wool dealer, 97


Illinois units: Second Cav., 267; Second Light Arty., 239n; Thirty-ninth Inf., 152, 160; 118th Inf., 189, 271, 278, 279

Immigrants, vii, 2

Indiana Inf. Regts.: Seventh, 79; Thirteenth, 40, 86, 152; Forty-ninth, 213, 214, 271; Sixty-ninth, 189, 266, 272; Ninety-fifth, 243

Ingels, col. of U.S. Regulars, 181

Irvine, John, 25

Irvine, William H., 44, 113


Jackson, Andrew, 11

Jackson, Thomas Jonathan, gen., 26, 47, 68, 74, 82, 83, 88, 110, 116

Jackson, Miss.: siege of, 300–301

Jewish Manual Training School, Chicago, 339

Jews: discriminated against, vii–viii, 1–2, 191–92; as soldiers, vii–viii; as immigrants, 2; in N.Y., 2–3; in Chicago, 3–4, 5–7, 175, 338–39; in Millersburg, 11; in Virginia, 106, 163; in Cincinnati, 180–81; in Memphis, 189, 191–92, 201–2, 227; in Baton Rouge, 331; in Akron, 338–39. See also Anti-Semitism; Spiegel, Marcus M.

Johnson, William H., pvt., 150

Johnston, Joseph E., gen., 110, 277, 280, 282, 284, 291, 296, 297, 300

Jones, Benjamin T., sgt., 242n, 247n, 256, 309, 327, 332, 335

Joseph, Moses, 46, 153, 157

Joss, N. F., of Weinsberg, 130, 130n

Judaism. See Jews; Reform Judaism

Jüdische Reformverein, Chicago, 4n


Kauffmann, H. K., civilian, 289

Kehilah Anshe Maariv, Congregation, Chicago, 4n

Keigwin, James, col., 271, 277

Keller, Christian, pvt., 41

Kentucky Inf. Regts.: Seventh, 278, 279, 314; Twenty-second, 189, 310, 314, 315

Kenyon House, Mt. Vernon, Ohio, 13

Keplar, John A., 91–92, 106

Kernstown, battle of, 82–91, 256–57

Kernstown, Va.: described, 75

Keyes, Erasmus D., gen., 123, 133, 169

Killbuck Rangers, Millersburg, 167n

Kimball, Nathan, col., 67, 70, 71–72, 74, 86, 87, 95, 96, 104, 176

Kolbe, Carl F., 44


Lander, Frederick W., gen.: compliments Spiegel, 48; death of, 52, 53; funeral, 56–57; mentioned, 29, 38, 50, 65, 70

Lander, Jean Davenport, 56–57

Lanphere, Charles H., capt., 268, 271, 300

Leadbetter, D. P., politician, 130, 169, 171

Lee, Albert L., gen., 278, 281, 284, 298

Lee, Robert E., gen., 110, 117, 294, 297

Lemmons, Marge J., sgt., 89, 89n, 150

Lever, Charles, 318

Levy, Memphis boardinghouse keeper, 202

Liebenstein, Henry, 117n, 211, 287

Liebenstein, Theresa, 1, 177n, 323

Limaville, Ohio: some inhabitants scorn Spiegels, 7

Lincoln, Abraham: Enos helps nominate, 12; inspects Sixty-seventh Ohio, 109; revokes order against Jews, 191; Spiegel on, 200; mentioned, 114, 115,

116, 174, 224, 225, 226, 230, 243–44, 250, 265, 295n, 297, 303, 312n, 320n
Lindsey, Daniel W., col., 210
Louisiana: storekeeping in, 308, 309, 312–14, 316, 319; "Black Code," 321
Lowman, Mrs., teacher (?), 319
Loy, Mrs., Virginia civilian, 42

McClellan, George B., gen.: Spiegel's admiration for, 108, 178, 198, 200, 261, 297; popularity of, 116, 117, 126, 127, 131, 146; mentioned, 71, 82, 88, 109, 110, 121, 132, 133, 140, 155, 209, 224
McClernand, John A., gen.: Spiegel respects, 220, 221, 222, 334; recommends Spiegel, 242; mentioned, 196, 207, 210, 217, 218, 227n, 240, 265, 270, 278n, 297, 298n, 329
McCormick, N. P. (?), watchmaker, 56, 73, 241
McDowell, Irvin, gen., 116
McEbright, Thomas, Dr. See Ebright, Thomas McBride
McGill, John, 113
McGregor, Archibald, 174
Mackey, John O., sgt., 285
Malvern Hill, engagement at, 146, 149–50
Manderback, Benjamin F., pvt., 21
Mansfield, Camp, Ohio, 171, 173, 174
Martin, Elbert S., 63n
Martinsburg, W. Va.: described, 63–65
Mason, John S., col., 96, 102, 103
Masons, 9, 12, 24, 25
Mayer, Leopold, 1, 2
Memphis, Tenn.: cotton trading at, 188–89, 191; Jews of, 201–2
Mennonites, 11
Michigan, Seventh Arty. Bty., 268, 271, 300
Middletown, Va.: described, 77
Miller, Benjamin F., lt., 315n, 327, 334
Millersburg, Ohio: described, 10–11; recruiting at, 15; politics in, 108–9, 146, 174, 295, 303; militia from, 167n
Millersburg Band, 21n, 29, 34, 44, 57, 90, 302
Millersburg Holmes County Farmer, 30, 97, 112, 145, 146n, 156, 224, 225, 265, 335

Millersburg Republican, 55, 286n, 290, 298, 303, 322
Milltown, Va.: described, 75
Mississippi River: boat trips on described, 197–204, 324–25
Mississippi Valley, map of, 199
Missouri Regts.: First Cav., 113; Sixth Cav., 266; Twelfth Inf., 239n
Moffitt, Valentine, capt., 293, 315
Morgan, George W., gen.: at Chickasaw Bluffs, 206, 210, 212, 213; praises Spiegel, 213, 235; mentioned, 189, 190, 195, 198, 201, 218, 231–32, 234
Mount Jackson, Va.: march toward, 101–5
Mount Union School, Ohio, 64
Mount Vernon, Ohio: Kenyon House, 13
Myers, William G., capt., 238, 250–51

National Council of Jewish Women, 339
Negroes. See Blacks; Slavery and Slaves
Nerney, Hattie Spiegel, 339
Nerney, Thomas, 339
New Market, Va.: march toward, 101–5
Newton, Va.: described, 77
New York, N.Y.: Jews in, 2–3
New York, Inf. Regts.: Fourth, 162; Eighty-third, 134
Nugen, Robert H., 115
Nutt, Haller, 254n
Nutt, Mrs., widow lady, 254–55

Odd Fellows, 9
Ohio First Lt. Arty. Bty., 25
Ohio Inf. Regts.: Fourth, 40, 102; Fifth, 84; Eighth, 32n, 40, 85; Sixteenth, 193, 250, 268, 303; Twenty-ninth, 21, 85; Forty-second, 189, 231, 271, 272; Forty-fifth, 14, 16, 17, 47; Fifty-sixth, 337n; Sixtieth, 43; Sixty-second, 124, 152; Sixty-seventh, 20–172 passim; 114th, 337; 115th, 179, 181n, 183; 120th, 171–337 passim
Ohio Militia, 14
Ord, Edward O. C., gen., 298
Orr, Thomas, pvt., 258, 292, 293
Osborn, Leroy, cpl., 48n, 84, 150, 151, 257
Osborn, Thomas O., col., 152

Osterhaus, Peter J., gen.: respects Spiegel, 231, 234–35, 242, 260, 304; characterized, 234, 269–70; mentioned, 218, 222, 230, 232, 239, 263, 266, 267, 276, 277, 280, 282, 294, 296, 300

Peck, John J., gen., 133, 137, 138, 142, 158, 169
Pemberton, John, gen., 297
Peninsula Campaign, Va., summarized: 109, 110, 116–17; map, 111
Pennsylvania, 110th Inf. Regt., 85
Pennsylvania Dutch, 92–93, 106–7
Perkins, Simon, 13n
Petry, Adam, 329n
Petry, Elizabeth. See Foust, Elizabeth
Phelan, Patrick, capt., 238
Plantations, 68, 76, 254–55, 267, 312, 320–21
Plaquemine, La.: described, 308, 311–12
Platt, Edwin S., capt., 25, 168–69, 171
Pomerene, Joel, surgeon, 285, 302
Pope, John, gen., 132
Port Gibson, battle of, 270–73
Porter, David Dixon, adm., 201, 204

Quakers, 4, 5, 93n

Red River Campaign: background, 306–7; defeats, 328, 329, 334; Spiegel's participation in, 335–37
Reform Judaism, 2–3, 4, 6
Remley, Christian, pvt., 21, 21n
Remley, Frederick C., pvt., 21, 21n
Republicans: attack war opponents, 174, 295n; attack Spiegel, 225; court Spiegel, 251, 303; reaction to City Belle attack, 337
Rex, George, 169, 259, 287
Richardson, William A., 115
Ritter, surgeon, 302
Rose, William B., pvt., 25
Rosecrans, William Starke, gen., 53, 71, 283
Roselles, soldier, 331, 334
Rosenbaum, Lewis, 106, 106n
Rosenbaum, Sarah, 106, 106n

Ruhman, Abraham, pvt., 190, 230, 232–33, 238–39, 241, 244, 261, 262

Schloss, Charley, 202
Schwartz, Adolph, col., 239–40, 242, 259–60
Sebrell, Ezra L., pvt., 181, 181n, 183, 187
Sebrell, Lewis C., 181, 181n, 183
Sedgwick, Charles B., 115
Sheldon, Lionel A., col.: characterized, 231; mentioned, 189, 190, 214n, 222, 315
Shenandoah Valley, map of, 27. See also Valley Campaign
Sherman, Charles Taylor, col., 173, 174, 201, 248n, 304
Sherman, Henry S., lt., 248, 256, 270, 273, 281–82, 304, 309
Sherman, John, 173, 201, 248n
Sherman, William T., gen.: at Chickasaw Bluffs, 206, 207, 210, 215n, 216; at Arkansas Post, 217, 218, 220; Spiegel criticizes, 220, 232; Spiegel respects, 311, 338; mentioned, 189, 195, 196, 197, 201, 204, 248, 294, 297, 300
Shields, James, gen., 69–70, 71, 78, 79, 82, 83, 86, 87, 88, 97, 102, 112, 116, 256
Shields's Division, 82, 83, 117, 118
Sigel, Franz, gen., 14n
Sinai, Temple, Chicago, 2–3, 4, 339
Sinsheimer, Aaron, 252, 254, 255, 263, 268, 269, 276, 287, 296, 297, 298, 308, 315, 317, 326, 328, 331
Slavery and Slaves: Spiegel's views on, 8, 204, 312, 315–16, 320–21. See also Emancipation
Slidell, John C., 114
Slocum, Williard, lt. col., 248, 256, 270, 273, 333, 336
Smith, Andrew J., gen., 176, 189, 206, 212, 232
Smith, David Goliath, 166
Smith, Morgan L., gen., 206, 212
Snaggy Point, battle at, 335
Snyder, William, cpl., 162
Solomon, Hannah Greenebaum, 339
Sons of Malta, 12
Southworth, Emma D. E. N., 29, 76, 131

Spiegel, Caroline F. (Marcus Spiegel's wife): preserves his letters, ix; early life, 4n, 5, 6; portraits of, 7, 36; concern over debts, 14; concern about Marcus's army career, 18, 129, 136, 194, 235, 262, 289, 304, 305, 309, 321–22; and Marcus's promotion, 169–71; birth of Hattie, 292; fifth pregnancy, 311, 319–20, 322, 328, 333, 338; reactions to Marcus's death, 337–38; postwar life, 338–41
Spiegel, Clara Marcus (Marcus Spiegel's daughter), 338, 339
Spiegel, Hamlin (Marcus Spiegel's son): portrait, 81; mentioned, 8, 335, 339
Spiegel, Hattie (Marcus Spiegel's daughter), 109, 292, 339
Spiegel, Hattie Goldstein (Hamlin Spiegel's wife), 339
Spiegel, Joseph (Marcus Spiegel's brother): birth of, 1; moves to Millersburg, 18; Marcus's concern for, 45, 72, 158–59; moves to Chicago, 177n; sutler, 204, 223, 230, 236, 240, 246, 249, 251–55, 263, 266, 269, 275, 287, 289, 296, 297, 298, 308, 309, 315, 316, 319, 320, 326, 328, 331, 333; with wounded brother, 302, 336; captured, 336, 337; postwar life, 339
Spiegel, Lizzie (Marcus Spiegel's daughter), 5, 8, 9, 304, 339; portrait, 81
Spiegel, Marcus M.: portraits, ii, 7; his letters, vii–x, 18–19, 30, 49; his significance, vii–viii, 341; early life, vii, 1–14; success in army, vii–viii, 17–18, 28n, 36, 81–82, 87n, 137–38, 142, 159, 189, 192–93, 213, 214n, 242; as Jew, ix, 1, 6, 13, 106, 163, 175, 180–81, 191–92, 202, 235, 250, 259, 331; on slavery and emancipation, ix, 62, 114–16, 200, 226, 230, 261, 315–16, 320–21; patriotism of, ix, 141, 147, 201, 243–44, 260–61; as husband, 6, 18, 37, 68, 93, 107–8, 127–29, 141, 148, 263, 276, 290–91, 309, 310–11, 332 (see also Spiegel, Caroline F.); as parent, 6, 39, 44–45, 50, 55–56, 80–81, 258–60, 311; politics of, 8–9, 108–9, 114–15, 106, 174, 225–26, 243–44, 249–51, 260–61, 269, 285–86, 288n, 290, 295, 299, 303; as Mason, 12, 24, 25; described, 17; and military promotions, 17, 22, 31, 47, 90, 125, 126–27, 136, 143, 151, 157–58, 168–71, 242, 266, 269, 304, 330; ailments, 31, 32, 34, 51, 121–22, 125, 126, 128, 132, 155, 178, 179, 180, 223, 252, 275, 331–32; debts, 14, 32, 45, 54, 98, 129, 262, 269, 276, 287, 314, 319; as brother, 39, 45, 82, 72–73 (see also Spiegel, Joseph); on army food, 39, 42–43, 48, 139, 227; affection of soldiers for, 41–42, 161, 191, 307–8, 327; army pay, 49, 50, 262, 275–76, 287, 296, 317; in Buerstenbinder quarrel, 34, 35, 38, 44, 54, 58, 60–61, 65, 66–70, 73, 131, 145; at Kernstown, 82–91, 256–57; at Chickasaw Bluffs, 204–18; at Arkansas Post, 219–22; as son, 246, 249; reminiscences of combat, 256–58; postwar plans, 266, 297, 314, 317, 318–19; at Port Gibson, 270–73; at Vicksburg attack, 277–81; wounds, 281, 284, 300–301, 302–5, 335–37; on marriage of Elizabeth Foust, 299, 308, 310–11; on gambling, 324–25; German relatives' pride in, 323; at Red River, 335–37; grave of, 338; monument, 340, 341
Spiegel, Meyer (Marcus Spiegel's ancestor), 1
Spiegel, Minna (Marcus Spiegel's sister), 1, 157
Spiegel, Moses (Marcus Spiegel's son), 9, 304, 339
Spiegel, Moses, Rabbi (Marcus Spiegel's father), 1, 2, 4, 9, 163, 202
Spiegel, Regina Herz (Marcus Spiegel's mother), 1, 141n, 195, 292, 322, 333, 339
Spiegel, Sarah (Marcus Spiegel's sister). See Greenebaum, Sarah
Spiegel, Theresa (Marcus Spiegel's sister). See Liebenstein, Theresa
Spiegel Catalogue Company, 339
Stanton, Benjamin, Dr., 270, 285
Stanton, Byron, surgeon, 248, 270, 285, 302, 309, 315, 327, 336
Stanton, Edwin M., 248n, 270, 323
Steel, Mrs., cook, 187
Steele, Clemens F., lt. col., 152
Steele, Frederick, gen., 206, 212

Steinbacher, E., and Co., 10
Steveson, surgeon, 302
Stouffer, Christopher C., surgeon, 182, 248–49
Strasburg, Va.: march to, 73–80
Suffolk, Va.: described, 162, 164
Sullivan, Jeremiah C., col., 40
Summit Post Office, Ohio, 8
Sumner, Charles, 114, 115
Sumner, Edwin V., gen., 140
Sumner, Louise, 76
Sussex County, Va., 5, 160
Sutlers: profits, 47; election of, 209; operations of, 230, 252, 254, 255; illustration of store, 253. See also Spiegel, Joseph
Suttlef, wool dealer, 97
Swick, Joseph W., Rev., 319n, 329n
Swift, Richard I., 3
Swiss: in Holmes County, 11

Taylor, wool dealer, 97
Taylor, Richard B., lt., 256
Thomlin, Sam, 76
Thompson's Hill. See Port Gibson, battle of Tod, David, gov., 22, 31n, 38, 44, 169, 170, 171, 262 Toledo, Ohio: Sixty-seventh Ohio recruited in, 16; influence of on promotions, 146, 169, 170
Tom Burk of "Ours," 318
Townsend, Samuel, pvt., 121
Troy, Hood, wool dealer, 97
Tuttle, James M., gen., 186
Tyler, Erastus B., gen., 33, 84, 85
Tyler, John, 159–60
Tysher, Mother, of Holmes Co., 29

Union League, 290n

Vallandigham, Clement L., 295n, 303
Valley Campaign, 88, 109, 110, 116n. See also Shenandoah Valley
Vandever, William, gen., 231
Vicksburg Campaign, 175, 265–300; map, 228–29. See also Chickasaw Bluffs, battle of
Virginia Regts. (Union): First Cav., 29, 40, 44; Seventh Inf., 40
Voorhees, Daniel W., 115

Voris, Alvin C., lt. col.: background, 16; Spiegel's friend, 26, 32, 44, 54, 70, 162, 164; promotion of, 90, 96, 146; at Kernstown, 84, 85, 86, 88; characterized, 153–54; backs Spiegel's promotion, 168, 169, 170; later career, 172, 195; mentioned, 20, 28n, 31, 37, 49, 57, 72, 74, 78, 79, 80, 97, 101, 103, 109, 120, 126, 132, 137, 139, 140, 149, 150, 152, 155, 157, 160, 161, 162, 167, 170

Wade, Benjamin F., 114
Wadsworth, James S., 116
Wallace, Robert P., lt., 284
Wallick, Henry M., sgt., 89, 135, 172
Washington, D.C.: described, 114–16
Waters, John W., sgt., 285
Wayne County, Ohio: political controversy in, 250–51
Weigam, George, cpl., 41, 46, 71, 93, 139
Weimer & Steinbacher, 10, 287
Weinsberg, Ohio: rally at, 12; dinner at, 108, 112
Welker, Martin, 15, 170
Wentworth, steamboat passenger, 325
Werner of Berlin, Ohio, 43
Westfall, James, surgeon, 42, 64, 147, 150, 154, 161
West Virginia, First Regt. Lt. Arty. Bty. (Bty. A), 84
Whitney, Bob, capt., 185
Wiggins, William J., sgt., 32, 48, 89n, 90
Williams, Thomas, gen., 227n
Winchester, Va., 68–71, 75
Winchester, battle of. See Kernstown, battle of
Winesburg, Ohio. See Weinsberg, Ohio
Wisconsin, Fourth Cav. Regt., 320
Wise, Isaac M., Rabbi, 181
Wise, William, 106, 107
Wolf, Simon, 192, 304, 330, 338
Women: with army, 187
Woodstock, Va.: described, 106
Woolf, Clara. See Spiegel, Clara Marcus
Woolf, Isaac, 339
Wooster Republican: controversy with Spiegel, 250–51, 288n
Wright, Horatio G., gen., 178

Yates, Samuel, 32